The RKO Features

THE RKO FEATURES

*A Complete Filmography of
the Feature Films Released or
Produced by RKO Radio Pictures,
1929–1960*

by JAMES L. NEIBAUR

McFarland & Company, Inc., Publishers
Jefferson, North Carolina, and London

The present work is a reprint of the library bound edition of The RKO Features: A Complete Filmography of the Feature Films Released or Produced by RKO Radio Pictures, 1929–1960, *first published in 1994 by McFarland.*

LIBRARY OF CONGRESS CATALOGUING-IN-PUBLICATION DATA

Neibaur, James L., 1958–
    The RKO features : a complete filmography of the feature
films released or produced by RKO Radio Pictures, 1929–1960 /
by James Neibaur.
        p.   cm.
    Includes index.

    ISBN 0-7864-2166-5 (softcover : 50# alkaline paper)

    1. RKO Radio Pictures, Inc.—Catalogs.   I. Title.
PN1999.R3N45   2005
016.79143'75'0973—dc20   92-56669

British Library cataloguing data are available

Cover: Ginger Rogers and Fred Astaire in *Roberta*.

Manufactured in the United States of America

McFarland & Company, Inc., Publishers
    Box 611, Jefferson, North Carolina 28640
        www.mcfarlandpub.com

Dedicated to the memory of
TIM HOLT
ORSON WELLES
MYRNA LOY
WHEELER AND WOOLSEY
LUCILLE BALL
RICHARD DIX
ANNE SHIRLEY
JOE PENNER

and to my friend
EMIL SITKA

Contents

Acknowledgments

My thanks to the following individuals and corporations who assisted me with photos, fact verification, materials, supplies, encouragement and friendship:

Ted Okuda, Gary Schneeberger, Emil Sitka, Joe Swaney, Leonard Maltin, Andrew McLean, Donald Key, Randy Skretvedt, Ann Martin, Bob King, the late Leslie Halliwell, Robert Andrews, John Cavallo, Gregory Revak, Tom White, Turner Network Television, Turner Home Entertainment, *Classic Images, VideoMania, Palmer Video News, Film Fan Monthly, The Big Reel, Past Times, Film Quarterly,* The Kenosha Historical Society, The Racine Public Library, The University of Wisconsin–Parkside, The Wisconsin Center for Film and Theater Research, and my son Max.

Introduction

Because RKO Radio Pictures is known for the many "B" westerns and gangster sagas they produced during the thirties and forties, the studio has often been dismissed as one which dealt mainly in second features. While the bulk of their releases were just that, RKO was also responsible for the Astaire-Rogers films, and for *Gunga Din, Citizen Kane,* and *King Kong,* as well as films featuring Cary Grant, Boris Karloff, Henry Fonda and John Wayne.

Their "B" products should also not be dismissed, as they featured the comedy team of Wheeler and Woolsey; the cowboy stars Harry Carey, George O'Brien, and Tim Holt; the earliest stars of talking pictures like Richard Dix, radio stars like Joe Penner, and future television stars like Lucille Ball. Unlike the poverty row studios, whose boasting of big names meant simply that a lot of former superstars went to the small studios to finish out their flickering careers, RKO had top performers who were at their height.

This reference work attempts to be the most comprehensive guide to the RKO features, from the final FBO part-talkies of 1928 and the first Radio Pictures releases of 1929 (see the Historical Overview which follows). The listing is restricted to feature films because the studio produced such a vast number of short subjects and cartoons; either of these categories deserves a book of their own. Along with the credits and synopses, entries often include interesting background information. For example, Lucy met Desi Arnaz while making the RKO feature *Too Many Girls.* Cary Grant met one of his wives, Betsy Drake, while starring in *Every Girl Should Be Married.* Frank Sinatra made his first films at this studio. Laurel and Hardy did *The Flying Deuces* here while waiting for their contract with Hal Roach to be renewed. And the Marx Brothers did *Room Service* for RKO through a deal engineered by their agent brother Zeppo.

Along with those films RKO produced and released are listed films released by the studio but produced elsewhere (e.g., many Disney features), those films RKO coproduced with other studios (usually Universal-International), and those the studio released through 1960, after production ceased in 1957. This listing also includes the much later films, like the 1982 remake of *The Cat People,* which really were not RKO films, but with which the studio was involved at least marginally. These are included for the sake of completeness.

Historical Overview

RKO studios originated with the import / export company of Robertson-Cole, which was founded by Englishman Harry F. Robertson and American Rufus Sidman Cole. Films were, originally, a sideline to Rohmer automobiles. The company began acquiring films around 1918, these efforts having been produced by Hawforth Pictures Corporation and distributed by Robertson-Cole through Exhibitors Mutual Distributing Corporation. In 1921, Robertson-Cole built a studio at 780 Gower Street, at the junction of Gower Street and Melrose Avenue in Hollywood, on 13.5 acres of land which had previously been owned by the Hollywood cemetery. The company then entered production with the feature *Kismet,* starring Otis Skinner who had achieved fame in the stage version, and *The Wonder Man,* starring Georges Carpentier. In 1922, Robertson-Cole became the Film Booking Office of America (FBO), producing mostly western, action, and melodramatic quickies featuring ace stuntman Yakima Canutt and early canine star Strongheart. The company was purchased by Joseph Kennedy in 1926. By 1928, Kennedy was experimenting with part-talkies, which led to the formation of RKO Radio Pictures as we know it.

RKO Radio Pictures was born in 1929 when Radio Corporation of America (RCA) President David Sarnoff joined forces with Kennedy, believing that the talking picture revolution would enable him to test his RCA sound system with motion pictures. Sarnoff and Kennedy merged the FBO studios with the Keith-Albee-Orpheum vaudeville circuit, providing the studio with theaters to show their films. FBO changed its name to Radio-Keith-Orpheum, or RKO Radio Pictures. Its first films, under the RKO auspices, included the features *Syncopation* and *Side Street.*

Between the years 1930 and 1942, RKO had several production heads, including David O. Selznick (1931–1933), Merian C. Cooper (1933–1934), B.B. Kahane (1934–1935), Samuel Briskin (1935–1938), Pandro S. Berman (1938–1939), and George Schaefer (1939–1942). Selznick left for the more prestigious MGM studios, but not before producing such great films as *A Bill of Divorcement* and *King Kong* and deciding, in 1931, to merge the production operations of RKO and Pathé under one staff and in one studio. Despite the rapid turnover of production heads during this period, RKO still managed to produce such exceptional films as *Top Hat, The Informer,* and *Gunga Din.* When Schaefer became head of production, he concentrated on freelancers and bringing new blood into the studio's films, which led the way for new-comers such as Robert Mitchum, and Orson Welles who produced the classic *Citizen Kane* for RKO in 1941. Schaefer also employed popular veterans like Boris Karloff and Bela Lugosi for a series of horror films produced by Val Lewton, while stars like John Wayne and William Powell were loaned to the studio for featured roles. When Schaefer left the studio in 1942, however, it was experiencing financial difficulties.

Charles Koerner became production head in 1942 and retained the title until his death in 1946, when he was replaced by Peter N. Rathvon, and, a year later, by Dore Schary. In 1948, millionaire Howard Hughes bought RKO. Hughes was generally a slave to his own impulses, resulting in many very bad creative and business decisions. These actions brought about the studio's downfall, and Hughes sold RKO to General Teleradio, Inc., in 1955. General Teleradio released the studio's backlog of features and short subjects to television the following year. That same year, William Dozier became head of production. RKO continued to produce feature films through 1957, ending with *The Unholy Wife.* Though no longer active in production, RKO continued to release films through 1960, many of them produced in Great Britain.

In the 1990s RKO Studios exists as a corporation dealing in the distribution of their films to the television and video markets. For years the RKO features were available to television only via grainy, edited prints distributed by C&C Television corporation. C&C even went so far as to replace the original RKO radio tower logo with their own Movietime time-piece logo. Then, in 1985, TV mogul Ted Turner bought the rights to the RKO library, and struck up new, complete, clear prints of all of the films; making these readily available via cable television, videocassette, and laser disc by the end of the decade. Turner not only released the RKO classics on video, he made available such interesting, often overlooked oddities as "Cockeyed Cavaliers," "Zombies on Broadway," and "Tuttles of Tahiti." Special packages released by Turner Home Entertainment included box sets commemorating the 50th anniversary of *Citizen Kane* (1991) and 60th anniversary of *King Kong* (1992). These packages offered the feature as well as such attractive items as a documentary tape on the making of the film, books on each movie's history, and copies of the original script. RKO's current address is 129 North Vermont Avenue, Los Angeles, California 90004. Many 16mm prints of RKO films are housed at the Wisconsin Center for Film and Theater Research (412 Historical Society, 816 State St., Madison, WI 53706). This center also holds the collections of Pandro S. Berman, and Orson Welles.

The Features

1 *Abe Lincoln in Illinois* (1940) Biographical drama. Running time: 110 minutes. Released in Great Britain as *Spirit of the People*. Black and white. Available on videocassette.

Produced by Max Gordon. Directed by John Cromwell. Written by Robert Sherwood (based on his play). Photographed by James Wong Howe. Music by Roy Webb.

Starring Raymond Massey (Abraham Lincoln), Gene Lockhart (Stephen Douglas), Ruth Gordon (Mary Todd Lincoln), Mary Howard (Ann Rutledge), Dorothy Tree (Elizabeth Edwards), Harvey Stephens (Ninian Edwards), Minor Watson (Joshua Speed), Alan Baxter (Billy Hemdon), Howard da Silva (Jack Armstrong), Maurice Murphy (John McNeil), Clem Bevans (Ben Battling), Herbert Rudley (Seth Gale), Roger Imhoff (Mr. Crimmin), Edmund Elton (Mr. Rutledge), George Rosener (Dr. Chandler), Trevor Bardette (John Hanks), Elisabeth Risdon (Sarah Lincoln), Napoleon Simpson (Gobey), Aldrich Bowker (Judge Bowling Green), Louis Jean Heydt (Mentor Graham), Harlan Briggs (Denton Offut), Andy Clyde (Stage Driver), Leona Roberts (Mrs. Rutledge), Florence Roberts (Mrs. Bowling Green), Fay Helm (Mrs. Seth Gale), Syd Saylor (John Johnston), Charles Middleton (Tom Lincoln), Alec Craig (Trem Cogdall).

Screen version of a popular play deals with Lincoln's life from young railsplitter to his election to the presidency in 1860. *Note:* Although this episodic film was a critical success, it was a failure at the box office, a loss of $750,000 for RKO.

2 *Ace of Aces* (1933) War drama. Running time: 76 minutes. Black and white.

Produced by Sam Jaffe. Directed by J. Walter Ruben. Written by John Monk Saunders and H.W. Hannemann (based on Saunders' story *Bird of Prey*). Photographed by Henry Cronjager. Edited by George Hively. Musical Director: Max Steiner.

Starring Richard Dix (Lt. Rex Thorne), Elizabeth Allan (Nancy Adams), Ralph Bellamy (Major Blake), Theodore Newton (Lt. Foster Kelly), Bill Cagney (Lt. Meeker), Clarence Stroud (Lt. Carroll Winstead), Joseph Sauers, Frank Conroy, Howard Wilson, Helmut Gorin, Art Jarrett, Anderson Lawlor, Frank Melton, Claude Gillingwater, Jr., Carl Eric Hanson, George Lollier.

A sculptor balks at having to go to war and fight people he does not personally hate. When his scruples are interpreted as cowardice by his fiancée, he enlists and becomes a ruthless killer, downing countless German planes. When he later meets up with his fiancée, a nurse, she is shocked by his callous attitude.

3 *Action in Arabia* (1944) Adventure. Running time: 75 minutes. Black and white.

Produced by Maurice Geraghty. Directed by Leonide Moguy. Written by Phillip MacDonald, Herbert Biberman.

Photographed by Roy Hunt. Edited by Robert Swink.

Starring George Sanders (Gordon), Virginia Bruce (Yvonne), Lenore Aubert (Mounrian), Gene Lockhart (Danesco), Robert Armstrong (Reed), H.B. Warner (Rashid), Alan Napier (Latimer), Andre Chalot (Leroux), Marcel Dalio (Chakka), Robert Anderson (Chalmers), Jamiel Hasson (Kareem), John Hamilton (Hamilton), Rafael Storm (Hotel Clerk), Michael Ansara (Hamid).

An American newspaperman in Damascus uncovers German spies trying to enlist the aid of Arab tribes.

Note: Much of the footage used here was originally shot by *King Kong* director Merian C. Cooper for an epic that was never filmed.

4 *Admirals All* (1935) Comedy. Running time: 75 minutes. Black and white. Made in England by Stafford productions, released in the U.S. by RKO.

Produced by John Stafford. Directed by Victor Hanbury. Written by Ian Hay and Stephen King-Hall, based on their play.

Starring Wynne Gibson (Gloria Gunn), Gordon Harker (Petty Officer Dingle), Anthony Bushell (Flag Lt. Steve Langham), George Curzon (Ping Hi), Joan White (Prudence Stallybrass), Henry Hewitt (Flag Captain Knox), Percy Walsh (Admiral Sir Westerham), Wilfrid Hyde-White (Mr. Stallybrass), Gwynneth Lloyd (Jean Stallybrass), Ben Welden (Adolph Klotz).

A standoffish actress is pursued by a low ranking Navy officer.

5 *The Admiral's Secret* (1934) Comedy. Running time: 71 minutes. Black and white. Produced in England by Real Art; released in the U.S. by RKO.

Produced by Julius Hagen. Directed by Guy Newall. Written by H. Fowler Mear (based on a play by Cyril Campion and Edward Dignon).

Starring Edmund Gwenn (Adm. Pitz-porter), James Raglan (Frank Bruce), Hope Davy (Pamela Pitzporter), Aubrey Mather (Capt. Brooke), Edgar Driver (Sam Hawkins), Abraham Sofaer (Don Pablo Y. Gonzales), Dorothy Black (Doona Teresa), Andrea Malandrinos (Guido d'Elvira), D.J. Williams (Questa).

A retired admiral steals jewels and is pursued by Spanish bandits.

6 *Adventure Girl* (1934) Docudrama. Running time: 69 minutes. Black and white.

Directed by Herman Raymaker. Narration written by Ferrin Fraser and delivered by Jane Lowell, based on her book of the same name.

A re-enactment of Jane Lowell's trek through Guatemala jungles with her 76-year-old father in search of a lost city.

7 *Adventure in Baltimore* (1949) Comedy. Running time: 89 minutes. British title: *Bachelor Bait*. Black and white.

Produced by Richard H. Berger. Directed by Richard Wallace. Written by Lionel Houser (based on a story by Lesser Samuels and Christopher Isherwood). Photographed by Robert De Grasse. Music by Frederick Hollander. Edited by Robert Swink.

Starring Robert Young (Dr. Sheldon), Shirley Temple (Dinah Sheldon), John Agar (Tom Wade), Albert Sharpe (Mr. Fletcher), Josephine Hutchinson (Mrs. Sheldon), Charles Kemper (Mr. Steuben), Johnny Sands (Gene Sheldon), John Miljan (Mr. Eckert), Norma Varden (H.H. Hamilton), Carol Brannan (Bernice Eckert), Charles Smith (Fred Beehouse), Josephine Whittell (Mrs. Eckert), Patti Brady (Sis Sheldon), Gregory Marshall (Mark Sheldon), Patsy Creighton (Sally Wilson).

A minister must contend with the townsfolk's reaction to his outspoken and liberal-minded daughter.

Note: Temple and Agar were real-life husband and wife when making this film.

8 *Adventures of a Rookie* (1943) Comedy. Running time: 64 minutes. Black and white.

Produced by Bert Gilroy. Directed by Leslie Goodwins. Written by Edward James (based on a story by William Bowers and M. Coates Webster). Photographed by Jack MacKenzie. Edited by Harry Marker.

Starring Wally Brown (Jerry Miles), Alan Carney (Mike Stager), Richard Martin (Bob Prescott), Erford Gage (Sgt. Burke), Margaret Landry (Peggy Linden), Patti Brill (Colonel), Ruth Lee (Mrs. Linden), Lorraine Krueger (Eve), Ercelle Woods (Margaret), Toddy Peterson (Betty), Byron Foulger (Mr. Linden).

A nightclub entertainer, a shipping clerk, and a rich playboy get drafted.

Note: RKO's answer to Universal's hot team of Bud Abbott and Lou Costello, this film was clearly inspired by the popularity of Bud and Lou's service comedies. This was the first of a handful of comic vehicles featuring Brown and Carney as a team to rival Abbott and Costello. Sequel: *Rookies in Burma.*

9 *Adventures of Ichabod and Mr. Toad* (1949). Running time: 68 minutes. Technicolor. Divided into two and available on videocassette and laser disc.

Produced by Walt Disney. Directed by Jack Kinney, Clyde Geronimi, and James Algar. Screenplay by Erdman Penner, Winston Hibler, Joe Rinaldi, Ted Sears, Homer Brightman, Harry Reeves (based on the stories "The Legend of Sleepy Hollow" by Washington Irving and "The Wind in the Willows" by Kenneth Graham.

Voices of Bing Crosby, Basil Rathbone, Eric Blore, Pat O'Malley, John Flyardt, Colin Campbell, Campbell Grant, Claude Allister, The Rhythmaires.

A feature-length cartoon, split into two sequences, detailing the stories of Mr. Toad in "The Wind in the Willows," and Ichabod Crane in "The Legend of Sleepy Hollow."

Review: "Superb family entertainment . . . one of Disney's finest efforts" — *The Motion Picture Guide.*

10 *Affair of a Stranger* (1953) Romantic drama. Running time: 89 minutes. Black and white.

Produced by Robert Sparks. Directed by Roy Rowland. Written by Richard Flournoy. Photographed by Harold J. Wild. Edited by George Amy. Music and lyrics: *Kiss and Run* by Sam Coslow (sung by Monica Lewis).

Starring Jean Simmons (Carolyn Parker), Victor Mature (Bill Blakely), Mary Jo Tarola (Dolly Murray), Monica Lewis (Janet Boothe), Jane Darwell (Ma Stanton), Dabbs Greer (Happy Murray), Wally Vernon (Joe), Nicholas Joy (George Craig), Olive Carey (Cynthia Craig), Victoria Horne (Mrs. Wallace), Lillian Bronson (Miss Crutcher), George Cleveland (Pop), Billy Chapin (The Older Timmy).

The ups and downs of a playwright and his wife, a model. Told in flashbacks as per their friends' reaction to an item about their breakup in a popular gossip column.

11 *Affairs of Annabel* (1938) Comedy. Running time: 73 minutes. Black and white. Available on videocassette.

Produced by Lou Lusty. Directed by Ben Stoloff. Written by Bert Granet and Paul Yawitz (based on a story by Charles Hoffman). Photographed by Russell Metty. Edited by Harry Marker.

Starring Jack Oakie (Morgan), Lucille Ball (Annabel), Ruth Donnelly (Josephine), Bradley Page (Webb), Fritz Feld (Vladmir), Thurston Hall (Major), Elisabeth Risdon (Mrs. Fletcher), Granville Bates (Mr. Fletcher), James Burke (Muldoon), Lee Van Atta (Robert Fletcher), Anthony Warde (Bailey), Edward Marr (Martin), Leona Roberts (Mrs. Hurley).

A publicity man tries to save his client's sagging movie career by dreaming up a publicity stunt which places her in a women's reformatory. When she is kidnapped by real gangsters and forced to participate in crimes, Hollywood does take notice and her press agent takes the credit.

Note: Sequel: *Annabel Takes a Tour.*

12 *After Tonight* (1933) Romantic drama. Running time: 70 minutes. Black and white.

Produced by Merian C. Cooper. Directed by George Archainbaud. Written by Jane Murfin, Albert Shelby LeVino and Worthington Miner (based on a story by Murfin). Photographed by Charles Rosher. Edited by William Hamilton. Musical director: Max Steiner.

Starring Constance Bennett (Carla), Gilbert Roland (Rudi), Edward Ellis (Col. Lieber), Sam Godfrey (Franz), Lucien Percival (Erlich), Mischa Auer (Adjutant Lehar), Ben Hendricks, Jr. (Probert), Leonid Snegoff (Pvt. Miller), Evelyn Carter Carrington (Frau Stengel), John Wray (Mitika).

World War I romance between a Russian spy and an Austrian captain.

13 *Age of Consent* (1932) Romantic drama. Running time: 100 minutes. Black and white.

Produced by David O. Selznick. Directed by Gregory La Cava. Written by Sarah Y. Mason and Francis Cockrell (based on the play *Cross Roads* by Martin Flavin). Photographed by J. Roy Hunt. Edited by Jack Kitchin.

Starring Dorothy Wilson (Betty), Richard Cromwell (Michael), Eric Linden (Duke), Arline Judge (Dora), John Halliday (David), Aileen Pringle (Barbara), Reginald Barlow (Swale).

Early look at sexuality between young people centering on a romance between a college boy and his underage girlfriend.

14 *Age of Innocence* (1934) Drama. Running time: 71 minutes. Black and white.

Produced by B.B. Kahane. Directed by Phillip Moeller. Written by Sarah Y. Mason and Victor Heerman (based on the novel by Edith Wharton). Photographed by James Van Trees. Edited by George Hively.

Starring Irene Dunne (Countess Ellen Olenska), John Boles (Newland Archer), Lionel Atwill (Julius Beaufort), Laura Hope Crews (Mrs. Welland), Helen Westley (Granny Mingott), Julie Haydon (May Welland), Herbert Yost (Mr. Welland), Theresa Maxwell-Conover (Mrs. Archer), Edith Van Cleve (Janey Archer), Leonard Carey (Butler).

Scandal occurs when a young lawyer dumps his socially acceptable fiancée and falls for a married woman.

15 *Aggie Appleby—Maker of Men* (1933) Comedy. Running time: 73 minutes. Black and white.

Produced by Pandro S. Berman. Directed by Mark Sandrich. Screenplay by Humphrey Pearson and Edward Kaufman (based on the play by Joseph O. Keserling). Photographed by J. Roy Hunt. Edited by Basil Wrangell.

Starring Charles Farrell (Adoniram Schlump), Wynne Gibson (Aggie Appleby), William Gargan (Red Branahan), ZaSu Pitts (Sybby), Betty Furness (Evangeline), Blanche Frederici (Aunt Katharine).

A society girl turns a hard guy into a sissy and a pampered lad into a roughneck, then must decide who she really loves.

16 *Alias French Gertie* (1930) Crime drama. Running time: 66 minutes. Black and white.

Directed by George Archainbaud. Written by Bayard Veiller (based on Veiller's *The Chatterbox*). Photographed by Roy Hunt.

Starring Bebe Daniels (Marie), Ben Lyon (Jimmy), Robert Emmett O'Connor (Kelcey), John Ince (Mr. Matson), Daisy Belmore (Mrs. Matson), Betty Pierce (Nellie).

A female crook, posing as French

maid, decides to rob her employer's home, but meets up with an old burglar acquaintance who is planning on doing the same. The two then decide to team up in Bonnie and Clyde fashion.

17 *Alice Adams* (1935) Drama. Running time: 99 minutes. Black and white.
Produced by Pandro S. Berman. Directed by George Stevens. Written by Dorothy Yost and Mortimer Offner (based on the novel by Booth Tarkington). Photographed by Robert De Grasse. Music by Max Steiner. Edited by Jane Loring.
Starring Katharine Hepburn (Alice Adams), Fred MacMurray (Arthur Russell), Fred Stone (Mr. Adams), Evelyn Venable (Mildred Palmer), Frank Albertson (Walter Adams), Ann Shoemaker (Mrs. Adams), Charley Grapewin (Mr. Lamb), Grady Sutton (Frank Dowling), Hedda Hopper (Mrs. Palmer), Jonathan Hale (Mr. Palmer), Janet McLeod (Henrietta Lamb), Virginia Howell (Mrs. Dowling), Hattie McDaniel (Malena).
Tarkington's story about a girl who lives just outside a posh area and strives to break free from the doldrums of her middle-class family's limitations.
Note: Previously filmed in 1923. Tarkington's ending was changed to a happy one for the Depression-era audiences, ensuring the film's box office appeal. Hepburn was nominated for an Oscar. Director Stevens was only 30 when he helmed this feature, his first major directorial assignment. He had worked as an assistant and cameraman on many Hal Roach silents including the classic Laurel and Hardy two-reeler *Two Tars* (1928).

18 *Alice in Wonderland* (1951) Animated fantasy. Running time: 75 minutes. Technicolor. A Walt Disney production released by RKO. Available on videocassette.
Produced by Walt Disney. Directed by Clyde Geronimi, Hamilton Luske, Will Jason. Screenplay by Winston Hiber, Bill Peet, Joe Rinaldi, Bill Cottrell, Joe Grant, Del Connell, Ted Sears, Erdman Penner, Milt Banta, Dick Kelsey, Dick Huemer, Tom Oreb, John Walbridge (based on the stories by Lewis Carroll). Animation directors: Milt Kahl, Ward Kimball, Franklin Thomas, Eric Larson, Houn Lounsberry, Oliver M. Johnston, Jr., Wolfgang Reitherman, Marc Davis, Les Clark, Norm Ferguson. Written by Winston Hibler, Bill Peet, Joe Rinaldi, Bill Cottrell, Joe Grant, Del Connell, Ted Sears, Erdman Penner, Milt Banta, Dick Kelsey, Dick Huemer, Tom Oreb, John Walbridge (based on the stories of Lewis Carroll). Animators: Hal King, Judge Whitaker, Hal Ambro, Bill Justice, Phil Duncan, Bob Carlson, Don Lusk, Cliff Nordberg, Harvey Toombs, Fred Moore, Marvin Woodward, Charles Nichols, Hugh Fraser. Effects animation: Joshua Meador, Dan McManus, George Rowley, Blaine Gibson. Color and Styling: John Hench, Mary Blair, Claude Coats, Ken Anderson, Don Da Gradi. Layout: Mac Stewart, Hugh Hennesey, Tom Codrick, Don Griffith, Charles Phillipi, Thor Putnam, A. Kendall O'Connor, Lance Nolley. Backgrounds: Ray Huffine, Ralph Hulett, Art Riley, Brice Mack, Dick Anthony, Thelma Witmer. Music by Oliver Wallace, Bob Hilliard, Sammy Fain, Gene DePaul, Mack David, Jerry Livingston, Al Hoffman. Orchestrations by Joseph Dubin. Vocal arrangements by Jud Conlon.
Songs: "Very Good Advice," "In a World of My Own," "All in a Golden Afternoon," "Alice in Wonderland," "The Walrus and the Carpenter," "The Caucus Race," "I'm Late," "Painting the Roses Red," "March of the Cards," "'Twas Brillig," "The Unbirthday Song," "We'll Smoke the Blighter Out," "Old Father William," "A E I O U."
Voices by Kathryn Beaumont (Alice), Ed Wynn (Mad Hatter), Richard Hayden (Caterpillar), Sterling Holloway (Cheshire Cat), Jerry Colonna (March Hare),

Verna Felton (Queen of Hearts), Pat O'Malley (Walrus, Carpenter, Tweedledee and Tweedledum), Bill Thompson (White Rabbit, Dodo), Heather Angel (Alice's sister), Joseph Kearns (Doorknob), Larry Grey (Bill), Queenie Leonard (Bird in the Tree), Dink Trout (King of Hearts), Doris Lloyd (The Rose), James MacDonald (Dormouse), The Mello Men (Card Painters), Pinto Colvig (Flamingoes), Ken Beaumont (Card Painter), Ed Penner (Baglet), Larry Grey (Card Painter), Queenie Leonard (Flower), Don Barclay.

Disney's version of the Lewis Carroll classic. *Notes:* The title was formally registered with the MPAA in 1938, after Disney had planned to do a film combining live action and animation, with Mary Pickford in the title role. In 1945, it was announced that Ginger Rogers would star. Then, after the success of *Song of the South* in 1946, Disney planned to star his new juvenile discovery Luana Patten. It was in 1946 that he finally decided to do an all-cartoon version. This idea was obviously inspired by Disney's *Alice in Cartoonland* series of the 1920s, which itself was based on the Carroll stories.

19 *All Mine to Give* (1957) Drama. Running time: 103 minutes. Color.

Produced by Sam Wiesenthal. Directed by Allen Reisner. Screenplay by Dale and Katherine Eunson (based on the *Cosmopolitan* magazine story "The Day They Gave Babies Away" by Katherine Eunson). Photographed by William Skall. Edited by Alan Crosland. Music by Max Steiner.

Starring Glynis Johns (Mamie), Cameron Mitchell (Robert), Rex Thompson (Robbie), Patty McCormack (Annabelle), Ernest Truex (Delbert), Hope Emerson (Mrs. Pugmir), Alan Hale (Tom Cullen), Sylvia Field (Leila Delbert), Royal Dano (Howard Tyler), Reta Shaw (Mrs. Runyon), Stephen Wooten (Jimmy), Butch Bernard (Kirk), Rosalyn Boulter (Mrs. Stephens), Francis DeSales (Mr. Stephens), Jon Provost (Bobby).

An older brother tries to find homes for his younger siblings on Christmas Day when their mother dies.

All That Money Can Buy see *The Devil and Daniel Webster*

20 *Allegheny Uprising* (1939) Action-adventure. Running time: 81 minutes. Black and white. Released in Great Britain under the title *The First Rebel*.

Produced by P.J. Wolfson. Directed by William Seiter. Written by P.J. Wolfson. Photographed by Nicholas Musuraca. Edited by George Croane.

Starring John Wayne (Jim Smith), Claire Trevor (Janie), George Sanders (Capt. Swanson), Brian Donlevy (Callendar), Wilfrid Lawson (MacDouglas), Robert Barrat (Duncan), John Hamilton (Professor), Moroni Olsen (Calhoon), Eddie Quillan (Anderson), Chill Wills (McCammon), Ian Wolfe (Poole), Wallis Clark (McGlashan), Monte Montague (Morris), Olaf Hytten (General Gage).

A frontiersman, just before the Revolutionary War, thwarts a tyrannical British captain and a crook who sells liquor and arms to Indians.

Note: Made just after Wayne's success in *Stagecoach.* Anti-British sentiments of the period were toned down for English audiences, but Native American stereotyping abounds.

21 *Almost a Gentlemen* (1939) Drama. Running time: 64 minutes. Black and white.

Produced by Cliff Reid. Directed by Leslie Goodwins. Screenplay by David Silverstein and Jo Pagano (based on a story by Harold Shumate). Photographed by J. Roy Hunt. Edited by Desmond Marquette.

Starring James Ellison (Dan Preston), Helen Wood (Shirley Haddon), Robert E. Kent (Robert Mabrey), June Clayworth (Marian), Robert Warwick (Major), Leonard Penn (Arthur), John Wray

(Crack Williams), Breandon (Tynan) (Jason), Earle Hodgins (Ira), Harlan Briggs (Doc), Ace the Wonder Dog.

A man's German shephard, whom he saves from the pound, implicates him in a murder.

22 *Along Came Jones* (1945)
Western satire. Running time: 90 minutes. Black and white. Available on videocassette.

Produced by Gary Cooper. Directed by Stuart Heisler. Screenplay by Nunnally Johnson (based on a story by Alan LeMay). Photographed by Milton Krasner. Music by Arthur Lange, Hugo Friedhofer, and Charles Maxwell. Edited by Thomas Neff. Costumes by Walter Plunkett.

Starring Gary Cooper (Melody Jones), Loretta Young (Cherry de Longpre), William Demarest (George Fury), Dan Duryea (Monte Jarrad), Frank Sully (Cherry's brother), Russell Simpson (Pop de Longpre), Arthur Loft (Sheriff), Willard Robertson (Luke Packard), Don Costello (Gledhill), Ray Teal (Kriendler), Walter Sande (Ira Waggoner), Lane Chandler (Boone), Frank Cordell (Coach Guard), Lou Davis, Ed Randolph, Tommy Coates (Coach Passengers), Tony Roux (Old Mexican), Erville Alderson (Bartender), Paul Sutton (Man at Bar), Herbert Heywood, Frank Hagney, Ralph Littlefield, Ernie Adams (Townsmen), Lane Watson (Town Character), Paul E. Burns (Small Man), Chris-Pin Martin (Store Proprietor), Jack Baxley (Rancher on Street), Douglas Morrow (Rifleman), Ralph Dunn (Cotton), Geoffery Ingham, John Merton, Tom Herbert (Card Players), Charles Morton (Fat Card Player), Lee Phelps (Deputy), Billy Engle (Wagon Driver), Bob Kortman, Frank McCarroll, Hank Bell, Chalky Williams (Posse).

A stumblebum cowboy is mistaken for a notorious bandit. When he sees the respect he suddenly receives, he keeps up the charade, much to the chagrin of his sardonic sidekick.

Note: A western satire similar in some ways to Bob Hope's later *The Paleface.* Cooper, as first-time producer, does a neat job parodying the type of cowpoke he'd played for years. Director Heisler is a former film editor who worked on many of Cooper's earlier films. Actor Demarest often cited this as his favorite among the many films in which he appeared. Produced by Cinema Artists/International Pictures for release by RKO.

23 *Along the Rio Grande* (1941)
Western. Running time: 65 minutes. Black and white.

Produced by Bert Gilroy. Directed by Edward Killy. Written by Arthur V. Jones and Morton Grant (based on a story by Stuart Anthony). Photographed by Frank Redman. Edited by Frederic Knudtson. Music by Fred Rose and Ray Whitley.

Starring Tim Holt (Jerry), Ray Whitley (Smokey), Betty Jane Rhodes (Mary), Emmett Lynn (Whopper), Robert Fiske (Doc Randall), Hal Taliaferro (Sheriff), Carl Stockdale (Turner), Slim Whitaker (Pete), Monte Montague (Kirby), Ruth Clifford (Paula), Harry Humphrey (Pop), Ernie Adams.

Two cowboys infiltrate a gang of outlaws in order to catch a rustler before he reaches the Mexican border.

Note: Holt's father Jack and sister Jennifer also appeared in many western films.

24 *The Americano* (1955) Western.
Running time: 85 minutes. Black and white.

Produced by Robert Stillman. Directed by William Castle. Screenplay by Guy Trosper (based on a story by Leslie T. White). Photographed by William Snyder. Edited by Harry Marker.

Starring Glenn Ford (Sam Dent), Frank Lovejoy (Benito Hermanny), Cesar Romero (Manuel), Ursula Thiess (Marianna), Abbe Lane (Teresa), Rodolfo Hoyos, (Cristiano), Salvador

Baguez (Capt. Gonzales), Tom Powers (Jim Rogers), Dan White (Barney Dent), Frank Marlowe (Captain), George Novarro (Tuba), Nyra Monsour (Tuba's Sister).

Farmers attempting to settle on grazing land become involved in a range war.

25 *Amos 'n' Andy* (1930) Comedy. Running time: 70 minutes. Black and white. Available on videocassette.

Directed by Melville Brown. Screenplay by J. Walter Ruben. Photographed by William Marshall. Music by Bert Kalmar and Harry Ruby.

Starring Freeman Gosden (Amos), Charles Correll (Andy), Sue Carol (Jean), Charles Morton (Richard Williams), Ralf Harolde (Ralph Crawford), Edward Martindel (John Blair), Irene Rich (Mrs. Blair), Russell Powell (Kingfish).

The famous radio team make their screen debut as workers in the taxi business.

Note: The same white actors who did the radio voices essay the title roles in blackface. Dated and offensive by today's standards, slow-moving and dull by any standards. Retitled *Check and Double Check.*

26 *Androcles and the Lion* (1952) Comedy. Running time: 98 minutes. Black and white.

Produced by Gabriel Pascal. Directed by Chester Erskine. Written by Erskine and Ken Englund (based on the play by George Bernard Shaw). Photographed by Harry Stradling. Music by Frederick Hollander. Edited by Roland Cross.

Starring Alan Young (Androcles), Jean Simmons (Lavinia), Victor Mature (Captain), Robert Newton (Ferrovious), Maurice Evans (Caesar), Elsa Lanchester (Megaera), Reginald Gardiner (Lentuluts), Gene Lockhart (Menagerie Keeper), Alan Mowbray (Editor), Noel Willman (Spintha), John Hoyt (Cato), Jim Backus (Centurion), Lowell Gilmore (Metellius).

Shaw's play is loosely adapted for the screen as animal lover Androcles removes a thorn from a lion's paw, and later is spared when that animal is among those in a lion's den feeding on captured Christians.

27 *Angel Face* (1953) Crime drama. Running time: 91 minutes. Black and white.

Produced and directed by Otto Preminger. Screenplay by Frank S. Nugent and Oscar Millard (based on a story by Chester Erskine). Photographed by Harry Stradling. Music by Dimitri Tiomkin. Edited by Frederic Knudtson.

Starring Jean Simmons (Diane), Robert Mitchum (Frank), Mona Freeman (Mary), Herbert Marshall (Mr. Tremayne), Leon Ames (Fred Barrett), Barbara O'Neill (Mrs. Tremayne), Kenneth Tobey (Bill), Raymond Greenleaf (Arthur Vance), Griff Barnett (The Judge), Robert Gist (Miller), Morgan Farley (Juror), Jim Backus (District Attorney Judson), Bess Flowers (Barrett's Secretary), Alex Gerry (Lewis, Frank's Attorney), Gertrude Astor (Matron).

A girl tries to kill her rich stepmother in an auto crash, implicating the family chauffeur, but her beloved father is killed as well.

28 *Animal Farm* (1955) Animated drama. Running time: 75 minutes. Technicolor. Copyright not renewed; now in the public domain. Available on videocassette.

Produced and directed by John Halas and Joy Batchelor. Screenplay by Halas, Batchelor, Lothar Wolff, Borden Mace and Phillip Stapp (based on the book by George Orwell). Photographed by S.J. Griffiths. Music by Matyas Seiber.

Narrated by Gordon Heath. All voice characterizations by Maurice Denham.

Animated British production of George Orwell's story about barnyard animals who engage in a revolution.

29 *Animal Kingdom* (1932)
Drama. Running time: 90 minutes.
Black and white.

Produced by David O. Selznick.
Directed by Edward H. Griffith.
Screenplay by Horace Jackson (based on
the play by Phillip Barry). Photographed
by George Folsey. Edited by Daniel
Mandell.

Starring Ann Harding (Daisy), Leslie
Howard (Tom), Myrna Loy (Cecilia),
Neil Hamilton (Owen), William Gargan
(Regan), Henry Stephenson (Rufus),
Ilka Chase (Grace), Donald Dillaway
(Joe).

A rich publisher leaves his mistress to
marry, but soon finds his new wife is unfaithful.

30 *Ann Vickers* (1933) Drama.
Running time: 73 minutes. Black and
white. Available on videocassette.

Produced by John Cromwell. Written
by Jane Murfin (based on the novel by
Sinclair Lewis). Photographed by David
Abel and Edward Cronjager. Edited by
George Nicholls, Jr. Music by Max Stei-
ner.

Starring Irene Dunne (Ann Vickers),
Walter Huston (Barney Dolphin), Conrad Nagel (Lindsay), Bruce Cabot (Res-
nick), Edna May Oliver (Malvina
Wormser), Sam Hardy (Russell Spalding), Mitchell Lewis (Capt. Waldo),
Helen Eby-Rock (Kitty Cignac), Gertrude Michael (Mona Dolphin), J. Carrol
Naish (Dr. Sorrell), Sarah Padden (Lil),
Reginald Barlow (Chaplain), Rafacla Ottiano (Feldermus), Irving Bacon
(Waiter), Edwin Maxwell (Defense Attorney), Jane Darwell (Mrs. Gates), Arthur Hoyt (Mr. Penny).

Loose screen adaptation of Sinclair
Lewis novel about a social worker who
fights for civil liberties.

31 *Anna of Brooklyn* (1958) Ro-
mance. Running time: 106 minutes.
Black and white. Produced by Cicero
Cinema for RKO release.

Directed by Reginald Denham and

Carlo Lasticati. Screenplay by Ettore
Margadonna and Dino Risi. Photographed by Giuseppe Rotunno. Music
by Alessandro Cicognini and Vittorio De
Sica.

Starring Gina Lollobrigida, Dale
Robertson, Vittorio De Sica, Peppino de
Felippo, Amedeo Nazzari, Gabriella
Palotta.

A wealthy widow leaves Brooklyn and
returns to Italy to find a husband, only to
fall for an American tourist.

32 *Annabel Takes a Tour* (1938)
Comedy. Running time: 66 minutes.
Black and white. Available on video-
cassette.

Produced by Lou Lusty. Directed by
Lew Landers. Screenplay by Bert Granet
and Olive Cooper (based on a story by
Joe Bigelow and characters created by
Charles Hoffman). Photographed by
Russell Metty. Edited by Harry Marker.

Starring Jack Oakie (Lanny Morgan),
Lucille Ball (Annabel), Ruth Donnelly
(Josephine), Bradley Page (Webb),
Ralph Forbes (Viscount), Frances Mercer
(Natalie), Donald MacBride (Thomp-
son), Alice White (Marcella), Pepito
(Poochy), Chester Clute (Pitcairn), Jean
Rouverol (Laura), Clare Verdera (Vis-
countess), Ed Gargan (Longshoreman),
Lee Phelps (Delivery Man), Major Sam
Harris, Robert Warwick (Race Track
Officials), Milton Kibbee (bit).

Sequel to *The Affairs of Annabel* features Ball as a wacky heiress who falls in
love with the songwriter with whom she's
romantically linked as a publicity stunt
to promote her latest film. The problem
is, he's already married.

Note: After the release of this film,
The New York Times said that Lucille
Ball was "rapidly becoming one of our
brightest comediennes," but it would be
another decade before she was able to
fully exhibit such abilities.

33 *Annapolis Salute* (1937) Drama.
Running time: 65 minutes. British title:
Salute to Romance. Black and white.

Jack Oakie in *Annabel Takes a Tour.*

Produced by Samuel Briskin. Directed by Christy Cabanne. Screenplay by John Twist (based on a story by Cabanne). Photographed by Russell Metty. Edited by Ted Cheesman.

Starring James Ellison (Bill Martin), Marsha Hunt (Julia Clemmens), Harry Carey (Chief Martin), Van Heflin (Clarke Parker), Ann Hovey (Bunny Oliver), Arthur Lake (Tex Clemmens).

Military drama dealing with the lives of Annapolis cadets learning adult responsibilities.

Note: A remake of *Midshipman Jack*

(1933), which also featured Arthur Lake, but in a different role. A year after this film was released, Lake would achieve lasting fame as Dagwood in the Blondie series at Columbia Pictures.

34 *Anne of Green Gables* (1934)

Drama. Running time: 80 minutes. Black and white. Available on video-cassette.

Directed by George Nicholls, Jr. Screenplay by Sam Mintz (based on the novel by L.M. Montgomery). Photographed by Lucien Andriot. Music by Max Steiner. Edited by Arthur Schmidt.

Starring Anne Shirley (Anne Shirley), Tom Brown (Gilbert Blythe), O.P. Heggie (Matthew Cuthbert), Helen Westley (Marilla Cuthbert), Sara Haden (Mrs. Barry), Murray Kinnell (Mr. Phillips), Gertrude Messinger (Diana), June Preston (Mrs. Blewett's daughter), Charley Grapewin (Dr. Tatum), Hilda Vaughn (Mrs. Blewitt).

Screen version of Montgomery's moving novel about a creative, imaginative girl's journey to young womanhood and the adults she encounters along the way.

Note: This version has become somewhat obsolete as a result of the 1985 Canadian production featuring Megan Follows and Colleen Dewhurst; a four-hour *Wonderworks* TV special. Ms. Shirley took her screen name from the character in this novel. Sequel: *Anne of Windy Poplars.*

35 *Anne of Windy Poplars* (1940)

Drama. Running time: 85 minutes. Black and white.

Produced by Cliff Reid. Directed by Jack Hively. Screenplay by Michael Kanin and Jerry Cady (based on the novel by L.M. Montgomery). Photographed by Frank Redman. Edited by George Hively.

Starring Anne Shirley (Anne Shirley), James Ellison (Tony Pringle), Henry Travers (Matey), Patric Knowles (Gilbert Blythe), Slim Summerville (Jabez Monkman), Elizabeth Patterson (Rebecca),

Louis Campbell (Katherine Pringle), Joan Carroll (Betty Grayson), Katherine Alexander (Ernestine Pringle), Minnie Dupree (Kate), Alma Kruger (Mrs. Stephen Pringle), Clara Blandick (Mrs. Morton Pringle), Gilbert Emery (Stephen Pringle), Wright Kramer (Morton Pringle), Jackie Moran (boy).

Sequel to *Anne of Green Gables* follows Anne Shirley's later years as town educator who manages to incur the wrath of a wealthy family, due to one of her snobby students.

Note: A 1985 Canadian remake, with Megan Follows and Colleen Dewhurst, for TV's *Wonderworks,* runs four hours and is titled *Anne of Avonlea.*

36 *Annie Oakley* (1935)

Western. Running time: 79 minutes. Black and white.

Produced by Cliff Reid. Directed by George Stevens. Screenplay by Joel Sayre and John Twist (based on a story by Joseph A. Fields and Ewart Adamson). Photographed by J. Roy Hunt. Edited by Jack Hively.

Starring Barbara Stanwyck (Annie Oakley), Preston Foster (Toby Walker), Melvyn Douglas (Jeff Hogarth), Moroni Olsen (Buffalo Bill), Pert Kelton (Vera Delmar), Andy Clyde (MacIvor), Chief Thundercloud (Sitting Bull), Margaret Armstrong (Mrs. Oakley), Delmar Watson (Wesley Oakley), Philo McCullough (Officer), Eddie Dunn and Ernie Adams (Wranglers), Harry Bowen (Father), Theodore Lorch (Announcer), Sammy McKim (Boy at Shooting Gallery).

A backwoods girl joins Buffalo Bill's Wild West Show as a sharpshooter and becomes its star attraction.

Note: Stanwyck's first appearance in a western; a genre in which she was to be successful through subsequent films, culminating in TV's *The Big Valley.*

37 *Another Face* (1935)

Comedy. Running time: 72 minutes. Black and white.

Produced by Cliff Reid. Directed by

Christy Cabanne. Screenplay by Ray Mayer, Thomas Fugan, Garrett Graham and John Twist. Photographed by Jack MacKenzie. Edited by George Hively. Music by Roy Webb.

Starring Wallace Ford (Joe Haynes), Brian Donlevy (Dawson Dutra), Phyllis Brooks (Sheila), Erik Rhodes (Asst. Director), Molly Lamont (Mary), Alan Hale (Kellar), Addison Randall (Tex), Paul Stanton (Director), Edward Burns (Cameraman), Charles Wilson (Capt. Spellman), Hattie McDaniel (Maid), Si Jenks (Janitor), Oscar Apfel (Doctor), Inez Courtney (Mamie), Emma Dunn (Sheila's Mother), Ethel Wales (Aunt Hattie), Frank Mills (Muggsie).

When a homely gangster has his face altered, he is so taken by his new-found good looks that he travels to Hollywood in hopes of becoming a leading man in movies.

38 *Appointment in Honduras* (1953) Adventure. Running time: 79 minutes. Technicolor.

Produced by Benedict Bogeaus. Directed by Jacques Tourneur. Screenplay by Karen De Wolf. Photographed by Joseph Biroc. Music by Louis Forbes. Edited by James Leicester.

Starring Glenn Ford (Steve Corbett), Ann Sheridan (Sylvia Shepherd), Zachary Scott (Harry Shepherd), Rodolfo Acosta (Reyes), Jack Elam (Castro), Ric Roman (Miminez), Rico Alaniz (Bermudez), Paul Zaramba (Juis), Stanley Andrews (Capt. McTaggart).

An adventurer, on a mission through Honduras to deliver money to an ousted *presidente*, takes along two hostages and treks through the hazards of the jungle.

39 *Arctic Fury* (1949) Adventure. Running time: 61 minutes. Black and white.

Produced by Boris Petroff. Directed by Norman Dawn and Fred Feishans. Screenplay by Charles F. Royal (based on a story by Dawn). Photographed by

Dawn, Jacob Hull, Edward Kull, William Thompson. Edited by Feitshans.

Starring Del Cambre (Dr. Thomas Barlow), Eve Miller (Mrs. Barlow), Gloria Petroff (Emily Barlow), Don Riss (Narrator), Merrill McCormack (Trapper), Fred Smith (Uncle Jim).

A doctor is lost in a plane crash while flying supplies to an Arctic village and must fight his way back across the tundra.

40 *Are These Our Children?* (1931) Crime drama. Running time: 75 minutes. Black and white.

Directed by Wesley Ruggles. Screenplay by Ruggles and Howard Estabrook. Photographed by Leo Tover. Edited by Jack Kitchin.

Starring Eric Linden (Eddie Brand), Rochelle Hudson (Mary), Arline Judge (Florence Carnes), Ben Alexander (Nick Crosby), Robert Quirk (Benni Gray), Roberta Gale (Giggles), Mary Kornman (Dumbell), William Orlamond (Heine Krantz), Beryl Mercer (Grandmother Morton), Billy Butts (Bobby Brand), Jimmy Wang (Sam Kong), Robert McKenzie (Taxi Driver), Earl Pingee (Charlie), Russell Powell (Sam), Harry Shutan (Defense Attorney), Ralf Harolde (Prosecutor).

A nice boy gets involved with a tough crowd, becomes a juvenile delinquent, and eventually commits a murder.

Note: Early look at peer pressure, the premise for so many movies of this sort that started to become especially popular during the fifties. Actor Linden reportedly was carrying on a romance with actress Frances Dee, but when she married Joel McCrea, he took a trip to Europe to forget her.

41 *Arizona Legion* (1939) Western. Running time: 58 minutes. Black and white.

Produced by Bert Gilroy. Directed by David Howard. Written by Oliver Drake (based on a story by Bernard McConville). Photographed by Harry Wild.

Edited by Frederic Knudtson. Music by Roy Webb.

Starring George O'Brien (Boone Yeager), Laraine Johnson (Letty Meade), Carlyle Moore, Jr. (Lt. Ives), Chill Wills (Whopper Hatch), Edward LeSaint (Judge Meade), Harry Cording (Whiskey Joe), Tom Chatterton (Commissioner Teagle), William Royle (Dutton), Glenn Strange (Kirby), Monte Montague (Dawson), Joe Rickson (Dakota), Robert Burns (Tucson Jones).

A group of federal agents go after an outlaw gang who have overtaken a small town. The leader of the agents decides to infiltrate the outlaw gang in an effort to uncover the brains behind the criminal activities.

42 *The Arizona Ranger* (1948)

Western. Running time: 64 minutes. Black and white. Available on videocassette.

Produced by Herman Schlom. Directed by John Rawlins. Screenplay by Norman Houston. Photographed by J. Roy Hunt. Music by Paul Sawtell. Edited by Desmond Marquette.

Starring Tim Holt (Bob Wade), Jack Holt (Rawhide), Nan Leslie (Laura Butler), Richard Martin (Chito Rafferty), Steve Brodie (Quirt), Paul Hurst (Ben Riddle), Jim Nolan (Nimino), Robert Bray (Jasper), Richard Benedict (Gil), William Phipps (Mae), Harry Harvey (Peyton).

Cowboy is discharged from serving with Theodore Roosevelt's Rough Riders, but, much to his father's chagrin, refuses to join the family ranching business upon his return home. He goes off on his own, haunted by the painful memories of war. He later gets involved with a battered woman and rescues her from her dangerous spouse.

Note: Tim and Jack Holt, here playing father and son, were so in real life.

43 *The Arizonian* (1935)

Western. Running time: 75 minutes. Black and white.

Produced by Cliff Reid. Directed by Charles Vidor. Screenplay by Dudley Nichols. Photographed by Harold Weinstrom. Edited by Jack Hively. Music by Roy Webb.

Starring Richard Dix (Clay Tallant), Margot Grahame (Kitty Rivers), Preston Foster (Tex Randolph), Louis Calhern (Make Mannen), James Bush (Orin Tallant), Ray Mayer (McClosky), Joseph Sauers (Pompey), Francis Ford (Comstock).

A marshall takes on an outlaw gang, but is heavily outnumbered. Thus, an ex-outlaw pitches in to help him subdue the bandits.

Note: Remade as *The Marshal of Mesa City.*

44 *Armored Car Robbery* (1950)

Crime drama. Running time: 67 minutes. Black and white.

Produced by Herman Schlom. Directed by Richard Fleischer. Screenplay by Earl Felton and Gerald Drayson Adams (based on a story by Robert Angus and Robert Leeds). Photographed by Guy Roe. Edited by Desmond Marquette.

Starring Charles McGraw (Cordell), Adele Jergens (Yvonne), William Talman (Purvus), Douglas Fowley (Benny), Steve Brodie (Mapes), Don McGuire (Ryan), Don Haggerty (Cuyler), James Flavin (Phillips), Gene Evans (Foster).

A cop seeks revenge on the gang that killed his friend during an armored car holdup.

45 *Army Surgeon* (1942)

War drama. Running time: 63 minutes. Black and white.

Produced by Bert Gilroy. Directed by A. Edward Sutherland. Screenplay by Barry Trivers and Emmet Lavery (based on a story by John Twist). Photographed by Russell Metty. Music by Roy Webb. Edited by Samuel E. Beetley.

Starring James Ellison (Capt. James Mason), Jane Wyatt (Beth Ainsley),

Kent Taylor (Lt. Phillip Harvey), Walter Reed (Bill Drake), James Burke (Brooklyn), Jack Briggs (Major Wishart), Cyril Ring (Major Peterson), Eddie Dew (Ship Orderly), Ann Codee (Flower Woman), Russell Wade (Soldier), Richard Martin (Soldier).

A lady doctor tells the Army she's a nurse so she will be sent to the front line.

Note: Jane Wyatt achieved great status on television's *Father Knows Best* in the 1950s.

46 *Around the World* (1943)

Musical. Running time: 90 minutes. Black and white.

Produced and directed by Allan Dwan. Screenplay by Ralph Spence. Photographed by Russell Metty. Edited by Theron Warth. Music and lyrics by Jimmy McHugh and Harold Adamson.

Songs: "Doodle-Ee-Doo," "He's Got a Secret Weapon," "Candlelight and Wine," "Great News in the Making," "They Chopped Down the Old Apple Tree," "A Moke from Shamokin."

Starring Kay Kyser (Kay), Mischa Auer (Mischa), Joan Davis (Joan), Marcy McGuire (Marcy), Wally Brown (Pilot), Alan Carney (Joe Gimpus), Georgia Carroll (Georgia), Harry Babbitt (Harry), Ish Kabibble (Ish), Sully Mason (Sully), Julie Conway (Julie), Diane Pendleton (Diane), Kay Kyser's Band (themselves), Jack and Max, Al Norman, Lucienne and Ashour, Little Fred's Football Dogs, Jadine Wong and Li Sun (Specialty acts), Robert Armstrong (General), John Barclay (Barclay), Margie Stewart (Marjorie), Barbara Hale (Barbara), Rosemary LaPlanche (Rosemary), Barbara Coleman (Coleman), Shirley O'Hara (Shirley), Sherry Hall (Clipper Steward), Joan Valerie (Countess Olga), Frank Puglia (Native Dealer), Peter Chong (Mr. Wong), Duncan Renaldo (Dragonman), Chester Conklin (Waiter), Selmer Jackson (Consul), Louise Curry (WAC), James Westerfield (Bashful Marine), Phillip Ahn (Foo).

Plotless musical which follows Kay Kyser and his band as they tour the world performing shows.

47 *At Sword's Point* (1951)

Adventure. Running time: 81 minutes. British title: *Sons of the Musketeers.* Technicolor. Available on videocassette.

Produced by Sid Rogell. Directed by Lewis Allen. Screenplay by Walter Ferris and Joseph Hoffman (based on a story by Aubrey Wisberg and Jack Pollexfen). Photographed by Ray Rennahan. Edited by Samuel E. Beetley and Robert Golden. Music by Roy Webb.

Starring Cornel Wilde (D'Artagnan), Maureen O'Hara (Claire), Robert Douglas (Lavalle), Gladys Cooper (Queen), June Clayworth (Claudine), Dan O'Herlihy (Armais), Alan Hale, Jr. (Porthos), Blanche Yurka (Mme. Michon), Nancy Gates (Princess Henriette), Edmond Breon (Queens Chamberlain), Peter Miles (Louis), George Petrie (Chalais), Moroni Olsen (Old Porthos), Boyd Davis (Dr. Fernand), Holmes Herbert (Mallard), Lucien Littlefield (Corporal Gautier), Claude Dunkin (Pierre).

An evil duke plans to marry a princess and removes her brother from the path of the throne by having him killed. His plot is foiled by the children of the original musketeers.

48 *The Avenging Rider* (1943)

Western. Running time: 56 minutes. Black and white.

Produced by Bert Gilroy. Directed by Sam Nelson. Screenplay by Harry O. Hoyt and Morton Grant. Photographed by J. Roy Hunt. Edited by John Lockert.

Starring Tim Holt (Brit), Cliff "Ukelele Ike" Edwards (Ike), Ann Summers (Jean), Davison Clark (Grayson), Norman Willis (Red), Karl Hackett (Sheriff Allen), Earle Hodgins (Deputy), Edward Cassidy (Sheriff Lewis), Kenneth Duncan (Blackie), Malcolm "Bud" McTaggert (Baxter), Bud Osborne (Wade), Bob Kortman (Harris).

When their old friend murders a local mine owner, a cowboy and his sidekick are jailed as members of his gang. They must break out to clear their name.

Note: Edwards was the voice of Disney cartoon character Jiminy Cricket.

49 *The Bachelor and the Bobby-Soxer* (1947)   Comedy. Running time: 95 minutes. British title: *Bachelor Bait.* Black and white.

Produced by Dore Schary. Directed by Irving Reis. Screenplay by Sidney Sheldon. Photographed by Robert de Grasse and Nicholas Musuraca. Music by Leigh Harline. Edited by Frederic Knudtson.

Starring Cary Grant (Dick), Myrna Loy (Margaret), Shirley Temple (Susan), Rudy Vallee (Tommy), Ray Collins (Beemish), Harry Davenport (Thaddeus), Johnny Sands (Jerry), Don Beddoe (Tony), Lillian Randolph (Bessie), Veda Ann Borg (Agnes Prescott), Dan Tobin (Walters), Ransom Sherman (Judge Treadwell), William Bakewell (Winters), Irving Bacon (Melvin), Ian Bernard (Perry), Carol Hughes (Florence), William Hall (Anthony Herman), Gregory Gaye (Maitre d'hotel).

When a handsome art teacher becomes the object of infatuation for one of his students, the girl's sister, a judge, orders the teacher to escort the adolescent everywhere until this crush subsides. Meanwhile, the art teacher falls for the judge.

Note: This film grossed five million dollars in its first theatrical release. It was producer Schary's last film before taking over as head of RKO.

50 *Bachelor Apartment* (1931)   Romantic comedy. Running time: 74 minutes. Black and white.

Directed by Lowell Sherman. Screenplay by J. Walter Ruben (based on a story by John Howard Lawson). Photographed by Leo Tover.

Starring Lowell Sherman (Wayne Carter), Irene Dunne (Helene Andrews), Mae Murray (Agatha Caraway), Norman Kerry (Lee Carlton), Claudia Dell (Lita Andrews), Ivan Lebedeff (Henri De Maneau), Noel Francis (Janet), Purnell Pratt (Henry Carraway), Charles Coleman (Rollins), Kitty Kelly (Miss Clark), Bess Flowers (Charlotte), Florence Roberts (Mrs. Holloran).

A New York working girl falls for an egotistical ladies' man.

Review: "It oversteps the reasonable limits of sophisticated art." — *Variety.*

51 *Bachelor Bait* (1934)   Romantic comedy. Running time: 80 minutes. Black and white. Available on videocassette.

Directed by George Stevens. Screenplay by Glenn Tryon (based on a story by Edward and Victor Halperin). Photographed by David Abel. Edited by James Morley. Music by Max Steiner.

Starring Stuart Erwin (Wilbur Fess), Rochelle Hudson (Linda), Pert Kelton (Allie Summers), Skeets Gallagher (Van Dusen), Berton Churchill (Big Barney), Grady Sutton (Don Belden), Clarence Wilson (District Attorney).

When a mild-mannered employee is fired from a marriage license bureau, he opens his own matchmaking agency so that he may continue to play Cupid.

Note: Stu Erwin achieved great success on TV in his own series *The Trouble with Father* during the early fifties.

52 *Bachelor Mother* (1939)   Comedy. Running time: 80 minutes. Black and white. Available on videocassette.

Produced by B.G. DeSylva and Pandro S. Berman. Directed by Garson Kanin. Screenplay by Norman Krasna (based on a story by Felix Jackson). Photographed by Robert De Grasse. Edited by Henry Berman and Robert Wise.

Starring Ginger Rogers (Polly Parish), David Niven (David Merlin), Charles Coburn (J.B. Merlin), Frank Albertson (Freddie Miller), E.E. Clive (Butler), Elbert Coplen, Jr. (Johnnie), Ferike Boros (Mrs. Weiss), Ernest Truex (Investigator), Leonard Penn (Jerome Weiss),

Paul Stanton (Hargraves), Frank M. Thomas (Doctor), Edna Holland (Matron), Dennie Moore (Mary), June Wilkins (Louise King), Donald Duck (Himself), Horace MacMahon and Murray Alper (Bouncers).

A shopgirl finds an abandoned baby and is mistaken for its mother, while the department store owner's son is mistaken for its father.

Review: "...just enough conviction to season its extravagance." — *New York Times*.

Note: Writer Krasna collaborated on the play *Time for Elizabeth* with Groucho Marx. Director Kanin collaborated on several screenplays with wife Ruth Gordon. Felix Jackson's original story was nominated for an Oscar. Remade as *Bundle of Joy* with Debbie Reynolds and Eddie Fisher.

53 Back from Eternity (1956)

Drama. Running time: 97 minutes. Black and white.

Produced and directed by John Farrow. Screenplay by Jonathan Latimer (based on the story by Richard Carroll). Photographed by William Meilor. Edited by Eda Warren.

Starring Robert Ryan (Bill), Anita Ekberg (Rita), Rod Steiger (Vasquez), Phyllis Kirk (Louise), Keith Andes (Joe), Gene Barry (Ellis), Fred Clark (Crimp), Beulah Bondi (Martha), Cameron Prudhomme (Henry), Jesse White (Pete), Adele Mara (Maria), Jon Provost (Tommy).

A plane crashes in a remote South American territory which is populated by headhunters. When the plane is repaired, only five of the eight survivors can be carried.

Note: A remake of *Five Came Back*.

54 Back to Bataan (1945) War.

Running time: 98 minutes. Black and white. Available on videocassette and in a colorized edition.

Produced by Robert Fellows. Directed by Edward Dmytryk. Screenplay by Ben Barzman and Richard Landau (based on a story by Aeneas MacKenzie and William Gordon). Photographed by Nicholas Musuraca. Edited by Marston Fay. Music by Roy Webb. Technical advisor: Col. George E. Clarke.

Starring John Wayne (Colonel Madden), Anthony Quinn (Capt. Andres Bonifacio), Beulah Bondi (Miss Bertha Barnes), Fely Franquelli (Dalisay Delgado), Richard Loo (Major Hasko), Phillip Ahn (Colonel Kuroki), J. Alex Havier (Sgt. Biernesa), "Ducky" Louie (Maximo), Lawrence Tierney (Lt. Commander Waite), Leonard Strong (General Homma), Paul Fix (Spindle Jackson), Abner Biberman (Japanese Captain/Japanese Diplomat), Vladimir Sokoloff (Buenaventura J. Bello), Benson Fong (Japanese Announcer), John Miljan (Gen. Jonathan M. "Skinny" Wainwright), Kenneth MacDonald (Major McKinley), Ray Teal (Lt. Col. Roberts), Angel Cruz, Bill Williams, Edmund Glover, Erville Alderson, and the actual American prisoners at the Japanese prison camp at Cambanatuan: Lt. (USN) Emmet L. Manson, Lt. (USN) Earl G. Baumgardner, Cpl. (USMC) Dennis D. Rainwater, Sgt. (USMC) Eugene C. Commander, Pvt. (USA) Jesus Santos, Lt. (USNR) George W. Greene, Sgt. (USMC) Kenneth W. Mize, Cpl. (USA) Max M. Greenberg, Pvt. (USA) Alfred C. Jolley, Pvt. (USA) Virgil H. Greenaway, PFC (USA) Lawrence C. Hall, Cpl. (USMC) Neil P. Iovino.

Told in flashback, story deals with a brave soldier who leads a company of Philippine scouts into guerrilla resistance when Bataan is cut off.

Note: Most of the war scenes were shot just outside San Bernardino. Wayne and Quinn reportedly played poker between takes with Filipino extras. The dealer was crooked, and Quinn lost hundreds of dollars, but refused to quit playing. Director Dmytryk fired the extra to save Quinn from losing his entire salary.

Reviews: "Good, sturdy WWII action

film."—Leonard Maltin, *TV Movies;* "Modestly made and rather dislikeable flagwaver."—Leslie Halliwell, *Film and Video Guide.*

55 Bad Company (1931) Crime drama. Running time: 65 minutes. Black and white. A Pathé production released by RKO.

Produced by Charles R. Rogers. Directed by Tay Garnett. Screenplay by Garnett and Thomas Buckingham (based on a story by Jack Lait, Jr.). Photographed by Arthur Miller. Edited by Claude Berkeley.

Starring Helen Twelvetrees (Helen), Ricardo Cortez (Goldie Gorio), John Garrick (Steve), Paul Hurst (Butler), Frank Conroy (Markham King), Frank McHugh (Doc), Edgar Kennedy (Buff), Kenneth Thompson (Barnes), Emma Dunn (Emma), William V. Mong (Henry), Wade Boteler (Monk), Al Iteman (Pearson), Harry Carey, Sr. (McBaine), Robert Keith (Professor).

A naïve girl gets mixed up with gangsters, who use her for their rackets while hiding the true facts of their shady dealings with her.

Note: Director-writer Garnett later did *The Postman Always Rings Twice* (MGM; 1946 version).

56 Bad Lands (1939) Western. Running time: 70 minutes. Black and white.

Produced by Robert Sisk. Directed by Lew Landers. Screenplay by Charles Upson Young. Photographed by Frank Redman. Edited by George Hively.

Starring Robert Barrat (Sheriff), Noah Beery, Jr. (Chile Lyman), Guinn "Big Boy" Williams (Billy Sweet), Douglas Walton (Mulford), Andy Clyde (Cliff), Addison Richards (Rayburn), Robert Coote (Eaton), Paul Hurst (Curley Tom), Francis Ford (Garth), Francis McDonald (Manuel Lopez).

A posse, in pursuit of Indians, is stranded in the desert and must battle for survival.

Note: Loosely based on *The Lost Patrol.*

57 Badman's Territory (1946) Western. Running time: 97 minutes. Black and white.

Produced by Nat Holt. Directed by Tim Whelan. Screenplay by Jack Natteford, Luci Ward, Clarence Upson Young, Bess Taffel. Photographed by Robert De Grasse. Edited by Phillip Martin, Jr. Music by Roy Webb.

Starring Randolph Scott (Mark Rowley), Ann Richards (Henrietta Alcott), George "Gabby" Hayes (Coyote), Ray Collins (Col. Farwell), James Warren (John Rowley), Morgan Conway (Bill Hampton), Virginia Sale (Meg), John Halloran (Hank McGee), Andrew Tombes (Doc Grant), Richard Hale (Ben Wade), Harry Holman (Hodge), Chief Thundercloud (Chief Tahlequah), Lawrence Tierney (Jesse James), Tom Tyler (Frank James), Steve Brodie (Bob Dalton), Phil Warren (Grant Dalton), William Moss (Bill Dalton), Nestor Paiva (Sam Bass), Isabel Jewell (Belle Starr), Emory Parnell (Bitter Creek), John Hamilton (Commissioner), Robert E. Homans (Trial Judge).

A Texas sheriff must enlist the help of famous outlaws in an effort to find his missing younger brother.

Review: "Unconvincing Western with good moments."—Leslie Halliwell, *Film and Video Guide.*

58 Ball of Fire (1941) Comedy. Running time: 111 minutes. Black and white. Available on videocassette.

Produced by Samuel Goldwyn. Directed by Howard Hawks. Screenplay by Charles Brackett and Billy Wilder (based on the story *From A to Z* by Thomas Monroe and Billy Wilder). Photographed by Gregg Toland. Edited by Daniel Manell. Music by Alfred Newman.

Song: "Drum Boogie," music by Gene Krupa.

Starring Gary Cooper (Prof. Bertram Potts), Barbara Stanwyck (Sugarpuss O'Shea), Oscar Homolka (Prof. Gurkakoff), Henry Travers (Prof. Jerome), S.Z.

"Cuddles" Sakall (Prof. Magenbruch), Tully Marshall (Prof. Robinson), Leonid Kinsky (Prof. Quintana), Richard Haydn (Prof. Oddly), Aubrey Mather (Prof. Peagram), Allen Jenkins (Garbage Man), Dana Andrews (Joe Lilac), Dan Duryea (Duke Patrami), Ralph Peters (Asthma Anderson), Kathleen Howard (Miss Bragg), Mary Field (Miss Totten), Charles Lane (Larson), Charles Arnt (McNeary), Elisha Cook, Jr. (Cook), Alan Rhein (Horseface), Eddie Foster (Pinstripe), Will Lee (Benny "The Creep"), Aldrich Bowker (Justice of the Peace), Addison Richards (District Attorney), Kenneth Howell, Tommy Ryan, Pat West, Ed Mundy, June Horne, Geraldine Fissette, Ethelreda Leopold, George Barton, Walter Shumway, Doria Caron, Marrilee Lannon, Chaterine Henderson, Helen Seamon, Jack Perry, Mildred Morris, Gerald Pierce, Francis Sayles, Lorraine Miller, Chet De Vito, Pat Flaherty, George Sherwood, Lee Phelps, Ken Christy, Del Lawrence, Eddie Chandler, Dick Rush, Johnnie Morris, Edward Clark (bits), Gene Krupa and His Orchestra (Themselves).

Seven professors compiling a new dictionary harbor a striptease dancer in an effort to learn more modern slang.

Note: Loosely based on *Snow White and the Seven Dwarfs.* Ginger Rogers was originally considered for the Barbara Stanwyck role. Remade by the same director as *A Song Is Born.*

Review: "It's played as if it were terribly bright, but it's rather shrill and tiresome." — Pauline Kael, *The New Yorker.*

59 *Bambi* (1942) Animation. Running time: 78 minutes. Technicolor. Available on videocassette.

Produced by Walt Disney and David D. Hand. Directed by David Hand and Perce Pearce. Screenplay by Larry Morey, George Stallings, Melvin Shaw, Carl Fallberg, Chuck Couch, Ralph Wright. Sequence directors: James Algar, Bill Roberts, Norman Wright, Sam Armstrong, Paul Satterfield, Graham Heid.

Supervising animators: Franklin Thomas, Milt Kahl, Eric Larson, Oliver M. Johnston, Jr. Animators: Fraser Davis, Bill Justice, Bernard Garbutt, Don Lusk, Retta Scott, Kenneth O'Brien, Louis Schmidt, John Bradbury, Joshua Meador, Phil Duncan, George Rowley, Art Palmer, Art Elliot. Backgrounds: Merle Cox, Tyrus Wong, Art Riley, Robert McIntosh, Travis Johnson, W. Richard Anthony, Stan Spohn, Ray Huffine, Ed Levitt, Joe Stahley. Music: Frank Churchill, Edward H. Plumb. Orchestrations: Charles Wolcott, Paul J. Smith. Conductor: Alexander Steinert. Choral arrangements: Charles Henderson.

Songs: "Love Is a Song," "Let's Sing a Gay Little Spring Song," "Little April Shower," "Looking for Romance (I Bring You a Song)."

Featuring the voices of Bobby Stewart (Bambi), Peter Behn (Thumper), Stan Alexander (Flower), Cammie King (Phylline), Donnie Dunagan, Hardie Albright, John Sutherland, Tim Davis, Sam Edwards, Sterling Holloway, Ann Gillis.

Animated classic tracing the life of a deer from fawn to buck.

Reviews: "This reviewer is of the opinion that, like many another work of art dealing with activities of the young, its greatest appeal will be for thoroughly adult minds." — Archer Winsten, *The New York Post;* "...a shade too much cuddly charm." — Bosley Crowther, *The New York Times;* "*Bambi* is a beautiful film, and the extraordinary effort that went into making it shows in the finished product." — Leonard Maltin, *The Disney Films.*

60 *The Bamboo Blonde* (1946) Romantic comedy. Running time: 68 minutes. Black and white.

Produced by Sid Rogell. Directed by Anthony Mann. Screenplay by Olive Cooper and Lawrence Kimble (based on a story by Wayne Wittaker). Photographed by Frank Redman. Edited by

Les Millbrook. Music by Mort Greene and Lou Pollack.

Starring Frances Langford (Louise Anderson), Ralph Edwards (Eddie Clark), Russell Wade (Patrick Ransom, Jr.), Iris Adrian (Montana), Richard Martin (Jim Wilson), Jane Greer (Eileen Sawyer), Glenn Vernon (Shorty Parker), Paul Harvey (Patrick Ransom, Sr.), Regina Wallace (Mrs. Ransom), Jean Brooks (Marsha), Tommy Noonan (Art Department), Dorothy Vaughan (Mom).

A nightclub singer is promoted when a likeness of her face is painted on a WWII bomber that goes on to sink Japanese battleships and down several enemy planes.

Note: Langford sings "Dreaming Out Loud."

61 *Bandit Ranger* (1942) Western. Running time: 58 minutes. Black and white.

Produced by Bert Gilroy. Directed by Lesley Selander. Screenplay by Bennett R. Cohen and Morton Grant (based on a story by Cohen). Edited by Les Millbrook. Music by Paul Sawtell.

Starring Tim Holt, Cliff Edwards, Joan Barclay, Kenneth Harlan, LeRoy Mason, Glenn Strange, Jack Rockwell, Bob Kortman, Dennis Moore, Frank Ellis, Bud Geary, Russell Wade, Ernie Adams, Lloyd Ingraham, Tom London.

Cowboy hero battles a band of cattle thieves single-handedly.

Note: One of six Holt westerns made between May and July, 1942, before Holt was drafted. Supporting actor Strange played Frankenstein's monster in *House of Frankenstein, House of Dracula,* and *Abbott and Costello Meet Frankenstein* at Universal. Cliff Edwards, as Ukelele Ike, sings "Move Along" and "Musical Jack."

62 *The Bandit Trail* (1941) Western. Running time: 59 minutes. Black and white.

Produced by Bert Gilroy. Directed by Ed Killy. Screenplay by Norton S. Parker

(based on a story by Arthur T. Horman). Photographed by Harry Wild. Edited by Frederic Knudtson.

Starring Tim Holt (Steve), Ray Whitley (Smokey), Janet Waldo (Ellen Grant), Lee "Lasses" White (Whopper), Morris Ankrum (Red), Roy Barcroft (Joel Nesbitt), J. Merrill Holmes (Sheriff Saunders), Eddy Waller (Tom Haggerty), Glenn Strange (Idaho), Frank Ellis (Al), Joseph Eggenton (Andrew Grant), Guy Usher (Mayor), Jack Clifford (Kurt Halliday), Bud Osborne (Tint).

A cowboy turns bad guy when a bank puts an unfair mortgage on his father's home. He robs the bank, later feels remorse, and becomes the town marshall, putting his former bandit comrades behind bars.

Note: The working title for this film is *Outlaw Trail,* which is the title of its lead song, sung by Ray Whitley, who also wrote it. Actress Waldo was the voice of TV's Judy Jetson.

63 *Banjo* (1947) Family drama. Running time: 67 minutes. Color.

Produced by Lillie Hayward. Directed by Richard Fleischer. Screenplay by Lillie Hayward. Photographed by George E. Diskant. Edited by Les Millbrook.

Starring Sharyn Moffett (Pat), Jacqueline White (Elizabeth), Walter Reed (Dr. Bob), Una O'Connor (Harriet), Herbert Evans (Jeffries), Louise Beavers (Lindy), Ernest Whitman (Jasper), Lanny Ross (Ned), Theron Jackson (Exodus), Howard McNeely (Genesis), Banjo (Himself).

When her father is killed, a peasant girl and her dog are sent to live with her cranky aunt.

64 *The Bashful Bachelor* (1942) Comedy. Running time: 78 minutes. Black and white.

Produced by Jack William Votion. Directed by Malcolm St. Clair. Screenplay by Chandler Sprague (based on a story by Chester Lauck and Norris Goff).

Photographed by Paul Ivano. Edited by Duncan Mansfield.

Starring Chester Lauck (Lum), Norris Goff (Abner), ZaSu Pitts (Geraldine), Grady Sutton (Cedric), Oscar O'Shea (Squire Skimp), Louise Currie (Marjorie), Constance Purdy (Widder Abernathy), Irving Bacon (Sheriff), Earle Hodgins (Joe), Benny Rubin (Pitch Man).

The radio team of Lum and Abner appear as their familiar characters in this story which has them trading a delivery truck for a race horse in an attempt to win big money at the track.

Note: Director St. Clair's career dates back to silent films. He helmed some of Laurel and Hardy's last features for 20th Century–Fox.

65 Beat the Band (1947) Musical comedy. Running time: 67 minutes. Black and white.

Produced by Michel Kraike. Directed by John H. Auer. Screenplay by Lawrence Kibble (based on the play by George Abbott). Photographed by Frank Redman. Edited by Samuel E. Beetley. Music by Mort Greene and Leigh Harline.

Songs include: "I'm in Love," "Kissing Well," "I've Got My Fingers Crossed," "Beat the Band."

Starring Frances Langford (Ann), Ralph Edwards (Eddie), Phillip Terry (Damon), June Clayworth (Wilow), Mabel Paige (Mrs. Peters), Andrew Tombes (Professor), Donald MacBride (Duff), Mira McKinney (Mrs. Rogers), Harry Harvey (Mr. Roberts), Grady Sutton (Harold).

A country girl with an operatic voice comes to the big city to take singing lessons, but falls for a bandleader who's after her money.

66 Beau Bandit (1930) Western. Running time: 71 minutes. Black and white.

Produced by William LeBaron. Directed by Lambert Hillyer. Screenplay by Wallace Smith. Photographed by Jack MacKenzie. Edited by Archie Marshek.

Starring Rod LaRocque (Montero), Mitchell Lewis (Coloso), Doris Kenyon (Helen), Charles Middleton (Perkins), George Duryea (Howard), Walter Long (Bobcat), James Donlan (Buck).

A dude cowboy hires a bandit to kill his rival so that he may marry the girl he loves.

Note: Actor Duryea later starred in many westerns under the name Tom Keene.

67 Beau Ideal (1931) Adventure. Running time: 82 minutes. Black and white.

Directed by Herbert Brenon. Screenplay by Elizabeth Meehan. Photographed by J. Roy Hunt.

Starring Frank McCormack (Carl Meyer), Ralph Forbes (John Geste), Lester Vail (Otis Madison), Otto Matieson (Jacob Levine), Don Alvarado (Ramon Gonzales), Bernard Siegel (Ivan Radinoff), Irene Rich (Lady Brandon), Myrtle Steadman (Mrs. Frank Madison), Loretta Young (Isobel Brandon), John St. Polls (Judge Advocate), Joseph de Stefani (Prosecuting Attorney), Paul McAllister (Sergeant Frederic), Hale Hamilton (Major Labaudy), George Rigas (The Emir), Leni Stengel (Zuleika).

The first sound version of *Beau Geste* (the original was a 1926 silent also featuring Forbes). This version lost $350,000.

68 Beauty for the Asking (1939) Drama. Running time: 68 minutes. Black and white.

Produced by B.P. Fineman. Directed by Glenn Tryon. Screenplay by Doris Anderson and Paul Jerrico. Photographed by Frank Redman. Edited by George Crone.

Starring Lucille Ball (Jean Russell), Patric Knowles (Denny Williams), Donald Woods (Jefferey Martin), Frieda Inescort (Flora Barton), Inez Courtney (Gwen Morrison), Leona Maricle (Eva

Harrington), Frances Mercer (Patricia Wharton), Whitney Bourne (Peggy Ponsby), Ann Evers (Lois Peabody), George Andre Beranger (Cyril).

Jealousies and marriage for money are the topics among women in a cosmetics showroom.

69 *Becky Sharp* (1935) Drama. Running time: 83 minutes. Color. Available on videocassette.

Produced by Kenneth MacGowan. Directed by Rouben Mamoulian. Screenplay by Francis Edwards Faragoh (based on the play by Langdon Mitchell and *Vanity Fair* by William Makepeace Thackeray). Photographed by Ray Rennahan. Edited by Archie Marshek. Music by Roy Webb.

Starring Miriam Hopkins (Becky Sharp), Frances Dee (Amelia Sedley), Sir Cedric Hardwicke (Marquis of Steyne), Billie Burke (Lady Bareacres), Alison Skipworth (Miss Crawley), Nigel Bruce (Joseph Sedley), Alan Mowbray (Rawdon Crawley), Colin Tapley (William Dobbin), George P. Huntley (George Osborne), William Stack (Pitt Crawley), George Hassell (Sir Pitt Crawley), William Faversham (Duke of Wellington), Charles Richman (General Tufto), Doris Lloyd (Duchess of Richmond), Leonard Mudie (Tarquin), Bunny Beatty (Lady Blanche), Charles Coleman (Bowles), May Beatty (Briggs), Finis Barton (Miss Floyers), Olaf Hytten, Pauline Caron, James "Hambone" Robinson, Elspeth Dudgeon, Tempe Pigott, Ottola Nesmith, Will Geer.

A scheming woman goes from rags to riches.

Note: The first all-color (Technicolor) movie, offering the closest color to real life. Critics believed this process would doom black and white films forever just as talkies sounded the death knell for silents. Miriam Hopkins was nominated for an Oscar as Best Actress. A Pioneer production released by RKO.

Reviews: "Beautiful cinematography, but weak on story." — *Variety;* "Audiences oohed and aahed at the (color), but came to sleep through the movie." — *Motion Picture Guide.*

70 *Bed of Roses* (1933) Drama. Running time: 70 minutes. Black and white.

Produced by Merian C. Cooper. Director by Gregory La Cava. Screenplay by Wanda Tuchock and Eugene Thackrey. Photographed by Charles Rosher. Edited by Basil Wrangell. Music by Max Steiner.

Starring Constance Bennett (Lorry Evans), Joel McCrea (Mike), John Halliday (Paige), Pert Kelton (Minnie), Samuel S. Hinds (Father Doran).

Two reform school girls fall for a couple of uptight men while on a steamer bound for New Orleans.

Reviews: "Adequate vehicle for a fading star who had played too many such roles." — Leslie Halliwell, *Filmgoers' Companion;* "Former Ziegfeld girl Kelton (gets) the best lines." — *The Motion Picture Guide.*

71 *Bedlam* (1945) Horror. Running time: 78 minutes. Black and white. Available on videocassette.

Produced by Val Lewton. Directed by Mark Robson. Screenplay by Robson, Carlos Keith. Photographed by Nicholas Musuraca. Edited by Lyle Boyer.

Starring Boris Karloff (Sims), Anna Lee (Neil), Billy House (Lord Mortimer), Glenn Vernon (Gilded Boy), Jason Robards, Sr. (Oliver), Joan Newton (Dorthea), Richard Fraser (Hannay), Ian Wolfe (Sidney).

A sadistic asylum master captures an actress.

72 *Before Dawn* (1933) Mystery. Running time: 60 minutes. Black and white.

Directed by Irving Pichel. Screenplay by Garrett Fort, Marion Dix and Ralph Block (based on a story by Edgar Wallace). Photographed by Lucien Andriot. Edited by William Hamilton. Music by Max Steiner.

Publicity poster for *Bedlam*.

Starring Stuart Erwin (Dwight Wilson), Dorothy Wilson (Patricia Merrick), Warner Oland (Dr. Cornelius), Dudley Digges (Horace Merrick), Gertrude W. Hoffman (Mattie), Oscar Apfel (O' Hara), Frank Reicher (Joe Valerie), Jane Darwell (Mrs. Marple).

Top detectives and fake mystics attempt to solve the murders at a mysterious mansion, all having to do with a million dollars that was supposedly buried there by a now deceased gangster.

73 *Behave Yourself* (1951) Comedy. Running time: 81 minutes. Black and white. Available on videocassette.

Produced by Jerry Wald, Norman Krasna, and Stanley Rubin. Directed by George Beck. Screenplay by Beck (based on a story by Beck and Frank Tarloff). Photographed by James Wong Howe. Edited by Paul Weatherwax. Music by Lew Spence and Buddy Ebsen.

Starring Farley Granger (Bill Denny), Shelley Winters (Kate Denny), Margalo Gilmore (Mrs. Carter), William Demarest (O'Ryan), Francis L. Sullivan (Fast Fred), Lon Chaney, Jr. (Pinky), Sheldon Leonard (Bert), Marvin Kaplan (Max), Henry Corden (Numi), Glenn Anders (Starn), Allen Jenkins (Detective), Elisha Cook, Jr. (Jonas), Hans Conried (Gillie).

A dog which criminals have trained wanders off and ends up in the care of a young married couple. When the crooks discover this, they set out to get the dog back.

Reviews: "The humor is spread too thin for success." — Leslie Halliwell, *Film and Video Guide;* "Strange casting of Granger and Winters detracts from comic potential." — Leonard Maltin, *TV Movies.*

74 *Behind Office Doors* (1931) Drama. Running time: 82 minutes. Black and white.

Directed by Melville Brown. Screenplay by Carey Wilson (based on a story by Alan Brener Schultz).

Starring Mary Astor (Mary Linden), Robert Ames (James Duneen), Ricardo Cortez (Bonnie Wales), Kitty Kelly (Delores Kogan), Edna Murphy (Daisy Presby), Catherine Dale Owen (Ellen Robison), Charles Sellon (Ritter), William Morris (Robinson).

A secretary who is the reason for her employer's success is taken for granted by him until she is lured away by a competitor.

75 *Behind the Headlines* (1937) Crime drama. Running time: 58 minutes. Black and white.

Produced by Cliff Reid. Directed by Richard Rosson. Screenplay by J. Robert Bren and Edmund L. Hartmann (based on a story by Thomas Ahearn). Photographed by Russell Metty. Edited by Harry Marker.

Starring Lee Tracy (Eddie Haines), Diana Gibson (Mary Bradley), Donald Meek (Potter), Paul Guilfoyle (Art Martin), Phillip Huston (Bennett), Frank M. Thomas (Naylor), Tom Kennedy (Tiny), Doodles Weaver (Duggan).

Male and female newspaper reporters compete for top stories until the man is forced to rescue the woman from the clutches of gangsters.

Note: Similar in concept to Warner Bros. feature *Front Page Woman* starring George Brent and Bette Davis. Actor Tracy was said to be RKO's answer to James Cagney. Actor Kennedy was at one time a Keystone Cop for Mack Sennett. Actor Weaver was a member of Spike Jones' City Slickers.

76 *Behind the Rising Sun* (1943) War. Running time: 88 minutes. Black and white. Available on videocassette.

Directed by Edward Dmytryk. Screenplay by Emmet Lavery (based on the book by James R. Young). Photographed by Russell Metty. Edited by Joseph Noriega. Music by Roy Webb.

Starring Margo (Tama), Tom Neal (Taro), J. Carrol Naish (Publisher), Robert Ryan (Lefty), Gloria Holden (Sara), Don Douglas (O'Hara), George

Givot (Boris), Adeline Reynolds (Grand-mother), Leonard Strong (Tama's Fa-ther), Iris Wong (Woman Secretary), Wolfgang Zilzer (Max), Shirley Lew (Ser-vant), Benson Fong (Japanese Officer), Lee Tung Foo (Dinner Guest), Mike Ma-zurki (Japanese Wrestler), William Yip (Japanese Officer), H.T. Tsiang (Police-man), Luke Chan (Officer), Bruce Wong (First Agent), Leon Lontoc (Japanese Guard), Mei Lee Foo (Geisha Girl), Allan Jung (Capt. Matsuda), Abner Biberman (Inspector), Connie Leon (Tama's Mother), Nancy Gates (Sister), Fred Essler (Takahashi), Phillip Ahn (Japanese Officer), Daisy Lee (Taka-hashi's Servant), Richard Loo (Japanese Officer), Barbara Jean Wong (Girl given dope), Beal Wong (Japanese major), Charles Lung (Broker), Robert Katcher (Prof. Namachi).

A Japanese publisher forces his son to join the Japanese army during WWII.

77 *Belle of the Yukon* (1944)

Western musical. Running time: 83 minutes. Technicolor.

Produced and directed by William Seiter. Screenplay by James Edward Grant (based on a story by Houston Branch). Photographed by Ray Renna-han. Edited by Ernest Nims. Music by Arthur Lange, Will Cobb, Jimmy Van Heusen, Gus Edwards.

Songs: "Like Someone in Love," "Sleigh Ride in July," "Belle of the Yukon," "Every Girl Is Different," "I Can't Tell Why I Love You But I Do Do Do."

Starring Randolph Scott (Honest John Calhoun), Gypsy Rose Lee (Belle De-valle), Dinah Shore (Lettie Candless), Charles Winninger (Pop Candless), Rob-ert Burns (Sam Slade), Florence Bates (Viola), Guinn "Big Boy" Williams (Marshall Maitland), William Marshall (Steve), Robert Armstrong (George), Victor Kilian (The Professor), Edward Fielding (C.V. Atterbury), Wanda McKay (Cherie Atterbury), Charles Soldani (Fire Chief).

A former con man who runs a legit dance hall tries to thwart a bad man who wants him to return to his crooked ways.

Note: The song "Sleigh Ride in July" was nominated for an Oscar. Director Seiter helmed Laurel and Hardy's classic *Sons of the Desert,* which was a classic due to the comedy team, not due to Seiter.

78 *The Bells of St. Mary's* (1945)

Drama. Running time: 126 minutes. Black and white. Available on videocas-sette. A Rainbow Production for RKO.

Produced and directed by Leo Mc-Carey. Screenplay by Dudley Nichols (based on a story by McCarey). Photo-graphed by George Barnes. Edited by Harry Marker. Music by Robert Emmet Dolan.

Starring Bing Crosby (Father O'Mal-ley), Ingrid Bergman (Sister Benedict), Henry Travers (Mr. Bogardus), Ruth Donnelly (Sister Michael), Joan Carroll (Patsy), Martha Sleeper (Patsy's Mother), William Gargan (Joe Gallagher), Rhys Williams (Dr. McKay), Dickie Tyler (Ed-die), Una O'Connor (Mrs. Breen), Bobby Frasco (Tommy), Matt McHugh (Clerk), Edna Wonacott (Delphine), Jimmy Crane (Luther), Minerva Urecal (Landlady), Cora Shannon (Old Lady), Gwen Crawford, Alma Constant, Eva Novak (The Sisters).

A priest is sent to St. Mary's parish to assist with its financial difficulties, and locks horns with the reigning Mother Superior.

Note: Sequel to *Going My Way,* which won Crosby an Oscar. At the time of this film's release, Crosby was the number one star in America, thus this film grossed nearly four million dollars, becoming the top box office hit of 1945. Producer-director-writer Leo McCarey is generally credited for teaming Laurel with Hardy, and also directed the Marx Brothers' classic *Duck Soup.* McCarey, Crosby, and Bergman had all won Oscars the previous year (Bergman and McCarey for *Gaslight,* Crosby for the aforementioned *Going My Way*). Art director William Flannery's set, consisting of a rebuilt St. Mary's cathedral, was used by Val Lewton the following year for his horror film *Bedlam.*

Oscar nominations: Best Picture, Best Director, Best Musical Score, Best Actor, Best Actress, Best Song ("Aren't You Glad That You're You" by Jimmy Van Heusen and Johnny Burke).

Review: "...a talented but desperate effort to repeat the unrepeatable." — James Agee.

79 *Beloved Imposter* (1936) Musical. Running time: 86 minutes. Black and white.

Produced by John Stafford. Directed by Victor Hanbury. Screenplay by Connery Chappell (based on the novel *Dancing Boy* by Ethel Mannin).

Starring Rene Ray (Mary), Fred Conygham (George), Germaine Aussey (La Lumiere), Penelope Parks (Connie), Edwin Ellis (Herbert), Charles Oliver (Pierre), Fred Groves (Jack Harding), Bela Mila (Mona), Tony de Lungo (Gavani), Lawrence Hanray (Arthur), Leslie "Hutch" Hutchinson, Caligray Brothers.

A stuck-up singing waiter becomes implicated in a murder.

Note: Filmed in England by Stafford productions for RKO release.

80 *Bengazi* (1955) Crime drama. Running time: 79 minutes. Black and white. A Panamint production for RKO release.

Produced by Sam Wisenthal and Eugene Tevlin. Directed by John Brahm. Screenplay by Endre Bohem, Louis Vittes (based on a story by Jeff Bailey). Photographed by Joseph Biroc. Edited by Robert Golden. Music by Roy Webb.

Starring Richard Conte (Gillmore), Victor McLaglen (Donovan), Richard Carlson (Levering), Mala Powers (Aileen), Richard Erdman (Selby), Hillary Brooke (Nora), Maury Hill (Peters), Jay Novello (Basim), Pedro Gonzales-Gonzales (Kamal).

Three outcasts team up and search for gold in the African desert.

Review: "Poor potboiler on predictable lines" — Leslie Halliwell, *Film and Video Guide.*

81 *Berlin Express* (1948) Drama. Running time: 86 minutes. Black and white. Available on videocassette.

Produced by Bert Granet. Directed by Jacques Tourneur. Screenplay by Harold Medford (based on a story by Curt Siodmak). Photographed by Lucien Ballard. Edited by Sherman Todd. Music by Frederick Hollander.

Starring Merle Oberon (Lucienne), Robert Ryan (Robert Lindley), Charles Korvin (Perrot), Paul Lukas (Dr. Bernhardt), Robert Coote (Sterling), Reinhold Schunzel (Walter), Roman Toporow (Lt. Maxim), Peter Von Zerneck (Hans Schmidt), Otto Waldis (Kessler), Fritz Kroner (Franzen), Michael Harvey (Sgt. Barnes), Tom Keene (Major), Jim Nolan (Train Captain), Arthur Dulac (Steward), Buddy Roosevelt (M.P.).

Three years after Hitler's death, a group of Nazis try to prevent reunification.

82 *The Best Little Whorehouse in Texas* (1982) Musical comedy. Running time: 114 minutes. Color. Available on videocassette.

Produced by Thomas Miller, Edward Milkis, Robert Boyett. Directed by Colin Higgins. Screenplay by Larry L. King, Peter Masterson, Higgins (based on their play). Photographed by William A. Fraker. Edited by Pembroke J. Herring, David Bretherton, Jack Hofstra, Nicholas Eliopoulous, H.W. Haneman.

Starring Burt Reynolds (Sheriff), Dolly Parton (Mona), Dom DeLuise (Melvin), Charles Durning (Governor), Jim Nabors (Fred), Robert Mandan (Senator Wingwood), Lois Nettleton (Dulcie Mae), Theresa Merritt (Jewel), Noah Beery, Jr. (Edsel), Raleigh Bond (Mayor), Barry Carbin (C.J.), Ken Magee (Mansel), Mary Jo Castlett (Rita), Mary Louise Wilson (Modene).

A sheriff has to close down a whore-house by orders of the governor.

Note: A Universal picture in which RKO was involved on paper only.

83 *Best of the Badmen* (1951)

Western. Running time: 83 minutes. Technicolor.

Produced by Herman Schlom. Directed by William D. Russell. Screenplay by Robert Hardy Andrews and John Twist (based on a story by Andrews). Photographed by Edward Cronjager. Edited by Desmond Marquette. Music by Paul Sawtell.

Starring Robert Ryan (Jeff Clanton), Claire Trevor (Lily Fowler), Jack Buetel (Bob Younger), Robert Preston (Matthew Fowler), Walter Brennan (Doc Burcher), Bruce Cabot (Cole Younger), John Archer (Curley Ringo), Lawrence Tierney (Jesse James), Barton MacLane (Joad), Tom Tyler (Frank James), Bob Wilke (Jim Younger), John Cliff (John Younger), Lee MacGregor (Lieutenant), Emmett Lynn (Oscar), Carleton Young (Wilson).

Post–Civil War western in which a law man, who tries to bust up Quantrill's Raiders, finds he needs their help.

84 *The Best Years of Our Lives*

(1946) Drama. Running time: 172 minutes. Black and white. Available on videocassette.

Produced by Samuel Goldwyn. Directed by William Wyler. Screenplay by Robert E. Sherwood (based on the blank verse novella *Glory for Me* by MacKinlay Kantor). Photographed by Gregg Toland. Edited by Daniel Mandell. Music by Hugo Friedhofer.

Starring Fredric March (Al Stephenson), Myrna Loy (Milly Stephenson), Dana Andrews (Fred Derry), Teresa Wright (Peggy Stephenson), Virginia Mayo (Marie Derry), Cathy O'Donnell (Wilma Cameron), Hoagy Carmichael (Butch Engle), Harold Russell (Homer Parrish), Gladys George (Hortense Derry), Roman Bohnen (Pat Derry), Ray Collins (Mr. Milton), Steve Cochran (Cliff), Minna Gombell (Mrs. Parrish), Walter Baldwin (Mr. Parrish), Dorothy Adams (Mrs. Cameron), Don Beddoe (Mr. Cameron), Erskine Sanford (Bullard), Marlene Aames (Luella Parrish), Michael Hall (Rob Stephenson), Charles Halton (Prew), Ray Teal (Mr. Mollett), Dean White (Novak), Howland Chamberlin (Thorpe), Victor Cutler (Woody Merrill), Pat Flaherty (Construction Foreman).

Three men come home from the war and try re-adjusting to civilian life, finding doing so very difficult. One married man with children tries to recapture the times he's lost forever. Another man discovers that his wife and family have little to offer him in the way of love or understanding. Finally, the third man, a wounded soldier who is returning home without hands, must adjust to this handicap and his loved ones' awkwardness around him.

Note: Oscars for Best Picture, Best Director, Best Screenplay, Best Music, Best Actor (March), and Best Supporting Actor (Russell; a real-life war vet whose hands were lost in combat. He also was awarded a special Oscar. He was not an actor and made only one other film — *Inside Moves* [1980]. That same year, Russell's son was convicted of murdering his girlfriend's husband and was sentenced to twenty years in prison. In 1987, Russell was diagnosed with cancer).

Comment: "I don't care if it doesn't make a nickel, I just want every man, woman and child in America to see it" — Samuel Goldwyn.

Reviews: "One of the best pictures of our lives" — *Variety;* "... Profoundly pleasing, moving, and encouraging" — James Agee; "Goldwyn was right; every man woman and child should see this film, from one generation to the next" — *The Motion Picture Guide.*

85 *Betrayal from the East* (1945)

War drama. Running time: 82 minutes. Black and white.

Dana Andrews and Teresa Wright in *The Best Years of Our Lives.*

Produced by Herman Schlom. Directed by William Berke. Screenplay by Kenneth Gamet and Aubrey Wisberg (based on the book by Alan Hynd). Photographed by Russell Metty. Edited by Duncan Mansfield. Music by Roy Webb.

Starring Lee Tracy (Eddie), Nancy Kelly (Peggy), Richard Loo (Tanni), Abner Biberman (Yamato), Regis Toomey (Scott), Phillip Ahn (Kato), Addison Richards (Capt. Bates), Bruce Edwards (Purdy), Hugh Hoo (Araki), Sen Yung (Omaya), Roland Varno (Kurt), Louis Jean Heydt (Marsden), Jason Robards, Sr. (Hildebrand).

An ex-G.I. thwarts a Japanese gang trying to sabotage the Panama Canal.

86 *Beware My Lovely* (1952)
Drama. Running time: 77 minutes. Black and white.

Produced by Collier Young. Directed by Harry Homer. Screenplay by Mel Dinelli (based on his story and play *The Man*). Photographed by George E. Dis-

kant. Edited by Paul Weatherwax. Music by Leith Stevens.

Starring Ida Lupino (Mrs. Gordon), Robert Ryan (Howard), Taylor Holmes (Mr. Armstrong), Barbara Whiting (Ruth Williams), James Williams (Mr. Stevens), O.Z. Whitehead (Mr. Franks), Dee Pollock (Grocery Boy).

A handyman holds a widow hostage and threatens to rape and kill her.

Reviews: "Inept characterizations and ludicrously repetitive situations will surely rank this among the silliest films of the year"—*MFB;* "...the kind of film they make for TV these days"—*The Motion Picture Guide.*

87 *Beyond a Reasonable Doubt*
(1956) Mystery. Running time: 80 minutes. Black and white.

Produced by Bert Friedlob. Directed by Fritz Lang. Screenplay by Douglas Morrow. Photographed by William Snyder. Edited by Gene Fowler, Jr. Music by Herschel Burke Gilbert.

Starring Dana Andrews (Tom Garrett),

Joan Fontaine (Susan Spencer), Sidney Blackmer (Austin Spencer), Phillip Bourneuf (Thompson), Shepperd Strudwick (Wilson), Arthur Franz (Hale), Edward Binns (Lt. Kennedy), Robin Raymond (Terry), Barbara Nichols (Sally), William Lecister (Charlie Miller), Dan Seymour (Greco), Rusty Lane (Judge), Joyce Taylor (Joan), Carleton Young (Kirk), Trudy Woe (Hat Check Girl), Joe Kirk (Clerk), Charles Evans (Governor), Wendell Niles (Announcer).

A writer and editor crusade to show the fallibility of circumstantial evidence after witnessing an execution.

88 *Beyond the Rockies* (1932) Western. 55 minutes. Black and white. Produced by Harry Joe Brown. Directed by Fred Allen. Screenplay by John McCarthy. Photographed by Ted McCord. Edited by William Clemens.

Starring Tom Keene, Rochelle Hudson, Marie Wells, Ernie Adams, Julian Rivero, Hank Bell, Tom London, William Welsh, Ted Adams.

A trio of do-gooders thwarts a woman's plans to rustle cattle.

89 *Beyond Tomorrow* (1940) Fantasy. Running time: 81 minutes. Black and white. Available on videocassette.

Produced by Lee Garmes. Directed by A. Edward Sutherland. Screenplay by Adele Comandini (based on a story by Mildred Cram and Comandini). Photographed by Lester White. Edited by Otto Ludwig. Music by Harold Spina and Charles Newman.

Songs include: "Jeannie with the Light Brown Hair" and "It's Raining Dreams."

Starring Harry Carey (George Melton), C. Aubrey Smith (Allan Chadwick), Charles Winninger (Michael O'Brien), Alex Melesh (Josef Butler), Maria Ouspenskaya (Madame Tanya), Helen Vinson (Arlene Terry), Rod La Rocque (Phil Hubert), Richard Carlson (James Houston), Jean Parker (Jean Lawrence), J. Anthony Hughes (Officer

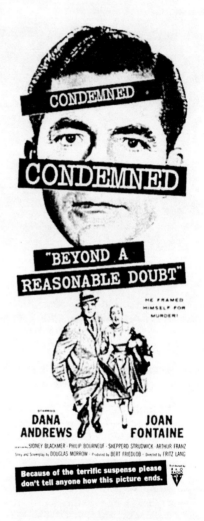

Promotion poster for *Beyond a Reasonable Doubt*.

Johnson), Robert Homans (Sergeant), Virginia McMullen (Radio Station Secretary), James Bush (Jace Taylor), William Bakewell (David Chadwick).

Two elderly ghosts return to help young lovers during the holidays.

90 *Beyond Victory* (1931) Drama. Running time: 70 minutes. Black and

white. A Pathé production for release by RKO.

Produced by E.B. Derr. Directed by John Robertson. Screenplay by Horace Jackson and James Gleason. Edited by Daniel Mandell. Music by Francis Romon.

Starring Bill Boyd (Bill), ZaSu Pitts (Fritzie), Lew Cody (Lew), Marion Shilling (Ina), James Gleason (Jim), Lissi Arna (Katherine), Theodore Von Eltz (Major Sparks), Mary Carr (Mother), Russell Gleason (Russell).

Four soldiers on the front line ponder their enlistment.

Note: Actor Russell Gleason, son of actor and co-writer James, jumped to his death when in the army during World War II. Actor Boyd was to become a household name as Hopalong Cassidy beginning in 1935 and throughout the forties and fifties, when he would buy the rights to all of his older films and bring the character to TV via the early works and new episodes filmed for the small screen. ZaSu Pitts was, at this time, appearing in two-reel comedies with Thelma Todd at the Hal Roach studios.

91 *The Big Brain* (1933) Directed by George Archainbaud. Screenplay by Sy Bartlett. Photographed by Arthur Edeson. Edited by Rose Loewinger.

Starring George E. Stone (Max), Phillips Holmes (Terry), Fay Wray (Cythia), Minna Gombell (Margy), Lillian Bond (Dorothy), Reginald Owen (Darlington), Berton Churchill (Higgenbottom), Reginald Mason (Latham), Sam Hardy (Slick), Randall Stake (Scoop), Edgar Norton (Butler), Charles McNaughton (Wallack), Lucien Littlefield (Justice of the Peace).

Barber becomes a phony stock promoter but is turned in.

92 *The Big Frame* (1953) Drama. Running time: 66 minutes. Black and white. British title: *The Last Hours.*

Produced by Robert S. Baker and Monty Brennan. Directed by David Mac-Donald. Screenplay by Steve Fisher and John Gilling. Photographed by Monty Berman. Edited by Reginald Beck. Music by William Hill-Rowan.

Starring Mark Stevens (Paul Smith), Jean Kent (Louise Parker), Garry Marsh (Foster), John Bentley (Clark Sutton), Dianne Foster (Dianne Wrigley), Jack Lambert (John Parker), Leslie Perrins (Dr. Morrison), Brian Coleman (Tom Wrigley), Duncan Lamont (Bristow), Cyril Smith (Roper), Thora Hird (Maid).

Smugglers attempt to rub each other out.

93 *The Big Gamble* (1931) Comedy. 65 minutes. Black and white. A Pathé production for RKO release.

Directed by Fred Niblo. Screenplay by Octavus Roy Cohen, Walter DeLeon, and F. McGrew Willis. Photographed by Hal Mohr. Edited by Joseph Kane. Music by Arthur Lange.

Starring Bill Boyd (Alan Beckwith), Dorothy Sebastian (Beverly), Warner Oland (Mr. North), William Collier, Jr. (Johnny), James Gleason (Squint), ZaSu Pitts (Nora), June MacCloy (May), Geneva Mitchell (Trixie), Ralph Ince (Webb), Fred Walton (Butler).

Gambler tries to fake his death in order to pay debts with his life insurance money.

94 *The Big Game* (1936) Sports drama. Running time: 73 minutes. Black and white.

Produced by Pandro S. Berman. Directed by George Nicholls, Jr. Screenplay by Irwin Shaw (based on the story by Francis Wallace). Photographed by Harry Wild. Edited by Frederic Knudtson.

Starring Phillip Houston (Clark), James Gleason (George), June Travis (Margaret), Bruce Cabot (Calhoun), Andy Devine (Pop), C. Henry Gordon (Brad Anthony), Guinn "Big Boy" Williams (Pete), John Arledge (Spike Adams), Frank M. Thomas (Jenins), Billy Gilbert (Fisher), Barbara Pepper

(Lois), Eddie Nugent (Drunk), Margaret Seddon (Mrs. Jenins), John Harrison (Dawson), Murray Kinnell (Dean), Jay Berwanger (U. of Chicago), William Shakespeare (Notre Dame), Robert Wilson (Southern Methodist), James Moscrip (Stanford), Irwin Klein (NYU), Gomer Jones (Ohio State University), Robert "Bones" Hamilton, Frank Alustiza.

Gamblers recruit coal miners as ringers for college football teams.

95 *The Big Shot* (1931) Comedy. Running time: 65 minutes. Black and white. A Pathé production for RKO release. British title: *The Optimist*.

Produced by Charles Rogers. Directed by Ralph Murphy. Screenplay by Joseph Fields and Earl Baldwin. Photographed by Arthur Miller. Edited by Charles Craft.

Starring Eddie Quillan (Ray), Maureen O'Sullivan (Doris), Mary Nolan (Fay Turner), Roscoe Ates (Barber), Belle Bennett (Mrs. Thompson), Arthur Stone (Old Timer), Otis Harlan (Dr. Peasley), Louis John Bartels (Mr. Howell), Edward McQuade (Uncle Ira), Frank Darien (Postmaster).

After a yokel is conned into buying worthless swamps, the crooks discover they contain priceless sulphur deposits and attempt to buy them back.

96 *The Big Shot* (1937) Comedy. Running time: 66 minutes. Black and white.

Directed by Edward Killy. Screenplay by Arthur T. Horman and Bert Granet (based on a story by Lawrence Pohle and Thomas Ahearn). Photographed by Nicholas Musuraca. Edited by Jack Hively.

Starring Guy Kibbee (Mr. Simms), Cora Witherspoon (Mrs. Simms), Dorothy Moore (Peggy), Gordon Jones (Chet), Russell Hicks (Drake), Frank M. Thomas (Murdock), Dudley Clements (McQuade), George Irving (Police Chief), Maxine Jennings (Gloria), Barbara Pepper (Mamie), Tom Kennedy (Bugs), John Kelly (Deuces), Eddie Gribbon (Soapy), Al Hill (Spots), Donald Kirke (Johnny Cullen).

A henpecked husband inherits a fortune and is besieged by gangsters who feel the money, left to him by their boss, is rightfully theirs. Meanwhile, the man's wife insists they move to Gotham to launch their daughter into society.

97 *The Big Sky* (1952) Adventure. Running time: 140 minutes. Black and white and colorized. A Winchester production for RKO release. Available on videocassette.

Produced and directed by Howard Hawks. Screenplay by Dudley Nichols (based on the novel by A.B. Guthrie). Photographed by Russell Harlan. Edited by Christian Nyby. Music by Dimitri Tiomkin.

Starring Kirk Douglas (Deakins), Dewey Martin (Boone), Elizabeth Threatt (Teal Eye), Arthur Hunnicutt (Zeb), Buddy Baer (Romaine), Steven Geray (Jourdonnais), Hank Worden (Poordevil), Jim Davis (Streak), Henri Letondal (Ladadie), Robert Hunter (Chouquette), Booth Coleman (Pascal), Paul Frees (MacMasters), Frank De Kova (Moleface), Guy Wilkerson (Longface), Don Beddoe (Horse Trader), George Wallace, Max Wagner, Sam Ash, Barbara Hawks, Frank Lackteen, Jay Novello, William Self.

Two mountain men encounter Indian conflicts while traveling up the Missouri.

Note: Russell Harlan and Arthur Hunnicut were nominated for Oscars.

Review: "It has the timeless, relentless quality of the long American historical novel" — Penelope Houston.

98 *The Big Steal* (1949) Crime drama. Running time: 71 minutes. Black and white. Available on videocassette.

Produced by Jack J. Gross. Directed by Don Siegel. Screenplay by Geoffrey Homes and Gerald Drayson (based on the novel *The Road to Carmichael's* by

Richard Wormser). Photographed by Harry J. Wild. Edited by Samuel E. Beetley. Music by Leigh Harline.

Starring Robert Mitchum (Duke), Jane Greer (Joan), William Bendix (Blake), Patric Knowles (Fiske), Ramon Novarro (Colonel Ortega), Don Alvarado (Lt. Ruiz), John Qualen (Seton), Pascual Garcia Pena (Manuel).

An army officer is accused of stealing a payroll, and sets out across Mexico after the real culprit. Meanwhile, he is pursued by another army representative.

Review: "Vigor and excellent craftsmanship" — Gavin Lambert.

99 *The Big Street* (1942) Comedy. Running time: 88 minutes. Black and white. Available on videocassette.

Produced by Damon Runyon. Directed by Irving Reiss. Screenplay by Leonard Spigelass (from the story *Little Pinks* by Runyon). Photographed by Russell Metty. Edited by William Hamilton. Music by Roy Webb.

Starring Henry Fonda (Little Pinks), Lucille Ball (Gloria), Barton MacLane (Case Ables), Eugene Pallette (Nicely Johnson), Agnes Moorehead (Violette), Sam Levine (Horsethief), Ray Collins (Professor B.), Marion Martin (Mrs. Venus), William Orr (Decauter Reed), George Cleveland (Col Venus), Hans Conried (Louie), Vera Gordon (Mrs. Lefkowitz).

A nightclub waiter falls for a selfish crippled singer.

100 *A Bill of Divorcement* (1932) Drama. Running time: 70 minutes. Black and white. Available on videocassette. A Selznick production for RKO release.

Produced by David O. Selznick. Directed by George Cukor. Screenplay by Howard Estabrook and Harry Wagstaff Gribble (based on the play by Clemence Dane). Photographed by Sid Hickox. Edited by Arthur Roberts. Music by Max Steiner.

Starring John Barrymore (Hillary Fair-

field), Billie Burke (Margaret Fairfield), Katharine Hepburn (Sydney Fairfield), David Manners (Kit Humphrey), Henry Stephenson (Doctor Alliot), Paul Cavanaugh (Gray Meredith), Elizabeth Patterson (Aunt Hester), Gayle Evers (Bassett), Julie Haydon (Party Guest).

A man escapes from a mental hospital on the day his wife is divorcing him, and meets, for the first time, his strong-willed daughter.

Note: Hepburn refused to ever again work with Barrymore after this film, which made her a star.

Review: "...the most potent tear jerker in many a moon" — *Variety.*

101 *A Bill of Divorcement* (1940) Drama. Running time: 70 minutes. Black and white.

Produced by Lee Marcus. Directed by John Farrow. Screenplay by Dalton Trumbo (based on the play by Clemence Dane). Photographed by Nicholas Musuraca. Edited by Harry Marker.

Starring Maureen O'Hara (Sydney), Adolphe Menjou (Hillary), Fay Bainter (Margaret), Herbert Marshall (Gray Meredith), Dame May Whitty (Hester Fairfield), Patric Knowles (John Strom), C. Aubrey Smith (Dr. Alliot), Ernest Cossart (Dr. Pumphrey), Kathryn Collier (Basset), Lauri Beatty (Susan).

Remake of the 1932 feature (above).

Note: Alternate title: *Never to Love.*

102 *Bird of Paradise* (1932) Romantic adventure. Running time: 80 minutes. Black and white. Available on videocassette.

Produced by David O. Selznick. Directed by King Vidor. Screenplay by Wells Root, Leonard Praskins, and Wanda Tuchock (based on the play by Richard Walton Tully). Photographed by Clyde DeVinna, Edward Cronjager and Lucien Andriot. Music by Max Steiner.

Starring Joel McCrea (Johnny Baker), Dolores Del Rio (Luana), John Halliday (Mac), Richard "Skeets" Gallagher

Henry Fonda and Lucille Ball in *The Big Street*.

(Chester), Creighton Chaney (Thornton), Bert Roach (Hector), Napoleon Pukui (The King), Sofie Ortega (Mahuamahu), Agostino Borgato (the Medicine Man).

An adventurer marries a native girl while on a South Sea island, eliciting trouble from their respective people.

Note: Filmed in Hawaii, the "kono wind" caused filming to be delayed while crew workers nailed branches back onto trees. Director Vidor was unhappy with the film's lack of story content, but Selznick was only interested in using the title and the climactic scene where Del Rio jumps into a volcano. Max Steiner's score was the first to run continuously throughout a film. The film cost a whopping (for the time) million dollars to produce, and was shot in only twenty-four days, as both McCrea and Del Rio had other commitments. The film was remade by 20th Century–Fox in 1951.

103 *The Bishop's Wife* (1947) Fantasy. Running time: 105 minutes. Black and white. Available on videocassette.

Produced by Samuel Goldwyn. Directed by Henry Koster. Screenplay by Robert E. Sherwood and Leonardo Bercovici (based on a novel by Robert Nathan). Photographed by Gregg Toland. Edited by Monica Collingwood. Music by Emil Newman.

Starring Cary Grant (Dudley), David Niven (Henry Brougham), Loretta Young (Julia Brougham), Monty Wooley (Professor Wutheridge), James Gleason (Sylvester), Gladys Cooper (Mrs. Hamilton), Elsa Lanchester (Matilda), Sara Haden (Mildred Casaway), Karolyn Grimes (Debby Brougham), Tito Vuolo (Maggenti), Regis Toomey (Mr. Miller), Sarah Edwards (Mrs. Duffy), Margaret McWade (Miss Trumbull).

When a bishop loses touch with people and thinks only of material gain, an angel is sent down to straighten him out.

Oscar nominations: Best Picture, Best Director, Best Music.

Review: "It is the Protestant comeback to the deadly successful RC propaganda of *Going My Way* and *The Bells of St. Mary's*. It surpasses in tastelessness, equals in whimsy, and in technique, falls well below those crooning parables. It is really quite a monstrous film" — Richard Winnington, *News Chronicle*.

104 *The Black Abbot* (1934) Crime drama. Running time: 56 minutes. Black and white. A British production by REA for RKO release.

Produced by Julius Hagen. Directed by George A. Cooper. Screenplay by H. Fowler Mear (based on the novel *The Grange Mystery* by Phillip Godfrey).

Starring John Stuart (Frank Brooks), Judy Kelly (Sylvia Hillcrest), Richard Cooper (Lord Jerry Pilkdown), Ben Welden (Charlie Marsh), Drusilla Wills (Mary Hillcrest), Edgar Norfolk (Brian Heslewood), Farren Soutar (John Hillcrest), Cyril Smith (Alf Higgins), John Turnbill (Inspector Lockwood).

A gang of crooks hold a wealthy man hostage.

105 *The Black Ghost* (1932) Adventure. Running time: 65 minutes. Black and white. Directed by Spencer Bennett and Thomas L. Storey. Screenplay by George Plympton and Robert Hill.

Starring Lon Chaney, Jr., Dorothy Gulliver, Richard Neill, LeRoy Mason, Francis X Bushman, Jr., Mary Jo Densmore, Joe Bonomo, Slim Cole, William Desmond, Yakima Canutt.

Feature version of "The Last Frontier," the only serial produced by RKO. Chaney plays heroic title character.

106 *Blackbeard the Pirate* (1952) Adventure. Running time: 98 minutes. Color. Available on videocassette.

Produced by Edmund Grainger. Directed by Raoul Walsh. Screenplay by Alan LeMay (based on a story by DeVallon Scott). Photographed by William Snyder. Edited by Ralph Dawson. Music by Victor Young.

Starring Robert Newton (Blackbeard), Linda Darnell (Edwina), William Bendix (Worley), Keith Andes (Maynard), Torin Thatcher (Sir Henry Morgan),

Irene Ryan (Alvira), Alan Mowbray (Noll), Richard Egan (Briggs), Skelton Knaggs (Gilly), Dick Wessel (Dutchman), Anthony Caruso (Pierre La Guard), Jack Lambert (Tom).

A reformed pirate is asked to rid the seas of the notorious title character.

107 *Blind Adventure* (1933) Crime drama. Running time: 65 minutes. Black and white.

Directed by Ernest B. Schoedsack. Screenplay by Ruth Rose. Photographed by Henry Gerard. Music by Max Steiner. Edited by Jack Kitchin.

Starring Robert Armstrong, Helen Mack, Roland Young, Ralph Belamy, John Miljan, Laura Hope Crews, Henry Stephenson, Phyllis Barry, John Warburton, Marjoreson Gateson, Beryl Mercer, Tyrell Davis, Desmond Roberts, Ivan Simpson.

An American becomes involved with kidnappers in London.

108 *Blind Alibi* (1938) Crime drama. Running time: 62 minutes. Black and white.

Produced by Cliff Reid. Directed by Lew Landers. Screenplay by Lionel Houser, Harry Segall, and Ron Ferguson (based on a story by William Joyce). Photographed by Nicholas Musuraca.

Starring Richard Dix (Paul Dover), Whitney Bourne (Julia Fraser), Eduardo Ciannelli (Mitch), Frances Mercer (Ellen Dover), Paul Guilfoyle (Taggart), Richard Lane (Bowers), Jack Arnold (Dick), Walter Miller (Maitland), Frank M. Thomas (Larcon), Solly Ward (Al), Tommy Bupp (Freddie), Ace the Wonder Dog.

A man feigns blindness to retrieve incriminating letters from a museum's collection.

Note: Actor Frank M. Thomas was the father of juvenile actor Frankie Thomas.

109 *Blind Folly* (1939) Comedy. Running time: 78 minutes. Black and white. A British production by George Smith for release by RKO.

Produced by George Smith. Directed by Reginald Denham. Screenplay by H.F. Maltby (based on John Hunter's story). Photographed by Geoffrey Faithfull.

Starring Clifford Mollison (George Bunyard), Lilli Palmer (Valerie), Leslie Perrins (Deverell), William Kendall (Raine), Gus McNaughton (Professor Zozo), Elliot Mason (Aunt Mona), David Home (Mr. Steel).

When a man inherits a roadhouse where a gang of thieves have hidden their money, the crooks are forced to steal their own loot.

110 *Blockade* (1929) Crime drama. Running time: 70 minutes. Black and white.

Directed by George B. Seitz. Screenplay by Harvey Thew (based on a story by Louis Sarecky and Harvey Thew). Photographed by Robert Martin. Edited by Archie Marshek.

Starring Anna Q. Nilsson (Bess), Wallace MacDonald (Vincent), James Bradbury, Sr. (Gwynn), Walter McGrail (Hayden).

Rum runners in Florida are captured by a tough female revenue agent.

111 *Blond Cheat* (1938) Comedy. Running time: 87 minutes. Black and white.

Produced by William Sistrom. Directed by Joseph Santley. Screenplay by Charles Kaufman, Paul Yawitz, Viola Brothers Shore, Harry Segall (based on the story by Aladar Lazlo).

Starring Cecil Kellaway, Joan Fontaine, Lillian Bond, Derrick de Marney, Cecil Cunningham, Robert Coote, Olaf Hytten, John Sutton, Gerald Hamer, Charles Coleman.

A millionaire agrees to back his daughter's stage show to keep her from marrying a well-known playboy.

112 *Blood on the Moon* (1948) Western. Running time: 88 minutes. Black and white. Available on videocassette.

Produced by Theron Worth. Directed by Robert Wise. Screenplay by Willie Howard (based on an adaptation by Harold Shumate of a novel by Luke Short). Photographed by Nicholas Musuraca. Edited by Samuel E. Beetley.

Starring Robert Mitchum (Jim Garry), Barbara Bel Geddes (Amy Lufton), Robert Preston (Tate Biling), Walter Brennan (Kris Barden), Phyllis Thaxter (Carol Lufton), Frank Faylen (Jake Pindalest), Tom Tully (Frank Reardon), George Cooper (Fred Borden), Richard Powers (Ted Eiser), Bud Osborne (Cap Willis), Zon Murray (Newls Titterton), Robert Bray (Bart Daniels).

After helping a rustler get rich on townsfolk, a gunfighter has a change of heart and sets out to destroy him.

113 *The Body Snatcher* (1945) Horror. Running time: 77 minutes. Black and white. Available on videocassette.

Produced by Val Lewton. Directed by Robert Wise. Screenplay by Phillip MacDonald and Carlos Keith (based on a short story by Robert Louis Stevenson). Photographed by Robert De Grasse. Edited by J.R. Whittridge.

Starring Boris Karloff (John Gray), Bela Lugosi (Joseph), Henry Daniell (Dr. MacFarlaine), Edith Atwater (Meg Camden), Russell Wade (Donald Fettes), Rita Corday (Mrs. Marsh), Sharyn Moffett (Georgina Marsh), Donna Lee (Street Singer).

When a doctor obtains supplies from grave robbers, the results are murder.

Review: "A humane sincerity and a devotion to good cinema.... However, most of the picture is more literary than lively" — *Time.*

114 *Bodyguard* (1948) Crime drama. Running time: 62 minutes. Black and white.

Produced by Sid Rogell. Directed by Richard Fleischer. Screenplay by Fred Niblo, Jr. and Harry Essex (based on a story by George W. George and Robert B. Altman). Photographed by Robert De Grasse. Edited by Elmo Williams.

Starring Lawrence Tierney (Mike Carter), Priscilla Lane (Doris Brewster), Phillip Reed (Freddie Dysen), June Clayworth (Connie), Elisabeth Risdon (Gene Dysen), Steve Brodie (Fenton), Frank Fenton (Lt. Borden), Charles Case (Captain Wayne).

A plainclothesman, protecting a young lady, finds that there are men on the force who want him dead.

115 *Bombadier* (1943) War drama. Running time: 97 minutes. Black and white. Available on videocassette.

Produced by Robert Fellows. Screenplay by John Twist (based on a story by Twist and Martin Rackin. Photographed by Nicholas Musuraca. Edited by Robert Wise. Music by Roy Webb.

Starring Pat O'Brien, Randolph Scott, Anne Shirley, Eddie Albert, Walter Reed, Robert Ryan, Barton MacLane, Richard Martin, Russell Wade, John Miljan, James Newell.

Cadet volunteers are introduced to the horrors of war during a series of raids over Japan, with conflicts between the conservative officer and a wildcat pilot.

Note: Filming began prior to the attack on Pearl Harbor, so there were extensive re-writes and revisions before it was finally released, three years later.

Review: "Totally routine recruiting poster heroics"—Leslie Halliwell, *Film and Video Guide.*

116 *Border Cafe* (1937) Western. Running time: 67 minutes. Black and white.

Produced by Robert Sisk. Directed by Lew Landers. Screenplay by Lionel Houser (based on a story by Thomas Gill). Photographed by Nicholas Musuraca. Edited by Jack Hively.

Starring Harry Carey (Tex), John Beal (Keith Whitney), Armida (Deminaga), George Irving (Senator Whitney), Leona Roberts (Mrs. Whitney), J. Carrol Naish (Rocky), Marjorie Lord (Janet), Lee Patrick (Ellie), Paul Fix (Dolson), Max Wagner (Shaky), Walter Miller (Evans).

Big city folks travel west and try changing the ways of the westerners.

117 *Border G-Man* (1938) Western. Running time: 58 minutes. Black and white.

Produced by Bert Gilroy. Directed by David Howard. Screenplay by Oliver Drake (based on a story by Bernard McConville). Photographed by Joseph H. August. Edited by Frederic Knudtson.

Starring George O'Brien, Laraine Johnson, Ray Whitley, John Miljan, Edgar Dearing, Robert Burns.

Criminals try organizing an army of bandits in South America, so a government agent is sent there to investigate.

118 *Border Treasure* (1950) Western. Running time: 60 minutes. Black and white.

Produced by Herman Schlom. Directed by George Archainbaud. Screenplay by Norman Houston. Photographed by J. Roy Hunt. Edited by Desmond Marquette.

Starring Tim Holt (Ed Porter), Jane Nigh (Stella), John Doucette (Bat), House Peters, Jr. (Rod), Inez Cooper (Anita), Julian Rivero (Felipe), Kenneth MacDonald (Sheriff), Vince Barnett (Pokey), Robert Payton (Del), David Leonard (Padre), Tom Monroe (Dimmick), Richard Martin (Chito Rafferty).

A cowboy hero and his sidekick thwart bandits' plans to rob a jewel shipment whose wares are intended to aid victims of a Mexican earthquake.

119 *Born to Be Bad* (1950) Drama. Running time: 93 minutes. Black and white.

Produced by Robert Sparks. Directed by Nicholas Ray. Screenplay by Edith Sommer, Robert Soderberg and George Oppenheimer (based on the novel *All Kneeling* by Anne Parrish, adapted by Charles Schnee). Photographed by

Nicholas Musuraca. Edited by Frederic Knudtson.

Starring Joan Fontaine (Christabel), Robert Ryan (Nick), Zachary Scott (Curtis), Joan Leslie (Donna), Mel Ferrer (Gabby), Harold Vermilyea (John Caine), Virginia Farmer (Aunt Clara), Kathleen Howard (Mrs. Bolton), Dick Ryan (Arthur), Bess Flowers (Mrs. Worthington), Joy Halliward (Mrs. Porter), Hazel Boyne (Committee Woman), Irving Bacon (Jewelry Salesman), Gordon Oliver (Lawyer).

A scheming woman marries for money, but continues her affair with an idealistic writer.

Review: "Trash story too much for cast and director to live down" — *Variety.*

120 *Born to Kill* (1947) Crime drama. Running time: 92 minutes. Black and white. Available on videocassette.

Produced by Herman Schlom. Directed by Robert Wise. Screenplay by Eve Green and Richard MacCaulay (based on the novel *Deadlier Than the Male* by James Gunn). Photographed by Robert De Grasse. Edited by Les Millbrook.

Starring Lawrence Tierney (Sam), Claire Trevor (Helen), Walter Slezak (Arnett), Phillip Terry (Fred), Audrey Long (Georgia), Elisha Cook, Jr. (Marty), Isabel Jewell (Laury Palmer), Esther Howard (Mrs. Kraft), Kathryn Card (Grace), Tony Barrett (Danny), Grandon Rhodes (Inspector Wilson).

A cold blooded killer murders two men, leaves town, and meets up with a woman with whom he falls in love. Later, when she turns from him, he marries her sister and begins implicating her in his crimes as police come looking for him.

Note: Released in Great Britain as *Lady of Deceit.*

Reviews: "Unusual heavy-going, well-acted melodrama" — Leslie Halliwell, *Film and Video Guide;* "Depressing, confusing film noir" — *The Motion Picture Guide.*

121 *Born to Love* (1931) Directed by Paul L. Stein. Screenplay by Ernest Pascal. Photographed by John Mescall. Edited by Claude Berkeley.

Starring Constance Bennett (Doris Kendall), Joel McCrea (Barry Craig), Paul Cavanagh (Sir Wilfred Drake), Frederick Kerr (Lord Ponsonby), Anthony Bushell (Leslie Darrow), Louise Closser Hale (Lady Agatha Posonby), Mary Forbes (Duchess), Elizabeth Forrester (Evelyn Kent), Edmond Breon (Tom Kent), Reginald Sharland (Foppish Gentleman), Daisy Bellmore (Tibbets), Marsha Mattox (Head Nurse), Fred Esmelton (Butler), Eddie Chandler (Captain Peters), Billy Bevan (Departing British Soldier), Bill Elliot (Extra).

A woman's fighter pilot husband is reported missing just before she gives birth to their first child. Later, once she has fallen for another man, her husband returns.

Review: "A useful compendium of thirties romantic cliches, quite attractively packaged" — Leslie Halliwell, *Film and Video Guide.*

122 *Boy Slaves* (1938) Social drama. Running time: 70 minutes. Black and white. Available on videocassette.

Produced and directed by P.J. Wolfson. Screenplay by Albert Bein and Ben Orkow (based on a story by Bein). Photographed by J. Roy Hunt. Edited by Desmond Marquette.

Starring Anne Shirley (Annie), Roger Daniel (Jesse), James McCallion (Tim), Alan Baxter (Graff), Johnny Fitzgerald (Knuckles), Walter Ward (Miser), Charles Powers (Lollie), Walter Tetley (Pee Wee), Frank Malo (Tommy), Paul White (Atlas), Arthur Hohl (Sheriff), Charles Lane (Albee), Norman Willis (Drift Boss), Roy Gordon (Judge).

A runaway boy finds himself placed in a forced labor camp and attempts to break free so that he may expose the brutal conditions.

Review: "Devoid of essential entertainment factors for general theater showings" — *Variety*.

123 *The Boy with Green Hair*
(1949) Drama. Running time: 82 minutes. Technicolor. Available on videocassette.

Produced by Dore Schary and Stephen Ames. Directed by Joseph Losey. Screenplay by Ben Barzman and Alfred Lewis Levitt (based on a story by Betsy Beaton). Photographed by George Baines. Edited by Frank Doyle.

Starring Dean Stockwell (Peter), Pat O'Brien (Gramp), Robert Ryan (Dr. Evans), Barbara Hale (Miss Brand), Richard Lyon (Michael), Walter Catlett (The King), Samuel S. Hinds (Dr. Knudson), Regis Toomey (Mr. Davis), Charles Meredith (Mr. Piper), David Clarke (Barber), Billy Sheffield (Red), John Clanks (Danny), Teddy Infuhr (Timmy), Dwayne Hickman (Joey), Eilene Janssen (Peggy), Charles Arnt (Mr. Hammond), Russ Tamblyn, Curtis Jackson (Students).

A war orphan awakens one day to find his hair has turned green, and thereafter learns to use his odd appearance as an anti-war statement.

Review: "Muddled, pretentious, and unpersuasive fantasy, typical of this producer's do-goodery" — Leslie Halliwell, *Film and Video Guide*.

124 *The Brave One* (1956) Children's. Running time: 100 minutes. Black and white.

Produced by Maurice and Frank King. Directed by Irving Rapper. Screenplay by Robert Rich, Harry Franklin, Merrill White. Original story by Robert Rich. Photographed by Jack Cardiff. Music by Victor Young. Edited by Merrill G. White.

Starring Michel Ray, Rodolfo Hoyos, Elsa Cartenas, Carlos Novarro, Joi Lansing, Fermin Rivera.

A young boy saves his pet bull from being slaughtered in the bull ring.

Note: Robert Rich won an Oscar for Best Original Story, which is ironic in that the mysterious Mr. Rich was actually a pseudonym for blacklisted writer Dalton Trumbo.

125 *Break of Hearts* (1935) Drama. Running time: 78 minutes. Black and white. Available on videocassette.

Produced by Pandro S. Berman. Directed by Phillip Moeller. Screenplay by Sarah Y. Mason and Anthony Veiller (based on a story by Lester Cohen). Photographed by Robert De Grasse. Edited by William Hamilton. Music by Max Steiner.

Starring Katharine Hepburn (Constance), Charles Boyer (Roberti), John Beal (Johnny), Jean Hersholt (Talma), Sam Hardy (Marx), Inez Courtney (Miss Wilson), Helene Millard (Sylvia), Ferdinand Gottschalk (Pazzini), Susan Fleming (Elise), Lee Kohlmar (Schubert), Jean Howard (Didi), Anne Grey (Phyllis).

A woman composer falls for a great conductor, but finds after marrying him that he enjoys carrying on with other women. When she leaves him, he plunges into alcoholic despair.

Note: Actress Susan Fleming was married to Harpo Marx.

Review: "A stale turnip story that relies entirely upon characterization to hide the basic dullness" — *Variety*.

126 *Breakfast for Two* (1937) Comedy. Running time: 67 minutes. Black and white.

Produced by Edward Kaufman. Directed by Alfred Santell. Screenplay by Charles Kaufman, Paul Yabwitz, and Viola Brothers Shore (uncredited contribution from Jack Mintz and Lawrence Pohle). Photographed by J. Roy Hunt. Edited by George Hively.

Starring Barbara Stanwyck (Valentine Ransome), Herbert Marshall (Jonathan Blair), Glenda Farrell (Carol Wallace), Eric Blore (Butch), Etienne Girardot (Meggs), Donald Meek (Justice of Peace), Frank M. Thomas (Sam Ransome), Pierre

Publicity poster for *The Brave One*.

Watkin (Gordon Faraday), Sidney Bracey (Butler), Harold Goodwin (Chauffeur), George Irving, Larry Starrs, Bobby Barber, Edward LeSaint, Tom Ricketts (Bits).

A wealthy heiress is attracted to a rich playboy, but must contend with his gold-digging fiancee.

Review: "Heaps of laughs in breezily paced comedy"—*Variety.*

127 *Breaking the Ice* (1938) Musical. Running time: 80 minutes. Black and white. Available on videocassette.

Produced by Sol Lesser. Directed by Edward F. Cline. Screenplay by Fritz Flakenstein, N. Brewster Morse, Mary McCall, Jr., Manuel Seff, and Bernard Schubert. Photographed by Jack MacKenzie. Edited by Arthur Hilton. Music and lyrics by Frank Churchill, Victor Young, and Paul Webster.

Starring Bobby Breen (Tommy Martin), Charles Ruggles (Samuel Terwillger), Dolores Costello (Martha Martin), Robert Barrat (William Decker), Dorothy Peterson (Annie Decker), John King (Henry Johnson), Billy Gilbert (Mr. Small), Margaret Hamilton (Mrs. Small), Charlie Murray (Janitor), Jonathan Hale (Kane), Spencer Charters (Farmer Smith), Maurice Cass (Mr. Jones).

A young boy tries to earn money for his mother by singing, soon becoming a celebrity.

Oscar nomination: Best Music.

Review: "Moderately engrossing" — *Variety.*

128 Bride by Mistake (1944) Comedy. Running time: 81 minutes. Black and white.

Produced by Bert Granet. Directed by Richard Wallace. Screenplay by Phoebe and Henry Ephron (based on a story by Norman Krasna). Photographed by Nicholas Musuraca. Edited by Les Millbrook.

Starring Alan Marshal (Tony), Laraine Day (Norah), Marsha Hunt (Sylvia), Allyn Joslyn (Phil Vernon), Edgar Buchanan (Connors), Michael St. Angel (Corey), Marc Cramer (Ross), William Post, Jr. (Donald), Bruce Edwards (Chaplain), Nancy Gates (Jane), Slim Summerville (Samuel), John Miljan (Maj. Harvey), Robert Anderson (Lt. Wilson).

A rich woman poses as her own secretary to question would-be suitors.

Note: Remake of *The Richest Girl in Town.* The screenwriters are the parents of screenwriter Nora Ephron (*Sleepless in Seattle, When Harry Met Sally*).

129 Bride for Sale (1949) Comedy. Running time: 87 minutes. Black and white.

Produced by Jack H. Skirball. Directed by William D. Russell. Screenplay by Bruce Manning and Islin Auster (based on a story by Joseph Fields). Photographed by Joseph Valentine. Edited by William Knudtson.

Starring Claudette Colbert (Nora Shelly), Robert Young (Steven Adams), George Brent (Paul Martin), Max Baer (Litka), Gus Schilling (Timothy), Charles Arndt (Dobbs), Mary Bear (Miss Stone), Ann Tyrell (Misas Swanson), Paul Maxey (Gentry), Burk Symon (Sitley), Stephen Chase (Drake), Anne O'Neal (Mrs. Jennings), Eula Guy (Miss Clarendon), John Michaels (Terry), William Vedder (Brooks), Thurston Hall (Mr. Trisby), Michael Brandon (Archie Twitchell), Patsy Moran (Sarah), Harry Cheshire (Haskins), Hans Conried (Jewelry Salesman).

An accounting expert uses her company's files to find the perfect husband.

Review: "Skittish romantic comedy for aging stars"—Leslie Halliwell, *Film and Video Guide.*

130 The Bride Walks Out (1936) Comedy. Running time: 75 minutes. Black and white. Available on videocassette.

Produced by Edward Small. Directed by Leigh Jason. Screenplay by P.J. Wolfson and Phillip G. Epstein (based on a story by Howard Emmett Rogers). Photographed by J. Roy Hunt. Edited by Arthur Roberts. Music by Roy Webb.

Starring Barbara Stanwyck (Carolyn Martin), Gene Raymond (Michael Martin), Robert Young (Hugh McKenzie), Ned Sparks (Paul Dodson), Helen Broderick (Mattie Dodson), Anita Colby and Vivian Oakland (Salesladies), Willie Best (Smoky), Robert Warwick (Mr. McKenzie), Billy Gilbert (Donovan), Eddie Dunn (Milkman), Ward Bond (Taxi Driver), Edgar Dearing (Cop), Wade Boteler (Field Manager), James Farley (Store Detective), Margaret Morris (Secretary), Hattie McDaniel (Mammy).

A couple separates when the woman spends more than her husband earns, soon latching onto a rich playboy.

131 The Brighton Strangler (1945) Crime drama. Running time: 67 minutes. Black and white. Available on videocassette.

Produced by Herman Schlom. Directed by Max Nosseck. Screenplay by Nosseck and Arnold Phillips. Photographed by J. Roy Hunt. Edited by Les Millbrook. Music by Leigh Harline.

Starring John Loder (Reginald), June Duprez (Mapril), Michael St. Angel (Bob), Miles Mander (Allison), Rose Hobart (Dorothy), Gilbert Emery (Dr. Manby), Rex Evans (Shelton), Matthew Boulton (Inspector Graham), Olaf Hytten (Banke), Lydia Bilbrook (Mrs. Manby), Ian Wolfe (Mayor).

An actor in a horror play assumes the identity of his stage character.

132 *Bring 'Em Back Alive* (1932)
Documentary. Running time: 67 minutes. Black and white.

Directed by Clyde Elliot. Photographed by Carl Berger and Nick Cavaliere.

Frank Buck searches the Malayan jungles for wild animals.

Note: One of the highest grossing films of 1932.

133 *Bringing Up Baby* (1938)
Comedy. Running time: 102 minutes. Black and white. Available on videocassette.

Produced and directed by Howard Hawks. Screenplay by Dudley Nichols and Hagar Wilde (based on a story by Wilde) (uncredited scenarists: Robert McGowan and Gertrude Purcell). Photographed by Russell Metty. Edited by George Hively. Music by Roy Webb.

Starring Katharine Hepburn (Susan Vance), Cary Grant (David Huxley), Charles Ruggles (Major Horace Applegate), May Robson (Aunt Elizabeth, Mrs. Carlton Random), Barry Fitzgerald (Mr. Gogarty), Walter Catlett (Constable Slocum), Fritz Feld (Dr. Fritz Lehman), Leona Roberts (Hannah Gogarty), George Irving (Alexander Peabody), Virginia Walker (Alice Swallow), Tala Birell (Mrs. Lehman), John Kelly (Elmer), Edward Gargan, Buck Mack (Zoo Officials), Billy Benedict, Buster Slaven (Caddies), Geraldine Hall (Maid), Stan-

ley Blystone (Doorman), Frank Marlowe (Joe), Pat West (Mac), Jack Carson (Roustabout), Richard Lane (Circus Manager), Frank M. Thomas (Circus Barker), Ruth Adler (Dancer), Ward Bond (Motorcycle Cop), Pat O'Malley (Deputy), Adalyn Asbury (Mrs. Peabody), Judith Ford, Jeanne Martel (Cigarette Girls), George Humbert (Louis), Billy Bevan (Bartender), D'Arcy Corrigan (Professor LaTouche), Asta (George), Nissa (Baby).

An eccentric heiress with a pet leopard gets involved with a shy, eccentric paleontologist.

Note: Considered a classic of its kind, it is said to have disappointed audiences of the period, in spite of critical acclaim, due to its relentless nuttiness, which was apparently considered overkill at the time.

Reviews: "Harum-Scarum farce comedy" — *Variety;* "Funny from the word go..." — Otis Fergusson; "It may be the American movies' closest equivalent to Restoration comedy" — Pauline Kael; "Overrated..." — David Denby, *Premiere.*

134 *Brothers in the Saddle* (1949)
Western. Running time: 60 minutes. Black and white.

Produced by Herman Schlom. Directed by Lesley Selander. Screenplay by Norman Houston. Photographed by J. Roy Hunt. Edited by Sam Beetley.

Starring Tim Holt (Tim Taylor), Richard Martin (Chito Rafferty), Steve Brodie (Steve Taylor), Virginia Cox (Nancy Austin), Carol Forman (Flora Trigby), Richard Powers (Nash Prescott), Stanley Andrews, Robert Bray, Francis McDonald, Emmett Vogan, Monte Montague (bits).

Two brothers find themselves on opposite sides of the law.

135 *Bullet Code* (1940) Western.
Running time: 56 minutes. Black and white.

Produced by Bert Gilroy. Directed by

David Howard. Screenplay by Doris Schroeder. Photographed by Harry Wild. Edited by Frederic Knudtson.

Starring George O'Brien (Steve Condon), Virginia Vale (Molly Matthews), Slim Whitaker (Pop Norton), Howard Hickman (John Matthews), Harry Woods (Cass Clantine), William Haade (Scar Atwood), Walter Miller (Gorman), Robert Stanton (Bud Matthews).

When a cowboy shoots a rustler he mistakes him for the neighbor's son. When he attempts to apologize, he ends up saving the neighbor from crooks and romancing the neighbor's daughter.

136 *Bunco Squad* (1950) Crime drama. Running time: 67 minutes. Black and white.

Produced by Lewis J. Rachmil. Directed by Herbert Leeds. Screenplay by George Callahan (based on a story by Reginald Taviner). Photographed by Henry Freulich. Edited by Desmond Marquette.

Starring Robert Sterling, Joan Dixon, Ricardo Cortez, Douglas Fowley, Elisabeth Risdon, Vivian Oakland.

Phony seance racket is exposed by the title unit.

137 *Bundle of Joy* (1956) Musical. Running time: 100 minutes. Technicolor. Available on videocassette.

Produced by Edmund Grainger. Directed by Norman Taurog. Screenplay by Norman Krasna, Robert Carson, and Arthur Sheekman (based on a story by Felix Jackson). Photographed by William Snyder. Edited by Harry Marker. Music by Andre Joseph Myrow and Max Gordon.

Songs: "I Never Felt This Way Before," "Bundle of Joy," "Lullaby in Blue," "Worry About Tomorrow," "All About Love," "Someday Soon," "What's So Good About Morning," "You're Perfect in Every Department."

Starring Eddie Fisher (Dan Merlin), Debbie Reynolds (Polly Parrish), Adolphe Menjou (J.B. Merlin), Tommy Noonan (Freddie Miller), Nita Talbot

(Mary), Una Merkel (Mrs. Dugan), Melville Cooper (Adams), Bill Goodwin (Mr. Creely), Howard McNear (Mr. Appleby), Robert H. Harris (Mr. Hargraves), Mary Treen (Matron), Edward Brophy (Dance Contest Judge), Gil Stratton (Mike Clancy), Scott Douglas (Bill Rand).

Musical remake of *Bachelor Mother;* a 1939 RKO feature (q.v.).

Review: "Some laughs, but poor numbers"—Leslie Halliwell, *Film and Video Guide.*

138 *Bunker Bean* (1936) Comedy. Running time: 65 minutes. Black and white.

Produced by William Sistrom. Directed by William Hamilton and Edward Kelly. Screenplay by Edmund North, James Gow, and Dorothy Yost (based on the novel by Harry Leon Wilson and the play by Lee Wilson Dodd). Photographed by David Abel. Edited by Jack Hively.

Starring Owen Davis, Jr. (Bunker Bean), Louise Latimer (Mary Kent), Robert McWade (J.C. Kent), Jessie Ralph (Grandmother), Eddie Nugent (Mr. Glab), Lucille Ball (Miss Kelly), Berton Churchill (Professor Balthazer), Hedda Hopper (Mrs. Kent), Pierre Watkin (Mr. Barnes), Joan Davis (Telephone Operator), Edgar Dearing (Cop).

A shy office clerk's personality changes dramatically when he is told by a fortune teller that he is Napoleon's incarnate.

Note: Filmed before in 1917 by Paramount and in 1925 by Warner Bros. In Great Britain, known as *His Majesty Bunker Bean.*

139 *By Your Leave* (1935) Comedy. Running time: 81 minutes. Black and white.

Produced by Pandro S. Berman. Directed by Lloyd Corrigan. Screenplay by Allan Scott (based on the play by Gladys Hurlbut and Emma B.C. Wells). Photographed by Nick Musuraca and Vernon Walker.

Starring Frank Morgan (Henry Smith), Genevieve Tobin (Ellen Smith), Neil Hamilton (David Mackenzie), Marian Nixon (Andree), Glenn Anders (Freddy Clark), Gene Lockhart (Skeets), Margaret Hamilton (Whiffen), Betty Grable (Frances Gretchill), Lona Andre (Miss Purcell), Charles Ray (Leonard).

A bored couple, fearing the onslaught of middle-age, agree to take separate vacations.

Review: "Once the customers are in they'll get some laughs, but they're not going to be easy to entice" — *Variety.*

140 *Call Out the Marines* (1942) Musical comedy. Running time: 66 minutes. Black and white. Available on videocassette.

Produced by Howard Benedict. Directed by Frank Ryan. Screenplay by Ryan and William Hamilton. Photographed by Nicholas Musuraca and J. Roy Hunt. Edited by Theron Warth. Music by Mort Greene and Harry Revel.

Songs: "The Light of My Life," "Zana Zarenda," "Beware," "Hands Across the Border."

Starring Victor McLaglen (McGinnis), Edmund Lowe (Harry Curtis), Binnie Barnes (Vi), Paul Kelly (Jim Blake), Robert Smith (Billy Harrison), Dorothy Lovett (Mitzi), Franklin Pangborn (Wilbur), Corinna Mura (Rita), George Cleveland (Bartender), The King's Men, Six Hits and a Miss.

Two rival marines compete against each other while stationed in San Diego in an effort to please women.

141 *Captain Hurricane* (1935) Drama. Running time: 72 minutes. Black and white.

Directed by John Robertson. Screenplay by Joseph Lovett (based on the novel *The Taming of Zenas Henry* by Sara Ware Bassett). Photographed by Lucien Andriot. Edited by George Hively.

Starring James Barton (Zenas Henry), Helen Westley (Abbie), Helen Mack (Matie), Gene Lockhart (Captain Jeremiah), Douglas Walton (Jimmy), Henry Travers (Captain Ben), Otto Hoffman (Silas Coffin), J. Farrell MacDonald, Forrest Henry, Stanley Fields.

A trio of males find their friendship strained when one of the men's old girlfriend becomes the trio's housekeeper.

142 *Captive Women* (1952) Science fiction. Running time: 67 minutes. Black and white.

Produced by Aubrey Wisberg and Jack Pollexfen. Directed by Stuart Gilmore. Screenplay by Wisberg and Pollexfen. Photographed by Paul Ivano. Edited by Fred Feitshans.

Starring Robert Carle (Rob), Margaret Field (Ruth), Gloria Saunders (Catherine), Ron Randell (Riddon), Stuart Randall (Gordon), Paula Dorety (Captive), Robert Bice (Bram), William Schallert (Carver).

Three tribes battle in Manhattan after a nuclear holocaust.

Note: Alternate title: *1000 Years from Now.*

143 *The Capture* (1950) Western. Running time: 67 minutes. Black and white.

Produced by Niven Busch. Directed by John Sturges. Screenplay by Busch. Photographed by Edward Cronjager. Edited by George Amy. Music by Daniel Amfitheatrof.

Starring Lew Ayres (Vanner), Teresa Wright (Ellen), Victor Jory (Father Gomez), Jacqueline White (Luana), Jimmy Hunt (Mike), Barry Kelley (Mahoney), Duncan Renaldo (Carlos), William Bakewell (Tobin), Milton Parsons (Thin Man), Frank Matts (Juan), Felipe Turich (Valdez), Edwin Rand (Tevlin).

A man on the run hides out in a priest's cabin and tells him his story, which is shown in flashback.

Note: Producer-writer Busch also authored *Duel in the Sun* (Selznick, 1946).

144 *Career* (1939) Drama. Running time: 79 minutes. Black and white.

Produced by Robert Sisk. Directed by Leigh Jason. Screenplay by Dalton Trumbo (based on the story by Phil Strong, adapted by Bert Granet). Photographed by Frank Redman. Edited by Arthur Roberts.

Starring Anne Shirley (Sylvia), Edward Ellis (Cruthers), Samuel S. Hinds (Bartholomew), Janet Beecher (Mrs. Cruthers), Leon Errol (Mudcat), Alice Eden (Merta), John Archer (Ray), Raymond Hatton (Deacon), Maurice Murphy (Mel), Harrison Greene (Burnett), Charles Drake (Chaney), Hobart Cavanaugh (Bronson).

The long standing rivalry of two midwestern small-town men escalates when their children fall in love.

Note: Alice Eden and John Archer were in this film after winning a Hollywood screen test competition sponsored by CBS radio and Doublemint gum. Archer went on to appear in many Hollywood films, was at one time married to actress Marjorie Lord, and is the father of Anne Archer. Eden made only one more film, *Kit Carson* (1940), this time using her real name, Rowena Cook, then disappeared from the Hollywood scene.

Review: "Small town story will sell better outside major playdates" — *Variety*.

145 *Carefree* (1938) Produced by Pandro S. Berman. Directed by Mark Sandrich. Screenplay by Allan Scott and Ernest Pagano (story and adaption by Dudley Nichols, Hagar Wilde, based on an original idea by Marian Ainslee and Guy Endore). Photographed by Robert de Grasse. Edited by William Hamilton. Music by Irving Berlin.

Starring Fred Astaire (Tony Flagg), Ginger Rogers (Amanda Cooper), Ralph Bellamy (Stephen Arden), Luella Gear (Aunt Cora), Jack Carson (Connors), Clarence Kolb (Judge Travers), Franklin Pangborn (Roland Hunter), Walter Kingsford (Dr. Powers), Kay Sutton (Miss Adams), Tom Tully (Policeman), Hattie McDaniel (Maid), Robert B. Mitchell and His St. Brendan's Boys (Themselves).

Songs: "I Used to Be Color Blind," "Since They Turned Loch Lomond Into Swing," "The Yarn," "The Night Is Filled with Music," "Change Partners."

A man, crazy about a radio singer, sends her to a psychiatrist so she'll fall for him — but she falls for the psychiatrist!

Note: The last of RKO's Astaire-Rogers films, this one concentrates on comedy and has only five musical numbers. Rogers went on to retain full stardom at the studio, but Astaire's contract lapsed and the studio let him move on. RKO was no longer financially capable of producing big budget musicals, especially since Astaire-Rogers as a team had just slipped out of the Top Ten box office draws — a list they'd headed only two years before. The song "Change Partners" was nominated for an Oscar.

Review: "Perhaps their poorest musical . . . a disappointing story but perhaps the stars alone may save it" — *Variety*.

146 *Carnival Boat* (1932) Drama. Running time: 61 minutes. Black and white. A Pathé production for RKO release.

Directed by Albert Rogell. Screenplay by James Seymour (based on a story by Marion Jackson and Don Ryan). Photographed by Ted McCord. Edited by John Link.

Starring Bill Boyd (Buck Gannon), Ginger Rogers (Honey), Fred Kohler, Sr. (Hack), Hobart Bosworth (Jim Gannon), Marie Prevost (Babe), Edgar Kennedy (Blady), Harry Sweet (Stubby), Charles Sellon (Lane), Walter Percival (DeLacey), Jack Carlyle (Assistant to DeLacey), Joe Marba (Windy), Eddie Chandler (Jordan), Bob Perry (Bartender).

A logger falls for a showgirl, much to his father's chagrin.

Note: Actress Prevost, a former Sennett Bathing Beauty, died in her home in 1936. When her body was discovered, several days later, her pet dog had consumed most of it. This incident was immortalized by rock singer Nick Lowe's misspelled song "Marie Provost."

147 *Carnival Story* (1954) Drama. Running time: 94 minutes. Technicolor. Available on videocassette.

Produced by Maurice and Frank King. Directed by Kurt Neumann. Screenplay by Hans Jacoby, Neumann (from a story by Marcel Klauber and C.B. Williams). Photographed by Ernest Haller. Music by Will Schmidt-Gentner. Edited by Merrill White and Rudolf Briesbach.

Starring Anne Baxter (Willie), Steve Cochran (Joe), Lyle Bettger (Frank), George Nader (Vines), Jay C. Flippen (Charley), Helene Stanley (Peggy), Adi Berber (Groppo).

A circus high diver leaves her seedy boyfriend and marries a fellow performer. Her former boyfriend arranges her husband's death in an aerial accident, and makes a play for her once again in order to steal her husband's savings.

148 *Cartouche* (1957) Adventure. Running time: 85 minutes. Black and white. An Italian production distributed in the U.S. by RKO.

Produced by John Nasht. Directed by Steve Sekely. Screenplay by Louis Stevens (based on a treatment by Tullio Pinelli).

Starring Richard Basehart, Patricia Roc, Massimo Serato, Akim Tamiroff, Isa Barzizza, Nerio Bernardi, Nino Marchetti, Aldo De Franchi.

A swashbuckler accused of murdering a prince tries to clear his name.

149 *Casanova Brown* (1944) Comedy. Running time: 93 minutes. Black and white.

Produced by Nunnally Johnson. Directed by Sam Wood. Screenplay by Johnson (based on the play *The Little Accident* (aka *Bachelor Father*) by Floyd Dell and Thomas Mitchell). Photographed by John Seitz. Edited by Thomas Neff. Music by Arthur Lange.

Starring Gary Cooper (Casanova Brown), Teresa Wright (Isabel Drury), Frank Morgan (Mr. Ferris), Anita Louise (Madge Ferris), Patricia Collinge (Mrs. Drury), Edmond Breon (Mr. Drury), Jill Esmond (Dr. Zernerke), Emory Parnell (Frank), Isobel Elsom (Mrs. Ferris), Mary Treen (Monica), Halliwell Hobbes (Butler), Larry Joe Olsen (Junior), Byron Foulger (Fletcher), Sarah Padden (Landlady), Eloise Hardt (Doris Ferris), Grady Sutton (Tod), Frederick Burton (Reverend Dean), Robert Dudley (Marriage Clerk), Isabel La Mal (Clerk's Wife), Florence Lake (Nurse Phillips), Ann Evers (Nurse Petheridge), Frances Morris (Nurse Gillespie), Nell Craig (Nurse), Lane Chandler (Orderly), Kay Deslys (Fat Woman Patient), Irving Bacon (Hotel Manager), Snub Pollard (Father at Baby Window).

A shy English teacher discovers after divorcing his wife that she is pregnant.

Review: "There is so much clowning with so little subject that one is exposed to the impression that anything went for a laugh"—Bosley Crowther, *The New York Times*.

150 *The Case of Sergeant Grischa* (1930) Drama. Running time: 82 minutes. Black and white.

Produced by William LeBaron. Directed by Herbert Brenon. Screenplay by Elizabeth Meehan (based on a novel by Arnold Zweig). Photographed by Roy Hunt. Edited by Marie Halvey.

Starring Chester Morris (Grischa), Betty Compson (Babka), Jean Hersholt (Posanski), Alan B. Francis (Gen. von Lychow), Gustav von Seyffertitz (Gen. Schieffenzahn), Paul McAllister (Col. Sacht), Leyland Hodgson (Lt. Winifred), Bernard Siegel (Verressieff), Frank McCormack (Capt. Spierauge/Kolja).

A Russian POW escapes from a German prison camp during WWI.

Review: "No sympathy, no fan appeal,

Publicity poster for *Cash on Delivery*.

and no entertainment. Can only be exploited as 'a fine production' or 'a new era in pictures.'" – *Variety*.

151 *Cash on Delivery* (1956) Comedy. Running time: 79 minutes. Black and white.

Produced by Peter Rogers. Directed by Muriel Box. Screenplay by Rogers (based on the play by Roger MacDougal. Photographed by Ernest Steward. Edited by Alfred Roome.

Starring Shelley Winters (Myrtle), John Gregson (Tony), Peggy Cummins (Dorothy), Wilfrid Hyde-White (Starke), Mona Washbourne (Appleby), Hal Osmond (Livingstone Potts), Harley Power (Cy).

An American nightclub singer in England will inherit a large sum if her ex-husband does not sire a son by a certain date.

Note: British title: *To Dorothy, a Son.*

152 *Cat People* (1942) Horror. Running time: 73 minutes. Black and white. Available on videocassette.

Produced by Val Lewton. Directed by Jacques Tourneur. Screenplay by DeWitt Bodeen. Photographed by Nicholas Musuraca. Edited by Mark Robson. Music by Roy Webb.

Starring Simone Simon (Irene Dubrovna), Kent Smith (Oliver Reed), Tom Conway (The Psychiatrist), Jane Randolph (Alice Moore), Jack Holt (Commodore), Alan Napier (Carver), Elizabeth Dunne (Miss Plunkett), Elizabeth Russell (The Cat Woman).

A beautiful girl believes she is turning into a panther and killing her friends.

Note: Lewton cut costs in this, the first of his horror films for RKO, by using the remains of Orson Welles' *Magnificent Ambersons* set. The film grossed $200,000 its first time out. It was the first monster film to refrain from showing its monster. Sequel (sort of): *Curse of the Cat People* (q.v.). Remake: *Cat People* (q.v.; a Universal production which involved RKO at least on paper).

Review: "...revolutionized scare movies with suggestion, imaginative sound effects, and camera angles, leaving everything to the fear-filled imagination"—Pauline Kael, 1968.

153 *Cat People* (1982) Horror/fantasy. Running time: 118 minutes. Color.

Produced by Charles Fries. Directed by Paul Schrader. Screenplay by Alan Ornsby (based on the story by DeWitt Bodeen). Photographed by John Bailey. Edited by Jacqueline Cambas. Music by David Bowie.

Starring Natassia Kinski (Irena Gallier), Malcolm McDowell (Paul Gallier), John Heard (Oliver Yates), Annette O'Toole (Alice Perrin), Ruby Dee (Female), Ed Begley, Jr. (Joe Creigh), Scott Paulin (Bill Searle), Frankie Faison (Detective Brandt), Ron Diamond (Detective Diamond), Lynn Lowry (Ruthie), John Larroquette (Bronte Judson), Tessa Richarde (Billie), Patricia Perkins (Taxi Driver), Berry Berenson (Sandra), Neva Gage (Cat-like woman).

A variation on the original, this time the lady having an incestuous relationship with her brother and only transforms and kills after sex.

Note: A Universal feature which lists as a tandem production with RKO. Thus, the studio whose work is compiled herein must have been involved at least marginally.

Review: "The final impression is of a phantasmagoric indulgence in sound and vision by a filmmaker who fears sex and is excited by violence"—*Sunday Times.*

154 *Cattle Queen of Montana* (1954) Western. Running time: 92 minutes. Technicolor. Available on videocassette.

Produced by Benedict Bogeaus. Directed by Allan Dwan. Screenplay by Robert Blees and Howard Estabrook (based on a story by Thomas Blackburn). Photographed by John Alton. Edited by Carl Lodato and Jim Lekester. Music by Louis Forbes.

Starring Barbara Stanwyck (Sierra Nevada Jones), Ronald Reagan (Farrell), Gene Evans (Tom McCord), Lance Fuller (Colorados), Anthony Caruso (Nachakos), Jack Elam (Yost), Yvette Dugay (Starfire), Morris Ankrum (J.I. "Pop" Jones), Chubby Johnson (Nat), Myron Healey (Hank), Rodd Redwing (Powhani), Paul Birch (Col. Carrington), Byron Foulger (Land Office Employee), Burt Mustin (Dan).

A tough woman battles cattle rustlers after inheriting her father's range.

Note: Stanwyck did her own stunts on this film and so impressed members of the Blackfoot tribe working as extras, they gave her the Indian name of Princess Many Victories. To the day she died, Reagan addressed her by this name whenever he would see or correspond with her.

155 *Caught Plastered* (1930) Comedy. Running time: 68 minutes. Black and white.

Produced by Douglas MacLean. Directed by William Seiter. Screenplay by Ralph Spence (based on a story by MacLean). Photographed by Jack MacKenzie.

Song: "I'm That Way About You" by Victor Schetzinger.

Starring Bert Wheeler (Tommy Tanner), Robert Woolsey (Egbert Higginbottom), Dorothy Lee (Peggy Morton), Lucy Beaumont (Mother Talley), Jason Robards, Sr. (Watters), DeWitt Jennings (Chief Morton), Charles Middleton (Flint), William Scott (Clarke).

Wheeler and Woolsey help save an old woman's store from foreclosure and, later, a gang of bootleggers.

A Certain Mr. Scratch see *The Devil and Daniel Webster*

156 *Chance at Heaven* (1933) Drama. Running time: 71 minutes. Black and white.

Produced by Merian C. Cooper. Directed by William Seiter. Screenplay by Julian Josephson and Sarah Y. Mason (based on a story by Vina Delmar). Photographed by Nicholas Musuraca. Edited by James Morely. Music by Max Steiner.

Starring Joel McCrea (Blackie Gorman), Ginger Rogers (Marge Harris), Marian Nixon (Glory Franklin), Andy Devine (Al), Virginia Hammond (Mrs. Franklin), Lucien Littlefield (Mr. Harris), Ann Shoemaker (Mrs. Harris), George Meeker (Sid Larrick), Herman Bing (Chauffeur), Betty Furness (Betty), Harry Bowen (First Reporter).

A gas station attendant falls for a rich society snob, leaving his girl behind to marry into wealth.

157 *Chasing Yesterday* (1935) Drama. Running time: 78 minutes. Black and white.

Produced by Cliff Reid. Directed by George Nicholls, Jr. Screenplay by Francis Edwards Faragoh (based on the novel *The Crime of Sylvestre Bannard* by Anatole France). Photographed by Lucien Andriot. Edited by Arthur Schmidt.

Starring Anne Shirley (Jeanne), O.P. Heggie (Sylvestre Bonnard), Helen Westley (Therese), Elizabeth Patterson (Prefers), John Qualen (Coccoz), Trent Durkin (Henri), Etienne Girardot (Mouche), Doris Lloyd (Mme. De Gabry).

An archaeologist tries to recapture his lost youth through the daughter of a woman he once loved — but lost.

158 *Chatterbox* (1936) Drama. Running time: 68 minutes. Black and white.

Produced by Robert Sisk. Directed by George Nicholls, Jr. Screenplay by Sam Mintz (based on a play by David Carb). Photographed by Robert De Grasse. Edited by Arthur Schmidt.

Starring Anne Shirley (Jenny Yates), Phillips Holmes (Phillip Green, Jr.), Edward Ellis (Uriah Lowell), Erik Rhodes (Archie Fisher), Margaret Hamilton (Emily Tipton), Granville Bates (Phillip Greene, Sr.), Allen Vincent (Harrison), Lucille Ball (Lillian Temple), George Offerman, Jr. (Michael Arbuckle).

A Vermont country girl attempts a stage career.

Review: "Discounting the nice job all around, the picture isn't there" — *Variety.*

Check and Double Check see *Amos 'n' Andy*

159 *The Cheyenne Kid* (1933) Western. Running time: 61 minutes. Black and white.

Directed by Robert Hill. Screenplay by Jack Curtis (based on the story *Sir Peagan Passes* by W.C. Tuttle).

Starring Tom Keene, Mary Mason, Roscoe Ates, Al Bridge, Otto Hoffman, Alan Roscoe, Anderson Lawlor.

A good guy cowboy is mistaken for a bandit named "Denver Ed."

160 *Child of Divorce* (1946) Drama. Running time: 62 minutes. Black and white.

Produced by Lillie Hayward. Directed by Richard Fleischer. Screenplay by Hayward (based on the play *Wednesday's Child* by Leopold L. Atlas). Photographed by Jack MacKenzie. Edited by Samuel E. Beetley. Music by Leigh Harline.

Starring Sharyn Moffett (Bobby), Regis Toomey (Ray), Madge Meredith (Joan), Walter Reed (Michael), Una O'Connor (Nora), Doris Merrick (Louise), Harry Cheshire (Judge), Selmer Jackson (Dr. Sterling), Lillian Randolph (Carrie), Pat Prest (Linda), Gregory Muradian (Freddie), George MacDonald (Donnie), Patsy Converse (Betty), Ann Carter (Peggy).

The pain a child suffers when her parents divorce.

Note: Moffett was eight years old at the time she did this film, would act until she was thirteen, and leave films without a trace.

161 *China Passage* (1937) Mystery-adventure. Running time: 63 minutes. Black and white.

Produced by Cliff Reid. Directed by Edward Killy. Screenplay by Edmund L. Hartmann and J. Robert Bren (based on a story by Taylor Caven). Photographed by Nicholas Musuraca. Edited by Desmond Marquette.

Starring Constance Worth (Jane Dunn), Vinton Haworth (Tom Baldwin), Leslie Fenton (A. Durand), Gordon Jones (Joe Dugan), Alec Craig (Harvey), Dick Eliot (Phillip Burton), Frank M. Thomas (Captain Williams), George Irving (Dr. Sibley), Billy Gilbert (Bartender), Joyce Compton (Mrs. Collins), Eddie Dunn (Ship's Waiter), Alan Curtis, Edgar Dearing (Ship's Officers), Phillip Ahn (Dr. Fang Tu).

Government agents search for stolen diamonds aboard a steamer bound for China.

162 *China Sky* (1945) War drama. Running time: 78 minutes. Black and white.

Produced by Maurice Geraghty. Directed by Ray Enright. Screenplay by Brenda Weisberg and Joseph Hoffman (based on the novel by Pearl Buck). Photographed by Nicholas Musuraca. Edited by Gene Milford.

Starring Randolph Scott (Thompson), Ruth Warrick (Sara), Ellen Drew (Louise), Anthony Quinn (Chen Ta), Carol Thurston (Siu Mei), Richard Loo (Col. Yasuda), Ducky Louie (Little Goat), Phillip Ahn (Dr. Kim), Benson Fong (Chung), Kermit Maynard (Bit).

A male and female doctor must face the trouble of living with Chinese guerrillas, as well as the problems caused by the male doctor's jealous and selfish wife.

163 *Christopher Strong* (1933) Drama. Running time: 77 minutes. Black and white. Available on videocassette.

Produced by David O. Selznick and Pandro S. Berman. Directed by Dorothy Arzner. Screenplay by Zoe Akins (based on the novel by Gilbert Frankau). Photographed by Bert Glennon. Music by Max Steiner. Edited by Arthur Roberts.

Starring Katharine Hepburn (Cynthia), Colin Clive (Christopher Strong), Billie Burke (Elaine), Helen Chandler (Monica), Ralph Forbes (Harry Rawlinson), Jack La Rue (Carlo), Irene Browne (Carrie), Gwendolyn Logan (Bradford), Desmond Roberts (Bryce Mercer), Agostino Borgato (Fortune Teller), Margaret Lindsay (Girl at Party), Donald Ogden Stewart (Mechanic), Zena Savina (Second Maid).

A courageous woman aviator has an affair with a married businessman, soon finding herself pregnant.

Note: Hepburn's second film; it was not a box office success.

Review: "Draggy society play with circusy airplane stunt incidentals" — *Variety*.

164 *Cimarron* (1931) Western. Running time: 131 minutes. Black and white. Available on videocassette.

Produced by William LeBaron. Directed by Wesley Ruggles. Screenplay by Howard Estabrook (based on the novel by Edna Ferber). Photographed by Edward Cronjager. Edited by William Hamilton.

Starring Richard Dix (Yancy Cravat), Irene Dunne (Sabra Cravat), Estelle Taylor (Dixie Lee), Nance O'Neil (Felice Venable), William Collier, Jr. (The Kid), Roscoe Ates (Jess Rickey), George E. Stone (Sol Levy), Robert McWade (Louie Heffner), Edna May Oliver (Mrs. Tracy Wyatt), Frank Darien (Mr. Bixby), Eugene "Pineapple" Jackson (Isaiah), Dolores Brown (Baby Big Elk "Eldest"), Gloria Vonic (Baby Big Elk "Youngster"), Otto Hoffman (Murch Rankin), William Orlamond (Grat Gotch), Frank Beal (Louis Venable), Nancy Dover (Donna Cravat "Eldest"), Helen Parrish (Donna Cravat "Youngster"), Scott Douglas (Cim "Youngest"), Reginald Streeter (Yancy, Jr.), Lois Jane Campbell (Felice, Jr.), Anna Lee (Aunt Cassandra), Tyrone Brereton (Dabney Venable), Lillian Lane (Cousin Bella), Henry Rocquemore (Jouett Goforth), Nell Craig (Arminta Greenwood), Robert McKenzie (Pat Leary), Bob Kortman (Killer), Clara Hunt (Indian Girl), William Janney (Worker), Dennis O'Keefe (Extra).

The life of an Oklahoma homesteader is traced from 1890 to 1915.

Note: Budgeted at $1,433,000, this was the most expensive production the studio ever tackled up to this time. In spite of rave reviews and being awarded Oscars for Best Picture and Best Screenplay, it lost more than a half million. It was to be the only RKO Oscar winner for Best Picture along with *The Best Years of Our Lives* (q.v.). Remade in 1960 by MGM.

Review: "An elegant example of super filmmaking"—*Variety.*

165 *Cinderella* (1950) Animated feature. Running time: 74 minutes. Technicolor. Available on videocassette. A Walt Disney Production released through RKO.

Produced by Walt Disney. Directed by Wilfred Jackson, Hamilton Luske, Clyde Geronimi. Screenplay by William Peet, Ted Sears, Homer Brightman, Kenneth Anderson, Erdman Penner, Winston Hibler, Harry Reeves, and Joe Rinaldi (based on the original story by Charles Perrault). Music by Oliver Wallace and Paul J. Smith. Character animators: Marvin Woodward, Hal Ambro, George Nicholas, Hal King, Judge Whitaker, Fred Moore, Hugh Fraser, Phil Duncan, Cliff Nordberg, Kenneth O'Brien, Harvey Toombs, Don Lusk.

Songs: "Bibbidi Bobbidi Boo," "So This Is Love," "A Dream Is a Wish Your Heart Makes," "Cinderella," "The Work Song," "Oh Sing, Sweet Nightingale."

Voices: Ilene Woods (Cinderella), William Phipps (Prince Charming), Eleanor Audley (Stepmother), Verna Felton (Fairy Godmother), James MacDonald (Jacques and Gus-Gus), Rhoda Williams (Anastasia), Lucille Bliss (Drusilla), Luis Van Rooten (King and Grand Duke), Don Barclay, Claire DuBrey.

Animated Disney feature based on the popular story.

Note: The song "Bibbidi Bobbidi Boo" was nominated for an Oscar.

166 *Cinderella Swings It* (1942) Comedy. Running time: 70 minutes. Black and white.

Produced by Jerrold T. Brandt. Directed by Christy Cabanne. Screenplay by Michael L. Simmons (based on the Scattergood Baines stories by Clarence Buddington Kelland). Photographed by Arthur Martinelli. Edited by Richard Cahoon.

Starring Guy Kibbee (Scattergood Baines), Gloria Warren (Betty Palmer), Helen Parrish (Sally Burton), Dick Hogan (Tommy Stewart), Leonard Kinsky (Vladimir Smitkin), Billy Lenhart and Kenneth Brown (Butch and Buddy), Dink Trout (Pliny Picett), Willie Best (Hipp), Pierre Watkin (Brock Harris), Lee "Lasses" White (Ed Potts), Fern Emmett (Clara Potts), Eddy Waller (Lem), Kay Linaker (Mme. Dolores), Christine McIntyre (Secretary), Grace Costello (Tap Dancer).

Scattergood Baines tries assisting a young singer with her career.

Note: Last of the Scattergood Baines series, the title was changed from *Scattergood Swings It* due to the poor box office generated by the previous entries.

167 *The Circus Kid* (1928) Drama. Running time: 61 minutes. Black and white.

Directed by George B. Seitz. Screenplay by Melville Baker and Randolph Bartlett (based on a story by James Ashmore Creelman). Photographed by Phillip Tannura. Edited by Ann McKnight.

Starring Frankie Darro, Poodles Hanneford, Joe E. Brown, Helene Costello, Sam Nelson, Lionel Belmore, Charles Miller, Johnny Gough, Sid Crosley, Charles Gemora, Frank Hemphill, Clarence Moorehouse.

An orphan joins the circus as an acrobat where a down-and-out animal trainer is vying for the affections of a bareback rider, who loves the big top's rising star instead.

Note: An FBO part-talkie, and direct precursor to RKO. This is basically a silent film with a sound prologue and snippets of dialogue throughout.

168 *Citizen Kane* (1941) Drama. Running time: 119 minutes. Black and white. Available on videocassette.

Produced and directed by Orson Welles. Screenplay by Welles and Herman J. Mankiewicz. Photographed by Gregg Toland. Music by Bernard Herrman. Edited by Robert Wise.

Starring Orson Welles (Charles Foster Kane), Joseph Cotten (Jedediah Leland), Dorothy Comingore (Susan Alexander), Everett Sloane (Mr. Bernstein), Ray Collins (Boss J.W. "Big Jim" Gettys), George Coulouris (Walter Parks Thatcher), Agnes Moorehead (Mrs. Mary Kane), Paul Stewart (Raymond, Head Butler), Ruth Warrick (Mrs. Emily Norton Kane), Erskine Sanford (Herbert Carter), William Alland (Jerry Thompson, Chief Reporter), Fortunio Bonanova (Matisti), Gus Schilling (Head Waiter), Phillip Van Zandt (Mr. Rawlston), George Bacus (Miss Anderson), Harry Shannon (Jim Kane), Sonny Bupp (Kane III), Buddy Swan (Kane at age 8), Alan Ladd, Arthur O'Connell (Reporter).

The rise and fall of a powerful newspaper magnate.

Note: Considered by many to be the greatest film of all time. Loosely based on the life of William Randolph Hearst, co-writer Mankiewicz was a former reporter and intimate of the publisher. Hearst tried to have the negative of the film burned prior to its release, offering the studio double its production costs.

Fortunately, the studio refused. Thus, Hearst ordered his newspaper enterprise to refrain from mentioning any RKO film in any context, including advertising. He also forced theater chains to refuse to book the film, this being the reason the movie lost money. It was, is, and shall always be a true milestone in cinematic technique, to which every film made since has been compared. This is an especially amazing achievement in that Welles was only 25 at the time. Upon its 50th anniversary, Turner Home Entertainment released a collector's package containing the film, a documentary of its rocky production, a book, and a copy of the script. Ted Turner made some attempt to colorize it, but reneged when Welles, on his death bed, begged that Turner not "ruin my movie with his crayons." This is a film that must be seen by everybody.

Review: "...if the cinema could do that, it could do anything"—Penelope Houston.

Orson Welles in *Citizen Kane*.

169 *Clash by Night* (1952) Drama. Running time: 105 minutes. Black and white. Available on videocassette.

Produced by Harriet Parsons. Directed by Fritz Lang. Screenplay by Alfred Hayes and David Dortort (based on the play by Clifford Odets). Photographed by Nicholas Musuraca. Edited by George J. Amy. Music by Roy Webb.

Starring Barbara Stanwyck (Mae Doyle), Paul Douglas (Jerry D'Amato), Robert Ryan (Earl Pfeiffer), Marilyn Monroe (Peggy), J. Carrol Naish (Uncle Vince), Keith Andes (Joe Doyle), Silvio

As brutally outspoken as the words this betrayed husband hurls at his wife!

"Livin' in my house!
Lovin' another man!
Is that what you call
bein' honest? That's
just givin' it a
nice name!"

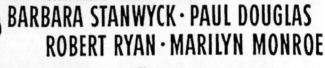

JERRY WALD & NORMAN KRASNA present

**BARBARA STANWYCK · PAUL DOUGLAS
ROBERT RYAN · MARILYN MONROE**

CLASH BY NIGHT

with J. CARROL NAISH · KEITH ANDES · produced by HARRIET PARSONS · directed by FRITZ LANG · screenplay by ALFRED HAYES

Publicity poster for *Clash by Night*.

Minciotti (Papa), Diane Stewart, Deborah Stewart (Twins), Julius Tannen (Sad-Eyed Waiter), Tony Dante (Fisherman at Pier).

A hardened girl returns from the big city to her small home town.

Review: "The sub-plot involving Monroe and Andes plays like *Gidget Faces an Identity Crisis*"—Kit Parker catalogue.

170 *The Clay Pigeon* (1949) Drama. Running time: 63 minutes. Black and white.

Produced by Herman Schlom. Directed by Richard Fleischer. Screenplay by Carl Foreman. Photographed by Robert De Grasse. Edited by Samuel Beetley.

Starring Bill Williams (Jim Fletcher), Barbara Hale (Martha Gregory), Richard Quine (Ted Niles), Richard Loo (Tokoyama), Frank Fenton (Lt. Cmdr. Prentice), Frank Wilcox (Hospital Doctor), Marya Marcho (Helen Minoto), Robert Bray (Blake), Martha Hyer (Receptionist), Harold Landon (Blind Veteran), James Craven (John Wheeler), Grandon Rhodes (Clark).

A sailor, suffering from amnesia, is court-martialed for treason.

Note: The first feature produced with Howard Hughes as studio head.

171 *Cockeyed Cavaliers* (1934)
Comedy. Running time: 72 minutes. Black and white. Available on videocassette.

Directed by Mark Sandrich. Screenplay by Edward Kaufman and Ben Holmes. Photographed by Nicholas Musuraca. Edited by Jack Kitchin. Music by Roy Webb.

Starring Bert Wheeler (Bert), Robert Woolsey (Bob), Thelma Todd (Genevieve), Dorothy Lee (Mary Ann), Noah Beery, Sr. (Baron), Robert Grief (Duke of Weskit), Henry Sedley (Baron's Friend), Franklin Pangborn (Town Crier), Jack Norton, Snub Pollard, Billy Gilbert.

The boys are mistaken for the king's physicians in this 16th century saga.

Note: Considered, along with *Diplomaniacs* to be the duo's best film.

172 *Code of the West* (1947)
Western. Running time: 57 minutes. Black and white.

Produced by Herman Schlom. Directed by William Berke. Screenplay by Norman Houston (based on a novel by Zane Grey). Photographed by Jack MacKenzie. Edited by Ernie Leadlay. Music by Lew Pollack and Harry Harris.

Starring James Warren (Bob Wade), Debra Alden (Ruth), John Laurenz (Chito), Steve Brodie (Saunders), Rita Lynn (Pepita), Robert Clarke (Harry), Carol Forman (Milly), Harry Woods (Hatfield), Raymond Burr (Carter), Harry Harvey (Stockton), Phil Warren (Wescott), Emmett Lynn (Doc Quinn).

A young cowboy hero leads settlers on a quest for land rights.

173 *Come On Danger!* (1932)
Western. Running time: 60 minutes. Black and white.

Directed by Robert Hill. Screenplay by Bennett Cohen. Photographed by Nicholas Musuraca.

Starring Tom Keene, Julie Haydon, Roscoe Ates, Robert Ellis, Wade Boteler, William Scott, Harry Tenbrook, Bud Osborne, Roy Stewart, Frank Lackteen, Nell Craig, Monte Montague, Flash the Horse.

A woman becomes an outlaw to save her ranch, and is implicated in the murder of a cowboy hero's brother.

Note: Keene's first feature for RKO. Remade with George O'Brien as *Renegade Ranger* in 1938, and again as *Come On Danger* with Tim Holt in 1942.

174 *Come On Danger* (1942)
Western. Running time: 56 minutes. Black and white.

Produced by Bert Gilroy. Directed by Edward Killy. Screenplay by Norton S. Parker (based on a story by Bennett Cohen). Photographed by Harry Wild. Edited by Frederic Knudtson.

Starring Tim Holt (Johnny), Frances Neal (Ann), Ray Whitley (Smokey), Lee "Lasses" White (Whopper), Karl Hackett (Ramsey), Malcolm "Bud" McTaggart (Russ), Glenn Strange (Sloan), Evelyn Dodson (Aunt Fanny), Davison Clark (Blake), John Elliott (Saunders), Slim Whitaker (Sheriff), Kate Harrington (Maggie), Henry Rocquemore (Jed).

Remake of the above Tom Keene western.

175 *The Common Law* (1931) Drama. Running time: 72 minutes. Black and white.

Produced by Charles R. Rogers. Directed by Paul Stein. Screenplay by John Farrow and Horace Jackson (based on the novel by Robert W. Chambers). Photographed by Hal Moore. Edited by Jack Kitchin.

Starring Constance Bennett (Valerie), Joel McCrea (Neville), Lew Cody (Cardemon), Robert Williams (Sam), Hedda Hopper (Mrs. Clare Collins), Marion Shilling (Stephanie).

A sophisticated lady leaves her sugar daddy boyfriend for the love of an idealistic artist.

Note: Filmed before in 1916 and 1923. This was a Depression-era moneymaker for RKO.

176 *The Company She Keeps* (1950) Drama. Running time: 82 minutes. Black and white.

Produced by John Houseman. Directed by John Cromwell. Screenplay by Ketti Frings. Photographed by Nicholas Musuraca. Edited by Robert Swink.

Starring Lizabeth Scott (Joan), Jane Greer (Diane), Dennis O'Keefe (Larry), Fay Baker (Tilly), John Hoyt (Judge Kendall), James Bell (Mr. Nelley), Don Beddoe (Jamieson), Bert Freed (Smitty), Irene Tedrow (Mrs. Seeley), Marjorie Wood (Mrs. Haley), Marjorie Crossland (Mrs. Griggs), Virginia Farmer (Mrs. Harris).

A girl makes a play for her parole officer's boyfriend.

177 *Condemned Women* (1938) Drama. Running time: 77 minutes. Black and white.

Produced by Robert Sisk. Directed by Lew Landers. Screenplay by Lionel Houser. Photographed by Nicholas Musuraca. Edited by George Hively.

Starring Sally Eilers (Linda Wilson), Louis Hayward (Phillip Duncan), Anne Shirley (Millie Anson), Esther Dale (Matron Glover), Lee Patrick (Big An-nie), Leona Roberts (Kate), George Irving (Warden Miller), Richard Bond (David), Netta Packer (Sarah), Rita LaRoy (Cora), Florence Lake (Susan).

A murder occurs in a women's prison.

178 *The Conqueror* (1956) Adventure. Running time: 111 minutes. Technicolor Cinemascope. Available on videocassette.

Produced and directed by Dick Powell. Screenplay by Oscar Millard. Photographed by Joseph LaShelle, Leo Tover, Harry J. Wild, and William Snyder. Edited by Robert Ford and Kenneth Marstella. Music by Victor Young.

Starring John Wayne (Temujin), Susan Hayward (Bortai), Pedro Armendariz (Jamuga), Agnes Moorehead (Hunlun), Thomas Gomez (Wang Kahn), John Hoyt (Shaman), William Conrad (Kasar), Ted De Corsia (Kumlek), Leslie Bradley (Targutai), Lee Van Cleef (Chepei), Peter Mamakos (Bogurchi), Leo Gordon (Tartar Captain), Richard Loo (Captain of Wang's Guard), Billy Curtis (Midget Tumbler).

Romantic early adventures of Genghis Khan.

Note: The film was shot about 136 miles from a hugh atomic test site, and of the 220 people who worked on this film, 90 contracted cancer. Among those who died as a result are Wayne, Hayward, Powell, Armendariz, and Moorehead. Wayne allegedly loved the script and demanded to play the lead, although it was so obviously a poor piece of casting. The result was that the film has yet to make its money back.

Reviews: "John Wayne as Genghis Khan—history's most improbable piece of casting unless Mickey Rooney were to play Jesus in *King of Kings*"—Jack Smith, *L.A. Times;* "An RKO Radioactive picture"—*The Motion Picture Guide.*

179 *The Conquerors* (1932) Historical drama. Running time: 88 minutes. Black and white.

Jane Greer and Lizabeth Scott in *The Company She Keeps.*

Produced by David O. Selznick. Directed by William Wellman. Screenplay by Robert Lord (based on a story by Howard Estabrook). Photographed by Edward Cronjager. Edited by William Hamilton. Music by Max Steiner.

Starring Richard Dix (Roger Standish), Ann Harding (Caroline Ogden Standish), Edna May Oliver (Matilda Blake), Guy Kibbee (Dr. Daniel Blake), Julie Haydon (Frances Standish), Donald Cook (Warren Lennox), Harry Holman (Stubby), Skeets Gallagher (Benson), Walter Walker (Mr. Ogden), Wally Albright and Marilyn Knowlden (Twins).

Nebraska settlers begin banking empire in the 1870s.

Note: Alternate title: *Pioneer Builders.*

Review: "As good as a Depression story can be, which isn't much box office" — *Variety.*

180 Consolation Marriage (1931) Drama. Running time: 82 minutes. Black and white.

Directed by Paul Sloane. Screenplay by Humphrey Pearson (based on a story by William Cunningham). Photographed by J. Roy Hunt. Music by Max Steiner and Myles Connolly.

Starring Irene Dunne (Mary), Pat O'Brien (Steve), John Halliday (Jeff), Matt Moore (The Colonel), Lester Vail (Aubrey), Myrna Loy (Elaine), Pauline Stevens (Baby).

Melodrama about a cheating husband, and his wife's strength during the situation.

Note: Only other time O'Brien and Loy worked together was as Burt Reynolds' parents in *The End* (1978). O'Brien always considered this film a favorite of his "because of that head of hair and my speed at running up stairs." At the premiere for this film, O'Brien stepped up to the microphone and thanked every cast and crew member by name. British title: *Married in Haste.*

Review: "...will satisfy with good stage support" — *Variety.*

181 Conspiracy (1930) Mystery. Running time: 69 minutes. Black and white.

Produced by Bertram Millhauser. Directed by Christy Cabanne. Screenplay by Beulah M. Dix (based on the play by Robert Baker and John Emerson). Photographed by J. Roy Hunt.

Starring Bessie Love, Ned Sparks, Hugh Trevor, Rita LaRoy, Ivan Lebedeff, Gertrude Howard, Otto Matieson, Walter Long, Donald MacKenzie.

A man and woman attempt to expose the drug ring responsible for their father's death.

182 Conspiracy (1939) Spy drama. Running time: 58 minutes. Black and white.

Produced by Cliff Reid. Directed by Lew Landers. Screenplay by Jerome Chodorov (based on a story by John McCarthy and Faith Thomas). Photographed by Frank Redman. Edited by George Hively. Music by Frank Tours, Lew Brown and Sammy Fain.

Starring Allan Lane (Steve), Linda Hayes (Nedra), Robert Barrat (Tio), Charles Foy (Studs), Lionel Royce (Lieutenant), J. Farrell MacDonald (Captain), Lester Matthews (Gair), Henry Brandon (Carlson), William Von Brincken (Wilson).

Intrigue surrounding poison gas shipment.

183 Cornered (1945) Thriller. Running time: 102 minutes. Black and white.

Produced by Adrian Scott. Directed by Edward Dmytryk. Screenplay by John Paxton (based on a story by John Wexley and a title by Ben Hecht). Photographed by Harry J. Wild. Edited by Joseph Noriega. Music by Roy Webb.

Starring Dick Powell (Gerard), Walter Slezak (Incza), Micheline Cheirel (Mme. Jarmac), Nina Vale (Senora Camargo), Morris Carnovsky (Santana), Edgar Barrier (DuBois), Steven Geray (Senor Mcargo), Jack La Rue (Diego), Luther Adler (Marcel Jarnac), Gregory Gaye (Perchon), Jean Del Val (1st Prefect), Georges Renevant (2nd Prefect), Nelson Leigh (Dominion Official), Leslie Dennison (Finance Officer), Tanis Chandler (Airline Hostess), Egon Brecher (Insurance Man), Gloria DeGuardia, Beverly Bushe (Girls), Hans Moebus, Joaquin Elizondo, Warren Jackson (Men), Byron Foulger (Night Clerk), Michael Mark (Elevator Operator), Kenneth MacDonald (Businessman), Al Murphy (Bartender), Al Walton, Milton Wallace (Waiters), Cy Kendall (Detective), Belle Mitchell (Hotel Maid), Simone LaBrusse (Maria), Carlos Barbe (Regules), Hugh

Prosser (Police Assistant), Jerry de Castro (Taxi Driver), Stanley Price (Hotel Clerk), Nestor Paiva (Police Official), Frank Mills (Stumblebum), Carl DeLora (Mean-faced Man), Richard Clark (Cab Driver), Paul Bradley (Policeman), Rob De Medici (Bellboy).

An ex–Canadian officer and POW survivor tracks down those responsible for his wife's death in France.

Review: "Well-made, but humorless, revenge thriller" — Leslie Halliwell, *Film and Video Guide.*

184 *Count the Hours* (1953) Crime drama. Running time: 74 minutes. Black and white.

Produced by Benedict Bogeaus. Directed by Don Siegel. Screenplay by Doane R. Hoag and Karen De Wolf. Photographed by John Alton. Edited by James Leicester.

Starring Teresa Wright (Ellen Braden), MacDonald Carey (Doug Madison), Dolores Mason (Paula), Adele Mara (Gracie), Edgar Barrier (Gillespie), John Craven (George Braden), Jack Elam (Max), Ralph Sanford (Alvin Taylor).

A lawyer tries to prove the innocence of a migrant worker accused of murder.

Note: British title: *Every Minute Counts.*

185 *The Courageous Dr. Christian* (1940) Drama. Running time: 67 minutes. Black and white. Available on videocassette.

Produced by William Stephens. Directed by Bernard Vorhaus. Screenplay by Ring Lardner, Jr., and Ian Hunter. Photographed by John Alton. Edited by Edward Mann.

Starring Jean Hersholt (Dr. Christian), Dorothy Lovett (Judy Price), Robert Baldwin (Roy Davis), Tom Neal (Dave Williams), Maude Eburne (Mrs. Hatings), Vera Lewis (Mrs. Stewart), George Meader (Harry Johnson), Bobby Larson (Jack Williams), Babette Bentley (Ruth Williams), Reginald LeBow (Sam), Jacqueline DeRiver (Martha), Edmund Glover (Tommy Wood), Mary Davenport (Jane Wood), Earle Ross (Grandpa), Sylvia Andrews (Mrs. Sam), Catherine Courtney (Mrs. Morris), Alan Bridge (Sheriff), James C. Morton (Bailey), Heinie Conklin (Pinball Addict).

Second in the six film series about the saintly Dr. Paul Christian, this time finding him crusading against conditions in the slums when a spinal meningitis epidemic breaks out.

Note: This was later a TV series starring MacDonald Carey in a much different variation of the role.

Cowpoke see *The Lusty Men*

186 *Crack-Up* (1946) Mystery. Running time: 93 minutes. Black and white.

Produced by Jack J. Gross. Directed by Irving Reis. Screenplay by John Paxton, Ben Bengal, and Ray Spencer (based on the short story *Madman's Holiday* by Fredric Brown). Photographed by Robert De Grasse. Edited by Frederic Knudtson. Music by Leigh Harline.

Starring Pat O'Brien (George Steele), Claire Trevor (Terry Cordeau), Herbert Marshall (Traybin), Ray Collins (Dr. Lowell), Wallace Ford (Cochrane), Dean Harens (Reynolds), Damian O'Flynn (Stevenson), Erskine Sanford (Mr. Barton), Mary Ware (Mary), Harry Harvey (Moran), Robert Bray (Man with Drunk), Tommy Noonan (Vendor), Bob White and Eddie Parks (Drunks), Chef Milani (Joe), Si Hill, Carl Hanson, Roger Creed, Gloria Jetter (Gamblers), Horace Murphy (Conductor), Alvin Hammer (Milquetoast), Tiny Jones and Dorothea Wolbert (Old Ladies), Sam Lufkin and Carl Faulkner (Detectives).

An art expert whose expertise runs to the revealing of forgeries is made to look incompetent by crooks.

187 *Cracked Nuts* (1931) Comedy. Running time: 65 minutes. Black and white. Available on videocassette.

Produced by Douglas MacLean. Directed by Edward F. Cline. Screenplay by Ralph Spence and Al Boasberg (based on

The picture of uncounted thrills!

Count the Hours!

More shocking than murder!

...were the things they whispered about them!

She loves deeply enough to do almost anything!

He lies to trap a killer and...to save his love!

Her jealousy drives her on to desperate deeds!

co-starring
TERESA WRIGHT · MACDONALD CAREY

with **DOLORES MORAN · ADELE MARA ·** Produced by **BENEDICT BOGEAUS ·** Directed by **DON SIEGEL ·** Screenplay by **DOANE R. HOAG** and **KAREN DeWOLF**

Publicity poster for *Count the Hours*.

a story by MacLean and Boasberg).
Photographed by Nicholas Musuraca.

Starring Bert Wheeler (Wendell Graham), Robert Woolsey (Zander U. Parkhurst), Edna May Oliver (Aunt Van Warden), Dorothy Lee (Betty Harrington), Leni Stengel (Carlotta), Stanley Fields (General Bogardus), Boris Karloff, Ben Turpin, Frank Lackteen, Wilfred Lucas (Bits).

Two Americans become rival leaders during a revolution in a mythical country.

Review: "As a two-reeler, it would be fair entertainment" — *Variety*.

188 *Crashing Hollywood* (1937)

Comedy. Running time: 60 minutes. Black and white.

Produced by Cliff Reid. Directed by Lew Landers. Screenplay by Paul Yawitz and Gladys Atwater (based on the play *Lights Out* by Paul Dickey and Mann Page). Photographed by Nicholas Musuraca and Frank Redman. Edited by Harry Marker.

Starring Lee Tracy (Michael), Joan Woodbury (Barbara), Paul Guilfoyle (Norman), Lee Patrick (Goldie), Richard Lane (Wells), Bradley Page (Darey Hawk), Tom Kennedy (Al), George Irving (Peyton), Frank M. Thomas (Decker), Jack Carson (Dickson).

A screenwriter selects a criminal as a collaborator, only to have the crook get himself in trouble by writing true life accounts of his own exploits.

Review: "Completely satisfactory picture" — *Variety*.

189 *The Crime Doctor* (1934)

Mystery. Running time: 75 minutes. Black and white.

Directed by John Robertson. Written by Jane Murfin (based on a story by Israel Zangwell). Photographed by Lucien Andriot. Edited by William Hamilton.

Starring Otto Kruger, Karen Morley, Nils Asther, Judith Wood, William Frawley, Donald Crisp, Frank Conroy, J. Farrell MacDonald, Fred Kelsey, G. Pat Collins, Willie Fung, Pat O'Malley, Wallis Clark, Samuel S. Hinds, Ethel Wales.

A mastermind detective plots the perfect crime.

Note: A remake of a 1928 part-talkie of the same name. Has nothing to do with the Crime Doctor detective series at Columbia during the forties.

190 *Crime Ring* (1938) Crime

drama. Running time: 69 minutes. Black and white.

Produced by Cliff Reid. Directed by Leslie Goodwins. Screenplay by J. Robert Bren and Gladys Atwater (based on a story by Reginald Taviner). Photographed by Jack MacKenzie. Music by Roy Webb.

Starring Allan Lane (Joe), Frances Mercer (Judy Allen), Clara Blandick (Phoebe Sawyer), Inez Courtney (Kitty), Bradley Page (Whitmore), Ben Welden (Nate), Walter Miller (Jenner), Frank M. Thomas (Redwine), Jack Arnold (Buzzell), Morgan Conway (Taylor), George Irving (Clifton), Leona Roberts (Mrs. Wharton), Charles Trowbridge (Marvin), Tom Kennedy (Dummy), Paul Fix (Slim), Jack Mulhall (Brady).

A reporter battles phony clairvoyants.

191 *Criminal Court* (1946) Crime

drama. Running time: 63 minutes. Black and white.

Produced by Martin Mooney. Directed by Robert Wise. Screenplay by Lawrence Kimble (based on a story by Earl Felton). Photographed by Frank Redman. Edited by Robert Swink.

Starring Tom Conway (Steve Baines), Martha O'Driscoll (Georgia Gale), June Clayworth (Joan Mason), Robert Armstrong (Vic Wright), Addison Richards (District Attorney), Pat Gleason (Joe West), Steve Brodie (Frankie), Robert Warwick (Marquette), Phil Warren (Bill Brannegan), Joe Devlin (Brownie), Lee Bonnell (Gil Lambert), Robert Clarke (Dance Director).

Well-liked lawyer accidentally kills a not-so-well-liked saloon owner.

Note: Producer Mooney was a crime reporter.

192 *Criminal Lawyer* (1937) Crime drama. Running time: 72 minutes. Black and white.

Produced by Cliff Reid. Directed by Christy Cabanne. Screenplay by G.V. Atwater and Thomas Lennon (based on the story by Louis Stevens). Photographed by David Abel. Edited by Jack Hively.

Starring Lee Tracy (Brandon), Margot Grahame (Madge Carter), Eduardo Ciannelli (Larkin), Erik Rhodes (Bandini), Betty Lawford (Molly Walker), Frank M. Thomas (William Walker), Wilfred Lucas (Brandon's Assistant), William Stack (District Attorney Hopkins).

When a district attorney is promoted with the help of a mob kingpin, he finds it difficult to send that same criminal to prison.

Note: Remake of *State's Attorney* (q.v.). Tracy was RKO's answer to James Cagney at Warner Bros.

Review: "Strong fronter for a dual, but can go solo where Tracy's name will draw" — *Variety.*

193 *Cross Country Romance* (1940) Romantic comedy. Running time: 67 minutes. Black and white.

Produced by Cliff Reid for Lee Marcus. Directed by Frank Woodruff. Screenplay by Jerry Cady and Bert Granet (based on the novel *Highway to Romance* by Eleanor Browne). Photographed by J. Roy Hunt. Edited by Harry Marker.

Starring Gene Raymond (Larry), Wendy Barrie (Diane), Hedda Hopper (Mrs. North), Billy Gilbert (Orestes), George P. Huntley (Walter Corbett), Berton Churchill (Conway), Tom Dugan (Pete), Edgar Dearing, Frank Sully (Cops), Cliff Clark (Captain Burke), Dorothea Kent (Millie).

A doctor finds that his pretty traveling companion is soon to be wed.

Note: This was Raymond's first film in two years; a hiatus taken while married to Jeanette MacDonald.

194 *Crossfire* (1933) Crime drama. Running time: 54 minutes. Black and white.

Produced by David O. Selznick. Directed by Otto Brower. Screenplay by Harold Shumate and Tom McNamara. Photographed by Nick Musuraca. Edited by Frederic Knudtson.

Starring Tom Keene (Tom Allen), Betty Furness (Patricia Plummer), Edgar Kennedy (Ed Wimpy), Edward Phillips (Bert King), Lafe McKee (Daniel Plummer), Nick Cogley (Doxc Stiels), Jules Cowan, Tom Brown, Murdock McQuarrie, Stanley Blystone (Bits).

A World War I vet returns home and find that one friend has been murdered and another friend is falsely accused of the crime.

195 *Crossfire* (1947) Mystery. Running time: 85 minutes. Black and white.

Produced by Adrian Scott (for Dore Schary). Directed by Edward Dmytryk. Screenplay by John Paxton (based on the novel *The Brick Foxhole* by Richard Brooks). Photographed by J. Roy Hunt. Edited by Harry Gerstad.

Starring Robert Young (Friday), Robert Mitchum (Keeley), Robert Ryan (Montgomery), Gloria Grahame (Ginny), Paul Kelly (The Man), Sam Levene (Joseph Samuels), Jacqueline White (Mary Mitchell), Steve Brodie (Floyd), George Cooper (Mitchell), Richard Benedict (Bill), Richard Powers (Detective), William Phipps (LeRoy), Lex Barker (Harry), Marlo Dwyer (Miss Lewis/Miss White), Phillip Morris (Sergeant), Kenneth MacDonald (Major), George Meader (Surgeon).

A Jew is murdered in a New York hotel and three soldiers are suspects.

Note: The first Hollywood film to lash out against bigotry.

Academy Award nominations for Best Picture, Best Screenplay, Best Director,

Best Supporting Actor (Robert Ryan), Best Actress (Gloria Grahame).

196 *The Crouching Beast* (1936)

Mystery. Running time: 68 minutes. Black and white.

Produced by John Stafford. Directed and written by Victor Hanbury (based on the novel *Clubfoot* by Valentine Williams). Photographed by James Wilson.

Starring Fritz Kortner (Ahmed Bay), Wynne Gibson (Gail Dunbar), Richard Bird (Nigel), Andrews Englemann (Prince Dmitri), Isabel Jeans (The Pellegrini), Fred Conygham (Rudi Von Linz).

An American newswoman becomes involved with a Turkish spy ring.

Note: Released in 1935 in Britain, was cut by 12 minutes for its American release a year later.

197 *Cry Danger* (1951) Mystery.

Running time: 79 minutes. Black and white.

Produced by Sam Wisenthal. Directed by Robert Parrish. Screenplay by William Bowers (based on an unpublished story by Jerry Cady). Photographed by Joseph F. Biroc. Edited by Bernard W. Burton. Music by Emil Newman.

Starring Dick Powell (Rocky), Rhonda Fleming (Nancy), Richard Erdman (Delong), William Conrad (Castro), Regis Toomey (Cobb), Jean Porter (Darlene), Jay Adler (Williams), Joan Banks (Alice Fletcher), Gloria Saunders (Cigarette Girl), Hy Averback (Bookie), Renny McEvoy (Taxi Driver), Lou Lubin (Hank), Benny Burt (Bartender).

After serving five years for robbery, a man gets paroled and sets out to prove his innocence.

198 *The Cuckoos* (1930) Comedy.

Running time: 90 minutes. Black and white with color sequences.

Directed by Paul Sloane and Louis Sarecky. Screenplay by Cyrus Wood (based on the play *The Ramblers* by Phillip H. Goodman). Songs by Harry Ruby and Bert Kalmar.

Starring Bert Wheeler, Robert Woolsey, June Clyde, Dorothy Lee, Ivan Lebedeff, Mitchell Lewis, Jobyna Howland.

Two fortune tellers attempt to rescue a kidnapped heiress.

Reviews: "One of the funniest silly movies ever" — *The Motion Picture Guide;* "It holds little between the laughs and doesn't need anything else" — *Variety.*

199 *The Curse of the Cat People*

(1944) Horror/fantasy. Running time: 70 minutes. Black and white.

Produced by Val Lewton. Directed by Robert Wise and Gunther V. Fritsch. Screenplay by DeWitt Bodeen. Photographed by Nicholas Musuraca. Edited by J.R. Whittridge.

Starring Simone Simon (Irena), Kent Smith (Oliver Reed), Jane Randolph (Alice Reed), Ann Carter (Amy), Elizabeth Russell (Barbara), Eve March (Miss Callahan), Julia Dean (Julia Farren), Erford Gage (State Trooper Captain), Sir Lancelot (Edward), Joel Davis (Donal), Juanita Alvarez (Lois).

Supposedly a sequel to the Lewton-Tournier *Cat People*, this is actually a fantasy involving a little girl who can communicate with the ghost of her father's dead wife.

Note: Wise took over the film's direction from Fritsch after filming had just commenced.

Reviews: "Full of the poetry and danger of childhood" — James Agee; "Its disturbingly Disneyesque fairy tale qualities have perplexed horror fans for decades" — Joe Dante.

200 *Curtain Call* (1940) Comedy.

Running time: 61 minutes. Black and white.

Produced by Howard Benedict. Directed by Frank Woodruff. Screenplay by Dalton Trumbo (based on a story by Howard J. Green). Photographed by Russell Metty. Edited by Harry Marker.

Starring Barbara Read (Helen Middleton), Alan Mowbray (Donald Avery), Helen Vinson (Charlotte Morley), Donald MacBride (Jeff Crandall), John Archer (Ted Palmer), Leona Maricle (Miss Smith), Frank Faylen (Spike Malone), Tom Kennedy (Attendant), Ralph Forbes (Leslie Barrivale), J.M. Kerrigan (Mr. Middleton), Ann Shoemaker (Mrs. Middleton), Tommy Kelly (Fred Middleton).

Two Broadway producers buy a sure-miss play for an annoyingly stuck-up star, but it turns out that she likes it and makes it a hit.

Note: Remade as *Footlight Fever.* Similar in theory to Mel Brooks' *The Producers.*

201 Cyclone on Horseback (1941)

Western. Running time: 58 minutes. Black and white.

Produced by Bert Gilroy. Directed by Edward Killy. Screenplay by Norton S. Parker (based on a story by Tom Gibson. Photographed by Harry Wild. Edited by Frederic Knudtson. Music by Fred Rose and Ray Whitley.

Songs: "Bangtail," "Tumbleweed Cowboy," "Blue Nightfall."

Starring Tim Holt, Marjorie Reynolds, Ray Whitley, Lee "Lasses" White, Harry Worth, Dennis Moore, Eddie Dew, Monte Montague, Slim Whitaker, Max Wagner, John Dilson, Lew Kelly, Terry Frost.

A rancher must decide to whom he will sell his herd.

202 A Damsel in Distress (1937)

Musical. Running time: 100 minutes. Black and white. Available on videocassette.

Produced by Pandro S. Berman. Directed by George Stevens. Screenplay by P.G. Wodehouse, S.K. Lawrence, and Ernest Pagano (based on a play by Wodehouse and Ian Hay, as well as a novel by Wodehouse). Photographed by Joseph H. August. Edited by Henry Berman. Music by George and Ira Gershwin.

Songs: "The Jolly Tar and Milkmaid," "Stiff Upper Lip," "I Can't Be Bothered Now," "Put Me to the Test" (instrumental), "Sing of Spring," "Things Are Looking Up," "Ah Che a Voi Perdoni Iddio" (from Flotow's *Marta*).

Starring Fred Astaire (Jerry), George Burns (George), Gracie Allen (Gracie), Joan Fontaine (Lady Alyce Marshmorton), Reginald Gardiner (Keggs), Ray Noble (Reggie), Constance Collier (Lady Caroline Marshmorton), Montague Love (Lord John Marshmorton), Harry Watson (Albert), Jan Duggan (Miss Ruggles), Mario Berini (Singing Voice of Gardiner), Bill O'Brien (Chauffeur), Mary Gordon (Cook), Fred Kelsey and Ralph Brooks (Sightseers).

An American dancer falls for an upper class English aristocrat.

Review: "...dancing, comedy, marquee values, the usual sumptuous investiture accorded by Pandro Berman, and those Gershwin songs"—*Variety.*

203 Dance, Girl, Dance (1940)

Musical. Running time: 88 minutes. Black and white.

Produced by Harry E. Edington and Erich Pommer. Directed by Dorothy Arzner. Screenplay by Tess Slesinger and Frank Davis (based on a story by Vicki Baum). Photographed by Russell Metty. Edited by Robert Wise. Music by Edward Ward, Chet Forrest, Bob Wright.

Songs: "Jitterbug Bite," "Morning Star," "Mother, What Do I Do Now."

Starring Maureen O'Hara (Judy), Louis Hayward (Jimmy Harris), Lucille Ball (Bubbles), Virginia Field (Elinor Harris), Ralph Bellamy (Steve Adams), Maria Ouspenskaya (Madame Lydia Basilova), Mary Carlisle (Sally), Katherine Alexander (Miss Olmstead), Edward Brophy (Dwarfie), Walter Abel (Judge), Harold Huber (Hoboken Gent), Ernest Truex and Chester Clute (Bailey 1 and Bailey 2), Lorraine Krueger (Dolly), Lola Jensen (Daisy), Emma Dunn (Mrs. Simpson), Sidney Blackmer

(Puss 'n Boots), Virginia Fay (Ballerina), Ludwig Stossel (Caesar), Erno Verebes (Fitch), Lee "Lasses" White (Stage Manager), Robert Emmett O'Connor, Clyde Cook, Gino Corrado, Milton Kibbee.

Problems of a nightclub dancing group.

Note: Roy Del Ruth left the directorial chores after a few weeks because he felt the script was too awful to be saved. RKO lost more than $400,000 on this one.

204 *Dance Hall* (1929) Drama.
Running time: 65 minutes. Black and white.

Directed by Melville Brown. Screenplay by Jane Murfin and J. Walter Ruben (based on a story by Vina Delmar). Photographed by Jack MacKenzie. Edited by Ann McKnight.

Starring Olive Borden (Gracie Nolan), Arthur Lake (Tommy Flynn), Margaret Seddon (Mrs. Flynn), Ralph Emerson (Ted Smith), Joseph Cawthorn (Bremmer), Helen Kaiser (Bee), Lee Moran (Ernie), Tom O'Brien (Truck Driver).

A shipping clerk and a taxi driver both vie for the same woman.

205 *Dancing Pirate* (1936) Musical.
Running time: 83 minutes. Color.

Produced by John Speaks. Directed by Lloyd Corrigan. Screenplay by Ray Harris, Jack Wagner, Boris Ingster, and Francis Edwards Faragoh (based on a story by Emma Lindsay-Squier). Photographed by William Skall. Edited by Archie Marshek. Music by Rodgers and Hart.

Songs: "Are You My Love," "When You're Dancing the Waltz."

Starring Charles Collins, Frank Morgan, Steffi Duna, Luis Alberni, Victor Varconi, Jack LaRue, Ala Real, William V. Mong, Mitchell Lewis, Cy Kendall, Julian Rivero, Harold Waldridge, Vera Lewis, Nora Cecil, Ellen Lowe, John Eberts, Max Wagner, James Farley, The Royal Casinos.

A dance teacher is shanghaied onto a pirate ship.

206 *Danger Lights* (1930) Drama.
Running time: 87 minutes. Black and white. Available on videocassette.

Produced by William LeBaron. Directed by George B. Seitz. Screenplay by James Ashmore Creelman and Hugh Herbert. Photographed by Karl Struss and John Boyle. Edited by Archie Marshek.

Starring Louis Wolheim (Dan Thorn), Robert Armstrong (Larry Doyle), Jean Arthur (Mary Ryan), Hugh Herbert (Professor), Frank Sheridan (Ed Ryan), Robert Edeson (Engineer), Alan Roscoe (General Manager), William P. Burt (Chief Dispatcher), James Farley (Joe Geraghty).

The story of a family-owned railroad and its workings, centering around the romance of the kindly owner and his girl, who falls for a young conductor.

Note: Shown in a new wide-screen system called Spoor-Bergen Natural Vision, needing a projector which cost $22,000 and required a three-person crew. Soaring costs of talking picture technology during the Depression would not allow the expense for this idea to last long.

207 *Danger Patrol* (1937) Drama.
Running time: 59 minutes. Black and white.

Directed by Lew Landers. Screenplay by Sy Bartlett (based on a story by Helen Vreeland and Hilda Vincent). Photographed by Nicholas Musuraca. Edited by Ted Cheesman.

Starring Sally Eilers (Cathie Street), John Beal (Dan Loring), Harry Carey ("Easy" Street), Frank M. Thomas (Rocky Saunders), Crawford Weaver (Eric Truble), Lee Patrick (Nancy Donovan), Ed Gargan (Gabby Donovan), Paul Guilfoyle (Tim), Solly Ward (Julius), Ann Hovey (Ada), Richard Lane (Pilot).

Nitro carriers, who use the explosive to thwart oil field blazes, are at odds when one of them wants to marry a co-worker's daughter.

208 *Dangerous Corner* (1935) Mystery. Running time: 65 mintues. Black and white.

Produced by Arthur Sibcom. Directed by Phil Rosen. Screenplay by Anne Morrison Chapin and Madeline Ruthven (based on a play by J.B. Priestly). Photographed by J. Roy Hunt. Edited by Archie Marshek.

Starring Melvyn Douglas, Conrad Nagel, Virginia Bruce, Erin O'Brien Moore, Ian Keith, Betty Furness, Henry Wadsworth, Doris Lloyd.

Detectives must find missing bonds and evidence that the suspect, who committed suicide, is actually guilty.

209 *Dangerous Mission* (1954) Crime drama. Running time: 75 minutes. Technicolor 3-D. Available on videocassette.

Produced by Irwin Allen. Directed by Louis King. Screenplay by Horace McCoy, W.R. Burnett, and Charles Bennett (based on a story by McCoy and James Edmiston). Photographed by William Snyder. Edited by Gene Palmer. Music by Roy Webb.

Starring Victor Mature (Matt Hallett), Piper Laurie (Louise Graham), William Bendix (Joe Parker), Vincent Price (Paul Adams), Betta St. John (Mary Tiller), Steve Darrell (Kattonai), Marlo Dwyer (Mrs. Elster), Walter Reed (Dobson), Dennis Weaver (Pruitt), Harry Cheshire (Elster), George Sherwood (Mr. Jones), Maureen Stephenson (Mrs. Jones), Fritz Apking (Hawthorne), Kem Dibbs (Johnny Yonkers/Killer), John Carlyle (Bellhop), Frank Griffin (Tedd), Trevor Bardette (Kicking Bear), Roy Engel (Hume), Grace Hayle (Mrs. Alvord), Jim Potter (Cobb), Mike Lally (Fletcher), Sam Shack, Craig Moreland, Ralph Vokie (Firefighters).

A policeman tries to protect a girl witness from gangsters.

Review: "...terribly edited, cheap imitation of a Hitchcock film"— *The Motion Picture Guide.*

210 *A Dangerous Profession* (1949) Crime drama. Running time: 79 minutes. Black and white.

Produced by Robert Sparks. Directed by Ted Tetzlaff. Screenplay by Martin Rackin and Warren Duff. Photographed by Robert De Grasse. Edited by Frederic Knudtson.

Starring George Raft (Kane), Ella Raines (Lucy), Pat O'Brien (Farley), Bill Williams (Brackett), Jim Backus (Ferrone), Roland Winters (McKay), Betty Underwood (Elaine), Robert Gist (Collins), David Wolfe (Dawson), Mack Gray (Fred, Taxi Driver), Lynne Roberts (Miss Wilson), Jonathan Hale (Lennert), Paul Maxey (Judge Thompson), Charmienne Harker (Helen), Gloria Gabel (Kane's Secretary).

An ex-cop turned bail bondsman must come up with the money to free the husband of the woman he loves.

Note: Grey, who plays a cab driver, was in reality George Raft's (and later Dean Martin's) manager. This was Pat O'Brien's last film for RKO.

Comment: "...a dog!"—Pat O'Brien.

211 *Daniel Boone* (1936) Adventure. Running time: 75 minutes. Black and white. Available on videocassette.

Produced by George A. Hirliman. Directed by David Howard. Screenplay by Dan Jarrett (based on a story by Edgecumb Pinchon). Photographed by Frank Good. Edited by Ralph Dixon.

Starring George O'Brien (Daniel Boone), Heather Angel (Virginia), John Carradine (Simon Girty), Ralph Forbes (Stephen Marlowe), Clarence Muse (Pompey), George Regas (Black Eagle), Dickie Jones (Jerry), Huntley Gordon (Sir John Randolph), Harry Cording (Joe Birch), Aggie Herring (Mrs. Burnch), Crauford Kent (Attorney General), Keith Kenneth (Commissioner).

Daniel Boone leads settlers from North Carolina to the wilds of Kentucky.

212 *Darts Are Trumps* (1938) Comedy. Running time: 72 minutes. Black and white.

Produced by George Smith. Directed by MacLean Rogers. Screenplay by Kathleen Butler. Photographed by Geoffrey Faithfull.

Starring Eliot Makeham, Nance O'Neil, Ian Colin, Muriel George, H.F. Maltby, Paul Blake, Johnny Singer, Michael Ripper, George Pembroke, Bryan Powley.

A clerk uses his dart playing skills to capture a criminal.

213 *A Date with the Falcon* (1941) Mystery. Running time: 63 minutes. Black and white.

Produced by Howard Benedict. Directed by Irving Reis. Screenplay by Lynn Root and Frank Fenton (based on a character created by Michael Arlen). Photographed by Robert De Grasse. Edited by Harry Marker.

Starring George Sanders (Falcon), Wendy Barrie (Helen Reed), James Gleason (O'Hara), Allen Jenkins (Goldy), Mona Maris (Rita Mara), Victor Kilian (Max), Frank Moran (Dutch), Russ Clark (Needles), Ed Gargan (Bates), Alec Craig (Waldo Sampson), Eddie Dunn (Grimes), Frank Martinelli (Louie), Hans Conried (Hotel Clerk), Elizabeth Russell (Girl on Plane).

The second in the series has the detective setting up his fiancee in order to investigate the kidnapping of a brilliant scientist.

214 *The Day the Bookies Wept* (1939) Comedy. Running time: 53 minutes. Black and white. Available on videocassette.

Produced by Robert Sisk. Directed by Leslie Goodwins. Screenplay by Bert Granet and George Jeske (based on a story by Daniel Fuchs). Photographed by Jack MacKenzie. Edited by Desmond Marquette.

Starring Joe Penner (Ernest Ambrose), Betty Grable (Ina Firpo), Richard Lane (Ramsey Firpo), Tom Kennedy (Pinky Brophy), Thurston Hall (Col. March), Bernadene Hayes (Margie), Carol Hughes (Patsy March), William Wright (Harry), Prince Albert (Horse), Emory Parnell (Cop).

A taxi driver buys a racehorse that needs beer to win races.

Note: Penner was a radio comedian who achieved equal success in films, his radio catch phrases being "Wanna Buy a Duck" and "Oh, you nasty man!" When his career began faltering slightly, the nervous Penner began worrying with such intensity it impaired his health. He dropped dead of a heart attack, brought about by his nervous condition, at the age of only 36.

215 *Days of Glory* (1944) Drama. Running time: 86 minutes. Black and white. Available on viceocassette.

Produced by Casey Robinson. Directed by Jacques Tourneur. Screenplay by Casey Robinson (based on a story by Melchoir Lengyel). Photographed by Tony De Gaudio. Edited by Joseph Noriega.

Starring Tamara Toumanova (Nina), Gregory Peck (Vladimir), Alan Reed (Sasha), Maria Palmer (Yelena), Lowell Gilmore (Semyon), Hugo Haas (Fedor), Dena Penn (Olga), Glenn Vernon (Mitya), Igor Dogoruki (Dimitri), Edward L. Durst (Petrov), Lou Crosby (Johann Straub).

Russian peasants battle invading Nazis.

Note: Toumanova was a prima ballerina who made this and four more films before marrying producer Robinson. This was Peck's film debut.

216 *Deadline at Dawn* (1946) Mystery. Running time: 83 minutes. Black and white. Available on videocassette.

Produced by Adrian Scott. Directed by Harold Clurman. Screenplay by Clifford Odets (based on a novel by William Irish [Cornell Woolrich]). Photographed by Nicholas Musuraca. Edited by Roland Gross.

Starring Susan Hayward (June Goff), Paul Lukas (Gus), Bill Williams (Alex Winkley), Joseph Calleia (Bartelli), Osa

Massen (Helen Robinson), Lola Lane (Edna Bartelli), Jerome Cowan (Lester Brady), Marvin Miller (Sleepy Parsons), Roman Bohnen (Collarless Man), Steven Geray (Man with Gloves), Joe Sawyer (Babe Dooley), Constance Worth (Mrs. Raymond), Joseph Crehan (Lt. Kane), Jason Robards, Sr. (Policeman), Sammy Blum (Taxi Driver), Emory Parnell (Capt. Bender), Lee Phelps (Policeman), Ernie Adams (Waiter), Larry McGrath (Whispering Man), Connie Conrad (Mrs. Bender), Carl Faulkner (Policeman Drawing Diagram), Dorothy Curtis (Giddy Woman), Mike Pat Donovan (Sweating Trickster), Peter Breck (Bit).

A sailor on leave passes out, only to awaken and find the girl he was with has been murdered.

217 Death of a Scoundrel (1956) Drama. Running time: 119 minutes. Black and white. Available on videocassette.

Produced, directed, and written by Charles Martin. Photographed by James Wong Howe. Edited by Conrad Nervig. Music by Max Steiner.

Starring George Sanders (Clementi Sabourin), Yvonne DeCarlo (Bridget Kelly), Zsa Zsa Gabor (Mrs. Ryan), Victor Jory (Leonard Wilson), Nancy Gates (Stephanie North), Coleen Gray (Mrs. Van Renassalear), John Hoyt (Mr. O'Hara), Lisa Ferraday (Zina Monte), Tom Conway (Gerry Monte), Celia Lovsky (Mother Sabourin), Werner Klemperer (Lawyer), Justice Watson (Butler), John Sutton (Actor), Curtis Cooksey (Oswald Van Renassalear), Gabriel Curtiz (Max Freundlich).

A Czech becomes rich in New York through fraudulent means.

Review: "...a vehicle for a male Bette Davis" — Leslie Halliwell, *Film and Video Guide.*

218 Delightful Rogue (1929) Adventure/romance. Running time: 64 minutes. Black and white.

Produced by William LeBaron. Di-

rected by A. Leslie Pearce and Lynn Shores. Screenplay by Wallace Smith. Music by Oscar Levant and Sidney Clare.

Starring Rod La Rocque, Rita LaRoy, Charles Byer, Bert Moorehouse, Ed Brady, Harry Semels, Samuel Blum.

A pirate falls for a dance hall girl and must then contend with her jealous suitor.

219 Deluge (1933) Adventure. Running time: 68 minutes. Black and white.

Produced by Samuel Bischoff. Directed by Felix E. Feist. Screenplay by John Goodrich and Warren B. Duff (based on the novel by S. Fowler Wright).

Starring Peggy Shannon (Claire), Sidney Blackmer (Martin), Lois Wilson (Helen), Matt Moore (Tom), Fred Kohler, Sr. (Jephson), Ralf Harolde (Norwood), Edward Van Sloan (Prof. Carlysle), Samuel S. Hinds (Chief Forecaster), Lane Chandler (Survivor), Philo McCullough, Harry Semels (Renegades).

A solar eclipse causes a tidal wave which floods most of the world. A man whose family has perished in the flood then must fight off scavengers.

220 Desert Desperadoes (1959) Biblical drama. Running time: 81 minutes. Black and white.

Produced by John Nasht. Directed by Steve Sekely. Screenplay by Victor Stoloff and Robert Hill (based on a story by Stoloff and Hill). Photographed by Massimo Dallamano.

Starring Ruth Roman (The Woman), Akim Tamiroff (The Merchant), Othelo Toso (Verrus), Gianni Glori (Fabius), Arnoldo Foa (The Chaldean), Alan Furian (Rais), Nino Marchetti (Metullus).

A rich merchant falls for a woman he finds stranded in the desert.

Note: Venturi-Express-Nascht production for distribution by RKO and Franchise productions. Alternate title: *The Sinner.*

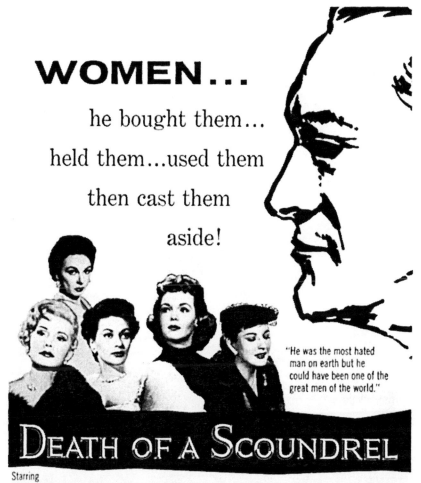

WOMEN...

he bought them...

held them...used them

then cast them

aside!

"He was the most hated man on earth but he could have been one of the great men of the world."

DEATH OF A SCOUNDREL

Starring
GEORGE SANDERS · YVONNE DeCARLO · ZSA ZSA GABOR
VICTOR JORY · NANCY GATES · COLEEN GRAY

Distributed by
R K O
RADIO
PICTURES

Written, Directed and Produced by CHARLES MARTIN   Music by MAX STEINER

Publicity poster for *Death of a Scoundrel*.

221 *Desert Passage* (1952) Western. Running time: 62 minutes. Black and white.

Produced by Herman Schlom. Directed by Lesley Selander. Screenplay by Norman Houston. Photographed by J. Roy Hunt. Edited by Paul Weatherwax.

Starring Tim Holt (Tim), Joan Dixon (Emily), Walter Reed (Carver), Dorothy Patrick (Rosa), John Dehner (Bronson), Clayton Moore (Warwick), Lane Bradford (Langdon), Michael Mark (Burley), Denver Pyle (Allen), Richard Martin (Chito Rafferty), Francis McDonald.

Cowboy hero is unwittingly hired by a gunman to drive him to Mexico.

Note: Holt's last western for RKO, as well as the last film for this studio of Herman Schlom and Lesley Selander.

222 *Desperate* (1947). Crime drama. Running time: 73 minutes. Black and white.

Produced by Michel Kraike. Directed by Anthony Mann. Screenplay by Harry Essex and Martin Rackin (based on a story by Dorothy Atlas and Mann). Photographed by George E. Diskant. Music by Paul Sawtell. Edited by Marston Fay.

Starring Steve Brodie (Steve Randall), Audrey Long (Ann Randall), Raymond Burr (Walt Radak), Douglas Fowley (Pete), William Challee (Reynolds), Jason Robards, Sr. (Ferrari), Freddie Steele (Shorty), Lee Frederick (Joe), Paul E. Buerns (Jan), Ilka Gruning (Aunt Clara), Larry Nunn (Al Radak), Ralf Harolde, Milton Kibbee, Dick Elliot, Eddie Parks.

A truck driver goes on the run when falsely accused of a crime.

Review: "Amazingly watchable within its formulary limits"—Tom Milne, MFB.

223 *Destination Murder* (1950) Crime drama. Running time: 72 minutes. Black and white.

Produced by Edward L. Cahn and Naurie M. Seuss. Directed by Cahn. Screenplay by Don Martin. Photographed by Jackson J. Rose. Edited by Phillip Cahn.

Starring Joyce MacKenzie (Laura Mansfield), Stanley Clements (Jackie Wales), Hurd Hatfield (Stretch Norton), Albert Dekker (Armitage), Myrna Dell (Alice Wentworth), James Flavin (Lt. Brewster), John Dehner (Frank Niles), Richard Emory (Sgt. Mulcahy), Norma Vance (Indebted Lady), Suzette Harbin (Harriet), Buddy Swan and Bert Wenland (Messenger Boys), Franklyn Farnum (Mr. Mansfield).

A woman enters the underworld to find the murderer of her father.

224 *The Devil and Daniel Webster* (1941) Fantasy. Running time: 112 minutes. Black and white. Available on videocassette.

Produced and directed by William Dieterle. Screenplay by Dan Totheroh and Stephen Vincent Benet (based on the story by Benet). Photographed by Joseph August. Edited by Robert Wise. Music by Bernard Herrmann.

Starring Edward Arnold (Daniel Webster), Walter Huston (Mr. Scratch), Jane Darwell (Ma Stone), Simone Simon (Bele), Gene Lockhart (Squire Slossum), John Qualen (Miser Stevens), Frank Conalan (Sheriff), Lindy Wade (Daniel Stone), George Cleveland (Cy Bibber), Anne Shirley (Mary Stone), James Craig (Jabez Stone), H.B. Warner (Justice Hawthorne), Jeff Corey (Tom Sharp), Sonny Bupp (Martin Van Aldrich), Eddie Dew (Farmer), Alec Craig (Eli), Fern Emmett (Wife), Robert Emmett Keene (Husband).

Rich man, who often exclaimed he'd sell his soul for the easy life, is finally called upon by the Devil.

Note: Original running time is 112 minutes, as stated above, but most prints now run about 85 minutes. A cult film, which is considered a classic by some, it lost $53,000 at the time of its initial release. Alternate titles: *All That Money Can Buy, Here Is a Man, A Certain Mr. Scratch.*

Oscar: Best Musical Score.

225 *The Devil and Miss Jones* (1941) Comedy. Running time: 92 minutes. Black and white. Available on videocassette.

Produced by Frank Ross and Norman Krasna. Directed by Sam Wood. Screenplay by Krasna. Photographed by Harry Stradling. Edited by Sherman Todd. Music by Roy Webb.

Starring Jean Arthur (Mary Jones), Robert Cummings (Joe O'Brien), Charles Coburn (John P. Merrick), Edmund Gwenn (Hooper), Spring Byington (Elizabeth Ellis), S.Z. "Cuddles"

Sakall (George), William Demarest (Detective), Walter Kingsford (Allison), Montague Love (Harrison), Richard Carle (Oliver), Charles Waldron (Needles), Edwin Maxwell (Withers), Ed Mc-Namara (Police Sergeant), Robert Emmett Keene (Tom Higgins), Florence Bates (Customer), Charles Irwin (Detective), Matt McHugh (Sam), Julie Warren (Dorothy), Ilene Brewer (Sally), Regis Toomey (Policeman).

A rich business owner poses as a lowly employee at one of his stores in order to spy on his workers.

Oscar nominations: Krasna and Coburn.

Reviews: "Elements of the crazy thirties and the more socially conscious forties" — Leslie Halliwell, *Film and Video Guide;* "A must!" — Leonard Maltin, *TV Movies.*

226 *The Devil Thumbs a Ride*

(1947) Crime drama. Running time: 63 minutes. Black and white.

Produced by Herman Schlom. Directed and written by Felix Feist (based on the novel by Robert C. DueSoe). Photographed by J. Roy Hunt. Edited by Robert Swink.

Starring Lawrence Tierney (Steve), Ted North (Jimmy), Nan Leslie (Carol), Betty Lawford (Agnes), Andrew Tombes (Joe Brayden), Harry Shannon (Owens), Glenn Vernon (Jack), Marian Carr (Diane), William Gould (Captain Martin), Josephine Whittell (Mother), Phil Warren (Pete), Robert Malcolm (Sheriff).

A man picks up some hitchhikers. One of them turns out to be a killer and holds them all hostage.

227 *Devil's Canyon* (1953) Western. Running time: 92 minutes. Technicolor 3-D.

Produced by Edmund Grainger. Directed by Alfred Werker. Screenplay by Frederick Hazlitt Brennan, Harry Essex.

Starring Virginia Mayo (Abby Nixon), Dale Robertson (Billy Reynolds), Stephen McNally (Jessie Gorman), Arthur Hunnicutt (Frank Taggert), Robert Keith (Steve Morgan), Jay C. Flippen (Captain Wells), George J. Lewis (Col. Gomez), Whit Bissell (Virgil), Morris Ankrum (Sheriff), James Bell (Dr. Betts), William Phillips (Red), Earl Holliman (Joe), Irving Bacon (Guard).

A marshall is unjustly convicted of a crime and sent to a brutal prison.

228 *Devotion* (1931) Drama. Running time: 80 minutes. Black and white. Available on videocassette.

Produced by Charles R. Rogers. Directed by Robert Milton. Screenplay by Graham John and Horace Jackson (based on the novel *A Little Flat in the Temple* by Pamela Wynne). Photographed by Hal Mohr. Edited by Dan Mandell.

Starring Ann Harding, Leslie Howard, Robert Williams, O.P. Heggie, Louise Closser Hale, Dudley Digges, Alison Skipworth, Olive Tell, Doris Lloyd, Ruth Weston, Joan Carr, Joyce Coad, Douglas Scott, Tempe Pigott, Forrester Harvey, Margaret Daily, Pat Somerset, Claude King, Donald Ogden Stewart, Cyril Delevanti.

A woman falls for a barrister, dons a disguise, and becomes his son's governess.

Review: "Much talk and little action" — *Variety.*

229 *Dick Tracy* (1945) Crime drama. Running time: 61 minutes. Black and white. Available on videocassette.

Produced by Herman Schlom. Directed by William Berke. Screenplay by Eric Taylor (based on the comic strip by Chester Gould). Photographed by Frank Redman. Edited by Ernie Leadlay. Music by Roy Webb.

Starring Morgan Conway (Dick Tracy), Anne Jeffreys (Tess Trueheart), Mike Mazurki (Splitface), Jane Greer (Judith Owens), Lyle Latell (Pat Patton), Joseph Crehan (Chief Brandon), Mickey Kuhn (Tracy, Jr.), Trevor Bardette (Professor Starling), Ralph Dunn (Manning), Tommy Noonan (Johnny Moko).

The famed detective tries tracking down a criminal with a disfiguring scar known as Splitface.

Note: First feature-length Dick Tracy film after several serials for Republic Pictures. Conway's first appearance as the square-jawed detective. The serials had him played by Ralph Byrd. Alternate titles: *Dick Tracy, Detective; Splitface.*

Dick Tracy, Detective see Dick Tracy

230 Dick Tracy Meets Gruesome (1947) Crime drama. Running time: 65 minutes. Black and white. Available on videocassette.

Produced by Herman Schlom. Directed by John Rawlins. Screenplay by Robertson White, Eric Taylor (based on a story by William H. Graffis and Robert E. Kent, from the comic strip by Chester Gould). Photographed by Frank Redman. Edited by Elmo Williams.

Starring Ralph Byrd (Dick Tracy), Boris Karloff (Gruesome), Anne Gwynne (Tess Trueheart), Ed Ashley (L.E. Thal), June Clayworth (Dr. I.M. Learned), Lyle Latell (Pat Patton), Tony Barrett (Melody), Skelton Knaggs (X-Ray), Jim Nolan (Dan Sterne), Joseph Crehan (Chief Brandon), Milton Parsons (Dr. A. Tomic).

Tracy goes after the title baddie who is using a knockout gas which freezes people in time and allows for easier bank heists.

Note: Last of the Tracy features, Byrd having played the detective in serials and later on TV. The character names were definitely inspired. Alternate titles: *Dick Tracy Meets Karloff, Dick Tracy's Amazing Adventure.*

Review: "Put it in the incinerator, boys" — Bosley Crowther, *The New York Times.*

Dick Tracy Meets Karloff see Dick Tracy Meets Gruesome

231 Dick Tracy Vs. Cueball (1946) Crime drama. Running time: 62 minutes. Black and white. Available on videocassette.

Produced by Herman Schlom. Directed by Gordon Douglas. Screenplay by Dane Lussier and Robert E. Kent (based on a story by Luci Eard, from the comic strip by Chester Gould). Photographed by George E. Diskant. Edited by Phillip Martin, Jr.

Starring Morgan Conway (Dick Tracy), Anne Jeffreys (Tess Trueheart), Lyle Latell (Pat Patton), Rita Corday (Mona Clyde), Ian Keith (Vitamin Flintheart), Dick Wessel (Cueball), Douglas Walton (Priceless), Esther Howard (Filthy Flora), Joseph Crehan (Chief Brandon), Byron Foulger (Little).

Tracy sets out after Cueball, who is on a killing spree, wasting those who have wronged him in the past.

Note: Conway's second and last appearance as Tracy. Considered by some the best of the features (if it makes a difference, this writer prefers Ralph Byrd).

Dick Tracy's Amazing Adventure see Dick Tracy Meets Gruesome

232 Dick Tracy's Dilemma (1947) Crime drama. Running time: 60 minutes. Black and white. Available on videocassette.

Produced by Herman Schlom. Directed by John Rawlins. Screenplay by Ralph Stephen Brode (based on the comic strip by Chester Gould). Photographed by Frank Redman. Edited by Marvin Coll.

Starring Ralph Byrd (Dick Tracy), Kay Christopher (Tess Trueheart), Lyle Latell (Pat Patton), Jack Lambert (The Claw), Ian Keith (Vitamin Flintheart), Bernadene Hayes (Longshot Lillie), Jimmy Conlin (Sightless), William B. Davidson (Peter Premium), Tony Barrett (Sam), Richard Powers (Fred).

Tracy stalks the leader of a gang who stole a shipment of furst after killing a guard.

Note: Byrd, star of the serials, returns to his role with this feature.

233 Ding Dong Williams (1946) Musical comedy. Running time: 61 minutes. Black and white.

Produced by Herman Schlom. Directed by William Berke. Screenplay by Brenda Weisberg and M. Coates Webster (based on *Collier's* magazine stories by Richard English). Photographed by Frank Redman. Edited by Les Millbrook.

Songs: "Candlelight and Wine," "I Saw You First," "Cool Water."

Starring Glenn Vernon (Ding Dong Williams), Marcy McGuire (Angela), Felix Bressart (Hugo), Anne Jeffreys (Vanessa), James Warren (Steve), William Davidson (Saul), Tommy Noonan (Zang), Cliff Nazarro (Zing), Ruth Lee (Laura Cooper), Bob Nolan and the Sons of the Pioneers.

A clarinetist is hired to compose a film.

234 *Diplomaniacs* (1933) Comedy. Running time: 59 minutes. Black and white. Available on videocassette.

Produced by H.N. Swanson. Directed by William Seiter. Screenplay by Joseph L. Mankiewicz and Henry Myers (based on a story by Mankiewicz). Photographed by Edward Cronjager. Edited by William Hamilton. Music by Max Steiner.

Starring Bert Wheeler (Willy), Robert Woolsey (Hercules), Marjorie White (Dolores), Phyllis Barry (Fifi), Louis Calhern (Winklereid), Hugh Herbert (Chinaman), Richard Carle (Captain), William Irving (Schmerzenpuppen), Neely Edwards (Puppenschmerzen), Billy Bletcher (Schmerzenschmerzen), Teddy Hart (Puppen Puppen), Charles Coleman (Butler), Edward Cooper (Chief Adoop), Dewey Robinson (Peter the Hermit).

The boys attend a peace conference on behalf of an Indian tribe.

Note: Along with *Cockeyed Cavaliers,* perhaps the duo's best film. Actress White, who the following year would appear with The Three Stooges in their first Columbia two-reeler, *Woman Haters,* was killed in an auto crash shortly after completing that film.

Reviews: "Often ferociously funny" — *The Motion Picture Guide;* "Memorable comic performances — endearing" — Leonard Maltin, *TV Movies;* "A baddie; rhymed dialogue no help for inane plot" — *Variety.*

235 *Dixiana* (1930) Musical. Running time: 100 minutes. Black and white with color sequences.

Produced by William LeBaron. Directed and written by Luther Reed (from a story by Anne Caldwell). Photographed by Roy Hunt. Edited by Jack Kitchin. Music by Victor Baravalle, Max Steiner.

Starring Bebe Daniels (Dixiana), Everett Marshall (Carl Van Horn), Bert Wheeler (Pee Wee), Robert Woolsey (Ginger), Joseph Cawthorn (Cornelius), Jobyna Howland (Mrs. Van Horn), Dorothy Lee (Poppy), Ralf Harolde (Royal Montague), Ed Chandler (Clondell), George Herman (Contortionist), Bill Robinson, Eugene "Pineapple" Jackson (Bits).

A Pennsylvania Dutchman tries to run a Louisiana plantation.

Review: "Not much but bigness for exploiting" — *Variety.*

236 *Dr. Christian Meets the Women* (1940) Drama. Running time: 65 minutes. Black and white.

Produced by William Stephens. Directed by William McGann. Screenplay by Marian Orth. Photographed by John Alton. Edited by Edward Mann.

Starring Jean Hersholt (Dr. Paul Christian), Dorothy Lovett (Judy Price), Edgar Kennedy (George Browning), Rod LaRocque (Professor Kenneth Parker), Frank Albertson (Bill Ferris), Marilyn Merrick (Kitty Browning), Maude Eburne (Mrs. Hastings), Veda Ann Borg (Carol Compton), Lelah Taylor (Martha Browning), William Gould (Dr. Webster), Heinie Conklin (Ed the Plumber).

The good doctor exposes a crooked weight loss program.

237 *A Dog of Flanders* (1935) Drama. Running time: 72 minutes. Black and white.

Produced by William Sistrom. Directed by Edward Sloman. Screenplay by Ainsworth Morgan and Dorothy Yost (based on the novel by Ouida). Photographed by J. Roy Hunt. Edited by George Crane.

Starring Frank M. Thomas (Nello), Helen Parrish (Maria), O.P. Heggie (Jehan), Richard Quine (Pieter), Christian Rub (Hans), DeWitt Jennings (Cogez), Ann Shoemaker (Frau Cogez), Lightning (Dog).

Belgian boy nurses sick dog back to health.

Note: Remade by Fox in 1959.

238 Don't Tell the Wife (1937) Comedy. Running time: 63 minutes. Black and white.

Produced by Robert Sisk. Directed by Christy Cabanne. Screenplay by Nat Perrin (based on the play *Once Over Lightly* by George Holland). Photographed by Harry Wild. Edited by Jack Hively.

Starring Guy Kibbee (Malcolm Winthrop), Una Merkel (Nancy Dorset), Lynne Overman (Steve Dorset), Thurston Hall (Major Manning), Guinn Williams (Cupid), William Demarest (Larry Tucker), Lucille Ball (Ann Howell), Harry Tyler (Mike Callahan), Charlie West (Joe Hoskins), Alan Curtis (Customer's Man).

A meek banker gets duped into a bad investment.

239 Don't Turn 'em Loose (1936) Crime drama. Running time: 68 minutes. Black and white.

Produced by Robert Sisk. Directed by Ben Stoloff. Screenplay by Ferdinand Reyher and Harry Segall (based on the story *Homecoming* by Thomas Walsh). Photographed by Jack MacKenzie. Edited by William Morgan.

Starring Lewis Stone (John Webster), James Gleason (Daniels), Bruce Cabot (Bat Roberts), Louise Latimer (Letty), Betty Grable (Mildred), Nella Walker (Mrs. Helen Webster), Grace Bradley (Grace), Frank M. Thomas (Attorney Pierce), Maxine Jennings (Mary), Frank Jenks (Pete), Harry Jans (Vic), John Arledge (Walter), Addison Randall (Al), Fern Emmett (Hattie), Arthur Hoyt (Judge Bass).

A high school principal and member of the parole board must decide the fate of his own son, a vicious criminal.

240 Double Danger (1938) Mystery. Running time: 61 minutes. Black and white.

Produced by Maury Cohen. Directed by Lew Landers. Screenplay by Arthur T. Horman and J. Robert Bren (based on a story by Horman). Photographed by Frank Redman. Edited by Desmond Marquette.

Starring Preston Foster (Robert Crane), Whitney Bourne (Carolyn Morgan), Samuel S. Hinds (David Theron), Donald Meek (Gordon Ainsley), Paul Guilfoyle (Taylor), Cecil Kellaway (Fentriss), June Johnson (Babs), Arthur Lake (Roy West), Edythe Elliott (Edith Theron), Harry Hayden (Dr. Hillard).

A jewel thief poses as a mystery writer and attempts to steal priceless diamonds from a police commissioner's home, only to find that their maid is a fellow jewel thief with similar ideas.

241 Double Deal (1950) Mystery. Running time: 64 minutes. Black and white. A Bel-Air production.

Produced by James T. Vaughn. Directed by Abby Berlin. Screenplay by Lee Berman and Charles S. Belden (based on a story by Don McGuire). Photographed by Frank Redman. Edited by Robert Swink.

Starring Marie Windsor (Terry), Richard Denning (Buzz), Taylor Holmes (Corpus), Fay Baker (Lilli), James Griffith (Karns), Carleton Young (Reno), Tom Browne Henry (Sheriff Morelli), Jim Hayward (Mike), Richard Reeves (Webber), Paul E. Burns (Razdik).

A petro engineer inherits a well when the owner is murdered.

Publicity poster for *Double Dynamite!*

242 *Double Dynamite!* (1951) Comedy. Running time: 80 minutes. Black and white. Available on videocassette.

Produced by Irving Cummings, Jr. Directed by Irving Cummings, Sr. Screenplay by Melville Shavelson and Harry Crane (based on a story by Leo Rostern and a character created by Mannie Manheim). Photographed by Robert De Grasse. Edited by Harry Marker.

Starring Frank Sinatra (Johnny Dalton), Jane Russell (Mibs Goodhug), Groucho Marx (Emil J. Keck), Don McGuire (Bob Pulsifer, Jr.), Howard Freeman (R.B. Pulsifer, Sr.), Nestor Paiva (Hot Horse), Lou Nova (Max), Joe Devlin (Frankie Boy), Frank Orth (Mr. Kofer), William Edmunds (Baganucci), Russ Thorson (Tailman), Charles Coleman (Santa Claus), Ida Moore (Little Old Lady), Hal K. Dawson (Mr. Hartman), George Chandler (Messenger), Jean De Briac (Maitre d'), Benny Burt (Waiter), Bill Snyder (Wire Service Man), Claire De Brey (Hatchet Faced Lady), Dickie Derrel (Boy).

A bank teller wins a fortune when a

man whose life he saves bets on a long-shot winning horse in his name.

Note: Howard Hughes oversaw the film, originally titled *It's Only Money,* but retitled it as a reference to Jane Russell's ample bust. Hughes didn't like Sinatra, who turned in a lackluster performance as a result. The film was produced in 1948, but held up for release.

243 Double Harness (1933) Comedy. Running time: 70 minutes. Black and white.

Produced by Merian C. Cooper. Directed by John Cromwell. Screenplay by Jane Murfin (based on the play by Edward Poor Montgomery). Photographed by J. Roy Hunt. Edited by George Nicholls, Jr.

Starring Ann Harding (Joan Colby), William Powell (John Fletcher), Henry Stephenson (Col. Colby), Lillian Bond (Monica Page), George Meeker (Dennis), Lucile Browne (Valerie Colby), Reginald Owen (Butler), Kay Hammond (Eleanor Weston), Leigh Allen (Leonard Weston), Hugh Huntley (Farley Drake), Wallis Clark (Postmaster General), Fred Santley (Shop Owner).

A girl tries to trick a rich man into marriage.

244 Down to Their Last Yacht (1934) Musical. Running time: 64 minutes. Black and white.

Produced by Lou Brock. Directed by Paul Sloane. Screenplay by Marion Dix and Lynn Starling (based on a story by Herbert Fields and Lou Brock). Photographed by Edward Cronjager and Vernon Walker. Edited by Arthur Roberts. Music by Max Steiner.

Songs: "Tiny Little Finger on Your Hand," "Funny Little World," "Queen March," "South Sea Bolero."

Starring Mary Boland (Queen of Malakamoukalu), Polly Moran (Nella Fitzgerald), Ned Sparks (Captain Don Roberts), Sidney Blackmer (Michael Forbes), Sidney Fox (Linda Straton), Sterling Holloway (Freddy Finn), Mar-

jorie Gateson (Mrs. Colt-Stratton), Irene Franklin (Mrs. Gilhooley), Charles Coleman (Sir Guy), Ramsey Hill (Mr. Colt-Stratton), Tom Kennedy (George Schultz), Gigi Parrish (Patricia).

An upper-class family, when hit by the Depression, charters its yacht to make extra money.

Note: British title: *Hawaiian Nights.*

245 Dreaming Out Loud (1940) Comedy. Running time: 81 minutes. Black and white. Available on videocassette.

Produced by Jack Votion and Sam Coslow. Directed by Harold Young. Screenplay by Howard J. Green, Barry Trivers, and Robert Andrews (based on a story by Trivers and Andrews). Photographed by Phillip Tannura. Edited by Otto Ludwig.

Starring Chester Lauck (Lum), Norris Goff (Abner), Frances Langford (Alice), Frank Craven (Dr. Walter Barnes), Bobs Watson (Jimmy), Irving Bacon (Wes Stillman), Clara Blandick (Jessica Spence), Robert Wilcox (Dr. Kenneth Barnes), Donald Briggs (Will Danielson), Robert McKenzie (Caleb).

Two small town store owners try to find a hit-and-run driver.

Note: Film debut for radio comedy team of Lum and Abner.

246 Drums in the Deep South (1951) Western. Running time: 87 minutes. Color.

Produced by Maurice and Frank King. Directed by William Cameron Menzies. Screenplay by Phillip Yordan and Sidney Harmon (based on a story by Hollister Noble). Photographed by Lionel Linden. Edited by Richard Heermance. Music by Dimitri Tiomkin.

Starring James Craig, Barbara Payton, Guy Madison, Barton MacLane, Craig Stevens, Tom Fadden, Robert Osterloh, Taylor Holmes, Robert Easton, Lewis Martin, Peter Brocco, Dan White, Louis Jean Heydt.

A Confederate officer finds he and his

best friend are on opposite sides of the Civil War.

Review: "Barely stimulating semi-western in appalling colour" — Leslie Halliwell, *Film and Video Guide.*

247 *Dude Cowboy* (1941) Western. Running time: 59 minutes. Black and white.

Produced by Bert Gilroy. Directed by David Howard. Screenplay by Morton Grant. Photographed by Harry Wild. Edited by Frederic Knudtson. Music by Ray Whitley and Fred Rose.

Songs: "Silver Rio," "Dude Cowboy," "End of the Canyon Trail," "Echo Singing in the Wild Wind."

Starring Tim Holt (Terry), Marjorie Reynolds (Barbara), Ray Whitley (Smokey), Lee "Lasses" White (Whopper), Louise Currie (Gail Sargent), Helen Holmes (Miss Carter), Eddie Kane (Gordon West), Eddie Dew (French), Byron Foulger (Mr. Adams), Tom London (Sheriff), Lloyd Ingraham (Pop Stebbens), Glenn Strange (Krinkle).

A U.S. Treasury agent sets out to stop a gang of counterfeiters.

248 *Dumbo* (1941) Animated feature. Running time: 64 minutes. Color. Available on videocassette.

Produced by Walt Disney. Directed by Ben Sharpsteen. Screenplay by Joe Grant and Dick Huemer (based on a book by Helen Aberson and Harold Pearl). Animators: Hugh Fraser, Howard Swift, Harvey Toombs, Down Towlsey, Milt Neil, Les Clark, Hicks Lokey, Claude Smith, Berny Wolf, Ray Patterson, Jack Campbell, Grant Simmons, Walt Kelly, Joshua Meador, Don Patterson, Bill Shull, Cy Young, Art Palmer. Music by Oliver Wallace, Frank Churchill, and Ned Washington.

Songs: "Look Out for Mr. Stork," "Baby of Mine," "All Aboard," "Pink Elephants on Parade," "When I See an Elephant Fly."

Voices: Ed Brophy (Timothy Mouse), Herman Bing (Ringmaster), Verna Felton (Elephant), Sterling Holloway (Stork), Cliff Edwards (Jim Crow).

A baby elephant with enormous ears finds his handicap is really beneficial.

Note: Disney's shortest feature film, and least expensive, costing less than $1 million.

Oscar: Best Musical Score.

249 *Dynamite Pass* (1950) Western. Running time: 60 minutes. Black and white. Available on videocassette.

Produced by Herman Schlom. Directed by Lew Landers. Screenplay by Norman Houston. Photographed by Nicholas Musuraca. Music by Paul Sawtell. Edited by Robert Swink.

Starring Tim Holt (Ross), Lynne Roberts (Mary), Regis Toomey (Dan), Robert Shayne (Wingate), Don Harvey (Mizzouri), Cleo Moore (Lulu), John Dehner (Thurber), Don Haggerty (Sheriff), Ross Elliot (Stryker), Denver Pyle (Whip), Richard Martin (Chito).

Cowboys build a toll free road, but are beset by problems caused by highwaymen.

250 *Easy Living* (1949) Drama. Running time: 77 minutes. Black and white. Available on videocassette.

Produced by Robert Sparks. Directed by Jacques Tourneur. Screenplay by Charles Schnee (based on the story *Education of the Heart* by Irwin Shaw). Photographed by Harry J. Wild. Edited by Frederic Knudtson. Music by Roy Webb.

Starring Victor Mature (Pete Wilson), Lucille Ball (Anne), Lizabeth Scott (Liza Wilson), Sonny Tufts (Tim McCarr), Lloyd Nolan (Lenahan), Paul Stewart (Argus), Jack Paar (Scoop Spooner), Jeff Donnell (Penny McCarr), Art Baker (Howard Vollmer), Gordon Jones (Bill Holloran), Don Beddoe (Jaegar), Dick Erdman (Buddy Morgan), William Phillips (Ozzie), Charles Lang (Whitey), Kenny Washington (Benny), Jim Backus (Dr. Franklin), Julia Dean (Mrs. Belle Ryan), Everett Glass (Virgil Ryan), The Los Angeles Rams (Themselves).

Lucille Ball, Victor Mature, and Paul Stewart in *Easy Living.*

An aging gridiron star must adjust to impending retirement.

Note: No relation to the similarly titled 1937 Preston Sturges feature, which was a Paramount release.

251 *Easy Riches* (1938) Comedy. Running time: 67 minutes. Black and white. A British-filmed GS Enterprises production, released by RKO.

Produced by A. George Smith. Directed by John Hunter. Photographed by Geoffrey Faithfull.

Starring George Carney (Sam Miller), Gus McNaughton (Joe Hicks), Marjorie Taylor (Dorothy Hicks), Tom Helmore (Harry Miller), Peter Gawthorne (Stacey Lang).

Two business rivals join forces to expose a ring of con men.

252 *Edge of Doom* (1950) Crime drama. Running time: 99 minutes. Black and white. A Samuel Goldwyn production for RKO.

Produced by Samuel Goldwyn. Directed by Mark Robson, with additional scenes by Charles Vidor. Screenplay by Phillip Yordan, additional scenes by Ben Hecht (based on the novel by Leo Brady). Photographed by Harry Stradling. Edited by Daniel Mandell.

Starring Dana Andrews (Father Roth), Farley Granger (Martin Lynn), Joan Evans (Rita Conroy), Robert Keth (Mandel), Paul Stewart (Craig), Mala Powers (Julie), Adele Jergens (Irene), John Ridgely, Douglas Fowley (Detectives).

A priest is murdered and several come under suspicion.

Note: British title: *Stronger Than Fear.*

253 *Emergency Call* (1933) Crime drama. Running time: 70 minutes. Black and white. Available on videocassette.

Produced by Sam Jaffe. Directed by Edward Cahn. Screenplay by John B. Clymer and Joseph L. Mankiewicz (based on a story by Clymer, James Ewens). Photographed by J. Roy Hunt. Edited by William Hamilton.

Starring Bill Boyd (Joe Bradley), Wynne Gibson (Mabel Weenie), William Gargan (Steven Brennan), Betty Furness (Alice Averill), Reginald Mason (Dr. Averill), Edwin Maxwell (Tom Rourke), George E. Stone (Sammie Jacobs), Merna Kennedy (File Clerk), Jane Darwell (Head Nurse).

Gangsters take over a hospital.

254 Enchanted April (1935) Drama. Running time: 66 minutes. Black and white.

Produced by Kenneth MacGowan. Directed by Harry Beaumont. Screenplay by Samuel Hoffenstein and Ray Harris (based on the novel *Elizabeth* by Mary Annette Beauchamp Russell, and a play by Kane Campbell). Photographed by Edward Cronjager. Edited by George Hively.

Starring Ann Harding (Lotty Wilkins), Frank Morgan (Mellersh Wilkins), Katherine Alexander (Rose Arbuthnot), Reginald Owen (Henry Arbuthnot), Jane Baxter (Lady Caroline), Ralph Forbes (Beppo), Jessie Ralph (Mrs. Fisher), Charles Judels (Domenico), Rafaela Ottiano (Francesca).

Four women encounter romance while vacationing in Italy.

Review: "Very British in background and proceeding at all times with a lifted eyebrow" — *Variety*.

255 Enchanted Cottage (1945) Drama. Running time: 92 minutes. Black and white. Available on videocassette.

Produced by Harriet Parsons. Directed by John Cromwell. Screenplay by DeWitt Bodeen and Herman J. Mankiewicz (based on the play by Sir Arthur Wing Pinero). Photographed by Ted Tetzlaff. Edited by Joseph Noriega. Music by Roy Webb.

Starring Dorothy McGuire (Laura), Robert Young (Oliver), Herbert Marshall (John Hillgrave), Mildred Natwick (Abigail Minnett), Spring Byington (Violet Pierce), Richard Gaines (Fred-

rick), Hillary Brooke (Beatrice), Alec Englander (Danny), Mary Worth (Mrs. Stanton), Josephine Whittell (Canteen Manager), Robert Clarke (Marine), Eden Nicholas (Soldier).

A disfigured war vet and a homely woman find beauty in each other.

Note: Originally on stage in 1922, filmed before with Richard Barthelmess and May McAvoy, in 1924. The original running time is above, although some prints run 78 minutes.

256 Enchantment (1948) Romantic drama. Running time: 102 minutes. Black and white.

Produced by Samuel Goldwyn. Directed by Irving Reis. Screenplay by John Patrick (from the novel *Take Three Tenses* by Runner Godden). Photographed by Gregg Toland). Edited by Daniel Mandell. Music by Emil Newman.

Starring David Niven (General Sir Roland Dane), Teresa Wright (Lark Ingoldsby), Evelyn Keyes (Grizel Dane), Farley Granger (Pilot Pax Masterson), Jayne Meadows (Selina Dane), Leo G. Carroll (Proutie), Phillip Friend (Pelham Dane), Shepperd Strudwick (Marchese del Laudi), Henry Stephenson (Gen. Fitzgerald), Colin Keth-Johnston (The Eye), Gigi Perreau (Lark as a Child), Peter Miles (Rollo as a Child), Sherlee Collier (Selina as a Child), Warwick Gregson (Pelham as a Child), William Johnstone (Narrator).

A London house remembers the three generations who lived there.

Review: "Deliberate in pace and artfully contrived as an emotional holiday, yet genuinely moving on its own terms" — *Newsweek*.

257 Escapade in Japan (1957) Adventure. Running time: 90 minutes. Color. Available on videocassette. A Universal-RKO tandem production.

Produced and directed by Arthur Lubin. Screenplay by Winston Miller. Photographed by William Snyder. Edited by George Walter. Music by Max Steiner.

Starring Teresa Wright (Mary Saunders), Cameron Mitchell (Dick Saunders), Jon Provost (Tony Saunders), Roger Nakagawa (Hiko), Phillip Ober (Lt. Col. Hargrave), Kuniko Miyake (Michiko), Susumu Fujita (Kei Tanaka), Katsuhiko Haida (Capt. Hibino), Clint Eastwood (Dumbo).

An American boy, en route to meet his parents, survives a plane crash and ends up in Tokyo.

258 *Escape* (1930)   Adventure. Running time: 70 minutes. Black and white. An Associated Talking Pictures production released by RKO.

Produced and directed by Basil Dean. Screenplay by Dean and John Galsworthy (based on a play by Galsworthy). Photographed by Jack MacKenzie. Edited by Milner Kitchin.

Starring Sir Gerald du Maurier (Capt. Matt Denant), Edna Best (Shingled Lady), Gordon Harker (Convict), Horace Hodges (Gentleman), Madeline Carrol (Dora), Mabel Poulton (Girl of the Town), Lewis Casson (Farmer), Ian Hunter (Detective), Austin Trevor (Parson), Marie Ney (Grace), Felix Aylmer (Governor), Ben Field (Captain), Fred Groves (Shopkeeper), Nigel Bruce (Constable).

An escaped convict's adventures.

Review: "A more careful work than most of the British talker product, but as an entertainment proposition it doesn't mean much" — *Variety.*

259 *Escape to Burma* (1955)   Adventure. Running time: 86 minutes. Color. Available on videocassette.

Produced by Benedict E. Bogeaus. Directed by Allan Dwan. Screenplay by Talbot Jennings and Hobart Donavan (based on the story *Bow Tamely to Me* by Kenneth Perkins). Photographed by John Alton. Edited by James Leicester.

Starring Robert Ryan (Jim Brecan), Barbara Stanwyck (Gwen Moore), David Farrar (Cardigan), Murvyn Vye (Mekash), Robert Warwick (Sawbwa), Reginald Denny (Commissioner), Lisa Montell (Andora), Peter Coe (Guard Captain), Anthony Numkena (Kasha), Alex Montoya (Dacoit), Robert Cabal (Kumat), Lal Chand Mehra (Pookan), William Benegal Raw (Young Horn Player), John Mansfield (Sergeant), Gavin Muir (Astrologer).

A man running from a false murder conviction finds solace on a remote plantation owned by a headstrong woman.

260 *Escape to Danger* (1943)   Spy drama. Running time: 92 minutes. Black and white.

Produced by William Sistrom. Directed by Victor Hanbury, Lance Comfort, and Mutz Greenbaum. Screenplay by Wolfgang Wilhelm and Jack Whittingham (based on a story by Patrick Kirwan). Photographed by Guy Greene.

Starring Eric Portman (Arthur Lawrence), Ann Dvorak (Joan Grahame), Karel Stepanek (Franz von Brinkman), Ronald Ward (Rupert Chessman), Ronald Adam (George Merrick), Lilly Kann (Karin Moeller), David Peel (Lt. Peter Leighton), Felix Aylmer (Sir Alfred Horton), Brefini O'Rorke (Security Officer), A.E. Matthews (Sir Thomas Leighton), Charles Victor (PO Flanagan), Marjorie Rhodes (Mrs. Pickles), Frederick Cooper (Goesta), Ivor Barnard (Henry Waud).

A British schoolmistress is sent to spy in England by Nazis, not realizing she is working for the Allies.

261 *Escape to Paradise* (1939)   Musical. Running time: 60 minutes. Black and white.

Produced by Barney Briskin. Directed by Erle C. Kenton. Screenplay by Weldon Melick (based on a story by Ian Hunter and Herbert Clyde Lewis). Photographed by Charles Schoenbaum. Edited by Arthur Hilton. Music by Nilo Melendez and Edward Cherkose.

Songs: "Tra-La-La," "Rhythm of the Rio," "Ay Ay Ay."

Starring Bobby Breen (Robertson), Kent Taylor (Fleming), Marla Shelton

Publicity poster for *Every Girl Should Be Married.*

(Juanita), Joyce Compton (Penelope Carter), Pedro de Cordoba (Don Miguel), Robert O. Davis (Alexander Komac), Rosina Galli (Duenna), Frank Yaconelli (Manuel), Anna Demetrio (Senora Ramos).

A singing motorcycle-taxi driver plays cupid in South America.

Note: Breen's last film for RKO.

262 *Every Girl Should Be Married* (1948) Comedy. Running time: 84 minutes. Black and white (colorized). Available on videocassette.

Produced and directed by Don Hart

man. Screenplay by Stephen Morehouse Avery and Hartman. Photographed by George E. Diskant. Edited by Harry Marker. Music by Leigh Harline.

Starring Cary Grant (Dr. Madison Brown), Franchot Tone (Roger Sanford), Diana Lynn (Julie Hudson), Betsy Drake (Anabel Sims), Alan Mowbray (Mr. Spitzer), Elisabeth Risdon (Mary Nolan), Richard Gaines (Sam McNutt), Harry Hayden (Gogarthy), Chick Chandler (Soda Clerk), Leon Belasco (Violinist), Fred Essler (Pierre), Anna Q. Nilsson (Saleslady), Charmienne Harker (Miss King), Marjorie Walker, Alvina Temin, Rosalie Cughenour, Joan Lybrook (Models), Louise Franklin (Elevator Girl), Dan Doster (Cigar Store Clerk), Gwyn Shipman (Mother), Carol Hughes (Girl at Counter).

A young girl aggressively pursues a bachelor pediatrician.

Note: Betsy Drake's film debut; she later became Mrs. Cary Grant.

Review: "In the past Cary Grant has shown a talent for quietly underplaying comedy. In this picture, he has trouble finding comedy to play"—*Time*.

263 *Everybody's Doing It* (1938)

Comedy. Running time: 66 minutes. Black and white.

Produced by William Sistrom. Directed by Christy Cabanne. Screenplay by J. Robert Bren, Edmund Joseph, Harry Segall (based on a story by George Beck). Photographed by Nicholas Musuraca. Edited by Ted Chessman.

Starring Preston Foster, Sally Eilers, Cecil Kellaway, Lorraine Krueger, William Brisbane, Richard Lane, Guinn "Big Boy" Williams, Arthur Lake, Solly Ward, Frank M. Thomas, Herbert Evans.

A puzzle creator goes on a drunken binge without leaving the answers to a nationwide breakfast cereal contest.

264 *Everything's on Ice* (1939)

Drama. Running time: 65 minutes. Black and white.

Produced by Sol Lesser. Directed by Erle C. Kenton. Screenplay by Adrian Landis and Sherman Lowe. Photographed by Russell Metty. Edited by Arthur Hilton. Ice numbers staged by Dave Gould.

Starring Irene Dare (Irene), Roscoe Karns (Felix), Edgar Kennedy (Joe), Lynne Roberts (Jane), Eric Linden (Leopold), Mary Hart (Elsie), Bobby Watson (Frenchie), George Meeker (Gregg).

A six year old figure skating champion is exploited by her uncle.

265 *Everything's Rosie* (1931)

Comedy. Running time: 60 minutes. Black and white.

Directed by Clyde Bruckman. Screenplay by Tim Whelan, Ralph Spence, and Al Boasberg (based on a story by Boasberg). Photographed by Nicholas Musuraca.

Starring Robert Woolsey (Dr. J. Dockweiler Droop), Anita Louise (Rosie), John Darrow (Billy Lowe), Florence Roberts (Mrs. Lowe), Frank Beal (Mr. Lowe), Alfred James (Oberdoff), Lita Chevret (Miss Van Dorn), Clifford Dempsey (Sheriff).

A medicine show man adopts a little girl.

Note: Woolsey's only film without partner Bert Wheeler. Wheeler did work alone in *Too Many Cooks* (q.v.) as well as several films after Woolsey's death in 1938.

266 *The Ex-Mrs. Bradford* (1936)

Comedy. Running time: 80 minutes. Black and white. Available on videocassette.

Produced by Edward Kaufman. Directed by Stephen Roberts. Screenplay by Anthony Veiller (based on a story by James Edward Grant). Photographed by J. Roy Hunt. Edited by Arthur Roberts. Music by Roy Webb.

Starring William Powell (Dr. Lawrence Bradford), Jean Arthur (Paula Bradford), James Gleason (Inspector Corrigan), Eric Blore (Stokes), Robert Armstrong (Nick Martel), Lila Lee (Miss Prentiss), Grant Mitchell (Mr. Summers), Erin O'Brien-Moore (Mrs. Summers), Ralph Morgan (Mr. Hutchins), Lucille Gleason (Mrs. Hutchins), Frank M. Thomas (Salsbury), Frank Reicher (Henry Strand).

A doctor's screwball wife gets him involved in a hunt for a murderer.

267 *Excess Baggage* (1933)

Comedy. Running time: 59 minutes. Black and white.

Produced by Julius Hagen. Directed by Redd Davis. Screenplay by H. Fowler Mear. Photographed by Stanley Blythe. A British Real Art production.

Starring Claud Allister, Frank Pettingell, Sydney Fairbrother, Rene Ray, Gerald Rawlinson, Viola Compton, O.B. Clarence, Maud Gill, Finlay Currie, Minnie Raymer, Ruth Taylor, Charles Groves.

A man believes he accidentally shot his boss, so he packs the body and dumps it into the river.

268 *Experiment Alcatraz* (1950) Drama. Running time: 58 minutes. Black and white. A Crystal production for RKO release.

Produced and directed by Edward L. Cahn. Screenplay by Orville H. Hampton (from a story by George W. George and George F. Slavin). Photographed by Jackson J. Rose. Edited by Phillip Kahn. Music by Irving Getz.

Starring John Howard (Dr. Ross Williams), Joan Dixon (Joan McKenna), Walter Kingsford (Dr. Finaly), Lynne Carter (Ethel Ganz), Robert Shayne (Barry Morgan), Kim Spalding (Duke Shaw), Sam Scar (Eddie Ganz), Kenneth MacDonald (Col. Harris), Frank Cady (Max Henry), Byron Foulger (Jim Carlton).

A doctor tests a radioactive drug on volunteer prisoners in return for a pardon.

269 *Experiment Perilous* (1944) Mystery. Running time: 90 minutes. Black and white.

Produced by Warren Duff and Robert Fellows. Directed by Jacques Tourneur. Screenplay by Duff (based on the novel by Margaret Carpenter). Photographed by Tony Gaudio. Edited by Ralph Dawson. Music by Roy Webb.

Starring Hedy Lamarr (Atilda Bedereaux), George Brent (Dr. Huntington Bailey), Paul Lukas (Mick Bedereaux), Albert Dekker (Claghorne), Carl Esmond (John Maitland), Olive Blakeney (Cissie Bedereaux), George N. Neise (Alec Gregory), Margaret Wycherly (Maggie), Stephanie Bachelor (Elaine), Mary Servoss (Miss Wilson), Julia Dean (Deria), William Post, Jr. (D.A. McDonald), Alan Ward (Shoes), Nolan Leary (Bellhop), Sam McDaniel (Porter), Charles McMurphy (Cop).

A woman becomes a suspect when her husband is mysteriously killed.

270 *The Face at the Window* (1932) Mystery. Running time: 52 minutes. Black and white.

Produced by Julius Hagen. Directed by Leslie Hiscott. Screenplay by H. Fowler Mear (based on a play by F. Brooke Warren).

Starring Raymond Massey (Paul le Gross), Isla Bevan (Marie de Brisson), Claude Hulbert (Peter Pomeroy), Eric Maturin (Count Fournal), Henry Mollison (Lucien Courtier), A. Bromley Davenport (Gaston de Brisson), Harold Meade (Dr. Renard), Dennis Wyndham (Lafonde).

A French detective fakes the revival of a dead man in order to capture a bank robbing count.

271 *Face to Face* (1952) Drama. Running time: 89 minutes. Black and white.

Produced by Huntington Hartford. Directed by John Brahm, Bretaigne Windstur. Screenplay by Aeneas MacKenzie, James Agee (based on stories by Joseph Conrad and Stephen Crane). Photographed by Karl Struss, George Diskant. Edited by Otto Meyer.

Starring James Mason, Gene Lockhart, Michael Pate, Albert Sharpe, Sean McClory, Alec Hartford, Robert Preston, Marjorie Steele, Minor Watson, Dan Seymour, Olive Carey, James Agee.

Two short story adaptions: Joseph Conrad's "The Secret Sharer" and Stephen Crane's "The Bride Comes to Yellow Sky."

272 *Faithful City* (1952) Drama. Running time: 86 minutes. Black and white. Produced in Israel by Molodeth productions for RKO release.

Produced, directed, and written by Joseph Leytes. Photographed by Gerald Gibbs. Edited by J.D. Guthridge.

Starring Jamie Smith (Sam), Ben Josef (Davidei), John Slater (Ezra), Rachel Markus (Sarah), Dina Peskin (Anna), Israel Hanin (Max), Juda Levi (Jean).

A group of Jewish children, orphaned during the war, come to idolize an American who befriends them.

273 *The Falcon and the Coeds*

(1943) Mystery. Running time: 67 minutes. Black and white.

Produced by Maurice Geraghty. Directed by William Clemens. Screenplay by Ardel Wray and Gerald Geraghty (based on an original story by Wray, from the character created by Michael Arlen). Photographed by Roy Hunt. Edited by Theron Worth.

Starring Tom Conway (Tom Lawrence/The Falcon), Jean Brooks (Vicky Gaines), Rita Corday (Marguerita Serena), Amelita Ward (Jane Harris), Isabel Jewell (Mary Phoebus), George Givot (Dr. Anatole Graelich), Cliff Clark (Timothy Donovan), Ed Gargan (Bates), Barbara Brown (Miss Keyes), Juanita Alvarez, Ruth Alvarez, Nancy McCullum (The Ughs), Patti Brill (Beanie Smith), Olin Howland (Goodwillie), Ian Wolfe (Eustace L. Harley), Margie Stewart (Pam), Margaret Landry (Sarey Ann), Dorothy Malone (Bit).

The sleuth is called in to investigate the murder of a professor at Bluecliff School.

Note: Made to take advantage of the plethora of female beauties available for films during WWII, when many men were fighting overseas.

274 *The Falcon in Danger* (1943)

Mystery. Running time: 69 minutes. Black and white.

Produced by Maurice Geraghty. Directed by William Clemens. Screenplay by Fred Niblo and Craig Rice (based on the character created by Michael Arlen). Photographed by Frank Redman. Edited by George Crone.

Starring Tom Conway (Falcon), Jean Brooks (Iris Fairchild), Elaine Shepard (Nancy Palmer), Amelita Ward (Bonnie Caldwell), Cliff Clark (Inspector Timothy Donovan), Ed Gargan (Bates), Clarence Kolb (Stanley Harris Palmer), Felix Basch (Morley), Richard Davis (Ken Gibson), Richard Martin (George Morley).

The sleuth attempts to track down two missing industrialists who disappeared with $100,000 and a private plane.

275 *The Falcon in Hollywood*

(1944) Mystery. Running time: 66 minutes. Black and white. Available on videocassette.

Produced by Maurice Geraghty. Directed by Gordon Douglas. Screenplay by Gerald Geraghty (based on the character created by Michael Arlen). Photographed by Nicholas Musuraca. Edited by Gene Milford.

Starring Tom Conway (Falcon), Barbara Hale (Peggy Callahan), Rita Corday (Lilli D'Allo), Jean Brooks (Roxanna), Veda Ann Borg (Billie), Konstantin Shayne (Alec Hoffman), John Abbott (Martin Dwyer), Emory Parnell (Inspector McBride), Frank Jenks (Lt. Higgins), Sheldon Leonard (Louie), Walter Soderling (Ed Johnson), Usef Ali (Nagari), Carl Kent (Art Director), Gwen Crawford and Patti Brill (Secretaries), Nancy Marlowe (Mail Clerk), Chester Clute (Hotel Clerk), Robert Clarke (Perc Saunders).

The Falcon takes a vacation in Tinseltown and ends up involved in a murder case.

Note: The film takes place on the RKO backlot, which allows the viewer to see what the studio looked like at the time.

276 *The Falcon in Mexico* (1944)

Mystery. Running time: 70 minutes. Black and white.

Produced by Maurice Geraghty. Directed by William Berke. Screenplay by George Worthington Yates and Gerald Geraghty (based on the character created by Michael Arlen). Photographed by Frank Redman. Edited by Joseph Noriega.

Starring Tom Conway (Falcon), Mona Maris (Raquel), Martha MacVicar (Barbara Wade), Nestor Paiva (Manuel Romero), Mary Currier (Paula Dudley), Cecilia Callejo (Dolores Ybarra), Emory Parnell (James Winthrop Hughes/Lucky Diamond), Pedro de Cordoba (Don Carlos Ybarra).

The Falcon is alerted when new paintings by a supposedly dead artist surface in New York City.

Note: Actress MacVicar later changed her name to Martha Vickers. Exterior footage from Orson Welles' aborted documentary *It's All True.*

277　*The Falcon in San Francisco*

(1945) Mystery. Running time: 66 minutes. Black and white.

Produced by Maurice Geraghty. Directed by Joseph H. Lewis. Screenplay by Robert E. Kent and Ben Markson (based on an original story by Kent, from the character created by Michael Arlen). Photographed by Virgil Miller and William Sickner. Edited by Ernie Leadlay.

Starring Tom Conway (Falcon), Rita Corday (Joan Marshall), Edward Brophy (Goldie Locke), Sharyn Moffett (Annie Marshall), Fay Helm (Doreen Temple), Robert Armstrong (De Forrest Marshall), Carl Kent (Rickey), George Holmes (Dalman), Myrna Dell (Bit), Esther Howard (Mrs. Peabody).

The Falcon investigates a silk smuggling operation.

278　*The Falcon Out West* (1944)

Mystery. Running time: 64 minutes. Black and white.

Produced by Maurice Geraghty. Directed by William Clemens. Screenplay by Billy Jones and Morton Grant (based on the character created by Michael Arlen). Photographed by Barry Wild. Edited by Gene Milford. Music by Roy Webb.

Starring Tom Conway (Falcon), Carole Gallagher (Vanessa), Barbara Hale (Marion), Joan Barclay (Mrs. Irwin), Cliff Clark (Inspector Donovan), Ed Gargan (Bates), Minor Watson (Caldwell), Don Douglas (Hayden), Lyle Talbot (Tex), Lee Trent (Dusty), Perc Launders (Red), Lawrence Tierney (Orchestra Leader), Chief Thunderbird (Eagle Feather), Norman Willis (Callahan), Slim Whitaker (Cowboy).

The Falcon investigates the murder of a Texas playboy.

279　*The Falcon Strikes Back*

(1943) Mystery. Running time: 63 minutes. Black and white.

Produced by Maurice Geraghty. Directed by Edward Dmytryk. Screenplay by Edward Dein and Gerald Geraghty (based on a character created by Michael Arlen). Photographed by Jack MacKenzie. Edited by George Crone.

Starring Tom Conway (Falcon), Harriet Hilliard (Gwynne Gregory), Jane Randolph (Marcia Brooks), Edgar Kennedy (Smiley Dugan), Cliff Edwards (Goldie), Rita Corday (Mia Bruger), Erford Gage (Rickey Davis), Wynne Gibson (Mrs. Lipton), Richard Loo (Jerry), Andre Charlot (Bruno Steffen), Ed Gargan (Bates), Byron Foulger (Argyle), Frank Faylen (Cecil), Jack Norton (Hobo), Joan Barclay (Bit).

The Falcon is wrongly accused of murdering a banker, so he hides in the mountains and uncovers a war bond racket.

Note: Perhaps the series entry with the best direction and best supporting cast.

280　*The Falcon Takes Over*

(1942) Mystery. Running time: 62 minutes. Black and white. Available on videocassette.

Produced by Howard Benedict. Directed by Irving Reis. Screenplay by Lynn Root and Frank Fenton (based on the character created by Michael Arlen and the novel *Farewell My Lovely* by Raymond Chandler). Photographed by George Robinson. Edited by Harry Marker.

Starring George Sanders (Falcon),

Lynn Bari (Ann Riodian), James Gleason (Inspector Mike O'Hara), Allen Jenkins (Goldie Locke), Helen Gilbert (Diana Kenyon), Ward Bond (Moose Malloy), Ed Gargan (Bates), Anne Revere (Jessie Floran), George Cleveland (Jerry), Harry Shannon (Grimes), Hans Conried (Lindsey Marriot), Mickey Simpson (Bartender), Selmer Jackson (Laird Burnett), Turhan Bey (Jules Amthor), Charlie Hall (Lovie).

Third in the Falcon series, this one based on Chandler's novel with the sleuth in the Phillip Marlowe role.

281 The Falcon's Adventure

(1946) Mystery. Running time: 61 minutes. Black and white. Available on videocassette.

Produced by Herman Schlom. Directed by William Berke. Screenplay by Aubrey Wisberg and Robert E. Kent (based on the character created by Michael Arlen). Photographed by Harry Wild and Frank Redman. Edited by Marvin Coil.

Starring Tom Conway (Falcon), Madge Meredith (Louisa Branganza), Edward Brophy (Goldie Locke), Robert Warwick (Kenneth Sutton), Myrna Dell (Doris Blanding), Steve Brodie (Benny), Ian Wolfe (Denison), Carol Forman (Helen), Joseph Crehan (Inspector Cavannaugh), Phil Warren (Mike Geary), Tony Barrett (Paolo), Harry Harvey (Duncan), Jason Robards, Sr. (Lt. Evans), David Sharpe (Crew Member).

The Falcon rescues a woman from a gang of kidnappers, but is soon framed for killing her father.

Note: The last appearance of Conway as the Falcon, and last of the "official" series.

282 The Falcon's Alibi

(1946) Mystery. Running time: 63 minutes. Black and white.

Produced by William Berke. Directed by Ray McCary. Screenplay by Paul Yawitz (from a story by Dane Lussier and Manuel Seff, based on a character created

by Michael Arlen). Photographed by Frank Redman. Edited by Phillip Martin.

Starring Tom Conway (Falcon), Rita Corday (Joan Meredith), Vince Barnett (Goldie Locke), Jane Greer (Lola Carpenter), Elisha Cook, Jr. (Nick), Emory Parnell (Metcalf), Al Bridge (Inspector Blake), Esther Howard (Gloria Peabody), Jean Brooks (Baroness Lena), Myrna Dell (Girl with Falcon), Paul Brooks (Alex).

A secretary hires the Falcon to guard her employer's valuable jewels.

283 The Falcon's Brother (1942)

Mystery. Running time: 63 minutes. Black and white. Available on videocassette.

Produced by Maurice Geraghty. Directed by Stanley Logan. Screenplay by Stuart Palmer and Craig Rice (based on the character created by Michael Arlen). Photographed by Russell Metty. Edited by Mark Robson.

Starring George Sanders (Gay Lawrence), Tom Conway (Tom Lawrence), Jane Randolph (Marcie Brooks), Don Barclay (Lefty), Cliff Clark (Donovan), Ed Gargan (Bates), Eddie Dunn (Grimes).

When the Falcon is killed, his brother Tom Lawrence assumes the sleuth's identity.

Note: Sanders' last appearance as the Falcon and Conway's first. The two were real-life brothers.

284 The Fall Guy (1930) Crime.

Running time: 66 minutes. Black and white.

Produced by William Le Baron. Directed by A. Leslie Pearce. Screenplay by Tim Whelan (based on a play by George Abbott and James Gleason). Photographed by Leo Tover. Edited by Archie Marshek.

Starring Jack Mulhall (Johnny Quinlan), Mae Clarke (Bertha Quinlan), Ned Sparks (Dan Walsh), Pat O'Malley (Charles Newton), Thomas Jackson (Nifty

Herman), Wynne Gibson (Lottie Quinlan), Ann Brody (Mrs. Bercowich), Elmer Ballards (Hutch), Alan Roscoe (Detective Keefe).

A naive clerk is used as patsy by a mobster dealing in narcotics.

285 *The Fallen Sparrow* (1943) Drama. Running time: 94 minutes. Black and white. Available on videocassette.

Produced by Robert Fellows. Directed by Richard Wallace. Screenplay by Warren Duff (based on the novel by Dorothy B. Hughes). Photographed by Nicholas Musuraca. Edited by Robert Wise. Music by Roy Webb.

Starring John Garfield (Kit), Maureen O'Hara (Toni), Walter Slezak (Skaas), Patricia Morrison (Barby), Martha O'Driscoll (Whitney), Bruce Edwards (Ab Parker), John Banner (Anton), John Miljan (Insp. Tobin), Sam Goldenberg (Prince Francois), Hugh Beaumont (Otto Skaas), George Lloyd (Sgt. Moore).

An American veteran of the Spanish Civil War finds himself haunted by Nazis in the U.S. who seek the Spanish flag of freedom.

Oscar nomination: Best Music.

286 *Fang and Claw* (1935) Produced, directed, narrated by Frank Buck.

Third documentary by Buck (the others are *Bring 'em Back Alive* and *Wild Cargo*), this one dealing with the capture of wild animals in Malaya.

287 *Fanny Foley Herself* (1931) Comedy. Running time: 73 minutes. Color.

Produced by John E. Burch. Directed by Melville Brown. Screenplay by Carey Wilson and Bernard Schubert (adapted from a story by Juliet Wilbur Tompkins). Photographed by Ray Rennahan. Edited by Nicholas Musuraca.

Starring Edna May Oliver (Fanny Foley), Hobart Bosworth (Seely), Helen Chandler (Lenore), John Darrow (Teddy), Rochelle Hudson (Carmen), Florence Roberts (Lucy), Robert Emmett O'Connor (Burns), Harry O. Stubbs (Crosby).

A wealthy man wants to take a vaudeville star's daughters away as he does not agree with her theatrical lifestyle.

Note: Ms. Oliver's first starring role, and an attempt at a projected series. Oliver, who was RKO's answer to Marie Dressler at MGM, fared better in supporting roles. RKO's faith in the actress is proven by the expensive two-strip technicolor used here. British title: *Top of the Hill.*

288 *Fantasia* (1940) Animated feature. Running time: 120 minutes. Technicolor. Available on videocassette.

Produced by Walt Disney. Directed by Samuel Armstrong, James Algar, Bill Roberts, Paul Satterfield, Hamilton Luske, Ford Beebe, Jim Handley, Norman Ferguson, Wilfred Jackson. Supervised by Ben Sharpsteen.

Musical compositions: Bach, "Tocatta and Fugue in D Minor"; Tchaikovsky, "The Nutcracker Suite"; Dukas: "The Sorcerer's Apprentice"; Stravinsky, "The Rites of Spring"; Beethoven, "The Pastoral Symphony"; Ponchielli, "Dance of the Hours"; Moussorgsky, "Night on Bare Mountain"; Schubert, "Ave Maria"; Leopold Stokowski and the Philadelphia Orchestra, "Deems Taylor."

Classical music compositions are set to music in this masterpiece of animation.

Note: Multiplane cameras, showing degrees of depth in animation, were used for the first time. The film was re-edited and re-released extensively, being released in its original form on video tape in 1991, after which the studio re-shot some scenes, adding new ones and dispensing with some old ones, calling it *Fantasia Continued* in an effort to update the film as per Disney's wishes.

Review: "It is ambitious and finely so, and one feels its vulgarities are at least unintentional"—James Agee.

John Garfield and Maureen O'Hara in *The Fallen Sparrow*.

289 *Farewell to Cinderella* (1937) Romance. Running time: 64 minutes. Black and white.

Produced by A. George Smith. Directed by MacLean Rogers. Screenplay by Rogers, Kathleen Butler, H.F. Maltby (based on a story by Arthur Richardson). Photographed by Geoffrey Faithfull.

Starring Anne Pichon (Margaret), John Robinson (Stephen Morley), Arthur Rees (Uncle William), Glynnis Lorimer (Betty Temperley), Sebastian

Smith (Andy Weir), Ivor Bernard (Mr. Temperley), Margaret Damer (Mrs. Temperley), Ena Grossmith (Emily).

A man helps his niece escape her life's drudgery and win the love of an artist.

290 The Fargo Kid (1941) Western. Running time: 63 minutes. Black and white.

Produced by Bert Gilroy. Directed by Edward Killy. Screenplay by Morton Grant and Arthur V. Jones (from a story by W.C. Tuttle). Photographed by Harry Wild. Edited by Frederic Knudtson. Music by Ray Whitley, Fred Rose, and Paul Sawtell.

Songs: "Crazy Ol' Trails," "Twilight on the Prairie."

Starring Tim Holt (Fargo Kid), Ray Whitley (Johnny), Emmett Lynn (Whopper), Jane Drummond (Jennie), Cy Kendall (Kane), Ernie Adams (Bush), Paul Fix (Mallory), Paul Scardon (Winters), Glenn Strange (Sheriff), Mary McLaren (Sarah).

When a lawman steals a gunman's horse, he is mistaken for the killer.

Note: Second in the Holt series, a remake of the 1933 western *The Cheyenne Kid* which itself was a remake of a 1928 silent entitled *Man in the Rough.*

291 The Farmer in the Dell (1936) Comedy. Running time: 67 minutes. Black and white.

Produced by Robert Sisk. Directed by Ben Holmes. Screenplay by Sam Mintz and John Grey (based on the novel by Phil Strong). Photographed by Nicholas Musuraca. Edited by George Hively.

Starring Fred Stone (Pa Boyer), Jean Parker (Adie Boyer), Esther Dale, (Ma Boyer), Moroni Olsen (Chester Hart), Frank Albertson (Davy Davenport), Maxine Jennings (Maud Durant), Ray Mayer (Spike), Lucille Ball (Gloria), Rafael Corio (Nicky Ranovitch), Frank Jenks (Crosby), Spencer Charters (Milkman), John Beck, Tony Martin (Bits).

An Iowa farm family moves to Hollywood.

Note: Leading role of Pa was originally slated for Will Rogers, who perished in a plane crash before production began.

292 The Farmer's Daughter (1947) Comedy. Running time: 97 minutes. Black and white. Available on videocassette.

Produced by Dore Schary. Directed by H.C. Potter. Screenplay by Allen Rivkin and Laura Kerr (from the play by Juhni Tevataa). Photographed by Milton Krasner. Edited by Harry Marker.

Starring Loretta Young (Katrin), Joseph Cotten (Glen Morley), Ethel Barrymore (Mrs. Morley), Charles Bickford (Clancy), Rose Hobart (Virginia), Rhys Williams (Adolph), Harry Davenport (Dr. Matthew Sutven), Tom Powers (Nordick), William Harrigan (Ward Hughes), Lex Barker (Olaf Holstrom), Thurston Hall (Wilbur Johnson), Art Baker (A.J. Finley), Don Beddoe (Einar), James (Arness) Aurness (Peter Holstrom), Anna Q. Nilsson (Mrs. Holstrom), Sven Hugo Borg (Dr. Mattsen), John Galludet (Van), William B. Davidson (Eckers), Cy Kendall (Sweeney), Frank Ferguson (Matternack), William Bakewell (Windor), Charles Lane (Jackson, Reporter), Douglas Evans (Silbey, Politician), Robert Clarke (Assistant Announcer), Bess Flowers (Woman).

A Swedish servant becomes involved in her employer's political activities.

Note: James Aurness later became James Arness. A TV series based on this film, starring the late Inger Stevens, was popular during the early-to-mid–sixties.

Oscar: Loretta Young, Best Actress.

Oscar nomination: Charles Bickford, Best Supporting Actor.

Review: "Patricians, politicans, even peasants are portrayed with unusual perception and wit"—James Agee.

293 Father Steps Out (1937) Comedy. Running time: 64 minutes. Black and white.

Produced by George Smith. Directed by Kathleen Butler. Photographed by

Geoffrey Faithfull. Edited by Andy Buchanan.

Starring George Carney, Dinah Sheridan, Bruce Seton, Vivienne Chatterton, Basil Langton, Peter Gawthorne, Zillah Bateman, Elizabeth Kent, Isobel Scaife.

A cheese manufacturer is swindled by con men, but gets even with the help of his cunning chauffeur.

294 *Father Takes a Wife* (1941)
Comedy. Running time: 80 minutes. Black and white.

Produced by Lee Marcus. Directed by Jack Hively. Screenplay by Dorothy and Herbert Fields. Photographed by Robert De Grasse. Edited by George Hively. Music by Roy Webb.

Starring Adolphe Menjou (Fredric Osborne, Sr.), Gloria Swanson (Leslie Colier), John Howard (Fredric Osborne, Jr.), Desi Arnaz (Carlos), Helen Broderick (Aunt Julie), Florence Rice (Enid), Neil Hamilton (Vincent Stewart), Grady Sutton (Tailor), George Meader (Henderson), Mary Treen (Secretary), Ruth Dietrich (Miss Patterson), Frank Reicher (Captain), Grant Withers (Judge Withers), Pierre Watkin (Mr. Fowler).

When a famous actress marries a shipping magnate, she finds being a wife and step-parent is not always fun.

Note: Swanson's return to the screen after a seven year hiatus. RKO publicized this comeback heavily, but the film grossed little over $100,000. Swanson later blamed director Hively for its failure.

Comment: "(Adolphe Menjou) was very helpful to me. He helped me with my lines, how to do the comedy bits, and my reactions. He was a lovely man" — Desi Arnaz, *A Book.*

295 *Fifth Avenue Girl* (1939)
Comedy. Running time: 82 minutes. Black and white. Available on videocassette.

Produced and directed by Gregory La-Cava. Screenplay by Allan Scott. Photographed by Robert De Grasse. Edited by Robert Wise. Music by Robert Russell Bennett.

Starring Ginger Rogers (Mary Grey), Walter Connolly (Mr. Borden), Verree Teasdale (Mrs. Martha Borden), James Ellison (Mike), Tim Holt (Tim Borden), Kathryn Adams (Katherine Borden), Franklin Pangborn (Higgins), Ferike Boros (Olga), Louis Calhern (Dr. Kessler), Theodore Von Eltz (Terwilliger), Alexander D'Arcy (Maitre D'Hotel), Bess Flowers (Woman in Nightclub), Jack Carson (Sailor in Park).

An unemployed girl is persuaded to pose as a golddigger by a rich playboy in an effort to annoy his stuffy family.

Note: Similar in theory to Cheech Marin's 1990 comedy *Shrimp on the Barbie.*

Review: "Substantial comedy drama for top grosses" — *Variety.*

296 *Fifty-Shilling Boxer* (1937)
Drama. Running time: 74 minutes. Black and white.

Produced by George Smith. Directed by MacLean Rogers. Screenplay by Guy Fletcher. Photographed by Geoffrey Faithfull.

Starring Bruce Seton (Jack Foster), Nance O'Neil (Moira Regan), Moore Marriott (Tim Regan), Eve Gray (Miriam Steele), Charles Oliver (Jim Pollett), Aubrey Mallalieu (Charles Day).

A circus performer longs to become a champion prizefighter, but can only land a job as a boxer in a movie.

297 *Fight for Your Lady* (1937)
Comedy. Running time: 67 minutes. Black and white.

Produced by Albert Lewis. Directed by Ben Stoloff. Screenplay by Ernest Pagano, Harry Segall, and Harold Kusell (based on a story by Isabel Leighton and Jean Negulesco). Photographed by Jack MacKenzie. Edited by George Croane.

Starring John Boles (Robert Densmore), Jack Oakie (Ham Hamilton), Ida Lupino (Marietta), Margot Grahame

Publicity poster for *Father Takes a Wife*.

(Marcia Trent), Gordon Jones (Mike Scanlon), Erik Rhodes (Spadissimo), Billy Gilbert (Boris), Paul Guilfoyle (Jimmy Trask), Georges Renavent (Joris), Charles Judels (Felix Janos), Maude Eburne (Nadya), Charles Coleman (Butler), Ward Bond (Wrestler), Gino Corrado (Waiter).

A singer, unlucky in love, is aided by a wrestling trainer.

Review: "This picture is going to entertain whether it sells or not" — *Variety.*

298 Fighting Father Dunne

(1948) Drama. Running time: 92 minutes. Black and white. Available on videocassette.

Produced by Jack J. Gross and Phil L. Ryan. Directed by Ted Tetzlaff. Screenplay by Frank Davis and Martin Rackin (from a story by William Rankin). Photographed by George E. Diskant. Edited by Frederic Knudtson. Music by Roy Webb, Constantin Bakaleinkoff.

Starring Pat O'Brien (Father Dunne), Darryl Hickman (Matt Davis), Charles Kemper (Emmett Mulvey), Una O'Connor (Miss O'Rourke), Arthur Shields (Mr. O'Donnell), Harry Shannon (John Lee), Joe Sawyer (Steve Davis), Anna Q. Nilsson (Mrs. Knudson), Don Gift (Jimmy), Myrna Dell (Paula), Ruth Donnelly (Kate Mulvey), Jim Nolan (Danny Briggs), Billy Cummings (Tony), Billy Gray (Chip), Eric Roberts (Monk), Gene Collins (Lefty), Lester Matthews (Archbishop), Ellen Corby (Secretary), Frank Ferguson (Kolpeck).

A priest who looks after wayward boys meets his match in a young delinquent. Set in the early 1900s.

Note: Based on a true story.

299 Fighting Frontier

(1943) Western. Running time: 57 minutes. Black and white.

Produced by Bert Gilroy. Directed by Lambert Hillyer. Screenplay by J. Benton Cheney and Norton S. Parker (based on a story by Bernard McConville). Photographed by Jack Greenhalgh. Edited by Les Millbrook. Music by Fred Rose and Ray Whitley.

Songs: "On the Outlaw Trail," "The Edwards and the Dews."

Starring Tim Holt (Kit), Cliff Edwards (Ike), Ann Summers (Jeannie), Eddie Dew (Walton), William Gould (Slocum), Davison Clark (Judge Halverson), Slim Whitaker (Sheriff), Tom London (Snap), Monte Montague (Pete), Jack Rockwell (Ira), Bud Osborne, Russell Wade (Bits).

A cowboy hero poses as an outlaw to get the goods on a gang of bandits, but is caught and almost hanged in the process.

300 The Fighting Gringo (1939)

Western. Running time: 59 minutes. Black and white.

Produced by Bert Gilroy. Directed by David Howard. Screenplay by Oliver Drake. Photographed by Harry Wild. Edited by Frederic Knudtson.

Starring George O'Brien (Wade Barton), Lupita Tovar (Nita), Lucio Villegas (Don Aliso), William Royle (Ben Wallace), Glenn Strange (Rance Potter), Slim Whitaker (Monty), LeRoy Mason (John Courtney), Mary Field (Sandra Courtney), Martin Garralaga, Dick Botiller, Bill Cody, Cactus Mack, Chris-Pin Martin, Ben Corbett, Forrest Taylor, Hank Bell (Bits).

A cowboy tries to clear the name of a Mexican rancher who is falsely accused of murder.

301 Finger of Guilt (1956) Drama.

Running time: 85 minutes. Black and white. An Anglo-Guild-Merton Park production for RKO release.

Produced by Alec Snowden. Directed by Joseph Walton. Screenplay by Howard Koch (based on the novel *Pay the Piper*). Photographed by Gerald Gibbs. Edited by Geoffrey Miller.

Starring Richard Basehart (Reggie Wilson), Mary Murphy (Evelyn Stewart), Constance Cummings (Kay Wallace), Roger Livesy (Ben Case), Faith Brook (Lesley Wilson), Mervyn Johns (Ernest Chapple).

An American ex-patriot working as a filmmaker in England is blackmailed by a woman from his past.

Note: The director and writer on this film were two of the self-exiled of the McCarthy era. Released in England as *The Intimate Stranger.*

Publicity poster for *Fighting Father Dunne.*

A scene from *Finishing School*.

302 ***Finishing School*** (1934)
Drama. Running time: 70 minutes.
Black and white. Available on videocassette.

Produced by Merian C. Cooper. Directed by Wanda Tuchock and George Nicholls, Jr. Screenplay by Tuchock and Laird Doyle (based on a story by David Hempstead and the play *These Days* by Katherine Clugston). Photographed by J. Roy Hunt. Edited by Arthur Schmidt.

Starring Frances Dee (Virginia Radcliffe), Billie Burke (Mrs. Radcliffe), Ginger Rogers (Pony), Bruce Cabot (MacFarland), John Halliday (Mr. Radcliff), Beulah Bondi (Miss Van Alstyn), Sara Haden (Miss Fisher), Marjorie Lytell (Ruth), Adalyn Doyle (Madeline), Dawn O'Day (Billie), Rose Coghlan (Miss Garland), Ann Cameron (Miss Schmidt).

Girl at a boarding school must cope with family troubles and her love of a young intern, while being aided by her wisecracking-yet-loving roommate.

Note: Actress Dawn O'Day soon became Anne Shirley.

Reviews: "Modest pap for the teenage audience"—Leslie Halliwell; "This one bombed badly at the time of its release despite a strong cast..."—*Motion Picture Guide*.

303 ***The First Traveling Saleslady*** (1956) Comedy. Running time: 92 minutes. Black and white.

Produced and directed by Arthur Lubin. Screenplay by Stephen Longstreet and Devery Freeman. Photographed by William Snyder. Edited by Otto Ludwig. Music by Irving Gertz.

Songs: "A Corset Can Do a Lot for a Lady," "The First Traveling Saleslady."

Starring Ginger Rogers (Rose Gilray), Barry Nelson (Charles Masters), Carol Hanning (Molly Wade), David Brian (James Carter), James Arness (Joel Kingdon), Clint Eastwood (Jack), Robert Simon (Cal), Frank Wilcox (Marshall Duncan), Dan White (Sheriff), Harry Cheshire (Judge Benson), John Eldredge (Gravy), Robert Hinkle (Pete), Jack Rice (Dowling), Kate Lawson (Annie Peachpit), Edward Cassidy (Theodore Roosevelt), Fred Essler

(Schlesinger), Bill Hale (Deputy), Hank Patterson (Cowhand), Lane Chandler (Rancher), Tris Coffin (Clerk), Pierce Lydon (Official), Clarence Muse (Amos).

A corset designer in the Gay Nineties heads west.

Note: One of Rogers' last films for RKO, and Eastwood's first for the studio. Although billed here as "Introducing Clint Eastwood," he had already appeared in a handful of unmemorable films for Universal (*Francis in the Navy, Revenge of the Creature,* etc.). He may have gotten this job through Producer-Director Lubin, who was also a Universal former and had directed the Francis films.

Review: "Carol and Clint make one of the oddest couples in screen history"—Leonard Maltin.

304 *First Yank into Tokyo* (1945)

War. Running time: 82 minutes. Black and white. Available on videocassette.

Produced by J. Robert Bren. Directed by Gordon Douglas. Screenplay by Bren (based on a story by Bren and Gladys Atwater). Photographed by Harry Wild. Edited by Phillip Martin, Jr.

Starring Tom Neal (Major Ross), Barbara Hale (Abby Drake), Marc Cramer (Jardine), Richard Loo (Col. Okanura), Keye Luke (Han-soo), Leonard Strong (Major Noirga), Benson Fong (Captain Tanahe), Clarence Lung (Ichibo), Keye Chang (Sato), Michael St. Angel (Kent), Bruce Edwards (Harris), Albert Law (Japanese Pilot), Russell Hicks (Thompson), Selmer Jackson (Blaine), John Hamilton (Dr. Stacy).

An American army pilot, raised in Japan, undergoes plastic surgery so that he can infiltrate Japanese opposition.

305 *Fisherman's Wharf* (1939)

Drama. Running time: 72 minutes. Black and white.

Produced by Sol Lesser. Directed by Bernard Vorhaus. Screenplay by Bernard Schubert, Ian Hunter, Herbert Clyde Lewis. Photographed by Charles Schoenbaum. Edited by Arthur Hilton.

Starring Bobby Breen (Tony), Leo Carrillo (Carlo), Henry Armetta (Beppo), Lee Patrick (Stella), Rosina Galli (Angelina), Tommy Bupp (Rudolph), George Humbert (Pietro), Leon Belasco (Luigi), Pua Lani, Leonard Kilbrick, Jackie Salling, Ronnie Paige, Milo Marchetti, Jr. (Tony's Gang), Slicker the Seal (Himself).

An orphan, adopted by a kindly fisherman, runs away when the man's sister and her spoiled son move in.

306 *Fit for a King* (1937)

Comedy. Running time: 73 minutes. Black and white. Available on videocassette.

Produced by David L. Loew. Directed by Edward Sedgwick. Screenplay by Richard Flournoy. Photographed by Paul C. Vogel. Edited by Jack Ogilvie.

Starring Joe E. Brown (Virgil Jones), Helen Mack (Jane Hamilton), Paul Kelly (Briggs), Harry Davenport (Archduke Julio), Halliwell Hobbes (Count Strunsky), John Qualen (Otto), Donald Briggs (Prince Michael), Frank Reicher (Kurtz), Russell Hicks (Hardwick), Charles Trowbridge (Marshall).

When a reporter is assigned to interview an aged duke, he falls for the crown princess and gets mixed up in a murder plot.

307 *Five Came Back* (1939)

Drama. Running time: 75 minutes. Black and white. Available on videocassette.

Produced by Robert Sisk. Directed by John Farrow. Screenplay by Jerry Cady, Dalton Trumbo, and Nathaniel West (adapted from a story by Richard Carroll). Photographed by Nicholas Musuraca. Edited by Harry Marker. Music by Roy Webb.

Starring Chester Morris (Bill), Lucille Ball (Peggy), Wendy Barrie (Alice), John Carradine (Crimp), Allen Jenkins (Peter), Joseph Calleia (Vasquez), C. Aubrey Smith (Professor Henry Spengler), Kent Taylor (Joe), Patric Knowles

(Judson Ellis), Elisabeth Risdon (Martha Spengler), Casey Johnson (Tommy), Dick Hogan (Larry).

A plane with twelve passengers crashes, but can only bring five back. Conflicts as to which five shall return safely while the remaining persons must face headhunters.

Note: Remade as *Back to Eternity* by the same director.

Review: "Exceptionally well-made adventure yarn. Looks like a solid click" — *Variety.*

308 *Fixer Dugan* (1939) Drama. Running time: 68 minutes. Black and white.

Produced by Cliff Reid. Directed by Lew Landers. Screenplay by Paul Yawitz and Bert Granet (adapted from a play by H.C. Potter). Photographed by J. Roy Hunt. Edited by Henry Berman.

Starring Lee Tracy (Charlie Dugan), Virginia Weidler (Terry), Peggy Shannon (Adgie), Bradley Page (Owner Barvin), William Edmunds (Smiley), Ed Gargan (Jake), Jack Arnold (Darlowe), Rita LaRoy (Patsy), Irene Franklin (Jane).

A circus fixer is given the custody of a little girl when her mother is killed in a circus accident.

Note: The lions in this film were fed ice cream cones between takes to keep them in a good humor. British title: *Double Daring.*

309 *Flaming Gold* (1934) Drama. Running time: 54 minutes. Black and white.

Produced by Merian C. Cooper. Directed by Ralph Ince. Screenplay by Malcolm Stuart Boylan and John Goodrich (based on a story by Houston Branch). Photographed by Charles Rosher. Edited by George Crone.

Starring Bill Boyd (Dan Manton), Pat O'Brien (Ben Lear), Mae Clarke (Claire Arnold), Rollo Lloyd (Banning), Helen Ware (Tess).

A group of oil magnates try strong-arming two wildcatters out of the desert, but will not divulge a reason.

310 *Flight for Freedom* (1943) Adventure. Running time: 101 minutes. Black and white.

Produced by David Hempstead. Directed by Lothar Mendes. Screenplay by Oliver H.P. Garrett, S.K. Lauren and Jane Murfin (based on a story by Horace McCoy). Photographed by Lee Garmes. Edited by Roland Gross. Music by Roy Webb.

Starring Rosalind Russell (Toni Carter), Fred MacMurray (Randy Britton), Herbert Marshall (Paul Turner), Eduardo Ciannelli (Johnny Salvini), Walter Kingsford (Adm. Graves), Damian O'Flynn (Pete), Jack Carr (Bill), Matt McHugh (Mac), Richard Loo (Mr. Yokohata), Charles Lung, Bud McTaggart, Donald Dillaway, Eddie Dew (Fliers).

An aviatrix falls for an aviator but soon surpasses him in her exploits.

Note: Based on the life of Amelia Earhart. Earhart's widower was paid $7,500 for permission to use his wife's story, with the understanding that her name not be used.

311 *Flight from Glory* (1937) Adventure. Running time: 66 minutes. Black and white.

Produced by Robert Sisk. Directed by Lew Landers. Screenplay by David Silverstein and John Twist (based on a story by Robert Andrews). Photographed by Nicholas Musuraca. Edited by Harry Marker.

Starring Chester Morris (Smith), Whitney Bourne (Lee Wilson), Onslow Stevens (Ellis), Van Heflin (George Wilson), Richard Lane (Hanson), Paul Guilfoyle (Jones), Solly Ward (Itzky), Douglas Walton (Hilton), Walter Miller (Old Timer), Rita LaRoy (Molly), Pasha Khan (Pepi).

A group of pilots accepts a dangerous mission of flying supplies from the Andrean mountains.

312 *Flood Tide* (1935) Romantic drama. Running time: 63 minutes. Black and white.

Produced by Julius Hagen. Directed by John Baxter. Screenplay by Ernest Anson Dryer.

Starring George Carney (Captain Buckett), Peggy Novak (Mabel), Leslie Hatton (Ted), Janice Adair (Betty), Wilson Coleman (Ben Salter), Minnie Rayner (Sarah), Mark Daly (Scotty).

A lockkeeper's son falls for a bargeman's daughter.

313 *The Flying Deuces* (1939)

Comedy. Running time: 67 minutes. Black and white and colorized. Available on videocassette.

Produced by Boris Morros. Directed by A. Edward Sutherland. Screenplay by Ralph Spence, Alf Schiller, Charles Rogers, Harry Langdon. Photographed by Art Lloyd. Edited by Jack Dennis.

Starring Stan Laurel and Oliver Hardy (Themselves), Jean Parker (Georgette), Reginald Gardiner (Francois), Charles Middleton (Commandant), Jean Del Val (Sergeant), James Finlayson (Jailer), Richard Cramer (Truck Driver), Michael Visaroff (Innkeeper), Christy Cabanne, Sam Lufkin, Arthur Housman (Bits).

In order to forget a failed love, Oliver decides to join the Foreign Legion and insists Stan accompany him. When they find the rigors of Legion life too taxing, they decide to escape.

Note: Director Sutherland did not enjoy working with Stan Laurel, stating, "I'd rather work with a tarantula." Screenwriter Langdon is the famed silent movie comic. This was a partial reworking of the duo's 1931 Hal Roach production *Beau Hunks,* released by MGM. Hardy sings "Shine On Harvest Moon."

314 *Flying Devils* (1933)

Drama. Running time: 60 minutes. Black and white.

Produced by David Lewis. Directed by Russell Birdwell. Screenplay by Byron Morgan and Louis Stevens (based on a story by Stevens). Photographed by Nicholas Musuraca. Edited by Arthur Roberts.

Starring Arline Judge (Ann Hardy), Bruce Cabot (Ace Murray), Eric Linden (Bud Murray), Ralph Bellamy (Speed Hardy), Cliff Edwards (Screwy), Frank LaRue (Kearns), June Brewster (Bit as Girlfriend).

The ups and downs of an aerial act's members.

Note: British title: *The Flying Circus.*

315 *Flying Down to Rio* (1933)

Musical. Running time: 89 minutes. Black and white. Available on videocassette.

Produced by Lou Brock for Merian C. Cooper. Directed by Thorton Freeland. Screenplay by Cyril Hume and H.W. Hanemann. Photographed by J. Roy Hunt. Edited by Jack Kitchin. Music by Max Steiner, Vincent Youmans.

Songs: "The Carioca," "Music Makes Me," "Orchids in the Moonlight," "Flying Down to Rio."

Starring Dolores Del Rio (Belinha de Rezende), Gene Raymond (Roger Bond), Raul Roulien (Julio Rberio), Ginger Rogers (Honey Hale), Fred Astaire (Fred Ayers), Blanche Frederici (Dona Elena), Walter Walker (Senor de Rezende), Etta Moten (Singer), Maurice Black, Roy D'Arcy, Armand Kaliz (Three Greeks), Paul Porcasi (Mayor), Reginald Barlow (Banker), Eric Blore (Butterball the Headwaiter), Franklin Pangborn (Hammersmith the Hotel Manager), Luis Alberni (Carioca Casino Manager), Jack Goode, Jack Rice, Eddie Borden (Yankee Clippers), Ray Cooke (Banjo Player), Gino Corrado (Messenger), Lucile Browne and Mary Kornman (Girlfriends of Belinha), Clarence Muse (Caddy), The American Clippers Band (Themselves).

A dance band achieves great success in Rio de Janeiro.

Note: Astaire and Rogers' first film together. Astaire's second film and first for RKO. Rogers' part originally slated for Dorothy Jordan, who bowed out when she married Merian C. Cooper. Last screen work of composer Youmans, who was suffering from incurable T.B. and would soon move to Denver, where he died in 1946.

Oscar nomination: The song "The Carioca."

Review: "...an irresistible period piece"—Leslie Halliwell; "Its main point is the screen promise of Fred Astaire"—*Variety.*

316 *Flying Fifty-five* (1939) Drama. Running time: 72 minutes. Black and white. A British production for Admiral films, released by RKO.

Produced by Victor M. Greene. Directed by Reginald Denham. Screenplay by Greene, Vernon Clancey, and Kenneth Horne (based on the novel by Edgar Wallace). Photographed by Ernest Palmer. Edited by Andrew Buchanan.

Starring Derrick De Marney (Bill Urquart), Nancy Burne (Stella Barrington), Marcus Goring (Charles Barrington), John Warwick (Jebson), Peter Gawthorne (Jonas Urquart), D.A. Clarke-Smith (Jacques).

A jockey hooks up with a crooked racehorse owner.

317 *Flying Fool* (1929) Comedy. 73 minutes. Black and white.

Directed by Tay Garnett. Screenplay by James Gleason (based on the story by Elliot Clawson). Photographed by Arthur Miller.

Starring William Boyd, Marie Prevost, Russell Gleason, Tom O'Brien, James Gleason.

Two brothers battle over the affections of a nightclub singer.

318 *The Flying Irishman* (1939) Biographical drama. Running time: 70 minutes. Black and white.

Produced by Pandro S. Berman. Directed by Leigh Jason. Screenplay by Ernest Pagano and Dalton Trumbo. Photographed by J. Roy Hunt. Edited by Arthur Roberts.

Starring Douglas "Wrong Way" Corrigan (Himself), Paul Kelly (Butch), Robert Armstrong (Joe Alden), Donald MacBride (Thompson), Eddie Quillan (Henry), J.M. Kerrigan (Mr. Corrigan), Dorothy Peterson (Mrs. Corrigan), Gene Reynolds (Corrigan as Young Boy), Scotty Beckett (Henry as a Young Boy), Joyce Compton (Sally), Dorothy Appleby (Maybelle), Minor Watson (Personnel Manager).

True story of Corrigan, pilot who acquired his nickname by landing in Ireland when attempting to fly cross-country.

Note: Corrigan's only screen appearance.

319 *Flying Leathernecks* (1951) War. Running time: 102 minutes. Color. Available on videocassette.

Produced by Ed Grainger for Howard Hughes. Directed by Nicholas Ray. Screenplay by James Edward Grant (based on a story by Kenneth Gamet). Photographed by William Snyder. Edited by Sherman Todd. Music by Roy Webb and Constantin Bakaleinkoff.

Starring John Wayne (Kirby), Robert Ryan (Griffin), Don Taylor (Blithe), William Harrigan (Curan), Janis Carter (Joan), Jay C. Flippen (Clancy), Carleton Young (McAllister), Brett King (Lt. Stark), Maurice Jara (Vegay), Steve Flagg (Jorgensen), Barry Kelly (General), Sam Edwards (Junior).

Two marine officers on Guadalcanal must deal with their own rivalry while fighting the Japanese.

Note: The first film for RKO where Howard Hughes took credit. Wayne was paid $30,000 for his performance.

320 *Follow Me Quietly* (1949) Mystery. Running time: 60 minutes. Black and white.

Produced by Herman Schlom. Directed by Richard Fleischer. Screenplay by Lillie Hayward (from a story by Anthony Mann and Francis Rosenwald). Photographed by Robert De Grasse. Edited by Elmo Williams.

Starring William Lundigan (Grant),

Fred Astaire and Ginger Rogers in *Follow the Fleet.*

Dorothy Patrick (Ann), Jeff Corey (Colins), Nestor Paiva (Benny), Charles D. Brown (Mulvaney), Paul Guilfoyle (Overbeck), Edwin Max (The Judge), Frank Ferguson (McGill), Marlo Dwyer (Waitress), Michael Brandon (Dixon), Doug Spencer (Phony Judge).

A mysterious killer, known only as The Judge, kills anyone whom he considers worthless.

321 *Follow the Fleet* (1936) Musical. Running time: 110 minutes. Black and white. Available on videocassette.

Produced by Pandro S. Berman. Directed by Mark Sandrich. Screenplay by

Dwight Taylor and Allan Scott (based on the play *Shore Leave* by Hubert Osborne). Photographed by David Abel. Music by Max Steiner, composed by Irving Berlin. Edited by Henry Berman.

Songs: "Let's Face the Music and Dance," "We Saw the Sea," "I'm Putting All My Eggs in One Basket," "But Where Are You?" "I'd Rather Lead a Band," "Let Yourself Go," and "Get Thee Behind Me Satan."

Starring Fred Astaire (Bake), Ginger Rogers (Sherry Martin), Randolph Scott (Bilge), Harriet Hilliard (Connie Martin), Astrid Allwyn (Iris Manning), Harry Beresford (Captain Hickey), Russell Hicks (Jim Nolan), Brooks Benedict (Sullivan), Ray Mayer (Dopey), Lucille Ball (Kitty), Jack Randall (Williams), Betty Grable, Tony Martin, Frank Jenks (Bits).

Sailors on shore leave romance two female singers.

Note: A remake of the 1925 Richard Barthelmess silent *Shore Leave*, which was once before filmed as a musical in 1930, entitled *Hit the Deck*.

Reviews: "(Randolph) Scott is about as funny as a rain-out at a ballgame" — *The Motion Picture Guide;* "The running time is way overboard" — *Variety*.

322 *Footlight Fever* (1941) Comedy. Running time: 69 minutes. Black and white.

Produced by Howard Benedict. Directed by Irving Reis. Screenplay by Ian Hunter and Bert Granet (based on a story by Granet). Photographed by Robert De Grasse. Edited by Theron Warth.

Starring Alan Mowbray (Avery), Donald MacBride (Crandall), Elisabeth Risdon (Hattie), Lee Bonnell (Carter), Elyse Knox (Eileen), Charles Quigley (Spike), Bradley Page (Harvey).

Two men try, through unscrupulous means, raising money to put on a show.

Note: This film lost $40,000.

Review: "...an old story which, if it were any moldier, would crawl away" — *The Motion Picture Guide*.

323 *Footlight Varieties* (1951) Musical variety. Running time: 77 minutes.

Jack Paar hosts a collection of novelty acts including comedy bits by Red Buttons and Leon Errol, as well as several musical numbers.

324 *Forever and a Day* (1943) Historical drama. Running time: 104 minutes. Black and white. Available on videocassette.

Produced and directed by Rene Clair, Ed Goulding, Sir Cedric Hardwicke, Frank Lloyd, Victor Saville, Robert Stevenson, and Herbert Wilcox. Screenplay by Charles Bennett, C.S. Forester, Lawrence Hazard, Michael Hogan, W.P. Lipscomb, Alice Duer Miller, John Van Druten, Alan Campbell, Peter Godfrey, S.M. Herzig, Christopher Isherwood, Gene Lockhart, R.C. Sheriff, Claudine West, Norman Corwin, Jack Harfield, James Hilton, Emmet Lavery, Fredrick Lonsdale, Donald Ogden Stewart, Keith Winters. Photographed by Robert De Grasse, Lee Garmes, Russell Metty, Nicholas Musuraca. Edited by Elmo J. Williams and George Crone. Music by Anthony Collins.

Starring Anna Neagle, Ray Milland, Claude Raines, C. Aubrey Smith, Dame May Whitty, Gene Lockhart, Ray Bolger, Edmund Gwenn, Lumsden Hare, Stuart Robertson, Claude McAllister, Ben Webster, Alan Edmiston, Patric Knowles, Halliwell Hobbes, Helena Pickard, Doris Lloyd, Lionel Belmore, Louis Bissiner, Charles Coburn, Ian Hunter, Charles Laughton, Montague Love, Reginald Owen, Sir Cedric Hardwicke, Noel Madison, Buster Keaton, Edward Everett Horton, Wendy Barrie, Ida Lupino, Brian Aherne, Eric Blore, June Duprez, Merle Oberon, Roland Young, Kay Deslys, Richard Haydn, Una O'Connor, Nigel Bruce, Gladys Cooper, Robert Cummings, Elsa Lanchester, Robert Coote, Donald Crisp, Kent Smith, June Lockhart, Billy Bevan, Herbert Marshall, Victor McLaglen, Reginald Gardiner, Arthur Treacher, Anna Lee, Cecil Kellaway, Gerald Oliver Smith, Charlie Hall, Clyde Cook.

The history of a London house from 1804 to the blitz in World War II.

Note: Made for war charities by a combination of European talents in Hollywood. Notable as having the longest list of credited screenwriters in movie history.

Reviews: "One of the most brilliant casts of modern times has been assembled to bolster up one of the poorest pictures" — James Agee; "... superbly crafted, acted, and directed" — *The Motion Picture Guide.*

325 *Fort Apache* (1948) Western.
Running time: 127 minutes. Black and white and colorized. Available on videocassette.

Produced by John Ford and Merian C. Cooper. Directed by Ford with Cliff Lyons. Screenplay by Frank S. Nugent (based on the story *Massacre* by James Warner Bellah). Photographed by Archie Stout. Edited by Jack Murray.

Starring Henry Fonda (Lt. Col. Owen Thursday), John Wayne (Capt. Kirby York), Shirley Temple (Philadelphia), Ward Bond (Michael O'Rourke), John Agar (Mickey), George O'Brien (Capt. Sam Collingwood), Irene Rich (Mary O'Rourke), Victor McLaglen (Mulcahey), Anna Lee (Mrs. Collingwood), Pedro Armendariz (Beaufort), Guy Kibbee (Dr. Wilkens), Grant Withers (Silas Meachem), Jack Pennick (Sgt. Shattuck), Dick Foran (Sgt. Qyincannon), Mae Marsh (Martha Gates), Hank Worden, Frank Ferguson, Mickey Simpson (Bits).

A demoted cavalry commander is sent to the title fort to fight Indians.

Note: Latter-day Oscar winner Ben Johnson was Duke's stunt double. Agar's first film. This movie netted a profit of nearly a half million dollars.

Reviews: "Shirley Temple and her husband handle the love interest as though they were sharing a soda fountain special, and there is enough Irish comedy to make me wish Cromwell had done a more thorough job" — James Agee; "Stretches of it meander and there is some careless mismatching of shots due to haste, but much of it is first rate Ford..." — Tag Gallagher, *John Ford: The Man and His Films.*

326 *Forty Naughty Girls* (1937)
Mystery. Running time: 63 minutes. Black and white.

Produced by William Sistrom. Directed by Edward F. Cline. Screenplay by John Grey (based on a story by Stuart Palmer). Photographed by Russell Metty. Edited by John Lockert. Music by Roy Webb.

Starring James Gleason (Oscar Piper), Zasu Pitts (Hildegarde), Marjorie Lord (Joan), George Shelley (Bert), Joan Woodbury (Rita Marlowe), Frank M. Thomas (Jeff), Tom Kennedy (Casey).

Oscar and Hildegarde solve the backstage murder of a press agent.

Note: Last entry in the Withers/Piper mystery series.

Review: "Decidedly tame, and won't cause much ripple on either side of duals, where it'll undoubtedly land" — *Variety.*

327 *The Fountain* (1934) Drama.
Running time: 85 minutes. Black and white.

Produced by Pandro S. Berman. Directed by John Cromwell. Screenplay by Jane Murfin and Samuel Hoffenstein (based on a novel by Charles Morgan). Photographed by Henry Gerard. Edited by William Morgan. Music by Max Steiner.

Starring Ann Harding (Julie von Narwitz), Brian Aherne (Lewis Alison), Paul Lukas (Rupert von Narwitz), Jean Hersholt (Baron Von Leyden), Ralph Forbes (Ballater), Violet Kemble-Cooper (Baroness Von Leyden), Sara Haden

(Sophie), Richard Abbott (Allard), Rudolph Amendt (Goof), Barbara Barondess (Goof's Wife), Betty Alden (Allard's wife), Ian Wolfe (Van Arkel).

When a German officer leaves his wife and goes off to fight in WW1, she falls in love with a dashing Englishman. When the soldier returns home missing an arm, the woman guiltily nurses him, but he soon senses what had transpired while he was away.

328 *Four Jacks and a Jill* (1941) Musical. Running time: 67 minutes. Black and white.

Produced by John Twist. Directed by Jack Hively. Screenplay by Twist (story by Monte Brice, suggested by *The Viennese Charmer* by W. Carey Wonderly). Photographed by Russell Metty. Edited by George Hively. Songs by Mort Greene and Harry Revel.

Songs: "I'm in Good Shape for the Shape I'm In," "You Got Your Way and I'll Go Crazy," "I Haven't a Thing to Wear," "Wherever You Are," "Boogie Woogie Conga."

Starring Ray Bolger (Nifty), Anne Shirley (Nine), June Havoc (Opal), Desi Arnaz (Steve), Jack Durant (Noodle), Eddie Foy, Jr. (Happy), Fritz Feld (Hoople), Henry Daniell (Bobo), Jack Briggs (Nat), William Blees (Eddie), Robert Smith (Joe), Fortunio Bonanova (Mike).

A nightclub band is in a fix when its female singer quits.

329 *Framed* (1930) Drama. Running time: 62 minutes. Black and white.

Produced by William LeBaron. Directed by George Archainbaud. Screenplay by Paul Schofield and Wallace Smith. Photographed by Leo Tover. Edited by Jack Kitchin.

Starring Evelyn Brent (Rose Manning), Regis Toomey (Jim MacArthur), Ralf Harolde (Chuck), Maurice Black (Bing), William Holden (Inspector MacArthur), Robert Emmett O'Connor (Sgt. Schultz), Eddie Kane (Headwaiter).

A mobster's daughter is out to get revenge on a police inspector, but finds he is the father of her lover.

Note: Actor Holden is no relation to the star of *Sunset Boulevard* and *Network*. That William Holden made his film debut in 1939. This William Holden was primarily a silent screen actor who made few talkies, and died in 1932 at the age of 60. The 1947 and 1974 films by this same title are not remakes.

330 *Freckles* (1935) Drama. Running time: 69 minutes. Black and white.

Produced by Pandro S. Berman. Directed by Edward Killy. Screenplay by Dorothy Yost. Photographed by Robert De Grasse. Edited by Desmond Marquette.

Starring Tom Brown (Freckles), Virginia Weidler (Laurie Lou), Carol Stone (Mary), Lumsden Hare (McLean), James Bush (Barton), Dorothy Peterson (Mrs. Duncan), Addison Richards (Jack Carter).

A young man finds a job at a lumber camp and becomes a town hero by saving a little girl.

331 *The French Line* (1954) Musical. Running time: 102 minutes. Color. Available on videocassette.

Produced by Ed Grainger. Directed by Lloyd Bacon. Screenplay by Mary Loos and Richard Sale (based on a story by Matty Kemp and Isabel Dawn). Photographed by Harry Wild. Edited by Robert Ford. Music by Andre Joseph Myrow, Ralph Blane, and Robert Wells, directed by Constantin Bakaleinkoff.

Songs: "Comment Allez-Vous," "Well I'll Be Switched," "Any Gal from Texas," "What Is This That I Feel," "With a Kiss," "By Madame Fuelle," "Wait Till You See Paris," "Poor Andre," "The French Line." Note: The latter song was cut from the final release print.

Starring Jane Russell (Mary Carson), Gilbert Roland (Pierre), Arthur Hunnicutt (Waco), Mary McCarty (Annie Farrell), Joyce MacKenzie (Myrtle

Brown), Paul Corday (Celeste), Scott Elliott (Bill Harris), Craig Stevens (Phil Barton), Laurel Elliot (Katherine Hodges), Steven Geray (Francois), John Wengraf (1st Mate), Barbara Darrow (Donna Adams), Kim Novak (Model), Joi Lansing (Showgirl).

A Texas oil heiress finds a husband in France.

Note: This film was shot in 3-D, with the ads proclaiming that Ms. Russell will "knock *both* your eyes out."

Review: "Since no Catholic can, with a clear conscience, attend such an immoral movie, we feel it is our solemn duty to forbid our Catholic people under penalty of moral sin to attend this presentation" — Archbishop Ritter of St. Louis.

332 *Friends and Lovers* (1931)

Drama. Running time: 66 minutes. Black and white.

Produced by William LeBaron. Director Victor Schertzinger. Screenplay by Jane Murfin (based on the novel *The Sphinx Has Spoken* by Maurice de Korba). Photographed by J. Roy Hunt. Music by Max Steiner.

Starring Adolphe Menjou (Capt. Roberts), Lily Damita (Alva Sangrito), Erich Von Stroheim (Victor Sangrito), Laurence Olivier (Lt. Nichols), Hugh Herbert (McNewllis), Kay Delsys (Waitress).

A society wife blackmails men from India with the help of her unscrupulous husband.

Note: Screenplay often incorrectly credited to Wallace Smith.

Review: "Dumb sentimental romance..." — *Variety.*

333 *From This Day Forward*

(1946) Drama. Running time: 95 minutes. Black and white.

Produced by William L. Pereira. Directed by John Barry. Screenplay by Garson Kanin, Edith Sommer, Hugo Butler, and Charles Schnee (based on the novel *All Brides Are Beautiful* by Thomas

Bell). Photographed by George Barnes. Edited by Frank Doyle.

Starring Mark Stevens (Bill Cummings), Joan Fontaine (Susan), Rosemary DeCamp (Martha), Henry Morgan (Hank), Wally Brown (Jake), Arline Judge (Margie), Renny McEvoy (Charlie), Bobby Driscoll (Timmy), Queenie Smith (Mrs. Beesley), Doreen McCann (Barbara), Mary Treen (Alice), Ellen Corby (Mother).

Upon returning home from WWII, a veteran and his wife recall their struggles during the Depression.

Note: Actor Henry Morgan later became billed as Harry Morgan.

Review: "Hollywood professionalism makes this more memorable than it may sound" — Leslie Halliwell.

334 *The Fugitive* (1947) Drama.

Running time: 104 minutes. Black and white. Available on videocassette.

Produced by John Ford and Merian C. Cooper. Directed by Ford. Screenplay by Dudley Nichols (based on the novel *The Power and the Glory* by Graham Greene). Photographed by Gabriel Figueroa. Edited by Jack Murray.

Starring Henry Fonda (Fugitive), Dolores Del Rio (Mexican Woman), Pedro Armendariz (Police Lieutenant), Ward Bond (El Gringo), Leo Carillo (Chief of Police), J. Carrol Naish (Police Spy), Robert Armstrong (Police Sergeant), John Qualen (Doctor), Chris-Pin Martin (Organ Player).

A priest is on the run for his life in an anti-Catholic country.

Note: Remade for TV as *The Power and the Glory* with Laurence Olivier.

Reviews: "A powerful passion play" — *The Motion Picture Guide;* "...slow and rather boring..." — Leslie Halliwell; "The most pretentious travesty of a literary work since *For Whom the Bell Tolls*" — Richard Winnington.

335 *Fugitives for a Night* (1938)

Mystery. Running time: 63 minutes. Black and white.

Produced by Lou Lusty. Directed by Leslie Goodwins. Screenplay by Dalton Trumbo (based on a story by Richard Wormser). Photographed by Frank Redman. Edited by Desmond Marquette.

Starring Frank Albertson (Matt Ryan), Eleanor Lynn (Ann Wray), Allan Lane (Nelson), Bradley Page (Poole), Adrienne Ames (Eileen Baker), Jonathan Hale (Captain), Russell Hicks (Tenwright), Paul Guilfoyle (Monk).

When a studio exec is murdered, a fallen actor is suspected.

336 Full Confession (1939) Drama. Running time: 72 minutes. Black and white.

Produced by Robert Sisk. Directed by John Farrow. Screenplay by Jerry Cady (based on a story by Leo Birinski). Photographed by J. Roy Hunt. Edited by Harry Marker.

Starring Victor McLaglen (McGinnis), Sally Eilers (Molly), Joseph Calleia (Father Loma), Barry Fitzgerald (Michael O'Keefe), Elisabeth Risdon (Norah O'Keefe), Adele Pearce (Laura Mahoney), Malcolm McTaggart (Frank O'Keefe), John Bleifer (Weaver), William Haade (Moore), George Humbert (Mercantinio).

A priest is accused of murder.

Review: "Rather interesting, but not strong enough for the upper bracket"— *Variety*.

337 Fun and Fancy Free (1947) Animated feature. Running time: 73 minutes. Color. Available on videocassette. A Walt Disney Production released by RKO.

Produced by Walt Disney. Directed by Jack Kinney, W.O. Roberts, Hamilton Luske. Live action directed by William Morgan. Screenplay by Homer Brightman, Harry Reeves, Ted Sears, Lance Nolley, Eldon Dedini, Tom Oreb. Live action photographed by Charles P. Boyle. Edited by Jack Bachom.

Starring Edgar Bergen with Mortimer Snerd and Charlie McCarthy, Luana Patten, and the Voices of Dinah Shore, Anita Gordon, Cliff Edwards, Billy Gilbert, Clarence Nash, The King's Men, The Dinning Sisters, and The Starlighters.

Two Disney shorts strung together with Jiminy Cricket as a unifying thread. The first episode, narrated by Shore, tells of Bongo the Circus Bear who escapes to the wilderness. The second features Bergen and his dummies as well as Mickey Mouse, Donald Duck, and Goofy.

338 Gambling House (1950) Drama. Running time: 80 minutes. Black and white.

Produced by Warren Duff. Directed by Ted Tetzlaff. Screenplay by Marvin Borofsky and Allen Rivkin (based on a story by Erwin Gelsey). Photographed by Harry J. Wild. Edited by Roland Gross.

Starring Victor Mature (Marc Fury), Terry Moore (Lynn Warren), William Bendix (Joe Farrow), Zachary A. Charles (Willie), Basil Ruysdale (Judge Ravinek), Donald Randolph (Lloyd Crane), Damian O'Flynn (Ralph Douglas), Cleo Moore (Sally), Ann Doran (Della), Eleanor Audley (Mrs. Livingston), Gloria Winters (B.J. Warren), Don Haggerty (Sharky), William E. Green (Doctor), Jack Kruschen (Bit).

An immigrant gambler is threatened with deportation after becoming involved with a murder.

339 Game of Death (1945). Suspense. Running time: 72 minutes. Black and white.

Produced by Herman Schlom. Directed by Robert Wise. Screenplay by Norman Houston (based on a story by Richard Connell). Photographed by J. Roy Hunt. Edited by J.R. Whittridge.

Starring John Loder (Rainsford), Audrey Long (Ellen), Edgar Barrier (Krieger), Russell Wade (Robert), Russell Hicks (Whitey), Jason Robards, Sr. (Captain), Gene Roth (Pleshke), Noble Johnson (Carib).

A maniacal hunter of humans terrorizes a trio on his island.

Note: A remake of the 1932 RKO feature "The Most Dangerous Game." Johnson repeats his role from the 1932 original. Fay Wray's screams from the original are also used.

340 *Gay Diplomat* (1931) Drama. Running time: 66 minutes. Black and white.

Directed by Richard Boleslavsky. Screenplay by Doris Anderson (based on a story by Benn W. Levy). Photographed by Leo Tover.

Starring Ivan Lebedeff (Capt. Orloff), Genevieve Tobin (Diana Dorchy), Betty Compson (Baroness Corri), Ilka Chase (Blinis), Purnell Pratt (Co. Gorin), Rita LaRoy (Natalie), Colin Campbell (Gamble).

A Russian officer combats a Mata Hari type during World War I.

Review: "A picture almost without a merit" — *Variety.*

341 *The Gay Divorcee* (1934) Musical. Running time: 107 minutes. Black and white. Available on videocassette.

Produced by Pandro S. Berman. Directed by Mark Sandrich. Screenplay by George Marion, Jr., Dorothy Yost, and Edward Kaufman (based on the musical play *The Gay Divorcee* by Dwight Taylor and Cole Porter). Musical adaptation by Kenneth Webb and Samuel Hoffenstein. Photographed by David Abel. Edited by William Hamilton. Music by Max Steiner. Songs by Con Conrad and Herb Magidson, Harry Revel and Mack Gordon, and Cole Porter.

Songs: "The Continental," "Don't Let It Bother You," "Let's K-nock K-nees," "A Needle in a Haystack," "Night and Day."

Starring Fred Astaire (Guy Holden), Ginger Rogers (Mimi Glossop), Alice Brady (Hortense), Edward Everett Horton (Egbert Fitzgerald), Erik Rhodes (Rodolfo Tonetti), Eric Blore (Waiter), Lillian Miles (Hotel Guest), Charles Coleman (Valet), Betty Grable (Hotel Guest), William Austin (Cyril), R.R. Clive (Customs Inspector), Charlie Hall (Call Boy at Dock).

A woman seeking a divorce hires a correspondent to claim infidelity.

Note: Astaire and Rogers' first starring film together. Original title was changed when Hayes Office stated that divorces were not happy, although the divorcees may be. Producer Berman bought the stage property for only $20,000.

Oscar: Best song, "The Continental."

Oscar nominations: Best Picture and Best Musical Adaptation.

Review: "Cinch box office anywhere" — *Variety.*

342 *The Gay Falcon* (1941) Mystery. Running time: 67 minutes. Black and white.

Produced by Howard Benedict. Directed by Irving Reis. Screenplay by Lynn Root and Frank Fenton (based on the character created by Michael Arlen). Photographed by Nicholas Musuraca. Edited by George Crone.

Starring George Sanders (Falcon), Wendy Barrie (Helen Reed), Allen Jenkins (Goldy), Anne Hunter (Elinor), Gladys Cooper (Maxine), Ed Brophy (Bates), Arthur Shields (Waldeck), Damian O'Flynn (Weber), Turhan Bey (Retana), Eddie Dunn (Grimes), Lucille Gleason (Mrs. Gardiner), Willie Fung (Jerry), Hans Conried (Herman), Jimmy Conlin (Bartender), Bobby Barber (Waiter), Joey Ray (Orchestra Leader), Bonnie Bonnell (Bit).

An amateur detective goes after a gang of jewel thieves.

Note: First of the Falcon mysteries. Similar to The Saint, which Sanders played in an RKO series that ran from 1938 to 1941. Saint creator Louis Charteris sued upon seeing this film, believing it to be a rip-off of his sleuth creation. Sanders would pass the baton to real-life brother Tom Conway after a few more films (see *The Falcon's Brother*).

343 *Genius at Work* (1946) Comedy. Running time: 61 minutes. Black and white.

Produced by Herman Schlom. Directed by Leslie Goodwins. Screenplay by Robert E. Kent and Monte Brice. Photographed by Robert De Grasse and Vernon Walker. Edited by Marvin Coil.

Starring Wally Brown (Jerry), Alan Carney (Mike), Anne Jeffreys (Ellen), Lionel Atwill (Marsh), Bela Lugosi (Sloane), Marc Cramer (Rick), Ralph Dunn (Gilley), Robert Clarke, Phil Warren, Harry Harvey (Bits).

Two radio detectives turn real sleuths and hunt for a murderer known as The Cobra.

Note: A partial reworking of *Super Sleuth* (RKO, 1937) and Abbott and Costello's *Who Done It?* (Universal, 1942). Brown and Carney's last film as a team, Lugosi's last film for RKO, and Atwill's last film before his sudden death.

344 *George White's Scandals* (1945) Musical. Running time: 95 minutes. Black and white.

Produced by Jack J. Gross, Nat Holt, and George White. Directed by Felix E. Feist. Screenplay by Hugh Wedlock, Howard Snyder, Parke Levy, Howard Green (based on a story by Wedlock and Snuder). Photographed by Robert De Grasse. Edited by Joseph Noriega. Songs by Sammy Fain, Jack Yellen, Gene Krupa, Buddy De Sylva, Leigh Harline.

Songs: "Bolero in the Jungle," "E.H.S.," "Leave Us Leap," "I Want to Bee a Drummer in the Band," "How Did You Get Out of My Dreams," "I Wake Up in the Morning," "Who Killed Vaudeville," "Scandals," "Liza," "Wishing," "Life Is Just a Bowl of Cherries," "Bouquet and Lace."

Starring Joan Davis (Joan Mason), Jack Haley (Jack Williams), Phillip Terry (Tom McGrath), Marrtha Holliday (Jill Marin), Ethel Smith (Singing Organist), Margaret Hamilton (Clarabell), Glenn Tryon (George White), Jane Greer (Billie Randall), Audrey Young (Maxine Manner), Rose Murphy (Hilda), Fritz Feld (Montescu), Beverly Wills (Joan as a child), Rufe Davis (Impersonations), Sid Melton (Songwriter), Florence Lake (mother), Minerva Uceal (Teacher), Neely Edwards (Lord Quimby), Gene Krupa and His Orchestra.

Two Scandals couples get together, but one of the girls disappears before the show.

Comments: "Lively comedy-musical with vaudeville orientations"—Leslie Halliwell; "Slapstick helps hackneyed plot"—Leonard Maltin.

345 *The Ghost Ship* (1943) Suspense. Running time: 69 minutes. Black and white.

Produced by Val Lewton. Directed by Mark Robson. Screenplay by Donald Henderson Clarke. Photographed by Nicholas Musuraca. Edited by John Lockert.

Starring Richard Dix (Captain), Russell Wade (Tom), Edith Barrett (Ellen), Ben Bard (Bowens), Edmund Glover (Sparks), Skelton Knaggs (Finn), Tom Burton (Benson), Steven Winston (Ausman), Robert Bice (Raphael), Lawrence Tierney (Louie), Dewey Robinson (Boats), Charles Lung (Jim).

The captain of a ship is driven insane from his isolation, and takes it out on his third-mate.

Note: Long withheld from release when writers Samuel Golding and Norbert Faulkner believed the producer had stolen their similarly titled play. The court agreed in favor of the writers, and the film was withdrawn.

346 *Gigolette* (1935) Drama. Running time: 70 minutes. Black and white.

Produced by Burt Kelly. Directed by Charles Lamont. Screenplay by Gordon Kahn. Photographed by Joseph Ruttenberg. Edited by William Thompson.

Starring Adrienne Ames (Kay Parrish),

Ralph Bellamy (Terry Gallagher), Donald Cook (Gregg Emerson), Robert Armstrong (Chuck Ahearn), Harold Waldridge (Ginsy), Robert T. Haines (Emerson), Grace Hampton (Mrs. Emerson), Milton Douglas Orchestra.

A society lady, hit by the Depression, must now seek employment; she finds work as the title character in a gangster's nightclub.

Note: British title: *Night Club.*

347 *Gildersleeve on Broadway*

(1943) Comedy. Running time: 65 minutes. Black and white.

Produced by Herman Schlom. Directed by Gordon Douglas. Screenplay by Robert E. Kent. Photographed by Jack MacKenzie. Edited by Les Millbrook.

Starring Harold Peary (Gildersleeve), Billie Burke (Mrs. Chandler), Claire Carleton (Francine Gray), Richard LeGrand (Peavey), Freddie Mercer (Leroy), Ann Doran (Matilda), Hobart Cavannaugh (Homer), Lillian Randolph (Birdie).

Gildersleeve is pursued by several women in the Big Apple.

Note: Based on the popular radio character.

348 *Gildersleeve's Bad Day*

(1943) Comedy. Running time: 62 minutes. Black and white.

Produced by Herman Schlom. Directed by Gordon Douglas. Screenplay by Jack Townley. Photographed by Jack MacKenzie. Edited by Les Millbrook.

Starring Harold Peary (Gildersleeve), Jane Darwell (Aunt Emma), Nancy Gates (Margie), Charles Arnt (Judge Hooker), Freddie Mercer (Leroy), Russell Wade (Jimmy), Lillian Randolph (Birdie), Frank Jenks (Al), Douglas Fowley (Louie), Alan Carney (Toad), Grant Withers (Henry Potter), Harold Landon (George Peabody), Joan Barclay (Julie Potter), Jack Rice (Bit).

Gildersleeve is the lone holdout in a jury who believe a guilty man has committed the crime for which he's accused.

Note: Based on the popular radio character.

349 *Gildersleeve's Ghost* (1944)

Comedy. Running time: 63 minutes. Black and white.

Produced by Herman Schlom. Directed by Gordon Douglas. Screenplay by Robert E. Kent. Photographed by Jack MacKenzie. Edited by Millbrook.

Starring Harold Peary (Gildersleeve), Marion Martin (Terry Vance), Richard LeGrand (Peavey), Amelita Ward (Marie), Freddie Mercer (Leroy), Margie Stewart (Margie), Emory Parnell (Haley), Frank Reicher (John Wells), Joseph Vitale (Henry Lennox), Lillian Randolph (Birdie), Nicodemus Stewart (Chauncey).

Police commissioner candidate Gildersleeve spends a night in a haunted house, complete with a crooked inventor and a woman who can become invisible.

Note: Last of the Gildersleeve series; based on the popular radio character.

350 *A Girl, a Guy, and a Gob*

(1941) Comedy. Running time: 90 minutes. Black and white. Available on videocassette.

Produced by Harold Lloyd. Directed by Richard Wallace. Screenplay by Frank Ryan and Bert Granet (based on a story by Grover Jones). Photographed by Russell Metty. Edited by George Crone.

Starring George Murphy (Coffee Cup), Lucille Ball (Dot Duncan), Edmond O'Brien (Stephen Herrick), Henry Travers (Abel Martin), Franklin Pangborn (Pet Shop Owner), George Cleveland (Pokey), Kathleen Howard (Jawme), Marguerite Chapman (Cecilia Grange), Lloyd Corrigan (Pigeon), Mady Correll (Cora), Frank McGlynn (Parkington), Doodles Weaver (Eddie), Frank Sully (Salty), Nella Walker (Mrs. Grange), Richard Lane (Recruiting Officer), Irving Bacon (Mr. Merney).

A rich boy falls for a girl who has marriage plans with an obnoxious sailor.

Note: Producer Lloyd is the classic screen comic. British title: *The Navy Steps Out.*

Amelita Ward, in bed, Harold Peary and Nicodemus Stewart in *Gildersleeve's Ghost.*

351 *The Girl and the Gambler*
(1939) Western. Running time: 62
minutes. Black and white.

Produced by Cliff Reid. Directed by
Lew Landers. Screenplay by Joseph Fields
and Clarence Upson Young (based on
the play *The Dove* by Willard Mack).
Photographed by Russell Metty. Edited
by Desmond Marquette.

Starring Leo Carrillo (El Royo), Tim
Holt (Johnny Powell), Steffi Duna (Do-
lores), Donald MacBride (Mike), Chris-
Pin Martin (Pasqual), Edward Raquello
(Rodolfo), Paul Fix (Charlie).

A Mexican Robin Hood tries to woo a
dancer.

352 *Girl Crazy* (1932) Musical
comedy. Running time: 75 minutes.
Black and white.

Produced by William LeBaron. Directed by William Seiter. Screenplay by
Tim Whelan, Herman J. Mankiewicz,
Eddie Welch, and Walter DeLeon (based
on the Broadway play by John McGowan

and Guy Bolton). Photographed by J.
Roy Hunt. Edited by Artie Roberts.
Music by George and Ira Gershwin.

Songs: "Could You Use Me?" "But
Not for Me," "Embraceable You," "Sam
and Delilah," "I Got Rhythm," "Bidin'
My Time," "You've Got What Gets
Me."

Starring Bert Wheeler (Jimmy Dee-
gan), Robert Woolsey (Slick Foster), Ed-
die Quillan (Danny Churchill), Dorothy
Lee (Patsy), Mitzi Green (Tessie Dee-
gan), Kitty Kelly (Kate Foster), Arline
Judge (Molly Gray), Stanley Fields (Lank
Sanders), Lita Chevret (Mary), Chris-Pin
Martin (Pete), Brooks Benedict, Monte
Collins (Bits).

Two city slickers get mixed up in many
misadventures when they taxi west.

Note: Based on the Gershwin musical.
Remade by MGM in 1943 with Mickey
Rooney and Judy Garland, and re-
vamped once again as *When the Boys
Meets the Girls* in 1967.

Review: "A weak sister. After a while
it all becomes too silly"—*Variety.*

353 *The Girl from Mexico* (1939)
Comedy. Running time: 71 minutes.
Black and white.

Produced by Robert Sisk. Directed by
Leslie Goodwins. Screenplay by Lionel
Houser and Joseph Fields (based on a
story by Houser). Photographed by Jack
MacKenzie. Edited by Desmond Mar-
quette.

Starring Lupe Velez (Carmelita),
Donald Woods (Dennis), Leon Errol
(Matt), Linda Hayes (Elizabeth), Donald
MacBride (Renner), Edward Raquello
(Romano), Elisabeth Risdon (Aunt
Della), Ward Bond (Mexican Pete).

A female entertainer from Mexico
becomes a sensation with an ad agency.

Note: Spawned the *Mexican Spitfire*
series.

354 *A Girl in Every Port* (1952)
Comedy. Running time: 86 minutes.
Black and white. Available on videocas-
sette.

Produced by Irwin Allen and Irving
Cummings, Jr. Directed and written by
Chester Erskine (based on the story *They
Sell Sailors Elephants* by Frederick Haz-
litt Brennan). Photographed by Nicholas
Musuraca. Edited by Ralph Dawson.

Starring Groucho Marx (Benny Linn),
Marie Wilson (Jane Sweet), William
Bendix (Tim Dunnevan), Don DeFore
(Bert Sedgwick), Gene Lockhart (Gar-
vey), Dee Hartford (Millicent), Hanley
Stafford (Navy Lieutenant), Teddy Heart
(High Life), Percy Helton (Drive-in
Manager), George E. Stone (Skeezer),
Rodney Wooten (The Pearl).

Two sailors blow their savings on a
racehorse.

Review: "Dismally mechanic farce"—
Leslie Halliwell.

355 *The Girl Most Likely* (1957)
Musical. Running time: 98 minutes.
Color. Available on videocassette. An
RKO-Universal tandem production.

Produced by Stanley Rubin. Directed
by Mitchell Leisen. Screenplay by Devery
Freeman (based on an uncredited story

and screenplay by Paul Jerrico). Photographed by Robert Planck. Edited by
Harry Marker and Dean Harrison. Music
by Hugh Martin and Robert Blaine.

Songs: "The Girl Most Likely," "All
the Colors of the Rainbow," "I Don't
Know What I Want," "Balboa," "We
Gotta Keep Up with the Joneses,"
"Crazy Horse."

Starring Jane Powell (Dodie), Cliff
Robertson (Pete), Keith Andes (Neil),
Kaye Ballard (Marge), Tommy Noonan
(Buzz), Una Merkel (Mom), Kelly Brown
(Sam), Judy Nugent (Pauline), Frank
Cady (Pop), Joseph Kearns (Bit).

A girl must select from among three
suitors.

Note: Musical remake of *Tom, Dick,
and Harry*. Director Leisen's last film.
Sometimes incorrectly listed as RKO's
last production. Jerrico's being uncredited as writer of the original film
caused a problem with Writer's Guild
when this film was released.

356 *Girl of the Port* (1932) Drama.
Running time: 69 minutes. Black and
white.

Directed by Bert Glennon. Screenplay
by Beulah Marie Dix and Frank Reicher.
Photographed by Leo Tover.

Starring Sally O'Neill, Reginald Sharland, Mitchell Lewis, Donald Mackenzie, and Renee MacReady.

A cafe entertainer in Mexico romances
an American.

357 *Girl of the Rio* (1932) Drama.
Running time: 67 minutes. Black and
white.

Produced by Louis Sarecky. Directed
by Herbert Brenon. Screenplay by
Elizabeth Meehan (based on the play
The Dove by Willard Mack, from a story
by Gerald Beaumont). Photographed by
Leo Tover. Edited by Artie Roberts.

Starring Dolores Del Rio (Dolores),
Leo Carrillo (Don Jose Tostado), Nor-
man Foster (Johnny Powell), Lucille
Gleason (Matron), Ralph Ince (O'Grady),

Publicity poster for *The Girl Most Likely*.

Edna Murphy (Madge), Stanley Fields (Mike), Frank Campeau (Bill), Roberta Gale (Mabelle).

A girl falls for the man who sent her lover to prison.

358 *The Girl Rush* (1944) Musical comedy western. Running time: 65 minutes. Black and white.

Produced by John Auer. Directed by Gordon Douglas. Screenplay by Robert

E. Kent (based on a story by Laslo Vadnay and Aladar Laszlo. Photographed by Nicholas Musuraca. Edited by Duncan Mansfield. Music by Harry Harris and Lew Pollack.

Starring Wally Brown (Jerry Miles), Alan Carney (Mike Stager), Frances Langford (Flo Daniels), Vera Vague (Suzie Banks), Robert Mitchum (Jimmy Smith), Paul Hurst (Muley), Patti Brill (Claire), Sarah Padden (Emma), Cy Kendall (Bartlan), John Merton (Scully), Diana King (Martha).

Two vaudevillians are promised gold if they find women for men in a prospecting town.

Note: Remade in 1955 by Paramount.

359 *Go Chase Yourself* (1938)
Comedy. Running time: 70 minutes. Black and white.

Produced by Robert Sisk. Directed by Edward F. Cline. Screenplay by Paul Yawitz and Bert Granet (based on a story by Walter O'Keefe). Photographed by Jack MacKenzie. Edited by Desmond Marquette.

Starring Joe Penner (Wilbur Meely), Lucille Ball (Carol Meely), June Travis (Judith Daniels), Richard Lane (Nails), Fritz Feld (Count Pierre de Louis-Louis), Tom Kennedy (Icebox), Granville Bates (Halliday), Bradley Page (Frank), George Irving (Daniels), Arthur Stone (Warden), Jack Carson (Warren Miles), Frank M. Thomas (Police Chief), Clayton Moore (Reporter).

A bank teller unwittingly aids crooks.

Review: "Aimed at the duals, where it will do a modicum of biz"—*Variety.*

360 *Goin' to Town* (1944)
Comedy. Running time: 68 minutes. Black and white.

Produced by Jack William Votion. Directed by Leslie Goodwins. Screenplay by Charles E. Roberts and Charles E. Marion. Photographed by Robert Pittack. Edited by Hanson T. Fritch.

Starring Chester Lauck (Lum), Norris Goff (Abner), Barbara Hale (Patty),

Florence Lake (Abigail), Dick Elliot (Squire), Grady Sutton (Cedric), Herbert Rawlinson (Wentworth), Dick Baldwin (Jimmy Benton), Ernie Adams (Zeke), Jack Rice (Clarke), Sam Flint (Dr. Crane), Andrew Tombes (Parker).

A city slicker talks some rural folks into investing in an oil well.

361 *Goldie Gets Along* (1933)
Comedy. Running time: 65 minutes. Black and white.

Produced by J.G. Bachmann. Directed by Malcolm St. Clair. Screenplay by Hawthorne Hurst. Photographed by Merritt Gerstad. Edited by Jack Kitchin.

Starring Lili Dalmita (Goldie), Charles Morton (Bill), Sam Hardy (Muldoon), Nat Pendleton (Cassidy), Arthur Hoyt (Mayor), Bradley Page (Hawthorne).

A small-town girl heads for Tinseltown.

362 *Good Sam* (1948)
Comedy. Running time: 112 minutes. Black and white. Available on videocassette. A Rainbow production.

Produced and directed by Leo McCarey. Screenplay by Ken Englund (based on a story by McCarey and John Klorer). Photographed by George Barnes. Edited by James McKay.

Starring Gary Cooper (Sam Clayton), Ann Sheridan (Lu Clayton), Ray Collins (Rev. Daniels), Edmund Lowe (H.C. Borden), Joan Lorring (Shirley Mae), Clinton Sunderberg (Nelson), Minerva Urecal (Mrs. Nelson), Louise Beavers (Chloe), Dick Ross (Claude), Lora Lee Michel (Lulu), Bobby Dolan, Jr. (Butch), Matt Moore (Mr. Butler), Netta Packer (Mrs. Butler), Ruth Roman (Ruthie), Carol Stevens (Mrs. Adams), Todd Karns (Joe Adams), Irving Bacon (Tramp), William Frawley (Tom).

A small-town man goes broke helping others.

Review: "This was really Frank Capra's meat, but when McCarey chewed on it, nothing remained but a barebones comedy with a few funny highlights and a lot of missed opportunities" — *The Motion Picture Guide.*

363 Grand Old Girl (1935) Drama. Running time: 70 minutes. Black and white.

Produced by Cliff Reid. Directed by John Robertson. Screenplay by Milton Krims, John Twist, and Arthur T. Horman (based on a story by Wanda Turchock). Photographed by Lucien Andriot. Edited by George Crone.

Starring Fred MacMurray (Sandy), Alan Hale (Click), May Robson (Laura Bayles), Hale Hamilton (Killiane), Mary Carlisle (Gerry), Etienne Girardot (Mellis), William Burgess (Butts), Edward Van Sloan (Holland), Fred Kohler, Jr. (Bill Belden), Ben Alexander (Tom Miller), Theodore Von Eltz (New Principal).

A veteran schoolteacher is drummed out of the system by local gamblers.

364 Great Day in the Morning (1956) Western. Running time: 91 minutes. Color. Available on videocassette.

Produced by Edmund Grainger. Directed by Jacques Tourneur. Screenplay by Lesser Samuels (based on the novel by Robert Hardy Andrews). Photographed by William Snyder. Edited by Harry Marker.

Starring Virginia Mayo (Ann Merry Alaine), Robert Stack (Owen Pentecost), Ruth Roman (Boston Grant), Alex Nicol (Stephen Kirby), Raymond Burr (Jumbo), Leo Gordon (Zeff), Regis Toomey (Father Murphy).

Civil war battles centering around Colorado territory.

365 The Great Gildersleeve (1942) Comedy. Running time: 61 minutes. Black and white. Available on videocassette.

Produced by Herman Schlom. Directed by Gordon Douglas. Screenplay by Jack Townley and Julie Josephson.

Photographed by Frank Redman. Edited by John Lockert.

Starring Harold Peary (Gildersleeve), Jane Darwell (Aunt Emma), Nancy Gates (Margie), Charles Arndt (Judge Hooker), Freddie Mercer (Leroy), Thurston Hall (Governor Stafford), Lillian Randolph (Birdie), Mary Field (Amelia Hooker), George Carleton (Mr. Powers).

A small-town bachelor is pursued by the town judge's sister.

Note: First in the Gildersleeve series, based on the popular radio character which was also played by Peary. On TV, Peary lookalike Willard Waterman took the role.

366 The Great Jasper (1933) Drama. Running time: 83 minutes. Black and white.

Produced by Kenneth MacGowan. Directed by J. Walter Ruben. Screenplay by Samuel Ornitz and H.W. Hanemann (based on the novel by Fulton Oursler). Photographed by Leo Tover. Edited by Jack Kitchin.

Starring Richard Dix (Jasper Horn), Vera Engles (Norman McGowd), Edna May Oliver (Madame Talma), Florence Eldridge (Jenny Horn), Walter Walker (Mr. McGowd), Dave Durand (Andrew as a Boy), Bruce Line (Roger as a Boy), James Bush (Andrew), Bruce Cabot (Roger), Betty Furness (Sylvia).

The saga of a turn-of-the-century womanizer.

367 The Great Man Votes (1939) Drama. Running time: 70 minutes. Black and white.

Produced by Cliff Reid. Directed by Garson Kanin. Screenplay by John Twist (based on a story by Gordon Malherbe Hillman. Photographed by Russell Metty. Edited by Jack Hively.

Starring John Barrymore (Vance), Virginia Weidler (Joan), Peter Holden (Donald), Katherine Alexander (Miss Billow), Donald MacBride (Iron Hat), Bennie Bartlett (Davy), Elisabeth Risdon (Phoebe), Granville Bates (Mayor), William Demarest (Charles Dale).

John Barrymore and Virginia Weidler in *The Great Man Votes*.

An alcoholic college professor tries to make ends meet raising two children alone.

Note: Perhaps Barrymore's best performance of his later films.

Review: "It will be hailed by class audiences as a fine example of film art, yet carrying sock appeal for mass patronage" — *Variety*.

368 *Green Promise* (1949) Drama. Running time: 92 minutes. Black and white.

Produced by Robert Paige. Directed by William D. Russell. Screenplay by Monty F. Collins. Photographed by John Russell. Edited by Richard Farrell.

Starring Marguerite Chapman (Deborah Matthews), Walter Brennan (Mr. Matthews), Robert Paige (David Barkley), Natalie Wood (Susan Matthews), Ted Donaldson (Phineas Matthews), Connie Marshall (Abigail Matthews), Robert Ellis (Buzz), Jeanne LaDuke (Jessie Wexford), Irving Bacon (Julius Larkin).

A crusty farmer tries to raise his daughters alone.

369 *Gun Law* (1938) Western. Running time: 60 minutes. Black and white.

Produced by Bert Gilroy. Directed by David Howard. Screenplay by Oliver Drake. Photographed by Joseph H. August. Edited by Frederic Knudtson. Music by Roy Webb.

Starring George O'Brien (Tom O'Malley), Rita Oehmen (Ruth Ross), Ray Whitley (Singing Sam McGee), Paul Everton (Mayor Blaine), Robert Glecker (Flash Arnold), Ward Bond (Pecos), Francis McDonald (Nevada), Ed Pawley (Raven), Frank O'Connor (Parson).

A lawman is ambushed and robbed of his papers; the criminal poses as him thereafter.

370 *Gun Smugglers* (1948) Western. Running time: 61 minutes. Black and white. Available on videocassette.

Produced by Herman Schlom. Directed by Frank McDonald. Screenplay by Norman Houston. Photographed by J. Roy Hunt. Edited by Les Millbrook.

Starring Tim Holt (Tim), Richard Martin (Chito), Martha Hyer (Judy), Gary Gray (Danny), Paul Hurst (Hasty), Douglas Fowley (Steve), Robert Warwick (Col. Davis), Don Haggerty (Sheriff), Frank Sully (Clancy), Robert Bray (Dodge), Steve Savage (Bit).

Cowboy hero saves a young boy from the clutches of his outlaw brother.

371 *Gunga Din* (1939) Adventure. Running time: 117 minutes. Black and white and colorized. Available on video-cassette.

Produced by Pandro S. Berman. Directed by George Stevens. Screenplay by Joel Sayre and Fred Guiol (based on the story by Ben Hecht, Charles MacArthur, William Faulkner [uncredited], suggested by the poem by Rudyard Kipling). Photographed by John August. Edited by Henry Berman. Music by Alfred Newman.

Starring Cary Grant (Sgt. Cutler), Victor McLaglen (Sgt. Machesney), Douglas Fairbanks, Jr. (Ballantine), Sam Jaffe (Gunga Din), Eduardo Ciannelli (Guru), Joan Fontaine (Emmy Stebbins), Montague Love (Col. Weed), Robert Coote (Higginbotham), Abner Biberman (Chota), Lumsden Hare (Mitchell), Cecil Kellaway (Mr. Stebbins), Reginald Sheffield (Journalist), Ann Evers, Audrey Manners, Fay McKenzie (Girls at Party), Roland Varno (Lt. Markham), Charles Bennett (Telegraph Operator).

Three brawling sergeants take a troop of Indians and water carriers to the silent outpost.

Note: Similar in concept to *The Front Page.* Howard Hawks was initially slated to direct. Remade in 1951 as *Soldiers Three* and in 1961 as *Sergeants Three.*

Review: "One of the most enjoyable nonsense-adventure movies of all time" — Pauline Kael.

372 *Gunplay* (1951) Western. Running time: 60 minutes. Black and white.

Produced by Herman Schlom. Directed by Lesley Selander. Screenplay by Ed Earl Repp. Photographed by J. Roy Hunt. Edited by Douglas Biggs.

Starring Tim Holt (Tim), Joan Dixon (Terry), Harper Carter (Chip), Mauritz Hugo (Landry), Robert Brice (Sam), Marshall Reed (Dobbs), Jack Hill (Sheriff), Robert Wilkie (Winslow), Leo McMahon (Zeke), Richard Martin (Chito).

Two cowboys seek out the killer of a young orphan's parents.

Review: "This may be one of the few westerns to have an under-abundance of gunplay" — *The Motion Picture Guide.*

373 *Guns of Hate* (1948) Western. Running time: 61 minutes. Black and white.

Produced by Herman Schlom and Sid Rogell. Directed by Lesley Selander. Screenplay by Norman Houston and Ed Earl Repp. Photographed by George Diskant. Edited by Desmond Marquette.

Starring Tim Holt, Nan Leslie, Richard

Martin, Steve Brodie, Myrna Dell, Tony Barrett, Jim Nolan, Jason Robards, Sr., Robert Bray, Marilyn Mercer.

Two drifters are falsely accused of murder.

374 *Half-Breed* (1952) Western. 81 minutes. Color.

Produced by Herman Schlom. Directed by Stuart Gilmore. Screenplay by Harold Shumate and Richard Wormser. Photographed by William Skall. Edited by Samuel Beetley.

Starring Robert Young, Janis Carter, Jack Buetel, Barton MacLane, Reed Hadley, Porter Hall, Connie Gilchrist, Sammy White, Damian O'Flynn, Frank Wilcox, Judy Walsh, Tom Monroe.

A half-breed Apache tries to make peace between his people and the white men.

375 *Half-Marriage* (1929) Comedy. Running time: 68 minutes. Black and white.

Produced by William LeBaron. Directed by William J. Cowen. Screenplay by Jane Murfin (based on a story by George Kibbe Turner). Edited by Archie Marshek.

Starring Olive Borden (Judy Page), Morgan Farley (Dick Carroll), Ken Murray (Charles Turner), Ann Greenway (Ann Turner), Sally Blane (Sally), Richard Tucker (George Page), Hedda Hopper (Mrs. Page).

A society girl secretly marries a young architect out of her social set.

376 *The Half-Naked Truth* (1932) Comedy. Running time: 75 minutes. Black and white.

Directed by Gregory La Cava. Screenplay by Bartlett McCormack, Corey Ford, and La Cava (based on a story by Ben Markson and H.N. Swanson, from the book *Phantom Fame* by Harry Reichenbach). Photographed by Bert Glennon. Edited by C.K. Campbell.

Starring Lupe Velez, Lee Tracy, Eugene Pallette, Frank Morgan, Robert

Mckenzie, Shirley Chambers, Charles Dow, James Donlan.

A carnival barker turns a dancer into a sensation and becomes a successful entrepreneur himself.

377 *Half Shot at Sunrise* (1930) Comedy. Running time: 75 minutes. Black and white. Available on videocassette.

Directed by Paul Sloane. Screenplay by James Ashmore Creelman, Anne Caldwell, and Ralph Spence (based on a story by Creelman). Photographed by Nicholas Musuraca. Edited by Arthur Roberts. Music by Max Steiner.

Starring Bert Wheeler (Tommy), Robert Woolsey (Gilbert), John Rutherford (M.P. Sergeant), George MacFarlane (Col. Marshall), Roberta Robinson (Eileen), Leni Stengel (Olga), Dorothy Lee (Annette), Hugh Trevor (Lt. Jim Reed), Edna May Oliver (Mrs. Marshall), The Tiller Sunshine Girls.

Two enlisted men go AWOL in Paris.

Review: "Laugh programmer beyond ordinary" — *Variety*.

378 *Handle with Care* (1935) Comedy. Running time: 55 minutes. Black and white.

Produced by George King and Randall Faye. Directed by Redd Davis. Screenplay by Randall Faye. Photographed by Geoffrey Faithfull. Edited by Andy Buchanan.

Starring Molly Lamont (Patricia), Jack Hobbs (Jack), James Finlayson (Jimmy), Henry Victor (Count), Vera Bogetti (Fifi), Margaret Yarde (Mrs. Tunbody), Toni Edgar Bruce (Lady Deeping), Stanford Hilliard (Professor Deeping).

Two ex-cons get hold of a strength pill and go up against a gang of spies in England.

379 *Hans Christian Anderson* (1952) Musical. Running time: 120 minutes. Color. Available on videocassette.

Produced by Samuel Goldwyn. Directed by Charles Vidor. Screenplay by Moss Hart (based on a story by Myles Connolly). Photographed by Harry Stradling. Music by Frank Loesser. Edited by Daniel Mandell.

Songs: "I'm Hans Christian Anderson," "No Two People," "The Ugly Duckling," "Inchworm," "Thumbelina," "Wonderful Wonderul Copenhagen," "Anywhere I Wander," "The King's New Clothes."

Starring Danny Kaye (Hans Christian Anderson), Farley Granger (Niels), Renee Jeanmarie (Doro), Joseph Walsh (Peter), Phillip Tonge (Otto), Erik Bruhn (The Hussar), Roland Petit (The Prince), John Brown (Schoolmaster), John Qualen (Burgomaster), Jeanne Lafayette (Celine), Robert Malcolm (Stage Doorman), George Chandler (Farmer), Fred Kelsey and Gil Perkins (Gendarmes), Peter Votrian (Lars), Betty Uitti (Princess), Jack Klaus (Sea Witch).

A storyteller moves to Copenhagen to make shoes for a prima ballerina.

Note: Some TV prints run only 104 minutes.

Oscar nomination: Song "Thumbelina."

380 *Hat, Coat, and Glove* (1934)

Drama. Running time: 64 minutes. Black and white.

Directed by Worthington Miner. Screenplay by Francis Edwards Faragoh (based on a play by Wilhelm Speyer). Photographed by J. Roy Hunt. Edited by Ralph Dietrich.

Starring Ricardo Cortez (Robert Mitchell), Barbara Robbins (Dorthea Mitchell), John Beal (Jerry Hutchins), Margaret Hamilton (Madame DuBarry), Sara Haden (Mitchell's Secretary), Samuel Hinds (John Walters), Murray Kinnell (The Judge), Dorothy Burgess (Ann), Louise Beavers (Imogene), Irving Bacon, Paul Harvey, Tom Brown, Dave Durand (Bits).

A lawyer witnesses a woman's suicide at the home of an artist with whom his wife is having an affair.

Note: Intended as a vehicle for John Barrymore, who was ostensibly too drunk to work.

381 *Having Wonderful Crime*

(1945) Comedy. Running time: 70 minutes. Black and white. Available on videocassette.

Produced by Robert Fellows. Directed by A. Edward Sutherland. Screenplay by Howard J. Green, Stewart Sterling, and Parke Levy (based on a story by Craig Rice). Photographed by Frank Redman. Edited by Gene Milford.

Starring Pat O'Brien (Michael J. Malone), George Murphy (Jake Justus), Carole Landis (Helene), Lenore Aubert (Gilda), George Zucco (King), Anjie Berens (Phyllis), Richard Marin (Lance), Charles D. Brown (Winslow), Wee Willie Davis (Zacharias), Blanche Ring (Elizabeth Lenhart), Josephine Whittell (Myra), Ed Fielding (Dr. Newcomb), Frank Mayo (Cop), Cyril Ring (Hotel Clerk), Emory Parnell (Butler).

Three amateur detectives try solving the disappearance of a magician.

382 *Having Wonderful Time*

(1938) Comedy. Running time: 70 minutes. Black and white. Available on videocassette.

Produced by Pandro S. Berman. Directed by Alfred Santell. Screenplay by Arthur Kober (based on his play). Photographed by Robert De Grasse. Edited by William Hamilton. Music by Roy Webb.

Starring Ginger Rogers (Teddy Shaw), Douglas Fairbanks, Jr. (Chick), Peggy Conklin (Fay), Lucille Ball (Miriam), Lee Bowman (Buzzy), Eve Arden (Henrietta), Dorothea Kent (Maxine), Red Skelton (Itchy), Donald Meek (P.U. Rogers), Jack Carson (Emil Beatty), Clarence Wilson (Mr. G.), Allan Lane (Mac), Grady Sutton (Gus), Inez Courtney (Emma), Juanita Quigley (Mabel), George Meeker (Subway Masher), Elise Cavannah (Office Supervisor), Ann Miller

(Vivian), Dean Jagger (Charlie), Wesley Barry, Florence Lake, Russell Gleason, Vera Gordon (Bits).

A New York girl falls for a guy at a summer resort.

Note: Red Skelton's film debut.

383 *Hawaii Calls* (1938) Musical. Running time: 72 minutes. Black and white.

Produced by Sol Lesser. Directed by Edward F. Cline. Screenplay by Wanda Tuchock (based on a novel by Don Blanding). Photographed by Jack Mac-Kenzie. Edited by Arthur Hilton.

Starring Bobby Breen (Billy), Ned Sparks (Strings), Irwin S. Cobb (Capt. O'Hara), Warren Hull (Milburn), Gloria Holden (Mrs. Milburn), Juanita Quigley (Doris), Pua Lani (Pua), Raymond Paige (Himself), Herb Rawlinson (Harlow), Ward Bond (Muller), Cy Kendall (Policeman).

Two young stowaways end up as singers on a boat.

384 *He Knew Women* (1930) Drama. Running time: 86 minutes. Black and white.

Produced by Myles Connolly. Directed by Hugh Herbert. Screenplay by Herbert and William Jute. Photographed by Ed Cronjager. Edited by Ann McKnight and George Marsh.

Starring Lowell Sherman (Geoffrey), Alice Joyce (Alice), David Manners (Austin), Frances Dade (Monica).

A novelist tries to use a woman for her money.

385 *Headline Shooter* (1933) Drama. Running time: 60 minutes. Black and white.

Directed by Otto Brower. Screenplay by Agnes Christine Johnston, Allen Rivkin, and Arthur Kober (based on a story by Wallace West). Photographed by Nicholas Musuraca. Edited by Frederic Knudtson.

Starring William Gargan (Bill Allen), Frances Dee (Jane), Ralph Bellamy (Hal), Jack LaRue (Ricci), Gregory Ratoff (Gottlieb), Wallace Ford (Mike), Hobart Cavannaugh (Happy), June Brewster (Betty), Robert Benchley (Radio Announcer), Betty Furness (Secretary), Franklin Pangborn (Crocker).

A newsreel photographer is more obsessed with his job than his girl.

386 *Heartbeat* (1946) Comedy. Running time: 100 minutes. Black and white.

Produced by Robert and Raymond Hakim. Directed by Sam Wood. Screenplay by Morrie Ryskind and Rowland Leigh (based on the French screenplay *Battlement de Coeur* by Hans Wilhelm). Photographed by Joseph Valentine. Edited by Roland Gross.

Starring Ginger Rogers (Arlette), Jean-Pierre Aumont (Pierre), Adolphe Menjou (Ambassador), Basil Rathbone (Aristide), Melville Cooper (Medeville), Mikhail Rasummy (Cadubert), Eduardo Ciannelli (Dvorak).

A French gamin becomes a pickpocket.

Review: "The heartbeat is irregular and sadly ailing" — *Photoplay.*

387 *Heavenly Days* (1944) Comedy. Running time: 72 minutes. Black and white.

Produced by Robert Fellows. Directed by Howard Estabrook. Screenplay by Estabrook and Don Quinn (based on a story by Estabrook). Photographed by J. Roy Hunt. Edited by Robert Swink.

Starring Jim Jordan (Fibber McGee), Miriam Jordan (Molly), Eugene Pallette (Sewn Bigbee), Gordon Oliver (Dick), Raymond Walburn (Popham), Barbara Hale (Angie), Don Douglas (Dr. Gallop), Frieda Inescort (Mrs. Clark), Irving Bacon (Butler), Charles Trowbridge (Alvin Clark), Chester Carlisle and Bert Moorehouse (Sergeants at Arms), J.M. Sullivan (Detective), Ed Stanley (Vice President Wallace), Harry Humphrey (Southern Senator), George Reed (Servant).

Radio stars Fibber McGee and Molly travel to Washington to voice their opinions about affairs of state, when Fibber is celebrated as Mr. Average Man.

388 *Hell's Highway* (1932) Drama. Running time: 62 minutes. Black and white.

Produced by David O. Selznick. Directed by Rowland Brown. Screenplay by Samuel Ornitz, Robert Tasker, and Rowland Brown. Photographed by Edward Cronjager. Edited by William Hamilton.

Starring Richard Dix (Duke), Tom Brown (Johnny), Louise Carter (Mrs. Ellis), Rochelle Hudson (Mary Ellen), C. Henry Gordon (Blacksnake Skinner), Warner Richmond (Pop Eye Jackson), Sandy Roth (Blind Maxie), Charles Middleton (Matthew the Hermit), Clarence Muse (Rascal), Stanley Fields (Whiteside).

A convict in a brutal prison camp finds that his beloved younger brother is soon to become an inmate.

Note: This indictment of the prison systems was released a few months before Warner Bros. *I Am a Fugitive from a Chain Gang,* but was eclipsed by the later film. Audiences at the time were stunned by its brutality, but it did pave the way for later depictions of prison life, owing much to its realism.

Review: "Too sodden for general appeal" — *Variety.*

Here Is a Man see The Devil and Daniel Webster

389 *Here We Go Again* (1942) Comedy. Running time: 75 minutes. Black and white. Available on videocassette.

Produced and directed by Allan Dwan. Screenplay by Paul Gerard Smith and Joe Bigelow (based on a story by Smith and material for the "Fibber McGee and Molly" radio program by Don Quinn). Photographed by Frank Redman. Edited by Desmond Marquette.

Starring Jim Jordan (Fibber), Miriom Jordan (Molly), Edgar Bergen (Himself), Harold Peary (Gildersleeve), Ginny Simms (Jean), William Thompson (Whimple), Gale Gordon (Caldwalder), Ray Noble (Himself), Isabel Randolph (Mrs. Uppington).

The McGees decide to spend their 20th wedding anniversary at the Silver Tip Lodge, where Fibber is accosted by con men.

390 *Heroes All* (1931). Documentary. Running time: 65 minutes.

A compilation of World War One films prepared by Emile Gaureau and featuring the narration of Major General John J. Bradley. A Mendelsohn-Young production for RKO Radio Pictures.

391 *Hi, Gaucho* (1935) Musical drama. 60 minutes. Black and white.

Directed by Tommy Atkins. Screenplay by Adele Buffington (based on a story by Atkins).

Starring John Carroll, Steffi Duna, Rod La Roque, Montague Love, Ann Codee, Tom Ricketts, Paul Porcasi, Enrique De Rosas, Billy Gilbert.

A South American romances his girl despite their feuding families.

392 *Hideaway* (1937) Comedy. Running time: 60 minutes. Black and white.

Produced by Cliff Reid. Directed by Richard Rosson. Screenplay by J. Robert Bren and Edmund L. Hartmann (based on a play by Melvin Levy). Photographed by Jack MacKenzie. Edited by Harry Marker.

Starring Fred Stone (Frankie), Emma Dunn (Emma), Marjorie Lord (Joan), J. Carrol Naish (Clarke), William Carson (Bill), Ray Mayer (Eddie), Bradley Page (Al), Paul Guilfoyle (Norris), Tommy Bond (Oscar), Dudley Clements (Sheriff), Alec Craig (Nolan), Charles Withers (Yokum), Otto Hoffman (Hank), Bob McKenzie (Mooney), Lee Patrick (Martha).

A poor man moves his family into an abandoned house, but discovers it to be a gangster's hideout.

393 *High Flyers* (1937) Comedy. Running time: 70 minutes. Black and white.

Produced by Lee Marcus. Directed by Edward F. Cline. Screenplay by Benny Rubin, Bert Granet, and Byron Morgan (from a play by Victor Mapes). Photographed by John MacKenzie. Edited by John Lockert. Music by Dave Dreyer and Harry Ruby.

Songs: "I Always Get My Man," "Keep Your Head Above Water," "I'm a Gaucho."

Starring Bert Wheeler (Jerry), Robert Woolsey (Pierre), Lupe Velez (Juanita), Marjorie Lord (Arlene), Margaret Dumont (Mrs. Arlington), Jack Carson (Dave), Paul Harvey (Mr. Arlington), Charles Judels (Mr. Fontaine), Lucien Prival (Mr. Panzer), Herbert Evans (Mr. Hatley), Herbert Clifton (Stone), George Irving (Police Chief), Bud Geary (Bosun's Mate), Bruce Sidney (Ship Officer).

Two men posing as fliers find themselves in the midst of a jewel smuggling ring.

Note: Lupe Velez was said to have gotten into regular fist fights with her makeup man on this picture. This was Wheeler and Woolsey's last film together. Woolsey, who was already suffering from a debilitating kidney disease, found it painful to work. He died about eight months after this film's release.

394 *High Stakes* (1931) Drama. Running time: 69 minutes. Black and white.

Directed by Lowell Sherman. Screenplay by J. Walter Ruben (based on the play by Willard Mack).

Starring Lowell Sherman, Mae Murray, Karen Morley, Edward Martindel, Leyland Hodgson, Ethel Levey, Alan Roscoe, Maude Turner Gordon, Charles Coleman, Phillips Smalley.

An alcoholic tries to save his brother from a golddigger's wiles.

395 *Higher and Higher* (1943) Musical. Running time: 90 minutes. Black and white. Available on videocassette.

Produced and directed by Tim Whelan. Screenplay by Jay Dratler, Ralph Spence, William Bowers, and Howard Harris (based on the play by Gladys Hurlbut and Joshua Logan). Photographed by Robert De Grasse. Edited by Gene Milford. Music by Jimmy McHugh, Harold Adamson, Rodgers and Hart.

Songs: "You Belong in a Love Song," "A Most Important Affair," "The Music Stopped," "Today I'm a Debutante," "A Lovely Way to Spend an Evening," "I Couldn't Sleep a Wink Last Night," "You're on Your Own," "I Saw You First," "Disgustingly Rich."

Starring Michele Morgan (Millie), Jack Haley (Mike), Frank Sinatra (Frank), Leon Errol (Drake), Marcy McGuire (Mickey), Victor Borge (Fitzroy Wilson), Mary Wickes (Sandy), Elisabeth Risdon (Mrs. Keating), Barbara Hale (Catherine Keating), Mel Torme (Marty), Paul Hartman (Bingham), Grace Hartman (Hilda), Dooley Wilson (Oscar), Dorothy Malone (Bridesmaid).

Servants try to save the family fortune, knowing it means saving their jobs.

Note: Frank Sinatra's first major screen role.

396 *Highways by Night* (1942) Crime drama. Running time: 62 minutes. Black and white.

Produced by Herman Schlom (Uncredited). Directed by Peter Godfrey. Screenplay by Lynn Root and Frank Fenton (based on the serial *Silver Spoon* by Clarence Budington Kelland). Photographed by Robert De Grasse. Edited by Harry Marker.

Starring Richard Carlson (Tommy Van Steel), Jane Randolph (Peggy Fogarty), Jane Darwell (Grandma), Barton MacLane (Leo Bronson), Ray Collins (Uncle Ben), Gordon Jones (Footsy Fogarty), Renee Hall (Ellen Cromwell), George

Cleveland (Judkins), Jack La Rue (Johnny), Paul Fix (Gabby).

A millionaire goes slumming and winds up involved in a gangland murder.

397 *Hips, Hips, Hooray* (1934) Comedy. Running time: 68 minutes. Black and white. Available on videocassette.

Produced by H.N. Swanson. Directed by Mark Sandrich. Screenplay by Harry Ruby, Bert Kalmar, and Ed Kaufman. Photographed by David Abel. Edited by Harry Marker.

Songs: "Tired of It All," "Keep Romance Alive," "Keep On Doin' What You're Doin'."

Starring Bert Wheeler (Andy Williams), Robert Woolsey (Bob Dudley), Ruth Etting (Herself), Thelma Todd (Miss Frisbie), Dorothy Lee (Daisy), George Meeker (Beauchamp), James Burtis (Epstein), Matt Briggs (Sweeney), Spencer Charters (Mr. Clark).

Two salesmen attempt to push their flavored lipstick on the market.

Reviews: "Femme display chief asset" — *Variety;* "One of W&W's best vehicles" — Leonard Maltin.

398 *His Family Tree* (1935) Comedy. Running time: 69 minutes. Black and white.

Directed by Charles Vidor. Screenplay by Joel Sayre and John Twist (based on the play "Old Man Murphy" by Patrick Kearney and Harry Wagstaff Gribble).

Starring James Barton, Margaret Callahan, Addison Randall, Maureen Delaney, William Harrigan, Marjorie Gateson, Clifford Jones, Ray Mayer, Herman Bing, Pat Moriarty, Ferdinand Munier.

An Irishman changes his name and becomes involved in politics.

399 *His Greatest Gamble* (1934) Drama. Running time: 70 minutes. Black and white.

Produced by Myles Connolly. Directed by John Robertson. Screenplay by Sidney Buchman and Harry Hervey (based on a story by Salisbury Field). Photographed by Ted Tetzlaff. Edited by William Hamilton.

Starring Richard Dix (Phillip Eden), Dorothy Wilson (Alice as an Adult), Bruce Cabot (Stephen), Erin O'Brien-Moore (Florence), Edith Fellows (Alice as a Child).

A man serving a prison sentence for murder escapes to save his beloved daughter from her domineering mother.

400 *His Kind of Woman* (1951) Crime drama. Running time: 120 minutes. Black and white. Available on videocassette.

Produced by Robert Sparks. Directed by John Farrow. Screenplay by Frank Fenton and Jack Leonard (based on the story *Star Sapphire* by Gerald Drayson Adams). Photographed by Harry J. Wild. Music by Leigh Harline. Edited by Eda Warren and Frederic Knudtson.

Starring Robert Mitchum (Don Milner), Jane Russell (Lenore Brent), Vincent Price (Mark Cardigan), Tim Holt (Bill Lusk), Charles McGraw (Thompson), Marjorie Reynolds (Helen Cardigan), Raymond Burr (Nick Ferraro), Leslye Banning (Jennie Stone), Jim Backus (Myron Winton), Phillip Van Zandt (Jose Morro), John Mylong (Martin Krafft), Carleton G. Young (Hobson), Erno Verebes (Estavan), Dan White (Tex Kearns).

A gambler meets up with trouble when he arrives in a Mexican resort.

401 *Hit the Deck* (1930) Musical. Running time: 93 minutes. Black and white and color.

Directed and written by Luther Reed (based on the play by Herbert Fields). Photographed by Robert Kurrie.

Starring Jack Oakie (Bilge), Polly Walker (Looloo), Roger Gray (Mat), Frank Woods (Pat), Harry Sweet (Bunny), Marguerita Padula (Lavinia), June Clyde (Toddy), Ethel Clayton (Mrs.

Payne), George Ovey, Dell Henderson (Bits).

A cafe owner falls in love with a sailor.

Note: Based on a Broadway show which ran 352 consecutive performances, this was RKO's second attempt at a big budget musical, but it was not as successful as their first, *Rio Rita.*

402 *The Hitch-Hiker* (1953) Crime drama. Running time: 71 minutes. Black and white. Available on videocassette.

Produced by Collier Young. Directed by Ida Lupino. Screenplay by Young, Lupino, and Robert Joseph. Photographed by Nicholas Musuraca. Edited by Douglas Stewart.

Starring Edmond O'Brien (Roy Collins), Frank Lovejoy (Gilbert Bowen), William Talman (Emmet Myers), Jose Torvay (Capt. Alvarado), Sam Hayes (Sam), Wendell Niles (Wendell), Jean Del Val (Inspector General), Clark Howat (Government Agent), Natividad Vacio (Jose), Rodney Bell (William Johnson), Nacho Galindo (Proprietor), Martin Garallaga (Bartender).

Two men on a fishing holiday pick up a hitchhiker who turns out to be a dangerous criminal.

Note: Based on the real-life exploits of mass-murderer William Cook. Original story writer Daniel Mainwaring did not receive credit, due to his leftist leanings. RKO chief Howard Hughes refused to credit "radicals" for their work. Ms. Lupino was the only woman directing films at this time, and rarely was given the respect she richly deserved for her remarkable directing abilities.

403 *Hitler's Children* (1942) Drama. Running time: 80 minutes. Black and white. Available on videocassette.

Produced by Edward A. Golden. Directed by Edward Dmytryk. Screenplay by Emmet Lavery (based on the book *Education for Death* by Gregor Ziemer). Photographed by Russell Metty. Edited by Joseph Noriega.

Starring Tim Holt (Karl Bruner), Bonita Granville (Anna Muller), Kent Smith (Prof. Nichols), Otto Kruger (Col. Henkel), H.B. Warner (Bishop), Lloyd Corrigan (Franz Erhart), Gavin Muir (Nazi Major), Bill Burrud (Murph), Jimmy Zaner (Irwin), Richard Martin (Gestapo Man), Goetz Von Eyck (Sergeant).

A Nazi tries recruiting more children into the Third Reich, falling for a woman who is set for forced sterilization because of her anti–Hitler attitudes.

Note: This film garnered more profits for RKO than any other film it had produced to this date, including such classics as *King Kong* and *Top Hat.* This was among the very first nice girl roles for Granville and a real departure for good guy cowboy star Holt.

404 *Hitting a New High* (1937) Musical. Running time: 80 minutes. Black and white.

Produced by Jesse Lasky. Directed by Raoul Walsh. Screenplay by Gertrude Percell and John Twist. Photographed by J. Roy Hunt. Edited by Desmond Marquette.

Songs: "You're Like a Song," "I Hit a New High," "Let's Give Love Another Chance," "This Never Happened Before."

Starring Lily Pons (Suzette), Jack Oakie (Corby), Eric Blore (Cosmo), Edward Everett Horton (Blynn), John Howard (Jimmy), Eduardo Ciannelli (Mazzinni), Luis Alberni (Marlo), Jack Arnold (Haig), Leonard Carey (Jevons).

A night club singer dreams of being a star at the Met.

Commentary: "The film lost tons of money and effectively ended Pons' career in the movies. Lasky also left the studio shortly after this bomb's release"—*The Motion Picture Guide.*

405 *Hold 'em Jail* (1932) Comedy. Running time: 65 minutes. Black and white. Available on videocassette.

Produced by H.N. Swanson. Directed

Publicity poster for *The Hitch-Hiker*.

by Norman Taurog. Screenplay by S.J. Perelman, Walter DeLeon, Mark Sandrich, and Albert Ray (based on a story by Tim Whelan and Lew Lipton). Photographed by Len Smith. Edited by Artie Roberts. Music by Max Steiner.

Starring Bert Wheeler (Curly Harris), Robert Woolsey (Spider Robbins), Edna May Oliver (Violet Jones), Edgar Kennedy (Warden), Betty Grable (Barbara Jones), Roscoe Ates (Slippery Sam), Paul Hurst (Coach), Warren Hymer (Steel), Robert Armstrong (Announcer), John Sheehan (Mike Mahoney), Jed Prouty (Warden Charles Clarke), Spencer Charters (Governor), Monty Banks (Timekeeper).

Two novelty salesmen are framed into jail sentences and decide to help the warden form an all-convict football team to battle a rival prison.

Note: Considered one of the better Wheeler and Woolsey comedies, this one lost $55,000 at the box office.

406 *Holiday Affair* (1949) Holiday romance. Running time: 86 minutes. Black and white. Available on videocassette.

Produced and directed by Don Harman. Screenplay by Isobel Lennart (based on the story *A Christmas Gift* by John D. Weaver). Photographed by Milton Krasner. Edited by Harry Marker. Music by Roy Webb.

Starring Robert Mitchum (Steve), Janet Leigh (Connie), Griff Barnett (Mr. Ennis), Wendell Corey (Carl), Esther Dale (Mrs. Ennis), Henry O'Neil (Mr. Crowley), Henry Morgan (Police Lieutenant), Larry J. Blake (Plainclothesman), Helen Brown (Emily), Gordon Bergert (Timmy), Frank Johnson (Santa Claus).

A young widow with a six year old child falls for an aggressive sales clerk at Christmas time.

407 *Hollywood Cowboy* (1937) Comedy. Running time: 63 minutes. Black and white. Available on videocassette.

Produced by George A. Hirliman. Directed by Ewing Scott. Screenplay by Ewing Scott and Dan Jarrett. Photographed by Frank B. Good. Edited by Robert Crandall.

Starring George O'Brien, Cecilia Parker, Maude Eburne, Joe Caits, Frank Milan, Charles Middleton, Lee Shumway, Walter dePalma, Al Hill, William Royle, Al Herman, Frank Hagney, Dan Wolheim, Slim Balch, Lester Dorr, Harold Daniels.

A movie company becomes involved in range warfare when Chicago gangsters try to get tough out west.

Alternate title: *Wings Over Wyoming.*

408 *Honeymoon* (1947) Comedy. Running time: 74 minutes. Black and white.

Produced by Warren Duff. Directed by William Keighley. Screenplay by Michael Kanin (based on a story by Vicki Baum). Photographed by Edward Cronjager. Edited by Ralph Dawson. Music by Leigh Harline.

Starring Shirley Temple (Barbara Olmstead), Franchot Tone (David Flanner), Guy Madison (Phil Vaughn), Lina Romay (Raquel Mendoza), Grant Mitchell (Crenshaw), Julio Villareale (Sr. Mendoza), Manuel Arvide (Registar), Jose R. Goula (Dr. Diego), Carol Forman (Nurse), John Parrish (Gilhooley).

A young girl follows her soldier fiance to Mexico, only to fall for an older man.

Note: British title: *Two Men and a Girl.*

Review: "...one of the reasons for Shirley Temple's early retirement"—Leslie Halliwell.

409 *Hook, Line and Sinker* (1930) Comedy. Running time: 72 minutes. Black and white. Available on videocassette.

Produced by Myles Connolly. Directed by Edward F. Cline. Screenplay by Tim Whelan and Ralph Spence (based on a story by Whelan). Photographed by Nicholas Musuraca. Edited by Archie Marshek.

Starring Bert Wheeler (Wilbur Bos-

Bert Wheeler and Dorothy Lee in *Hook, Line and Sinker.*

well), Robert Woolsey (Addington Ganzy), Dorothy Lee (Mary Marsh), Jobyna Howland (Mrs. March), Ralf Harolde (John Blackwell), Natalie Moorhead (Duchess Bessie Venessie), George F. Marion, Sr. (Bellboy), Hugh Herbert (House Detective), Stanley Fields, William B. Davidson (Bits).

Two insurance men help a pretty girl restore a hotel she's just inherited.

Note: The similarly titled Jerry Lewis feature is not a remake.

Review: "Will tickle most in the spots where price is least"—*Variety.*

410 Hooray for Love (1935) Musical. Running time: 75 minutes. Black and white.

Produced by Felix Young. Directed by Walter Lang. Screenplay by Lawrence Hazard and Ray Harris (based on a story by Marc Lachmann). Photographed by Lucien Andriot. Edited by George Crone.

Starring Ann Sothern (Pat), Gene Raymond (Doug), Bill Robinson (Bill), Thurston Hall (Commodore), Pert Kelton (Trixie), Georgia Caine (Duchess), Lionel Stander (Chowsky), Etienne Girardot (Judge), Harry Kernell (Regan), Sam Hardy (Ganz), Eddie Kane (Grady), Fats Waller (Himself).

A wealthy college boy helps finance a stage show.

Review: "Trouble is entirely traceable to its terribly lethargic tempo and lack of any real production numbers"—*Variety.*

411 Hot Lead (1951) Western. Running time: 60 minutes. Black and white.

Produced by Herman Schlom. Directed by Stuart Gilmore. Screenplay by William Lively. Photographed by Nicholas Musuraca. Edited by Robert Golden.

Starring Tim Holt, Joan Dixon, Ross Elliot, John Dehner, Paul Marion, Lee

MacGregor, Stanley Andrews, Paul E. Burns, Kenneth MacDonald, Robert Wilke, Richard Martin.

Two cowboys go after train robbers.

412 *Hot Tip* (1935) Comedy. Running time: 70 minutes. Black and white.

Produced by William Sistrom. Directed by Ray McCarey and James Gleason. Screenplay by Hugh Cummings, Olive Cooper, and Louis Stevens (based on a story by William Slavens McNutt). Photographed by Jack MacKenzie. Edited by George Crone.

Starring ZaSu Pitts (Belle McGill), James Gleason (Jimmy McGill), Margaret Callahan (Jane McGill), Russell Gleason (Ben), Ray Mayer (Tyler), J.M. Kerrigan (Matt), Arthur Stone (Hooper), Donald Kerr (Spider), Kitty McHugh (Queenie).

A racetrack enthusiast gets into hot water when his friends bet on the same horses as he does—and lose.

413 *Hotel Reserve* (1946) Suspense. Running time: 79 minutes. Black and white.

Produced by Victor Hanbury. Directed by Hanbury, Lance Comfort, Max Greene (Mutz Greenbaum). Screenplay by John Davenport (based on the novel *Epitaph for a Spy* by Eric Ambler). Photographed by Max Greene. Edited by Syd Stone.

Starring James Mason (Peter Vadassy), Lucie Mannheim (Madame Koche), Raymond Lovell (Duclos), Julien Mitchell (Beghin), Clare Hamilton (Mary Skelton), Martin Miller (Herr Walter Vogel), Herbert Lom (Roux), Frederick Valk (Schimler).

A medical student is wrongfully accused of espionage.

Note: A hit in England in 1944, it did not do well in America two years later.

414 *The Hunchback of Notre Dame* (1939). Melodrama. Running time: 115 minutes. Black and white.

Produced by Pandro S. Berman. Directed by William Dieterle. Screenplay by Sonya Levien and Bruno Frank (based on the novel by Victor Hugo). Photographed by Joseph August. Edited by William Hamilton and Robert Wise. Available on videocassette.

Starring Charles Laughton (Hunchback), Sir Cedric Hardwicke (Frollo), Thomas Mitchell (Clopin), Maureen O'Hara (Esmerelda), Edmond O'Brien (Gringoire), Alan Marshal (Proebus), Walter Hampden (Claude), Harry Davenport (Louis XI).

The classic story of the doomed bellringer Quasimoto.

Note: Made for almost $2 million, this was a remake of a classic 1925 silent. Released at exactly the same time as *Gone with the Wind,* thus it had to take a back seat to that event. One of six film versions of Hugo's story, the others being *Esmerelda* (French, 1906), *Notre Dame de Paris* (French, 1911), *The Darling of Paris* (USA, 1917), the 1925 Lon Chaney film, this one, and then again in 1957 with Anthony Quinn.

415 *Hunt the Man Down* (1950) Drama. Running time: 68 minutes. Black and white. Available on video cassette.

Produced by Lewis Rachmil. Directed by George Archainbaud. Screenplay by Davallon Scott. Photographed by Nicholas Musuraca. Edited by Samuel Beetley.

Starring Gig Young, Lynne Roberts, Mary Anderson, Willard Parker, Carla Balenda, Gerald Mohr, James Anderson, John Kellogg, Harry Shannon, Cleo Moore, Christy Palmer, Paul Frees.

A public defender tries to clear the name of a fugitive who fled upon being found guilty for a murder he didn't commit.

416 *Hurry, Charlie, Hurry* (1941) Comedy. Running time: 65 minutes. Black and white. Available on videocassette.

Produced by Howard Benedict. Directed by Charles E. Roberts. Screenplay by Paul Gerard Smith (based on a story by Luke Short). Photographed by Nicholas Musuraca. Edited by George Hively.

Starring Leon Errol (Daniel Boone), Mildred Coles (Beatrice Boone), Kenneth Howell (Jerry Grant), Cecil Cunningham (Mrs. Boone), George Watts (Horace Morris), Edward Conrad (Wagon Track), Noble Johnson (Poison Arrow), Douglas Walton (Michael Prescott), Renee Haal (Josephine Whitley), Georgia Crane (Mrs. Whitley), Lalo Encinas (Frozen Foot).

A small town banker gets into a fight with his wife over his daughter's romantic plans for the future.

417 *I Dream Too Much* (1935)
Musical. Running time: 95 minutes. Black and white.

Produced by Pandro S. Berman. Directed by John Cromwell. Screenplay by James Gow and Edmund North (based on a story by Elsie Finn and David G. Wittels). Photographed by David Abel. Edited by William Morgan. Music by Max Steiner, Andre Kostalanetz, Jerome Kern, and Dorothy Fields.

Songs: "The Jockey on the Carousel," "I'm the Echo," "I Got Love," the title song, "The Bell Song," "Caro Nome."

Starring Lily Pons (Annette), Henry Fonda (Jonathan), Eric Blore (Roger), Osgood Perkins (Paul), Lucien Littlefield (Hubert Dilley), Esther Dale (Mrs. Dilley), Lucille Ball (Gwendolyn), Mischa Auer (Pianist), Scotty Beckett (Boy on Merry-Go-Round), Clarence Wilson (Detective), Oscar Apfel (Cafe Owner).

A husband tries to push his reluctant wife into a singing career.

I Married a Communist see
Woman on Pier 13

418 *I Married a Woman* (1958)
Comedy. Running time: 80 minutes. Black and white. Available on videocassette. A Universal-RKO tandem production.

Produced by William Bloom. Directed by Hal Kanter. Screenplay by

Goodman Ace. Photographed by Lucien Ballard. Edited by Otto Ludwig and Kenneth Marstella.

Starring George Gobel (Marshall "Mickey" Briggs), Diana Dors (Janice Briggs), Adolphe Menjou (Frederick Sutton), Jessie Royce Landis (Mother Blake), Nita Talbot (Miss Anderson), William Redfield (Eddie Benson), Steve Dunne (Bob Sanders), John McGiver (Felix Girard), Cheerio Meredith (Mrs. Wilkins), Steve Pendelton (Photographer), Stanley Adams (Cab Driver), Kay Buckley, Angie Dickinson (Bits), John Wayne (Cameo in color dream sequence).

An ad agency exec neglects his wife because of his business, so she determines to make him jealous.

419 *I Remember Mama* (1948)
Drama. Running time: 134 minutes. Black and white.

Produced by George Stevens and Harriet Parsons. Directed by Stevens. Screenplay by DeWitt Bodeen (based on the play by John Van Druten and the novel *Mama's Bank Account* by Kathryn Forbes). Photographed by Nicholas Musuraca. Edited by Robert Swink. Music by Roy Webb.

Starring Irene Dunne (Mama), Barbara Bel Geddes (Katrin), Oscar Homolka (Uncle Chris), Phillip Dorn (Papa), Sir Cedric Hardwicke (Mr. Hyde), Edgar Bergen (Mr. Thorkelson), Rudy Vallee (Dr. Johnson), Barbara O'Neil (Jessie Brown), Florence Bates, (Florence Dana Moorehead), Peggy McIntyre (Christine), June Hedin (Dagmar), Steve Brown (Nels), Ellen Corby (Aunt Trina), Hope Landin (Jenny).

A novelist looks back at her Norwegian-American upbringing.

Note: Later a TV series (1946–57) featuring Peggy Wood.

Oscar nominations: Best Photography, Irene Dunne, Barbara Bel Geddes, Oscar Homolka, Ellen Corby.

420 *I Walked with a Zombie*
(1943) Horror. Running time: 69 min-

George Gobel and Diana Dors in *I Married a Woman*.

utes. Black and white. Available on videocassette.

Produced by Val Lewton. Directed by Jacques Tourneur. Screenplay by Curt Siodmak and Ardel Wray (based on an original story by Inez Wallace). Photographed by J. Roy Hunt. Edited by Mark Robson. Music by Roy Webb.

Starring James Ellison (Wesley Rand), Frances Dee (Betsy), Tom Conway (Paul Holland), Edith Barnett (Mrs. Rand), James Bell (Dr. Maxwell), Christine Gordon (Jessica Holland), Theresa Harris (Alma), Sir Lancelot (Calypso Singer), Darby Jones (Carre Four), Jeni LeGon (Dancer), Richard Abrams (Clement), Martin Wilkins (Houngan), Jieno Moxer (Sabreur), Arthur Walker (Ti-Joseph).

A nurse must care for a woman cursed by voodoo.

421 *I Want You* (1951) Drama. Running time: 102 minutes. Black and white.

Produced by Samuel Goldwyn. Directed by Mark Robson. Screenplay by Irwin Shaw (based on stories by Edward Newhouse). Photographed by Harry Stradling. Edited by Daniel Mandell. Music by Leigh Harline.

Starring Dana Andrews (Martin Greer), Dorothy McGuire (Nancy Greer), Farley Granger (Jack Greer), Peggy Dow (Carrie Turner), Robert Keith (Thomas Greer), Mildred Dunnock (Sarah Greer), Ray Collins (Judge Jonathan Turner), Martin Milner (George Kress, Jr)., Jim Backus (Harvey Landrum), Marjorie Crossland (Mrs. Celia Turner), Walter Baldwin (George Kress, Sr.), Walter Sande (Ned Iversen), Peggy Maley (Gladys), Jerrilyn Flannery (Anne Greer), Erik Nielsen (Tony Greer), Ann Robin (Gloria), Carol Savage (Caroline Krupka), James Adamson (Train Porter), Frank Sully (Bartender).

Homefront reaction to the Korean conflict.

Note: Most reviewers unfairly compare this to Goldwyn's somewhat similar *Best Years of Our Lives* (q.v.).

Review: "A recruiting picture which seems to accept a third world war almost as a present reality"—Penelope Houston.

422 *If I Were Free* (1933) Drama. Running time: 65 minutes. Black and white.

Produced by Kenneth Macgowan and Merian C. Cooper. Directed by Elliott Nugent. Screenplay by Dwight Taylor (based on the play by John van Druten). Photographed by Edward Cronjager. Edited by Arthur Roberts.

Starring Irene Dunne, Clive Brook, Nils Asther, Henry Stephenson, Vivian Tobin, Tempe Pigott, Lorraine MacLean, Laura Hope Crews, Halliwell Hobbes, Mario Dominici.

An antique dealer and a lawyer, each in a bad marriage, fall in love.

423 *If I Were Rich* (1936) Comedy. Running time: 58 minutes. Black and white.

Produced and directed by Randall Faye. Screenplay by Brandon Fleming (based on the play *Humpty-Dumpty* by Horace Annesley Vachell). Photographed by Geoffrey Faithfull. Edited by Andrew Buchanan.

Starring Jack Melford (Albert Mott), Kay Walsh (Chrissie de la Mothe), Clifford Heatherly (Gen de la Noth), Minnie Rayner (Mrs. Mott), Henry Carlisle (Pauttick), Fred Bradshaw (Jack).

A Socialist barber quickly turns capitalist when he runs into a large sum of money.

424 *If You Knew Susie* (1948) Musical comedy. Running time: 90 minutes. Black and white. Available on videocassette.

Produced by Eddie Cantor. Directed by Gordon Douglas. Screenplay by Warren Wilson, Oscar Brodney, Bud Pearson, and Lester White. Photographed by Frank Redman. Edited by Phillip Martin. Music by George Tibbles, Buddy De Sylva, Jimmy McHugh, Harold Adamson.

Songs: "If You Knew Susie," "My Brooklyn Love Song," "What Do I Want with Money," "We're Living the Life We Love," "My How the Time Goes By."

Starring Eddie Cantor (Sam Parker), Joan Davis (Susie Parker), Allyn Joslyn (Mike Garrett), Charles Dingle (Mr. Whitley), Phil Brown (Joe Collins), Sheldon Leonard (Steve Garland), Joe Sawyer (Zero), Douglas Fowley (Marty), Margaret Kerrey (Marjorie), Dick Humphreys (Handy), Howard Freeman (Mr. Clinton), Sig Rumann (Count Alexis), Fritz Feld (Chez Henri), Bobby Driscoll (Junior), Addison Richards (Senator), George Chandler (Reporter), Don Beddoe (Editor), Ellen Corby (Bit), Tom Keene (Graham), Syd Saylor (Pet Store Owner), J. Farrell MacDonald (Policeman).

A vaudeville couple retire to a conservative community and are snubbed by their neighbors until they find the former vaudevillians are heir to a fortune.

425 *I'm from the City* (1938) Comedy. Running time: 65 minutes. Black and white.

Produced by William Sistrom. Directed by Ben Holmes. Screenplay by Nicholas Barrows, Robert St. Clair, and John Grey (based on the story by Holmes). Photographed by Frank Redman. Edited by Ted Cheesman.

Starring Joe Penner (Pete), Richard Lane (Ollie), Lorraine Krueger (Rosie), Paul Guilfoyle (Willie), Kay Sutton (Marlene), Kathryn Sheldon (Grandma), Ethan Laidlaw (Jeff), Lafe McKee (Bobby), Edmund Cobb (Red), Clyde Kinney (Butch).

A city slicker finds he is an expert bareback rider when under hypnosis.

426 *I'm Still Alive* (1940) Drama. Running time: 72 minutes. Black and white.

Produced by Fredric Ullman. Directed by Irving Reis. Screenplay by Edmund North. Photographed by J. Roy Hunt. Edited by Theron Warth. Music by Roy Webb.

Starring Kent Taylor (Steve Bonnett), Linda Hayes (Laura Marley), Howard da Silva (Red Garvey), Ralph Morgan (Walter Blake), Don Dillaway (Tommy Briggs), Fred Niblo (Director).

The romantic ups and downs of a stuntman and his actress wife.

Note: Former RKO actress Helen Twelvetrees sued over this film believing it to be based on her courtship with Jack Woody. The suit was settled out of court. Fred Niblo, cast as a director in a small role, was actually a top silent screen helmsman, responsible for the 1922 version of *Ben Hur.*

427 *In Name Only* (1939) Drama. Running time: 94 minutes. Black and white. Available on videocassette.

Produced by George Haight. Directed by John Cromwell. Screenplay by Richard Sherman (based on the novel *Memory of Love* by Bessie Brewer). Photographed by J. Roy Hunt. Edited by William Hamilton. Music by Roy Webb.

Starring Carole Lombard (Julie Eden), Cary Grant (Alec Walker), Kay Francis (Maida Walker), Charles Coburn (Mr. Walker), Katherine Alexander (Laura), Jonathan Hale (Dr. Gateson), Maurice Moscovich (Dr. Muller), Nella Walker (Mrs. Walker), Peggy Ann Garner (Ellen), Spencer Charters (Gardener).

A rich man falls for another woman, but his wife will not divorce him.

Review: "Stock romantic drama..." — *Variety.*

428 *In Person* (1935) Musical comedy. Running time: 90 minutes. Black and white. Available on videocassette.

Produced by Pandro S. Berman. Directed by William Seiter. Screenplay by Allan Scott (based on the novel by Samuel Hopkins Adams). Photographed by Edward Cronjager. Edited by Arthur Schmidt. Music by Oscar Levant and Dorothy Fields.

Songs: "Don't Mention Love to Me," "Got a New Lease on Life."

Starring Ginger Rogers (Carol Corliss), George Brent (Emory Muir), Alan Mowbray (Jay Holmes), Grant Mitchell (Judge Parks), Samuel S. Hinds (Dr. Aaron Sylvester), Joan Breslau (Minna), Louis Mason (Sheriff Twing), Spencer Charters (Parson Lunk), Lew Kelly (Mountain Man).

A movie star hides out from pesty fans by disguising herself and living in the mountains.

Review: "Inept starring debut for Ginger Rogers ... a very weak affair" — *Variety.*

429 *Indian Agent* (1948) Western. Running time: 70 minutes. Black and white.

Produced by Herman Schlom. Directed by Lesley Selander. Screenplay by

Norman Houston. Photographed by J. Roy Hunt. Edited by Les Millbrook.

Starring Tim Holt (Dave), Noah Beery, Jr. (Redfox), Richard Martin (Chito), Nan Leslie (Ellen), Harry Woods (Carter), Richard Powers (Hutchins), Claudia Drake (Turquoise), Robert Bray (Nichols), Lee "Lasses" White (Inky), Bud Osborne (Sheriff), Iron Eyes Cody (Wovoka).

Two bandits try diverting foodstuffs from the Indian reservations, but are stopped by a cowboy hero and Indian sympathizer.

430 *The Informer* (1935) Drama. Running time: 91 minutes. Black and white. Available on videocassette.

Produced by Cliff Reid. Directed by John Ford. Screenplay by Dudley Nichols (based on the novel by Liam O'Flaherty). Photographed by Joseph H. August. Edited by George Hively. Music by Max Steiner.

Starring Victor McLaglen (Gippo Nolan), Heather Angel (Mary McPhillip), Preston Foster (Dan Gallagher), Margot Grahame (Katie Madden), Wallace Ford (Frankie McPhillip), Una O'Connor (Mrs. McPhillip), J.M. Kerrigan (Terry), Jos Sawyer (Bartley Mulholland), Neil Fitzgerald (Tommy Conner), Donald Meek (Pat Mulligan), D'Arcy Corrigan (Blind Man), Leo McCabe (Donahue), Gaylord Pendleton (Daley), Francis Ford (Judge Flynn), May Boley (Mrs. Betty), Grizelda Harvey (An Obedient Girl), Denis O'Dea (Street Singer), Jack Mulhall (Lookout), Robert Parrish (Soldier), Clyde Cook (Bit).

A simple man is plagued by rebels and his conscience when he betrays the IRA.

Note: Ford and McLaglen were said to drink before some of the more emotional scenes. Ford spent five years trying to get this film made—studio heads found the subject matter too dark. It became a turning point in the director's career. The screenplay was written in only six days. It was not a successful film until the end of the year, when critics named it among the ten best films of 1935. Thereafter, audiences flocked to see it, making it a box office smash. The story was filmed in England in 1929, and with an all-black cast in 1968 under the title *Uptight*. Both were failures.

Oscars: Screenplay, Director, Music, Best Actor (McLaglen).

Oscar nomination: Best Picture.

Reviews: "A tough subject; a sure critic's picture, but dubious box office" — *Variety;* "Masterpiece study of human nature..." — Leonard Maltin.

431 *Inside the Lines* (1930) Drama. Running time: 72 minutes. Black and white.

Produced by William LeBaron. Directed by Roy J. Pomeroy. Screenplay by Ewart Adamson and John Farrow (based on the play by Earl Derr Biggers). Photographed by Nicholas Musuraca. Edited by Jack Kitchin.

Starring Betty Compson (Jane Gershon), Ralph Forbes (Eric Woodhouse), Montague Love (Governor of Gibraltar), Mischa Auer (Amahdti), Ivan Simpson (Capper), Betty Carter (Lady Crandall), Evan Thomas (Major Bishop), Reginald Sharland (Archie), William Von Brincken (Spy School Chief).

Two World War I spies fall in love.

Note: Writer Farrow is father of actress Mia Farrow. Original playwright Derr Biggers created Charlie Chan. The 1915 play on which this film is based flopped on Broadway.

432 *Irene* (1940) Musical comedy. Running time: 101 minutes. Black and white.

Produced and directed by Herbert Wilcox. Screenplay by Alice Duer Miller (based on the musical comedy by James H. Montgomery). Photographed by Russell Metty. Edited by Elmo Williams. Music by Harry Tierney and Joseph McCarthy.

Songs: "Irene," "Castle of Dreams," "You've Got Me Out on a Limb," "Alice Blue Gown," "Worthy of You," "There's

Something in the Air," "Sweet Vermosa Brown."

Starring Anna Neagle (Irene O'Dare), Ray Milland (Don Marshall), Roland Young (Mr. Smith), Alan Marshal (Bob Vincent), May Robson (Granny), Billie Burke (Mrs. Vincent), Arthur Treacher (Betherton), Marsha Hunt (Eleanor), Isabel Jewell (Jane McGee), Doris Nolan (Lillian), Stuart Robertson (Freddie), Ethel Griffies (Princess Minetti), Tommy Kelly (Michael), Juliette Compton (Emily), Roxanne Barkley (Helen), Johnny Long and His Orchestra (Themselves).

A poor Irish girl moves in with rich folks in Long Island.

Note: Based on a 1919 musical and filmed before in 1926. Leads were originally slated for Astaire and Rogers, both of whom turned the script down. Grand ball sequence shot in Technicolor.

433 The Iron Major (1943) Biographical drama. Running time: 85 minutes. Black and white. Available on videocassette.

Produced by Robert Fellows. Directed by Ray Enright. Screenplay by Aben Kandel and Warren Duff (based on a story by Florence Cavanaugh). Photographed by Robert De Grasse. Edited by Robert Wise. Music by Roy Webb.

Starring Pat O'Brien (Frank Cavanaugh), Ruth Warrick (Florence "Mike" Ayers Cavanaugh), Robert Ryan (Father Donovan), Leon Ames (Robert Stewart), Russell Wade (Pvt. Manning), Bruce Edwards (Lt. Jones), Richard Martin (Davis Cavanaugh), Robert Brice (Coach), Virginia Brissac (Mrs. Ayers), Lew Harvey (Lieutenant), Bud Geary (Sergeant), Walter Brooke (Stone), Louis Jean Heydt (Recruiting Sergeant), Frank Puglia (Nurse), Pierre Watkin (Col. White), Walter Fenner (Doctor).

The story of legendary coach Frank Cavanaugh of Dartmouth, Boston College and Fordham.

Note: Original story written by Cavanaugh's wife.

Review: "All the talk is in words of less than one syllable"—James Agee.

434 Is My Face Red? (1932) Drama. Running time: 67 minutes. Black and white.

Produced by Harry Joe Brown. Directed by William Seiter. Screenplay by Bartlett Comack and Casey Robinson (based on the play by Markson and Allen Rivkin. Photographed by Leo Tover. Edited by Joseph Kane.

Starring Helen Twelvetrees (Peggy Bannon), Ricardo Cortez (William Poster), Jill Esmond (Mildred Huntington), Robert Armstrong (Ed Maloney), Arline Judge (Bee), ZaSu Pitts (Telephone Operator), Sidney Toler (Tony Mugatti), Clarence Muse (Horace), Fletcher Norton (Angelo Spinello).

The saga of a tough journalist who prints stories without conscience.

435 Isle of Destiny (1940) Adventure. Running time: 83 minutes. Black and white.

Produced by Franklyn Warner. Directed by Elmer Clifton. Screenplay by Arthur Hoerl, M. Coates Webster, and Robert Hively (based on a story by Allan Vaughn Elston). Photographed by Edward Linden. Edited by John Rawlins and Robert Crandall.

Starring William Gargan (Stripes), Wallace Ford (Milly), June Lang (Virginia), Gilbert Roland (Barton), Etienne Giardot (Doc), Katherine DeMille (Inda), Grant Richards (Lt. Allerton), Tom Dugan (Sgt. Reikker), Ted Osborne (Max), Harry Woods (Lawson).

A society girl is kidnapped by gangsters.

436 Isle of the Dead (1945) Horror. Running time: 72 minutes. Black and white. Available on videocassette.

Produced by Val Lewton. Directed by Mark Robson. Screenplay by Ardel Wray, Josef Mischel, and Lewton (suggested by a painting by Arnold Boecklin). Photographed by Jack MacKenzie.

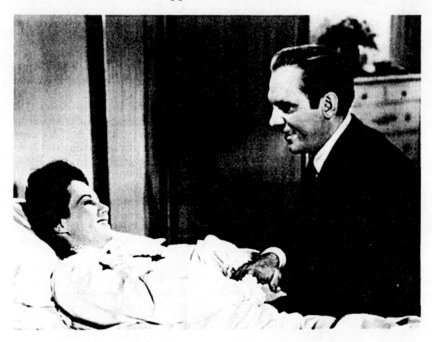

Ruth Warrick and Pat O'Brien in *The Iron Major*.

Edited by Lyle Boyer. Music by Leigh Harline.

Starring Boris Karloff (General Nikolas Pherides), Ellen Drew (Thea), Marc Cramer (Oliver Davis), Katherine Emery (Mrs. St. Aubyn), Helene Thmig (Kyra), Alan Napier (Mr. St. Aubyn), Jason Robards, Sr. (Albrecht), Skelton Knaggs (Henry Robbins), Sherry Hall (Colonel), Ernest Dorian (Dr. Drossos), Carl Eric Hanson (Officer).

A group of people on an island fear one of their members is a vampire.

Note: Banned in Britain at the time of its initial release. Karloff suffered back trouble during filming and underwent an emergency spinal operation. Actress Rose Hobart was originally slated to play Emery's role.

Review: "...quite different from any other horror film"—Leslie Halliwell.

437 *It Happened to One Man* (1941). Drama. Running time: 81 minutes. Black and white.

Produced by Victor Hanbury. Directed by Paul Stein. Screenplay by Paul Merzbach and Nina Jarvis (based on the play by Roland Pertwee and John Hastings Turner). Photographed by Walter Harvey.

Starring Wilfrid Lawson (Felton Quair), Nora Swinburne (Alice), Marta Labarr (Rita), Ivan Brandt (Leonard Drayton), Reginald Tate (Ackroyd), Brian Worth (Jack Quair), Edmond Breon (Adm. Drayton), Patricia Roc (Betty Quair), Thorley Walters (Ronnie), Athole Stewart (Lord Kenley).

A financier is exposed by his partner, whom he seeks when released from prison.

Made in Britain during World War Two with "frozen funds," which could not leave the country due to wartime restrictions.

438 *It's a Pleasure* (1945). Drama. Running time: 89 minutes. Color.

Produced by David Lewis. Directed by

William Seiter. Screenplay by Lynn Starling and Elliot Paul. Photographed by Ray Rennahan. Edited by Ernest Nims.

Starring Sonja Henie (Chris Linden), Michael O'Shea (Don Martin), Bill Johnson (Buzz Fletcher), Marie Mac-Donald (Mrs. Buzz Fletcher), Gus Schilling (Bill Evans), Iris Adrian (Wilma), Cheryl Walker (Loni), Peggy O'Neill (Cricket), Arthur Loft (Jack Weimar).

A former hockey star attempts a comeback as an ice-show performer but his problems with alcohol cause him to flounder while his wife emerges as a star.

439 *It's a Wonderful Life* (1946) Fantasy. Running time: 129 minutes. Black and white and colorized. Available on videocassette. A Liberty Films production for RKO release.

Produced and directed by Frank Capra. Screenplay by Frances Goodrich, Albert Hackett, Capra, and Jo Swerling (based on the story *The Greatest Gift* by Phillip Van Doren Stern). Photographed by Joseph Walker and Joseph Biroc. Edited by William Hornbeck. Music by Dimitri Tiomkin.

Starring James Stewart (George Bailey), Donna Reed (Mary Hatch), Lionel Barrymore (Mr. Potter), Thomas Mitchell (Uncle Billy), Henry Travers (Clarence), Beulah Bondi (Mrs. Bailey), Frank Faylen (Ernie), Ward Bond (Bert), Gloria Grahame (Violet Bix), H.B. Warner (Mr. Gower), Frank Albertson (Sam Wainwright), Samuel S. Hinds (Pa Bailey), Todd Karns (Harry Bailey), Mary Treen (Tilly), Virginia Patton (Ruth), Charles Williams (Eustace), Sarah Edwards (Mrs. Hatch), Bill Edmunds (Martini), Lillian Randolph (Annie), Sheldon Leonard (Nick), Charles Lane (Real Estate Agent), Carl Alfalfa Switzer (Freddie), Stanley Andrews (Mr. Welch), Ellen Corby, Lane Chandler, Larry Simms, Danny Mummert (Bits).

A small town man, eager to break out of his rut, is shown the meaning of life by his guardian angel when he attempts suicide on Christmas eve.

Note: This Yuletide perennial, seen now by virtually everybody, lost over a half million dollars when first released. Explained Stewart on *The Tonight Show:* "The war had ended and people were more interested in seeing Red Skelton or Jerry Lewis." Stewart has called it his favorite among his many fine films. He spoke out vehemently against its colorization in the mid to late 1980s. The film had long been in the public domain, and presumably every TV station, from network affiliates to small time cable outfits, owned a print, until 1993 when the film's copyright was attained by Republic Pictures for video sales and TV broadcasts.

Commentary: "I think it's the greatest film I ever made. Better yet, I think it's the greatest film *anybody* ever made" — Frank Capra.

440 *Jalna* (1935) Drama. Running time: 75 minutes. Black and white.

Produced by Kenneth MacGowan. Directed by John Cromwell. Screenplay by Anthony Veiller, Garrett Fort, and Larry Bachmann. Photographed by Edward Cronjager. Edited by William Morgan.

Starring Kay Johnson (Alayne), Ian Hunter (Renny), C. Aubrey Smith (Nicholas), Nigel Bruce (Maurice), David Manners (Eden), Peggy Wood (Meg), Jessie Ralph (Gran), Molly Lamont (Pheasant), Theodore Newton (Piers), George Offerman, Jr. (Finch), Clifford Severn (Wakefield).

The lives and loves of an eccentric family.

441 *The Jazz Age* (1929) Directed by Lynn Shores. Screenplay by Paul Gangelin and Randolph Bartlett. Photographed by Ted Pahle. Edited by Ann McKnight.

Starring Douglas Fairbanks, Jr., Marceline Day, Henry B. Walthall, Myrtle Steadman, Gertrude Messinger, Joel McCrea, William Bechtel, E.J. Ratcliffe, Ione Holmes, Edgar Dearing.

Part-talkie about a young man whose

JIMMY STEWART'S **NEW** PICTURE ... AND IT'S **WONDERFUL!**

JIMMY'S FIRST PICTURE IN FIVE YEARS!

James **STEWART** **DONNA REED** in Frank Capra's **IT'S A WONDERFUL LIFE** *with* Lionel BARRYMORE Thomas MITCHELL Beulah BONDI

Publicity poster for *It's a Wonderful Life*.

protected kid sister falls in with a bad crowd.

It's Only Money* see *Double Dynamite

442 *Jazz Heaven* (1929) Drama. Running time: 80 minutes. Black and white.

Produced by William LeBaron. Directed by Melville Brown. Screenplay by Cyrus Wood and J. Walter Ruben (based on a story by Dudley Murphy and Pauline Forney). Photographed by Jack MacKenzie. Edited by Ann McKnight and George Marsh. Music by Oscar Levant.

Starring Johnny Mack Brown (Barry Holmes), Clyde Cook (Max), Blanche Frederici (Mrs. Langley), Sally O'Neill (Ruth Morgan), Joseph Cawthorn (Herman Kemple), Albert Conti (Walter Klucke), Henry Armetta (Tony).

A poor songwriter falls in love with a girl at a boarding house.

443 Jet Pilot (1957) Adventure. Running time: 112 minutes. Color. Available on videocassette.

Produced by Jules Furthman. Directed by Josef von Sternberg. Screenplay by Furthman. Photographed by Winton C. Hoch. Edited by James Wilkinson.

Starring John Wayne (Shannon), Janet Leigh (Anna), Jay C. Flippen (Black), Paul Fix (Rexford), Hans Conried (Matoff), Roland Winters (Sokolov), Ivan Triessault (Langrad), Denver Pyle (Simpson), Ruth Lee (Mother), Phil Arnold (Bellboy), Gene Roth (Bit).

An American pilot falls for a Russian spy.

Note: Filmed for RKO under Howard Hughes' tutelage in 1949, finally released by Universal Pictures in 1957.

Review: "...all concerned should be thoroughly ashamed..."—Leslie Halliwell.

444 Joan of Arc (1948) Historical epic. Running time: 145 minutes. Color. Available on videocassette.

Produced by Walter Wanger. Directed by Victor Fleming. Screenplay by Maxwell Anderson and Andrew Solt (based on the play *Joan of Lorraine* by Anderson). Photographed by Joseph Valentine. Edited by Frank Sullivan.

Starring Ingrid Bergman (Jeanne d'Arc), Jose Ferrer (The Dauphin), Francis L. Sullivan (Pierre Cauchon), J. Carrol Naish (Count John of Luxemberg), Ward Bond (La Hire), Shepperd Strudwick (Father Jean Massieu), Gene Lockhart (Georges la Tremouille), Leif Erickson (Jean Dunois), Cecil Kellaway (Jean Le Maistre), Selena Royle (Isabelle d'Arc), Robert Barrat (Jacques d'Arc), James Lydon (Pierre d'Arc), Rand Brooks (Jean d'Arc), Roman Bohnen (Duran Lazxart), Irene Rich (Catherine LeRover), Nestor Paiva (Henri le Royer), Richard Derr (Jean De Metz), Ray Teal (Bertrand de Poulengy), David Bond (Jean Fournier), George Zucco (Constable of Clervaux).

The story of the 15th century peasant girl who led her people in battle against an invading British horde, and became a national hero.

445 Joan of Paris (1942). War drama. Running time: 93 minutes. Black and white.

Produced by David Hempstead. Directed by Robert Stevenson. Screenplay by Charles Bennett and Ellis St. Joseph (based on a story by Jacques Thery and Georges Kessel). Photographed by Russell Metty. Edited by Sherman Todd.

Starring Paul Henried (Lavallier), Michele Morgan (Joan), Thomas Mitchell (Father Antoine), Laird Cregar (Funk), May Robson (Rosay), Alan Ladd (Baby), Jimmy Monks (Splinter), Jack Briggs (Robin), Richard Fraser (Jeffrey).

A French barmaid, whose patron saint is Joan of Arc, helps downed pilots return to Allied lines.

Note: American film debuts of Henried and Morgan. Released in January 1942, just after Pearl Harbor was bombed, thus doing great business.

446 Johnny Angel (1945) Drama. Running time: 79 minutes. Black and white. Available on videocassette.

Produced by William L. Pereira. Directed by Edwin L. Marin. Screenplay by Steve Fisher and Frank Gruber (from the novel *Mr. Angel Comes Aboard* by Charles Gordon Booth). Photographed by Harry J. Wild. Music by Leigh Harline. Edited by Les Millbrook.

Starring George Raft (Johnny Angel), Claire Trevor (Lilah), Signe Hasso (Paulette), Lowell Gilmore (Sam Jewell), Hoagy Carmichael (Celestia O'Brien),

Marvin Miller (Gustafson), Margaret Wycherly (Miss Drumm), J. Farrell Mac-Donald (Capt. Angel), Mack Gray (Bartender), Jason Robards, Sr., and Marc Cramer (Officers), Bill Williams (Sailor).

A ship's captain sets out to find the men who murdered his father.

Note: Pereira's debut as producer. A box office success.

Review: "Tough, well-done melodrama..."—Leonard Maltin.

447 *Journey Into Fear* (1942) Drama. Running time: 71 minutes. Black and white. Available on videocassette.

Produced by Orson Welles. Directed by Norman Foster. Screenplay by Welles and Joseph Cotten (based on a novel by Eric Ambler). Photographed by Karl Struss. Edited by Mark Robson. Music by Roy Webb.

Starring Joseph Cotten (Graham), Dolores Del Rio (Josette), Ruth Warrick (Stephanie), Agnes Moorehead (Mme. Mathews), Jack Durant (Gogo), Everett Sloane (Kopeikin), Eustace Wyatt (Haller), Frank Readick (Mathews), Edgar Barrier (Kuvetli), Jack Moss (Banat), Stefan Schnaubel (Purser), Hans Conried (Oo Lang Sang), Orson Welles (Col. Haki).

Spy drama involving the smuggling of munitions into Turkey during WWII.

Note: Production was started by Welles, taken out of his hands. Apparently editor Robson worked for a year on the jumbled footage he was provided, and new scenes were added for the film's eventual release. This was the third and final Mercury production for RKO. The film was remade in Canada in 1975.

448 *Joy of Living* (1938) Musical comedy. Running time: 90 minutes. Black and white. Available on videocassette.

Produced by Felix Young. Directed by Tay Garnett. Screenplay by Gene Towne, Graham Baker, and Allan Scott (based on a story by Dorothy and Her-

bert Fields). Photographed by Joseph Walker. Edited by Jack Hively. Music by Jerome Kern and Dorothy Fields.

Songs: "You Couldn't Be Cuter," "A Heavenly Party," "What's Good About Goodnight?" "Just Let Me Look at You."

Starring Irene Dunne (Maggie), Douglas Fairbanks, Jr. (Dan Webster), Alice Brady (Minerva), Guy Kibbee (Dennis), Joan Dixon (Harrison), Eric Blore (Potter), Lucille Ball (Salina), Warren Hymer (Mike), Billy Gilbert (Cafe Owner), Frank Milan (Bert Pine), Dorothy Steiner (Dotsy), Estelle Steiner (Betsy), Phyllis Kennedy (Marie), Franklin Pangborn (Radio Broadcast Orchestra Leader), Grady Sutton (Florist), Charles Lane, Bert Roach, Fuzzy Knight (Bits).

A playboy sets his sights on a singing star.

Reviews: "Delightful screwball music comedy"—Leonard Maltin; "...a good way to fall asleep on one of those nights when you're fighting with your pillow"—*The Motion Picture Guide.*

449 *The Judge Steps Out* (1949) Comedy. Running time: 91 minutes. Black and white. Available on videocassette.

Produced by Michel Kraike. Directed by Boris Ingster. Screenplay by Ingster and Alexander Knox (based on a story by Ingster). Photographed by Robert De Grasse. Edited by Les Millbrook.

Starring Alexander Knox (Judge), Ann Sothern (Peggy), George Tobias (Mike), Sharyn Moffett (Nan), Florence Bates (Chita), Frieda Inescort (Evelyn Bailey), Myrna Dell (Mrs. Winthrop).

A pressured judge leaves all behind and runs away, finding a job as a short order cook.

Note: Completed in 1947 but released two years later. Knox was on loan from Columbia, Sothern from MGM. British title: *Indian Summer.*

450 *Keep 'Em Rolling* (1934). Comedy-drama. Running time: 65 minutes. Black and white.

Publicity poster for *Joan of Arc*.

Produced by William Sistrom. Directed by George Archainbaud. Screenplay by Albert Shelby LeVino and F. McGrew Willis (based on the story *Rodney* by Leonard Mason). Photographed by Harold Wenstrom. Edited by William Hamilton.

Starring Walter Huston, Frances Dee, Minna Gombell, Frank Conroy, G. Pat Collins, Robert Shayne, Ralph Remley, Army Personnel of the 16th Field Artillery.

A man goes AWOL when separated from the horse that saved his life in combat.

Ann Sothern and Alexander Knox in a scene from *The Judge Steps Out*.

451 *Kentucky Kernels* (1935) Comedy. Running time: 74 minutes. Black and white. Available on videocassette.

Produced by H.N. Swanson. Directed by George Stevens. Screenplay by Bert Kalmar, Harry Ruby, and Fred Guiol (based on a story by Kalmar and Ruby). Photographed by Edward Cronjager. Edited by James Morely. Music by Kalmar and Ruby.

Songs: "One Little Kiss," "Supper Song."

Starring Bert Wheeler (Willie), Robert Woolsey (Elmer), Mary Carlisle (Gloria), George McFarland (Spanky), Noah Beery, Sr. (Col. Wakefield), Lucille LaVerne (Hannah Milford), Willie "Sleep 'n' Eat" Best (Buckshot), William Pawley (John Wakefield), Louis Mason (Col. Ezra Milford), Margaret Dumont (Adoption Official).

A pair of small-time magicians adopt a little boy who's a missing heir to a wealthy Kentucky family. This family, however, is embroiled in a heated feud.

Note: British title: *Triple Trouble.*

Reviews: "Good vehicle for the team, with great slapstick finale"—Leonard Maltin; "One of their better efforts"—Leslie Halliwell.

452 *Kept Husbands* (1931) Drama. Running time: 76 minutes. Black and white.

Produced by William LeBaron. Directed by Lloyd Bacon. Screenplay by Alfred Jackson and Forrest Halsey (based on a story by Louis Sarecky). Photographed by Jack MacKenzie. Edited by Jack Kitchin.

Starring Dorothy Mackaill (Dot), Joel McCrea (Dick), Robert McWade (Parker), Florence Roberts (Mrs. Parker), Clara Kimball Young (Mrs. Post), Mary Carr (Mrs. Brunton), Lita Chevret (Gwenn), Ned Sparks (Hughie), Bryant Washburn (Bates), Freeman Wood (Mr. Post).

A steel worker marries and has his earnings spent frivolously by his new wife—the boss' daughter.

453 *The Kid from Brooklyn*
(1946) Comedy. Running time: 114 minutes. Color.

Produced by Samuel Goldwyn. Directed by Norman Z. McLeod. Screenplay by Don Hartman and Melville Shavelson (based on the screenplay by Grover Jones, Frank Butler, and Richard Connell from the play *The Milky Way* by Lynn Root and Harry Clork). Photographed by Gregg Toland. Edited by Daniel Mandell. Music by Jule Styne, Sammy Cahn, Sylvia Fine, and Max Liebman. Available on videocassette.

Starring Danny Kaye (Burleigh Sullivan), Virginia Mayo (Polly Pringle), Vera-Ellen (Susie), Walter Abel (Gabby), Eve Arden (Ann), Steve Cochran (Speed MacFarlane), Lionel Stander (Spider Schultz), Fay Bainter (Mrs. LeMoyne), Clarence Kolb (Wilbur Austin), Jerome Cowan (Fight Announcer).

A milkman is talked into becoming a prizefighter by a gang of crooks.

Note: A remake of Harold Lloyd's "The Milky Way" in which Lionel Stander also costarred.

454 *Killers from Space* (1954) Sci-fi. Running time: 71 minutes. Black and white. Available on videocassette. A Filmplays production for RKO release.

Produced and directed by Lee Wilder. Screenplay by Bill Raynor (based on a story by Myles Wilder). Photographed by William Clothier. Edited by William Faris.

Starring Peter Graves, James Seay, Frank Gerstle, Steve Pendleton, John Merrick, Barbara Bestar, Ben Welden, Shep Menken, Ruth Bennett, Ron Kennedy, and narrated by Mark Scott.

A dead scientist is revived by aliens and brainwashed to provide top secret information.

Note: Producer-director is brother to Billy Wilder.

Review: "Bad stock footage, bad costuming for the aliens, and bad acting for everyone involved"—*Motion Picture Guide.*

455 *King Kong* (1933) Adventure. Running time: 100 minutes. Black and white. Available on videocassette.

Produced and directed by Merian C. Cooper and Ernest B. Schoedsack. Screenplay by James Creelman and Ruth Rose (based on a story by Cooper and Edgar Wallace). Photographed by Edward Linden, Vernon Walker, and J. Taylor. Edited by Ted Cheesman. Music by Max Steiner. Special effects by Willis O'Brien, E.B. Gibson, Marcel Delgado, Fred Reefe, Orville Goldner, Carroll Shephard, Mario Larrinaga, and Byron L. Crabbe.

Starring Fay Wray (Ann Darrow), Robert Armstrong (Carl Denham), Bruce Cabot (John Driscoll), Frank Reicher (Capt. Englehorn), Sam Hardy (Charles Weston), Noble Johnson (Native Chief), Steve Clemente (Witch King), James Flavin (Briggs), Victor Wong (Charley), Paul Porcasi (Socrates), Russ Powell (Dock Watchman), Dick Curtis (Sailor), Vera Lewis (Theater Patron), Jim Thorpe (Native Dancer), Frank Mills & Lynton Brent (Reporters), George McQuarrie (Police Captain), Etta McDaniel (Native Woman), Merian C. Cooper (Flight Commander), Ernest Schoedsack (Chief Observer), Dorothy Gulliver, Carlotta Monti (Bits).

A showbiz entrepreneur travels to a remote island in search of a giant ape, which he plans to capture and bring back to the States, in spite of the monster's attachment to a young ingenue who is traveling with the entrepreneur.

Note: Although he received screen credit, writer Wallace died before making any contribution to the script. The film was budgeted at $400,000, but cost RKO $672,000 to produce. MGM offered to buy the film from the smaller studio, but RKO wisely refused. The film grossed $1,761,000 at the time of its

Bob Woolsey, Spanky McFarland, and Bert Wheeler in *Kentucky Kernels*.

initial release, singlehandedly saving RKO from bankruptcy. It was edited and toned down for a 1938 release, and it wasn't until thirty years later that the original was restored. The filmmakers tried to capture the same spirit with *Son of Kong* (1934) and *Mighty Joe Young* (1947), but these were lackluster by comparison. Low-budget efforts like *King Kong Escapes, King Kong Vs. Godzilla,* and *King Kong Lives!* were made throughout the sixties, seventies and eighties. In 1976, Dino DeLaurentiis produced a big-budgeted remake, but this was a dismal failure on all levels. Ray Harryhausen assisted Willis O'Brien with the animation. Considered one of the all-time greatest films ever made, it was, interestingly enough, Adolf Hitler's favorite movie.

456 *Kitty Foyle* (1940) Drama. Running time: 105 minutes. Black and white. Available on videocassette.

Produced by David Hempstead. Directed by Sam Wood. Screenplay by Dalton Trumbo and Donald Ogden Stewart (based on the novel by Christopher Morley). Photographed by Robert De Grasse. Edited by Henry Berman. Music by Roy Webb.

Starring Ginger Rogers (Kitty Foyle), Dennis Morgan (Wyn Stafford), James Craig (Mark), Eduardo Ciannelli (Giono), Ernest Cossart (Pop), Gladys Cooper (Mrs. Stafford), Odette Myrtil (Delphine Detaille), Mary Treen (Pat), Katharine Stevens (Molly), Walter Kingsford (Mr. Kennett), Cecil Cunningham (Grandmother), Nella Walker (Aunt Jessica), Edward Fielding (Uncle Edgar), Kay Linaker (Wyn's Wife), Richard Nichols (Wyn's Boy), Florence Bates, Heather Angel, Tyler Brooke, Hattie Noel, Doodles Weaver, Max Davidson, Spencer Charters, Gino Corrado, Brooks Benedict (Bits).

A hard-working girl dreams of marrying a rich man. When she falls for one, she is rejected by his snobbish family.

Note: Actress Stevens (later billed as

SENSATIONAL THRILL TO STARTLE MILLIONS!

MOST AMAZING SHOW ON ANY SCREEN!

Startling! Staggering! Stupendous! Nothing can approach this show-of-the-age!...The strangest story ever conceived by man!...Adventure to make you wonder if it's true... while your very eyes convince you that it *is*!

KING KONG

with **FAY WRAY**
ROBERT ARMSTRONG · BRUCE CABOT

a personally directed
CMERIAN C. **S**ERNEST B.
COOPER SCHOEDSACK
RKO RADIO **PRODUCTION**

Publicity poster for *King Kong*.

K.T. Stevens), is the daughter of director Wood.

Oscar: Ginger Rogers for Best Actress, among stiff competition (Hepburn, Davis, etc). *Oscar nominations:* Best Picture, Best Screenplay, and Best Sound.

457 *Laddie* (1935) Drama. Running time: 70 minutes. Black and white.

Produced by Pandro S. Berman. Directed by George Stevens. Screenplay by Ray Harris and Dorothy Yost (based on the novel by Gene Stratton-Porter).

Photographed by Harold Wenstrom. Edited by James Morley.

Starring John Beal (Laddie Stanton), Gloria Stuart (Pamela Pryor), Virginia Weidler (Little Sister), Charlotte Henry (Shelly Stanton), Donald Crisp (Mr. Pryor), Gloria Shea (Sally Stanton), Willard Robertson (Mr. Stanton), Dorothy Peterson (Mrs. Stanton), Jimmy Butler (Leon Stanton), Greta Mayer (Candace), Mary Forbes (Mr. Pryor), Grady Sutton (Peter Dover).

A farm boy falls for a city girl.

Note: Remake of a 1925 silent.

458 *Laddie* (1940) Drama. Running time: 69 minutes. Black and white.

Produced by Cliff Reid. Directed by Jack Hively. Screenplay by Bert Granet and Jerry Cady (based on the novel by Gene Stratton-Porter). Photographed by Harry Wild. Edited by George Hively. Music by Roy Webb.

Starring Tim Holt (Laddie), Virginia Gilmore (Pamela), Joan Carroll (Sister), Spring Byington (Mrs. Stanton), Robert Barrat (Mr. Stanton), Esther Dale (Bridgette), Miles Mander (Mr. Pryor), Sammy McKim (Leon), Joan Brodel (Shelly), Martha O'Driscoll (Sally), Rand Brooks (Peter Dover), Peter Cushing (Robert Brooks).

Third version of the above. Actress Brodel later was billed as Joan Leslie.

459 *Ladies' Day* (1943) Comedy. Running time: 62 minutes. Black and white.

Produced by Bert Gilroy. Directed by Leslie Goodwins. Screenplay by Charles E. Roberts and Dane Lussier (based on a play by Robert Considine, Edward Clark Lilley, and Bertrand Robinson). Photographed by Jack MacKenzie. Edited by Harry Marker. Music by Roy Webb.

Starring Lupe Velez (Pepita), Eddie Albert (Wacky), Patsy Kelly (Hazel), Max Baer, (Hippo), Jerome Cowan (Updyke), Iris Adrian (Kitty), Joan Barclay (Joan), Cliff Clark (Dan), Carmen Morales (Marianna), George Cleveland (Doc), Jack Briggs (Marty), Russ Clark (Smokey), Nedrick Young (Tony), Eddie Dew (Spike), Tom Kennedy (House Detective), Ralph Sanford, Frank Mills, Richard Martin, George O'Hanlon, Mary Stuart, Sally Wadsworth (Bits).

A baseball pitcher is having troubles on the mound as he thinks about his wife, so the other players' wives try kidnapping her until the championship is over.

460 *Ladies of the Jury* (1932) Comedy-drama. Running time: 65 minutes. Black and white.

Produced by William LeBaron. Directed by Lowell Sherman. Screenplay by Marion Dixon. Salisbury Field, John Frederick Ballard, and Eddie Welch (based on a play by Ballard). Photographed by Jack MacKenzie. Edited by Charles Kimball.

Starring Edna May Oliver (Mrs. Crane), Ken Murray (Wayne Dazy), Roscoe Ates (Andrew MacKaig), Kitty Kelly (Mayme Mixter), Guinn Williams (Steve Bromm), Kate Price (Mrs. McGuire), Charles Dow Clark (Jay J. Pressley), Cora Witherspoon (Lily Pratt), Jill Esmond (Mrs. Gordon), Robert McWade (Judge), Helene Miller (Evelyn Snow), Susan Fleming (Suzanne), Tom Francis (Jury Room Officer), Leyland Hodgson (Chauncey Gordon), Florence Lake (Bit).

A society woman is a lone holdout among jurists in a murder trial.

461 *The Lady Consents* (1936) Drama. Running time: 75 minutes. Black and white.

Produced by Edward Kaufman. Directed by Stephen Roberts. Screenplay by P.J. Wolfson and Anthony Veiller (based on the story *The Indestructible Mrs. Talbot* by Wolfson). Photographed by J. Roy Hunt. Edited by Charles Kimball.

Starring Ann Harding (Anne Talbot), Herbert Marshall (Dr. Michael Talbot),

Margaret Lindsay (Jerry Mannerly), Walter Abel (Stanley Ashton), Edward Ellis (Jim Talbot), Hobart Cavanaugh (Yardley), Ilka Chase (Susan), Paul Porcasi (Joe), Willie Best (Sam), Mary Gordon (Apple Lady).

A married man falls for a younger woman.

462 *Lady Luck* (1946) Comedy. Running time: 97 minutes. Black and white.

Produced by Warren Duff. Directed by Edwin L. Marin. Screenplay by Lynn Root and Frank Fenton (based on the story by Herbert Clyde Lewis). Photographed by Lucien Andriot. Edited by Ralph Dawson.

Starring Robert Young (Larry Scott), Barbara Hale (Mary Audrey), Frank Morgan (William Audrey), James Gleason (Sacramento Sam), Don Rice (Eddie), Harry Davenport (Judge Martin), Lloyd Corrigan (Little Joe), Teddy Hart (Little Guy), Joseph Vitale (Happy Johnson), Douglas Morrow (Dan Morgan), Robert Clarke (Southern Officer), Russell Simpson (Daniel Boone), Pat Priest, Mary Field, Dick Elliot, Myrna Dell (Bits).

A woman marries and tries to reform a gambler.

463 *A Lady Mislaid* (1958) Comedy. Running time: 60 minutes. Black and white.

Produced by Robert Hall. Directed by David Macdonald. Screenplay by Kenneth Horne. Photographed by Norman Warwick.

Starring Phyllis Calvert, Alan White, Thorley Walters, Gilian Owen, Richard Leech, Constance Fraser, Sheila Shand Gibbs.

Two spinsters on holiday get mixed up with detectives looking for a dead body.

464 *The Lady Refuses* (1931). Drama. Running time: 70 minutes. Black and white.

Produced by Bertram Millhauser. Directed by George Archainbaud. Screenplay by Wallace Smith (based on the story *Lady for Hire* by Robert Milton and Guy Bolton). Photographed by Leo Tover.

Starring Betty Compson, Gilbert Emery, John Darrow, Margaret Livingston, Ivan Lebedeff, Edgar Norton, Daphne Pollard, Reginald Sharland.

A millionaire hires a poor girl to woo his son from a golddigger, but the peasant girl ends up falling in love with the older man.

465 *Lady Scarface* (1941) Crime drama. Running time: 69 minutes. Black and white. Available on videocassette.

Produced by Cliff Reid. Directed by Frank Woodruff. Screenplay by Arnaud D'usseau and Richard Collins. Photographed by Nicholas Musuraca. Edited by Harry Marker.

Starring Dennis O'Keefe (Lt. Mason), Judith Anderson (Slade), Frances Neal (Ann Rogers), Mildred Coles (Mary Powell), Eric Blore (Mr. Hartford), Marc Lawrence (Lefty Landers), Damian O'Flynn (Onslow), Andrew Tombes (Seidel), Marion Martin (Ruby), Rand Brooks (Jimmy).

A police lieutenant stalks a criminal, unaware that she is a woman.

466 *A Lady Takes a Chance* (1943) Comedy. Running time: 86 minutes. Black and white. Available on videocassette.

Produced by Frank Ross. Directed by William Seiter. Screenplay by Robert Ardrey and Garson Kanin (based on the story by Jo Swerling). Photographed by Frank Redman. Edited by Theron Warth. Music by Roy Webb.

Starring Jean Arthur (Mollie Truesdale), John Wayne (Duke Hudkins), Charles Winninger (Waco), Phil Silvers (Smiley), Mary Field (Florrie Bendix), Don Costello (Drunk), John Philliber (Storekeeper).

A city girl falls for a rodeo rider.

Note: Screenwriter Arley went on to

publish best-selling books on behavioral evolution.

Review: "Wayne and Arthur make a fine comedy team..." — Leonard Maltin.

467 *Lady with a Past* (1932) Comedy. Running time: 70 minutes. Black and white.

Produced by Charles Rogers and Harry Joe Brown. Directed by Edward H. Griffith. Screenplay by Horace Jackson (based on the story by Harriet Henry). Photographed by Hal Mohr. Edited by Charles Craft.

Starring Constance Bennett (Venice Muir), Ben Lyon (Guy Bryson), David Manners (Donnie), Don Alvarado (The Argentine), Albert Conti (Rene), Merna Kennedy (Ann).

A bashful girl hires a private escort and heads for Europe in search of a more exciting life.

468 *Land of the Open Range* (1941) Western. Running time: 60 minutes. Black and white.

Produced by Bert Gilroy. Directed by Edward Killy. Screenplay by Morton Grant (based on the story *Homesteads of Hate* by Lee Bond). Photographed by Harry Wild. Edited by Frederic Knudtson. Music by Fred Rose and Ray Whitley.

Songs: "Hi-O My Horse Is So Slow," "K1-O," "Land of the Open Range."

Starring Tim Holt (Dave), Ray Whitley (Smokey), Janet Waldo (Mary Cook), Lee "Lasses" White (Whopper), Hobart Cavanaugh (Pinky Gardner), Lee Bonnell (Stuart), Roy Barcroft (Gil Carse), John Eliot (Dad Cook), Frank Ellis (Dude), Tom London (Tonton), J. Merrill Holmes (Sam Walton).

When a deceased landowner's will leaves his property to anyone serving at least two years in prison, many convicts descend upon the town.

469 *Las Vegas Story* (1952) Drama. Running time: 87 minutes. Black and white. Available on videocassette.

Produced by Robert Sparks. Directed by Robert Stevenson. Screenplay by Earl Felton and Harry Essex (based on the story by Jay Dratler). Photographed by Harry J. Wild. Edited by George Shrader.

Starring Jane Russell (Linda Rollins), Victor Mature (Dave Andrews), Vincent Price (Lloyd Rollins), Hoagy Carmichael (Happy), Brad Dexter (Thomas Hubler), Gordon Oliver (Drucker), Jay C. Flippen (Harris), Will Wright (Fogarty), William Welsh (Martin), Ray Montgomery (Desk Clerk), Colleen Miller (Mary), Robert Wilke (Clayton), Syd Silver (Matty), Jimmy Long, Paul Frees, Midge Ware, Brooks Benedict (Bits).

A newly married couple in Las Vegas have trouble when the woman's shady past is revealed.

Note: Paul Jarrico contributed to the script, but was denied credit by mogul Howard Hughes due to the writer's leftist leanings. This led to a battle between the Writer's Guild and Hughes.

470 *The Last Days of Pompeii* (1935) Historical epic. Running time: 96 minutes. Black and white. Available on videocassette.

Produced by Merian C. Cooper. Directed by Ernest B. Schoedsack. Screenplay by Ruth Rose and Boris Ingster (based on a story by James Ashmore Creelman and Melville Baker). Photographed by Edward Linden and Roy Hunt. Edited by Archie Marshek. Special effects by Willis O'Brien, Vernon Walker and Harry Redmond. Music by Roy Webb.

Starring Preston Foster (Marcus), Alan Hale (Burbix), Basil Rathbone (Pontius Pilate), John Wood (Falvius as a Man), Louis Calhern (Prefect), David Holt (Falvius as a Boy), Dorothy Wilson (Clodia), Wyrley Birch (Leaster), Gloria Shea (Julia), Frank Conroy (Gaius), William V. Mong (Cleon), Edward Van Sloan (Calvus), Henry Kolker (Warder), Ward Bond, Zeffie Tilbury, John Davidson (Bits).

Events in people's lives leading up to the eruption of Mount Vesuvius.

Note: This film lost nearly a quarter-million dollars when first released, not recouping that loss until its re-release in 1949, when paired with *She* (the 1935 version).

471 *The Last Outlaw* (1936). Western. Running time: 62 minutes. Black and white.

Produced by Robert Sisk. Directed by Christy Cabanne. Screenplay by John Twist, Jack Townley, and E. Murray Campbell (based on a story by Campbell and John Ford). Photographed by Jack MacKenzie. Edited by George Hively.

Starring Harry Carey (Dean Payton), Hoot Gibson (Chuck Wilson), Henry B. Walthall (Calvin Yates), Margaret Callahan (Sally Mason), Frank M. Thomas (Dr. Mason), Tom Tyler (Al), Frank Jenks (Tom), Fred Scott (Larry Dixon), Joe Sawyer (bit).

A cowboy emerges from a 25-year prison term to find his old cowtown has evolved into a big city.

Note: Story was filmed by John Ford as a two-reeler in 1919.

472 *Laugh and Get Rich* (1931) Comedy. Running time: 72 minutes. Black and white.

Produced by Douglas MacLean. Directed by Gregory La Cava. Screenplay by La Cava and Ralph Spence (based on a story by MacLean). Photographed by Jack MacKenzie. Edited by Jack Kitchin.

Starring Hugh Herbert (Joe Austin), Edna May Oliver (Sarah Austin), Dorothy Lee (Alice Austin), Robert Emmett Keane (Phelps), John Harron (Hepburn), Charles Sellon (Biddle), George Davis (Vincentini), Maude Fealy (Mrs. Teasdale), Russell Gleason (Larry).

A man drives his wife crazy with get-rich-quick schemes, even to the point of spending the family nest egg on an invention of his daughter's boyfriend.

Note: "Entertainment for the willing"—*Variety.*

473 *Law and Disorder* (1940) Comedy. Running time: 74 minutes. Black and white.

Produced by K.C. Alexander. Directed by David MacDonald. Screenplay by Roger MacDonald.

Starring Barry K. Barnes (Larry Preston), Diana Churchill (Janet), Alastair Sim (Samuel Blight), Edward Chapman (Inspector Bray), Austin Trevor (Heinrichs).

A young lawyer defends some saboteurs, then finds himself fighting them when he's drafted.

474 *Law of the Badlands* (1950) Western. Running time: 59 minutes. Black and white.

Produced by Herman Schlom. Directed by Lesley Selander. Screenplay by Ed Earl Repp. Photographed by George Diskant. Edited by Desmond Marquette.

Starring Tim Holt (Dave), Joan Dixon (Velvet), Robert Livingston (Dirkin), Leonard Penn (Cash), Harry Woods (Conroy), Kenneth MacDonald (McVey), Richard Martin (Chito).

Texas Rangers go undercover to capture counterfeiters.

475 *Law of the Underworld* (1938) Crime drama. Running time: 58 minutes. Black and white.

Produced by Robert Sisk. Directed by Lew Landers. Screenplay by Bert Granet and Edmund L. Hartmann (based on the play *Crime* by John B. Hymer and Samuel Shipman). Photographed by Nicholas Musuraca. Edited by Ted Cheesman.

Starring Chester Morris (Gene Filmore), Anne Shirley (Annabelle), Eduardo Ciannelli (Rocky), Walter Abel (Rogers), Richard Bond (Tommy), Lee Patrick (Dorothy), Paul Guilfoyle (Batsy), Frank M. Thomas (Capt. Gargan), Eddie Acuff (Bill), Jack Arnold (Eddie), Jack Carson (Johnny), Paul Stanton (Barton), George Shelley (Frank), Anthony Warde (Larry).

Two innocent young people get

involved in a respected man's underworld dalliances.

Note: A remake of *The Pay Off* (1930).

476 *The Law West of Tombstone* (1938) Western. Running time: 72 minutes. Black and white. Available on videocassette.

Produced by Cliff Reid. Directed by Glenn Tryon. Screenplay by John Twist and Clarence Upson Young (based on a story by Young). Photographed by J. Roy Hunt. Edited by Ted Cheesman.

Starring Harry Carey (Bill Parker), Tim Holt (The Tonto Kid), Evelyn Brent (Clara Martinez), Jean Rouverol (Nitta Moseby), Clarence Kolb (Sam Kent), Allan Lane (Danny), Esther Muir (Mme. Mustache), Bradley Page (Doc Howard), Paul Guilfoyle (Bud McQuinn), Kermit Maynard (Bit).

A young cowboy falls for the daughter of a local judge.

Note: Tim Holt's first cowboy appearance.

477 *Lawful Larceny* (1930) Drama. Running time: 66 minutes. Black and white.

Produced by William Le Baron. Directed by Lowell Sherman. Screenplay by Jane Murfin (based on the play by Samuel Shipman). Photographed by Roy Hunt. Edited by Marie Halvey.

Starring Bebe Daniels (Marion Dorsey), Kenneth Thompson (Andrew Dorsey), Lowell Sherman (Guy Tarlow), Olive Tell (Vivian Hepburn), Purnell B. Pratt (Judge Perry), Lou Payne (Davis), Bert Roach (French), Maude Turner Gordon (Mrs. Davis), Helene Millard (Mrs. French), Charles Coleman (Butler).

A fool loses his fortune to a sharp woman.

478 *Lawless Valley* (1938) Western. Running time: 59 minutes. Black and white.

Produced by Bert Gilroy. Directed by David Howard. Screenplay by Oliver Drake (based on the story *No Law in Shadow Valley* by W.C. Tuttle). Photographed by Harry Wild. Edited by Frederic Knudtson.

Starring George O'Brien (Larry Rhodes), Walter Miller (Bob North), Kay Sutton (Norma Rogers), Fred Kohler, Sr. (Jeff Marsh), George McQuarrie (Tim Wade), Lew Kelly (Fresno), Earle Hodgins (Sheriff), Chill Wills (Speedy), Dot Farley (Anna), Dick Hunter (Henchman), Robert Stanton (Bit).

When a man leaves prison he sets out to clear his name and find those who framed him.

479 *Lazybones* (1935) Comedy. Running time: 75 minutes. Black and white.

Produced by Julius Hagen. Directed by Michael Powell. Screenplay by Gerard Fairlie (based on the play by Ernest Denny). Photographed by Ernest Palmer.

Starring Claire Luce (Kitty), Ian Hunter (Sir Reginald), Sara Allgood (Bridget), Bernard Nedell (McCarthy), Michael Shipley (Hildebrand Pope), Pamela Carne (Lottie Pope).

An Englishman marries an American girl to recoup a lost fortune.

480 *Leathernecking* (1930) Musical. Running time: 72 minutes. Black and white and color.

Directed by Edward F. Cline. Screenplay by Alfred Jackson and Jane Murfin (based on the play *Present Arms* by Herbert Fields, Richard Rodgers and Lorenz Hart). Photographed by J. Roy Hunt. Edited by Victor Barraville. Music by Rodgers and Hart, Oscar Levant, Benny Davis, Harry Akst, Sidney Clare.

Songs: "You Took Advantage of Me," "A Kiss for Cinderella," "All My Life," "Careless Kisses," "Evening Star," "Brightly Nice and So Peculiar," "Shake It Off and Smile."

Starring Irene Dunne (Delphine), Ken Murray (Frank), Louise Fazenda (Hortense), Ned Sparks (Ned Sparks), Lilyan Tashman (Edna), Eddie Foy, Jr.

(Chick), Benny Rubin (Stein), Rita La Roy (Fortuneteller), Fred Stanley (Douglas).

A marine private pursues a socialite.

481 *Legion of the Lawless* (1940) Western. Running time: 59 minutes. Black and white. Available on videocassette.

Produced by Bert Gilroy. Directed by David Howard. Screenplay by Doris Schneider. Photographed by Harry Wild. Edited by Frederic Knudtson.

Starring George O'Brien (Jeff Toland), Virginia Vale (Ellen), Herbert Heywood (Doc Denton), Norman Willis (Leo Harper), Hugh Sothern (Henry Ives), William Benedict (Edwin), Eddy Waller (Lafe Barton), Delmar Watson, Monte Montague, Slim Whitaker, Mary Field, Richard Cramer, Martin Garralaga, Wilfred Lucas (Bits).

A vigilante group, set up by the mayor of a western town, gets out of hand.

482 *The Leopard Man* (1943) Thriller. Running time: 63 minutes. Black and white. Available on videocassette.

Produced by Val Lewton. Directed by Jacques Tourneur. Screenplay by Ardel Wray and Edward Dein (based on *Black Alibi* by Cornell Woodrich). Photographed by Robert De Grasse. Edited by Mark Robson. Music by Roy Webb.

Starring Dennis O'Keefe (Jerry Manning), Margo (Clo-Clo), Jean Brooks (Kiki Walaker), Isabel Jewell (Maria), James Bell (Dr. Galbraith), Margaret Landry (Teresa Delgado), Abner Biberman (Charlie How Come), Richard Martin (Raoul Belmonte), Tula Palma (Consuelo Contreras), Ben Bard (Chief Robles).

A leopard, rented by a P.R. man for a stunt, escapes and kills a child. Further murders are then attributed to the animal, but the P.R. man believes it to be a human murderer.

Review: "Proves once again that money is not the essential element in good filmmaking"—*The Motion Picture Guide.*

483 *Let's Make Music* (1940) Musical. Running time: 82 minutes. Black and white.

Produced by Howard Benedict. Directed by Leslie Goodwins. Screenplay by Nathaniel West. Photographed by Jack MacKenzie. Edited by Desmond Marquette.

Starring Bob Crosby (Himself), Jean Rogers (Abby Adams), Elisabeth Risdon (Malvina Adams), Joseph Buloff (Joe Beliah), Joyce Compton (Betty), Bennie Bartlett (Tommy), Louis Jean Heydt (Mr. Stevens), Bill Goodwin (Announcer), Frank Orth (Mr. Botts), Grant Withers (Head Waiter), Walter Tetley (Eddie), Benny Rubin (Music Publisher), Jacqueline Nash (Singer), Donna Jean Dolfer (Pianist), Bob Crosby's Orchestra with The Bobcats (Themselves).

Songs: "Fight On for Newton," "The Big Noise from Winnetka," "Central Park," "You Forgot About Me."

A spinster schoolteacher cannot impress her students with a song she wrote, until it is picked up and turned into a pop hit by Bob Crosby's band.

Note: Crosby, brother of Bing, makes his film debut here.

484 *Let's Sing Again* (1936) Musical. Running time: 70 minutes. Black and white. A Principal production for RKO release.

Produced by Sol Lesser. Directed by Kurt Neumann. Screenplay by Don Swift and Dan Jarrett. Photographed by Harry Neumann. Edited by Robert Crandall. Music by Jimmy McHugh, Gus Kahn, Hugo Risenfield, Selmak Hautzik, Charles Locke, Richard Tyler.

Songs: "Let's Sing Again," "Lullaby," "Farmer in the Dell."

Starring Bobby Breen (Billy Gordon), Henry Armetta (Joe Pasquale), George Houston (Leon Albe), Vivienne Osborne (Rosa Donelli), Grant Withers (Diablo), Inez Courtney (Marge), Lucien Littlefield (Perkins), Richard Carle (Carter),

Clay Clement (Jackson), Ann Doran (Alice Albe).

A boy runs away from an orphanage and joins a traveling show as a singer.

Note: Breen's film debut; first in a series.

485 *Let's Try Again* (1934) Drama. Running time: 64 minutes. Black and white.

Produced by Myles Connolly. Directed by Worthington Miner. Screenplay by Miner, Allan Scott (based on the play *Sour Grapes* by Vincent Lawrence). Photographed by J. Roy Hunt. Music by Max Steiner. Edited by Ralph Dietrich.

Starring Diana Wynyard (Alice), Clive Brook (Dr. Jack Overton), Irene Hervey (Marge), Helen Vinson (Nan), Theodore Newton (Paul), Arthur Hoyt (Phillips).

A physician and his wife each contemplate having an affair. During divorce proceedings they find their marriage has caused them to need each other.

486 *Life of the Party* (1937) Musical comedy. Running time: 86 minutes. Black and white.

Produced by Edward Kaufman. Directed by William Seiter. Screenplay by Bert Kalmar, Harry Ruby, Viola Brothers Shore (based on a story by Joseph Santley). Photographed by J. Roy Hunt. Edited by Jack Hively. Music by Herb Magidson, Allie Wrubel, George Jessel, Ben Oakland.

Songs: "So You Won't Sing," "Let's Have Another Chance," "The Life of the Party," "Chirp a Little Ditty," "Yankee Doodle Band," "Roses in December."

Starring Joe Penner (Penner), Gene Raymond (Barry Saunders), Parkyakarkus (Parky), Harriet Hilliard (Mitzi), Victor Moore (Loiver), Helen Broderick (Pauline), Billy Gilbert (Dr. Molnac), Ann Miller (Betty), Richard Lane (Hotel Manager), Franklin Pangborn (Beggs), Margaret Dumont (Mrs. Penner).

A wealthy fool is chosen as a beautiful singer's mate, but she prefers a handsome fellow singer.

Note: Hilliard is the Harriet of Ozzie and ... fame. Parkyakarkus is the father of Albert Brooks (whose real name is Albert Einstein!) and Bob "Super Dave Osborne" Einstein.

487 *The Life of Vergie Winters* (1934) Drama. Running time: 75 minutes. Black and white.

Produced by Pandro S. Berman. Directed by Alfred Santell. Screenplay by Jane Murfin (based on the novel *A Good Woman* by Louis Bromfield). Photographed by Lucien Andriot. Edited by George Hively. Music by Max Steiner.

Starring Ann Harding (Vergie Winters), John Boles (John Shadwell), Helen Vinson (Laura Shadwell), Betty Furness (Joan at age 19), Frank Albertson (Ranny Truesdale), Lon Chaney, Jr. (Hugo McQueen), Sara Haden (Winne Belle), Molly O'Day (Sadie), Ben Alexander (Barry Preston), Donald Crisp (Mike Davey), Maidel Turner (Ella Hennan), Cecil Cunningham (Pearl Turner), Josephine Whittell (Madame Claire), Wesley Barry (Somersby), Edward Van Sloan (Winters), Walter Brennan (Roscoe), Mary McLaren (Nurse), Betty Mack (Maid).

A politician marries, but retains his mistress and child.

488 *Lightning Strikes Twice* (1935) Mystery. Running time: 64 minutes. Black and white.

Produced by Lee Marcus. Directed by Ben Holmes. Screenplay by Joseph A. Fields and John Grey (based on a story by Holmes and Marion Dix). Photographed by Edward Cronjager. Edited by Arthur Roberts.

Starring Ben Lyon (Stephen Brewster), Skeets Gallagher (Wally Richards), Thelma Todd (Judy Nelson), Jonathan Hale (Capt. Nelson), Laura Hope Crews (Aunt Jane), Walter Catlett (Gus), Pert Kelton (Fay), Chick Chandler (Marty Hicks), Margaret Armstrong (Delia), John Davidson (Phillips), Fred Kelsey (Dugan), Edgar Dearing (Lt. Foster), Roger Gray (Casey), Walter Long (Cop).

Murder mystery surrounding a jewel theft.

489 *A Likely Story* (1947) Comedy. Running time: 89 minutes. Black and white.

Produced by Richard H. Berger. Directed by H.C. Potter. Screenplay by Bess Taffel (based on a story by Alexander Kenedi). Photographed by Roy Hunt. Music by Leigh Harline. Edited by Harry Marker.

Starring Barbara Hale (Vickie North), Bill Williams (Bill Baker), Lanny Rees (Jamie), Sam Levene (Louie), Dan Tobin (Phil Bright), Nestor Paiva (Tiny), Max Willenz (Mr. Slepoff), Henry Kulky (Tremendo), Robin Raymond (Ticket Girl), Mary Young (Little Old Lady), Nancy Saunders (Blonde on Train), Bill Shannon (Major), Jack Rice (Secretary), Joel Green (Senator), Cy Schindell (Trucker).

A former soldier believes he is dying, gets a group of gangsters to insure him and designates a woman he meets as the beneficiary.

490 *The Little Foxes* (1941) Drama. Running time: 116 minutes. Black and white. Available on videocassette.

Produced by Samuel Goldwyn. Directed by William Wyler. Screenplay by Lillian Hellman. Additional dialogue by Arthur Kober, Dorothy Parker, and Alan Campbell (based on the play by Hellman). Photographed by Gregg Toland. Edited by Daniel Mandell. Music by Meredith Wilson.

Starring Bette Davis (Regina Hubbard Giddens), Herbert Marshall (Horace Giddens), Teresa Wright (Alexandra Giddens), Richard Carlson (David Hewitt), Patricia Collinge (Birdie Hubbard), Dan Duryea (Leo Hubbard), Charles Dingle (Ben Hubbard), Carl Benton Reid (Oscar Hubbard), Jessica Grayson (Addie), John Marriott (Cal), Russell Hicks (William Marshall), Lucien Littlefield (Sam Naders), Virginia Brissac (Lucy Hewitt), Terry Nibert (Julia), Alan Bridge (Dawson), Kenny Washington (Servant).

Post–Civil War drama of a family's attempts to blackmail each other.

Note: Screen debuts of Dan Duryea and Teresa Wright.

Oscar nominations: Best Director, Best Actress, Best Screenplay, Best Supporting Actress, Best Scoring, Best Editing, Best Art/Set Design.

Reviews: "One of the really beautiful jobs in the whole range of movie making" — Otis Ferguson; "Superb film of a brilliant play" — Leslie Halliwell.

491 *Little Men* (1940) Drama. Running time: 84 minutes. Black and white. Available on videocassette.

Produced by Gene Towne. Directed by Norman Z. McLeod. Screenplay by Mark Kelly and Arthur Caesar (based on the novel by Louisa May Alcott). Photographed by Nicholas Musuraca. Edited by George Hively. Music by Roy Webb.

Starring Kay Francis (Jo), Jack Oakie (Willie), George Bancroft (Major Birdee), Jimmy Lydon (Dan), Ann Gillis (Nan), Carl Esmond (Professor), Richard Nichols (Teddy), Casey Johnson (Robby), Francesca Santoro (Bess), Johnny Burke (Silas), Lillian Randolph (Asia), Sammy McKim (Tommy), Stanley Blystone (Bartender).

Jo and her professor run a school for boys, attempting to teach them about life.

Note: Filmed before by Mascot Pictures in 1935, this is the weaker of the two versions.

492 *The Little Minister* (1934) Drama. Running time: 104 minutes. Black and white. Available on videocassette.

Produced by Pandro S. Berman. Directed by Richard Wallace. Screenplay by Jane Murfin, Sarah Y. Mason, Victor Heerman, Mortimer Offner, and Jack Wagner (based on the novel and play by James M. Barrie). Photographed by Henry Gerard. Edited by William Hamilton. Music by Max Steiner.

Starring Katharine Hepburn (Babbie),

John Beal (Gavin), Alan Hale (Rob), Donald Crisp (Dr. McQueen), Lumsden Hare (Tammas), Andy Clyde (Wearyworld), Beryl Mercer (Margaret), Billy Watson (Micah Dow), Dorothy Stickney (Jean), Mary Gordon (Nanny), Frank Conroy (Lord Rintoul), Eily Malyon (Evalina), Reginald Denny (Capt. Halliwell), Leonard Carey (Munn), Herbert Bunston (Carfrae), Harry Beresford (John Spiens), Barlowe Borland (Snecky), May Beatty (Maid).

A minister falls for an earl's wayward daughter.

"Miss Hepburn plays the part with likeable sprightliness and charm" — *The New York Times.*

493 *Little Orphan Annie* (1932) Drama. Running time: 60 minutes. Black and white. Available on videocassette.

Directed by John Robertson. Screenplay by Wanda Tuchock and Tom McNamara (based on the comic strip of Harold Gray and Al Lowenthal). Photographed by Jack MacKenzie. Edited by Jack Kitchin.

Starring Mitzi Green (Annie), Buster Phelps (Mickey), May Robson (Mrs. Stewart), Kate Lawson (Mrs. Brugin), Edgar Kennedy (Daddy Warbucks), Matt Moore (Dr. Griffith), Sidney Bracey (Butler).

A little girl is deserted by her poor father and ends up in an orphanage.

494 *Little Orvie* (1940) Drama. Running time: 65 minutes. Black and white.

Produced by William Sistrom. Directed by Ray McCarey. Screenplay by Lynn Root and Frank Fenton (based on the novel by Booth Tarkington). Photographed by Roy Hunt. Edited by Theron Warth.

Starring Johnny Sheffield (Orvie), Ernest Truex (Frank), Dorothy Tree (Clara), Ann Todd (Patsy), Emma Dunn (Mrs. Welty), Daisy Mothershed (Corbinia), Fay Helm (Mrs. Balliser), Dell

Henderson (Mr. Brown), Edgar Dearing (Policeman).

After being told he can't have a dog, a young boy brings home a stray.

495 *Little Women* (1933) Drama. Running time: 117 minutes. Black and white.

Produced by Kenneth MacGowan. Directed by George Cukor. Screenplay by Sarah Y. Mason and Victor Herman (based on the novel by Louisa May Alcott). Photographed by Henry Gerard. Edited by Jack Kitchin. Music by Max Steiner. Available on videocassette.

Starring Katharine Hepburn (Jo), Joan Bennett (Amy), Paul Lukas (Fritz), Edna May Oliver (Aunt March), Jean Parker (Beth), Frances Dee (Meg), Henry Stephenson (Mr. Lawrence), Douglass Montgomery (Laurie), Spring Byington (Marmee), Samuel S. Hinds (Mr. March).

Saga of four sisters, their lives and loves, during the Civil War era.

Note: Previously made as a silent, then again by MGM in 1949.

496 *The Locket* (1946) Drama. Running time: 86 minutes. Black and white.

Produced by Bert Granet. Directed by John Brahm. Screenplay by Sheridan Gibney. Photographed by Nicholas Musuraca. Edited by J.R. Whittridge.

Starring Laraine Day (Nancy), Brian Aherne (Dr. Blair), Robert Mitchum (Norman), Gene Raymond (John Willis), Sharyn Moffett (Nancy at Age 10), Ricardo Cortez (Mr. Bonner), Henry Stephenson (Lord Wyndham), Katherine Emery (Mrs. Willis), Reginald Denny (Mr. Wendall), Fay Helm (Mrs. Bonner), Myrna Dell (Thelma), Vivian Oakland (Mrs. Donovan), Nick Thompson (Waiter), Martha Hyer, Ellen Corby (Bits).

A psychiatrist tries to prevent a disturbed woman's marriage.

497 *Lonely Wives* (1931) Comedy. Running time: 87 minutes. Black and white. A Pathe production for RKO.

Matt Moore, Buster Phelps, and Mitzi Green in *Little Orphan Annie*.

Directed by Russell Mack. Screenplay by Walter DeLeon (based on the play by A.H. Woods). Photographed by Edward Snyder. Edited by Joseph Kane.

A lawyer tries to have an affair without being caught by his wife or mother-in-law, so he hires an impersonator to take his place.

498 *Long Lost Father* (1934) Drama. Running time: 64 minutes. Black and white.

Directed by Ernest B. Schoedsack. Screenplay by Dwight Taylor (based on the novel by G.B. Stern). Photographed by Nicholas Musuraca. Edited by Paul Weatherwax.

Starring John Barrymore (Carl Bellaire), Helen Chandler (Lindsey Lane), Donald Cook (Dr. Bill Strong), Alan Mowbray (Sir Anthony Gelding), Claude King (Inspector), Reginald Sharland (Lord Vivyan), Ferdinand Gottschalk (Lawyer), Phyllis Barry (Phyllis Mersey-Royds), Tempe Pigott (Flower), Herbert Bunston (Bishop), E.E. Clive (Bit).

A London nightclub owner finds that the daughter he abandoned years ago has arrived at his doorstep looking for work — but wants no part of him.

499 *Long Night* (1947) Drama. Running time: 101 minutes. Black and white.

Produced by Robert and Raymond Hakim and Anatole Litvak. Directed by Litvak. Screenplay by John Wexley (based on the screenplay *Le Jour Se Leve* by Jacques Viot). Photographed by Sol Polito. Edited by Robert Swank.

Starring Henry Fonda (Joe), Barbara Bel Geddes (Jo Ann), Vincent Price (Maximillian), Ann Dvorak (Charlene), Howard Freeman (Sheriff), Moroni Olsen (Chief of Police), Elisha Cook, Jr. (Frank), Queenie Smith (Janitor's Wife), Charles McGraw (Policeman).

A WW2 vet, adjusting to civilian life, commits a murder and then, through flashback, comes to grips with how and why he ended up a murderer.

Note: Fonda chose this role just after returning from the service in an effort to change his established image. Remake of *Daybreak* (1939).

500 *Look Who's Laughing* (1941) Comedy. Running time: 79 minutes. Black and white. Available on videocassette.

Produced and directed by Allan Dwan. Screenplay by James V. Kern, Don Quinn, Leonard L. Levinson, Zeno Klinker, and Dorothy Kingsley. Photographed by Frank Redman. Edited by Sherman Todd. Music by Roy Webb.

Starring Edgar Bergen (Himself), Charlie McCarthy (Himself), Jim Jordan (Fibber McGee), Miriam Jordan (Molly), Lucille Ball (Julie Patterson), Lee Bonnell (Jerry), Dorothy Lovett (Marge), Harold Peary (Gildersleeve), Isabel Randolph (Mrs. Uppington), Walter Baldwin (Bill), Neil Hamilton (Hilary Horton), Spencer Charters (Hotel Manager), George Cleveland (Mayor Kelsey), Jed Prouty (Mayor Duncan), Sterling Holloway (Rusty), Charles Lane (Club Secretary), Dell Henderson (Wentworth).

Radio star Bergen lands his plane in Fibber McGee's town of Wistful Vista and plans to build an airplane plant there.

Note: Characters from popular radio shows appear together.

501 *The Lost Patrol* (1934) War adventure. Running time: 74 minutes. Black and white. Available on videocassette.

Produced by Cliff Reid. Directed by John Ford. Screenplay by Dudley Nichols, Garrett Fort (based on the novel *Patrol* by Phillip MacDonald). Photographed by Harold Wenstrom. Edited by Paul Weatherwax. Music by Max Steiner.

Starring Victor McLaglen (Sergeant), Boris Karloff (Sanders), Wallace Ford (Morelli), Reginald Denny (George Brown), J.M. Kerrigan (Quincannon), Billy Bevan (Herbert Hale), Alan Hale (Cook), Brandon Hurst (Bell), Douglas Walton (Pearson), Sammy Stein (Abelson), Howard Wilson (Aviator), Neville Clark (Hawkins).

A small British army troop is lost in the desert under Arab attack.

Note: Shot on location in Yuma, Arizona, in 110 degree heat. Filmed before in England in 1929.

502 *The Lost Squadron* (1932) Adventure. Running time: 72 minutes. Black and white. Available on videocassette.

Produced by David O. Selznick. Directed by George Archainbaud. Screenplay by Wallace Smith, Herman J. Mankiewicz, and Robert Presnell (based on a story by Dick Grace). Photographed by Leo Tover, Ed Cronjager, Rob Robison and Elmer Dyer. Edited by William Hamilton.

Starring Richard Dix (Capt. Gibson), Mary Astor (Follete Marsh), Erich von Stroheim (Von Furst), Dorothy Jordan (Pest), Joel McCrea (Red), Robert Armstrong (Woody), Hugh Herbert (Fritz), Ralph Ince (Detective).

Ex–World War I pilots are hired as stunt fliers for a film studio.

Review: "A pretty good show ... whether it will get back what it cost is something else again" — *Variety*.

503 *Louisiana Territory* (1953) Drama. Running time: 65 minutes. Color.

Produced by Jay Bonafield. Directed by Harry Smith. Screenplay by Jerome Brondfield. Photographed by Smith. Edited by Milton Shifman. Music by George Bassman.

Starring Val Winter (Robert Livingston), Leo Zinser (Charles Talleyrand), Julian Meister (George Benton), Phyllis Massicto (Phyllis Caldwell), Marlene Behrens (Jane Benton).

The ghost of Livingstone, who helped

negotiate the Louisiana Purchase, returns to New Orleans, to see what has become of the land.

Note: Filmed in 3-D.

504 *Love Affair* (1939) Comedy. Running time: 87 minutes. Black and white. Available on videocassette.

Produced and directed by Leo McCarey. Screenplay by Delmer Daves, Donald Ogden Stewart (from a story by McCarey, Daves, and Mildred Cram). Photographed by Rudolph Mate. Edited by Edward Dmytryk and George Hively.

Starring Irene Dunne (Terry McKay), Charles Boyer (Michel Marnet), Maria Ouspenskaya (Grandmother Janou), Lee Bowman (Kenneth Bradley), Astrid Allwyn (Lois Clarke), Maurice Moscovich (Maurice Colbert), Scotty Beckett (Boy on Ship), Bess Flowers and Harold Miller (Couple on Deck), Joan Leslie (Autograph Seeker), Dell Henderson (Cafe Manager), Carol Hughes (Nightclub Patron), Gerald Mohr (Extra).

A New York girl and a European man's bumpy transatlantic romance.

Note: It won no Oscars, as this was the year of *Gone with the Wind* and *The Wizard of Oz*. Joan Leslie's fourth film; she was only fourteen. Writers on this project were creating new scenes daily, and the actors never had a finished script. Remade as *An Affair to Remember*. Now in public domain, some video distributors have planted a new music score on the soundtrack.

Oscar nominations: Best Picture, Best Screenplay, Best Actress, Best Supporting Actress.

505 *Love Comes Along* (1930) Drama. Running time: 77 minutes. Black and white.

Directed by Rupert Julian. Screenplay by Wallace Smith. Photographed by J. Roy Hunt. Edited by Archie Marshek.

Starring Bebe Daniels (Peggy), Lloyd Hughes (Johnny), Montague Love (Sangredo), Ned Sparks (Happy), Alma Tell (Carlotta), Lionel Belmore (Brown).

An actress, stranded on an island, has an affair with a sailor.

506 *Love in the Desert* (1929) Drama. Running time: 68 minutes. Black and white.

Directed by George Melford. Screenplay by Harvey Thew, Paul Percy, and Randolph Barlett. Photographed by Paul Perry. Edited by Mildred Richter.

Starring Olive Borden (Zarah), Hugh Trevor (Bob), Noah Beery, Sr. (Abdullah), Frank Leigh (Harim), Charles Brinley (Hassan), Pearl Varvell (Fatima), William H. Tooker (Winslow).

A spoiled young man is sent to the desert by his wealthy parents, where he is kidnapped by an Arab tribe, and saved by a princess.

Note: Originally silent, with dialogue added later.

507 *Love on a Bet* (1936) Comedy. Running time: 75 minutes. Black and white.

Produced by Lee Marcus. Directed by Leigh Jason. Screenplay by P.J. Wolfson and Phil G. Epstein. Photographed by Robert De Grasse. Edited by Desmond Marquette.

Starring Gene Raymond (Michael), Wendy Barrie (Paula), Helen Broderick (Aunt Charlotte), William Collier, Sr. (Uncle Carlton), Walter Johnson (Stephan), Addison Randall (Jackson Wallace), Eddie Gribbon (Donovan), Morgan Wallace (Morton), Billy Gilbert (Cop).

A man bets he can get from New York to Los Angeles with no money.

508 *Love Starved* (1932) Drama. Running time: 80 minutes. Black and white.

Produced by David O. Selznick and Harry Joe Brown. Directed by William Seiter. Screenplay by Garrett Fort, Ralph Murphy, and Jane Murfin. Photographed by Arthur Miller. Edited by Joseph Kane.

Starring Helen Twelvetrees, Eric

Linden, Arline Judge, Cliff Edwards, Roscoe Ates, Polly Walters, Blanche Frederici, Allan Fox.

A woman marries a man of the streets and finds that the union is unhappy.

Note: Alternate title: *Young Bride.*

509 *Lovin' the Ladies* (1930) Comedy. Running time: 65 minutes. Black and white.

Produced by William LeBaron. Directed by Melville Brown. Screenplay by J. Walter Ruben (based on the play *I Love You* by LeBaron). Photographed by Edward Cronjager. Edited by Archie Marshek.

Starring Richard Dix (Peter), Lois Wilson (Joan), Allen Kearns (Jimmy), Rita La Roy (Louise), Renee MacReady (Betty Duncan), Virginia Sale (Marie), Selmer Jackson (George Van Horne), Anthony Bushell (Brooks), Henry Armetta (Sagatelli).

A man, in order to win a bet, tries to get a young couple together and engaged to be married inside a month.

510 *Luck of the Turf* (1936). Comedy. Running time: 64 minutes. Black and white.

Produced and directed by Randall Faye. Screenplay by John Hunter. Photographed by Geoffrey Faithfull.

Starring Jack Melford (Sid), Moira Lynd (Letty), Wally Patch (Bill), Moore Marriott (Jackson).

A man who picks winning horses for his pals finally decides to place his own bet in order to afford to get married.

511 *Lucky Devils* (1933) Action. Running time: 64 minutes. Black and white.

Produced by David O. Selznick. Directed by Ralph Ince. Screenplay by Ben Markson and Agnes Christine Johnston. Photographed by J. Roy Hune. Edited by Jack Kitchin.

Starring Bill Boyd (Skipper), William Gargan (Bob), Bruce Cabot (Happy), William Bakewell (Slugger), Creighton

Chaney (Frankie), Bob Rose (Rusty), Dorothy Wilson (Fran), Sylvia Picker (Toots), Julie Haydon (Doris), Gladden James (Neville), Roscoe Ates (Gabby).

A behind-the-scenes look at Hollywood stuntmen.

512 *Lucky Partners* (1940) Comedy. Running time: 102 minutes. Black and white. Available on videocassette.

Produced by Harry Eddington. Directed by Lewis Milestone. Screenplay by Allan Scott, John Van Druten (based on the story *Bonne Chance* by Sacha Guitry). Photographed by Robert De Grasse. Edited by Henry Berman.

Starring Ronald Coleman (David Grant), Ginger Rogers (Jean Newton), Jack Carson (Freddie Harper), Spring Byington (Aunt), Cecilia Loftus (Mrs. Sylvester), Harry Davenport (Judge), Billy Gilbert (Charles), Hugh O'Connell (Niagara Clerk), Brandon Tynan (Mr. Sylvester), Leon Belasco (Nick #1), Edward Conrad (Nick #2), Olin Howard (Tourist), Benny Rubin (Spieler), Lucille Gleason (Ethel's Mother), Nora Cecil (Clubwoman), Edgar Dearing (Desk Sergeant), Al Hill (Motor Cop), Billy Benedict (Bellboy).

Two strangers share a sweepstakes ticket.

Review: "There's nothing duller than a dull comedy..." — *The Motion Picture Guide.*

513 *The Lusty Men* (1952) Western. Running time: 113 minutes. Black and white. Available on videocassette.

Produced by Jerry Wald, Norman Krasna. Directed by Nicholas Ray. Screenplay by Horace McCoy and David Dortort (based on a story by Claude Stanush). Photographed by Lee Garmes. Edited by Ralph Dawson. Music by Roy Webb.

Starring Susan Hayward (Louise Merritt), Robert Mitchum (Jeff McCloud), Arthur Kennedy (Wess Merritt), Arthur Hunnicutt (Booker Davis), Frank Faylen (Al Dawson), Walter Coy (Buster Burgess), Carol Nugent (Rusty Davis), Maria Hart (Rosemary Maddox), Lorna Thayer (Grace Burgess), Burt Mustin (Jeremiah), Karen King (Ginny Logan), Jimmy Dodd (Red Logan), Eleanor Todd (Babs), Riley Hill (Hoag), Bob Bray (Fritz), Sheb Wooley (Slim), Marshall Reed (Jim-Bob), Paul E. Burns (Waite), Sally Yarnell, Nancy Moore, Alice Kirby (Bit Girls), Chuck Roberson (Tall Cowboy), Lane Bradford (Tyler), Glenn Strange (Foreman), Lane Chandler (Announcer), Denver Pyle (Niko).

Rodeo champ becomes young man's mentor, but finds himself attracted to the man's wife.

Note: Originally titled *Cowpoke* then *This Man Is Mine* before being shelved for a year and released under its present title.

514 *Macao* (1952) Crime drama. Running time: 80 minutes. Black and white. Available on videocassette.

Produced by Alex Gottlieb. Directed by Josef Von Sternberg. Screenplay by Bernard C. Schoenfeld and Stanley Rubin. Photographed by Harry J. Wild. Edited by Samuel Beetley.

Starring Robert Mitchum (Nick Cochran), Jane Russell (Julie Benson), William Bendix (Lawrence Trumble), Thomas Gomez (Lt. Sebastian), Gloria Grahame (Margie), Brad Dexter (Halloran), Edward Ashley (Martin Stewart), Phillip Ahn (Itzumi), Vladmir Sokoloff (Kwan Sum Tang).

A wandering American in the Far East falls for a singer and helps a detective trap a killer.

Note: Some scenes directed, without credit, by Nicholas Ray.

515 *The Mad Miss Manton* (1938) Comedy-mystery. Running time: 80 minutes. Black and white. Available on videocassette.

Produced by Pandro S. Berman and P.J. Wolfson. Directed by Leigh Jason. Screenplay by Phillip G. Epstein and Hal Yates (based on a story by Wilson Collison). Photographed by Nicholas Musuraca. Edited by George Hively. Music by Roy Webb.

Starring Barbara Stanwyck (Melissa Manton), Henry Fonda (Peter Ames), Sam Levene (Lt. Brent), Frances Mercer (Helen), Stanley Ridges (Eddie), Whitney Bourne (Pat), Vicki Lester (Kit), Ann Evers (Lee), Catherine O'Quinn (Dora Fenton), Linda Terry (Myra), Eleanor Hanson (Jane), Hattie McDaniel (Hilda), James Burke (Sullivan), Paul Guilfoyle (Bat Regan), Penny Singleton (Frances), Leona Maricle (Sheila Lane), Kay Sutton (Gloria Hamilton), John Qualen (Subway Watchman), Grady Sutton (Secretary), Emory Parnell (Doorman), Jack Rice (Doctor), Matt McHugh (Waiter), Clarence Wilson, Otto Fries (Bit).

A socialite tries to uncover a murder mystery with the help of a group of friends.

Review: "Something ground out by people in a desperate mood"—Pauline Kael.

516 *Mad Wednesday* (1950) Comedy. Running time: 79 minutes. Black and white. Available on videocassette as *Sins of Harold Diddlebock*.

Produced, directed, and written by Preston Sturges. Photographed by Robert Pittack. Edited by Thomas Neff.

Starring Harold Lloyd (Harold Diddlebock), Frances Ramsden (Miss Otis), Jimmy Conlin (Wormy), Raymond Walburn (E.J. Waggleberry), Edgar Kennedy (Jake), Arline Judge (Manicurist), Franklin Pangborn (Formfit Franklin), Lionel Stander (Max), Margaret Hamilton (Flora), Al Bridge (Wild Bill), Frank Moran (Cop), Torben Meyer (Barber), Victor Potel (Potelle), Jack Norton (Smoke), Arthur Hoyt (Blackston), Georgia Caine (Bearded Lady), Gladys Forrest (Snake Charmer), Max Wagner (Doorman), Rudy Vallee (Banker Sargent), Julius Tannen (Banker with Glasses), Robert Dudley (MacDuff), Robert Grieg (Thomas), Dot Farley

Publicity poster for *Macao*.

Harold Lloyd in *Mad Wednesday*.

(Secretary), J. Farrell MacDonald (Desk Sergeant).

A former college football star, now a lowly bookkeeper, decides to live it up when he is fired from his job.

Note: Originally produced as *The Sin of Harold Diddlebock* by California Pictures, run by Sturges and Howard Hughes in 1947, and released that year by United Artists. The film bombed, so Hughes retitled it, edited out about twelve minutes, and re-released through RKO in 1950. Lloyd and Sturges did not get along during filming, and scenes had to be shot twice to please both parties. The opening contains the climactic football game from Lloyd's silent classic *The Freshman*. This was Lloyd's last film.

517 *Mademoiselle Fifi* (1944) Drama. Running time: 69 minutes. Black and white.

Produced by Val Lewton. Directed by Robert Wise. Screenplay by Josef Michel,

Peter Ruric (based on stories by Guy de Maupassant). Photographed by Harry Wild. Edited by J.R. Whittridge. Music by Werner Heyman.

Starring Simone Simon (Elizabeth Roussette), John Emery (Jean Cornudet), Kurt Kreuger (Lt. Von Eyrick), Alan Napier (Count de Breville), Helen Freeman (His Countess), Jason Robards, Sr. (Wholesaler in Wines), Norma Varden (His Wife), Romaine Callendar (Manufacturer), Fay Helm (His Wife), Edmund Glover (Young Priest), Charles Waldron (Cure of Cleresville).

French laundress refuses to sleep with Prussian officer although it will save stagecoach passengers.

518 *Magic Town* (1947) Comedy. Running time: 103 minutes. Black and white. Available on videocassette.

Produced by Robert Riskin. Directed by William Wellman. Screenplay by Riskin. Photographed by Joseph F.

Biroc. Edited by Sherman Todd. Music by Roy Webb and Constantin Bakaleinkoff.

Starring James Stewart (Rip), Jane Wyman (Mary Peterman), Kent Smith (Hoopendecker), Ned Sparks (Ike Sloane), Wallace Ford (Lou Dicketts), Regis Toomey (Ed Weaver), Ann Doran (Mrs. Weaver), Donald Meek (Mr. Twiddle), E.J. Ballantine (Moody), Ann Shoemaker (Ma Peterman), Mickey Kuhn (Hank Nickleby), Howard Freeman (Richard Nickleby), Harry Holman (Mayor), Mickey Roth (Bob Peterman), Mary Currier (Mrs. Frisby), George Irving (Sen. Wilton), Selmer Jackson (Charlie Stringer), Robert Dudley (Dickey, the Reporter), Julia Dean (Mrs. Wilton), Joel Friedkin (Dingle), Paul Scardon (Hodges), George Crane (Shorty), Richard Belding (Junior), Danny Mummert (Benny), Griff Bennett (Henry), Edna Holland (Secretary), Eddie Parks (Bookkeeper), Paul Maxey (Fat Man in Hallway), Lee "Lasses" White (Old Timer), Snub Pollard (Townsman), Wheaton Chambers (Electrician), Edgar Dearing (Gray-haired Man), Emmett Vogan (Reverend), Eddy Waller (Newcomer), Frank Fenton (Birch), Garry Owen, Dick Wessel, Dick Elliot (Bits).

An opinion pollster arrives in a small town which reflects the views of all Americans.

Review: "Doesn't always hit bullseye, but remains engrossing throughout" — Leonard Maltin.

519 *The Magnificent Ambersons*

(1942) Drama. Running time: 88 minutes. Black and white. Available on videocassette.

Produced by Orson Welles. Directed by Welles, Freddie Fleck, Robert Wise. Screenplay by Welles (based on the novel by Booth Tarkington). Photographed by Stanley Cortez, Russell Metty, Harry J. Wild. Edited by Robert Wise, Jack Moss, Mark Robson.

Starring Joseph Cotten (Eugene Morgan), Dolores Costello (Isabel), Anne Baxter (Lucy), Tim Holt (George), Agnes Moorehead (Fanny), Ray Collins (Jack), Richard Bennett (Major Amberson), Erskine Sanford (Benson), J. Louis Johnson (Butler), Donald Dillaway (Wilbur), Charles Phipps (Uncle John), Orson Welles (Narrator).

A snobbish family must deal with losing their wealth and position.

Note: Welles wrote the screenplay in nine days and edited as he filmed. It originally ran nearly two and one-half hours, but after a very shaky premiere, studio heads prevailed. The film was edited down to its present 88 minute length, and a new, more upbeat ending was tacked on. The film was then released as a throwaway to theaters, paired with *Mexican Spitfire's Elephant* as a double-bill. It was made for $1,125,000 and lost $625,000. Still, it is today considered brilliant.

Review: "Even in its truncated form, it is amazing and memorable" — Pauline Kael.

520 *Maid's Night Out* (1938)

Comedy. Running time: 64 minutes. Black and white. Available on videocassette.

Produced by Robert Sisk. Directed by Ben Holmes. Screenplay by Bert Granet. Photographed by Frank Redman. Edited by Ted Cheesman.

Starring Joan Fontaine (Sheila Harrison), Allan Lane (Bill Norman), Hedda Hopper (Mrs. Harrison), George Irving (Rufus Norman), William Brisbane (Wally Martin), Billy Gilbert (Popalopolis), Cecil Kellaway (Geoffrey), Vicki Lester (Adele), Hilda Vaughn (Mary), Eddie Gribbon (Hogan), Frank M. Thomas (McCarthy), Solly Ward (Mischa), Lee Patrick, Jack Carson, Edgar Dearing, Paul Guilfoyle (Bits).

A wealthy playboy becomes a milkman to prove to his father that he can hold down a regular job; en route he meets a wealthy girl whom he mistakes for a servant.

521 *Make a Wish* (1937) Musical. Running time: 75 minutes. Black and white.

Produced by Sol Lesser. Directed by Kurt Neumann. Screenplay by Gertrude Berg, Bernard Schubert, Al Boasberg, Earle Snell, and William Hurlburt (based on a story by Berg). Photographed by John Mescall. Music by Oscar Strauss. Edited by Arthur Hilton.

Songs: "Music in My Heart," "My Campfire Dreams," "Make a Wish," "Old Man Rip."

Starring Bobby Breen (Chip), Basil Rathbone (Selden), Marion Claire (Irene), Henry Armetta (Moreta), Ralph Forbes (Mays), Leon Errol (Brennan), Billy Lee (Pee Wee), Donald Meek (Joseph).

A young soprano goes to summer camp and aids a composer suffering from writer's block.

522 *Make Mine Music* (1946) Animated. Running time: 74 minutes. Color.

Produced by Joe Grant. Directed by Jack Kinney, Clyde Geronimi, Hamilton Luske, Robert Cormack, and Joshua Meador. Screenplay by Homer Brightman, Dick Huemer, Dick Kinney, John Walbridge, Tom Oreb, Dick Shaw, Eric Gurney, Sylvia Holland, T. Hee, Dick Kelsey, Jesse Marsh, Roy Williams, Erdman Penner, James Boldero, Cap Palmer, Erwin Graham. Music by Baron Friedrich von Flotow, Al Cameron, Ken Darby, Ray Gilbert, Ted Weems, Bobby Worth, Henry Creamer, Turner Leighton.

Voices of Nelson Eddy, Dinah Shore, Benny Goodman and His Orchestra, The Andrews Sisters, Jerry Colonna, Andy Russell, Sterling Holloway, The Pied Pipers, The King's Men, The Ken Darby Chorus, Tatiana Riabouchinska, David Lichine.

Ten part Walt Disney feature of animation and music.

Review: "A mixed bag to be sure" — Leonard Maltin.

523 *Make Way for a Lady* (1936) Comedy. Running time: 65 minutes. Black and white.

Produced by Zion Meyers. Directed by David Burton. Screenplay by Gertrude Purcell (based on the novel *Daddy and I* by Elizabeth Jordan). Photographed by David Abel. Edited by George Croane.

Starring Herbert Marshall (Christopher Drew), Anne Shirley (June Drew), Gertrude Michael (Miss Eleanor Emerson), Margot Grahame (Valerie Broughton), Clara Blandick (Miss Dell), Frank Coghlan, Jr. (Billy Hopkins), Mary Jo Ellis (Mildred Jackson), Maxine Jennings (Miss Moore), Taylor Holmes (George Terry).

A widower's daughter sets out to find him a new wife.

524 *Mama Loves Papa* (1945) Comedy. Running time: 61 minutes. Black and white.

Produced by Ben Stoloff and Sid Rogell. Directed by Frank Strayer. Screenplay by Charles E. Roberts and Monte Brice. Photographed by Jack MacKenzie. Edited by Edward W. Williams. Music by Leigh Harline.

Starring Leon Errol (Wilbur Todd), Elisabeth Risdon (Jessie Todd), Edwin Maxwell (Kirkwood), Emory Parnell (O'Leary), Charles Halton (Appleby), Paul Harvey (Mr. McIntosh), Charlotte Wynters (Mrs. McIntosh), Ruth Lee (Mabel), Lawrence Tierney (Sharpe), Joanne D. Mark (Bit).

A park commissioner finds faulty playground equipment.

Note: Remake of a 1933 Paramount film, RKO having purchased the rights for $85,000.

525 *Man About Town* (1947) Comedy. Running time: 89 minutes. Black and white. Made in France by Pathé, for RKO American release.

Produced and directed by Rene Clair. Screenplay by Clair, and Robert Pirosh (based on a story by Clair). Photographed by Armand Thirard. Song

Orson Welles produced, co-directed, and wrote *The Magnificent Ambersons.*

"Place Pigalle" written by M. Alstone and Maurice Chevalier.

Starring Maurice Chevalier (Emile), Francois Perier (Jacques), Marcelle Derrien (Madeline), Dany Robin (Lucette), Robert Pizani (Duperrier), Raymond Cordy (Curly).

Story of a French playboy with an eye for the ladies.

Note: This was Chevalier's first film in seven years, and Clair's first French film in twelve. The American version is in French, without subtitles, with Maurice translating occasionally. Winner of the Grand Prize at Brussels and the Critic's Circle Award at Locarno. Original French title: *Le Silence Est D'or.*

526 *Man Alive* (1945) Comedy. Running time: 70 minutes. Black and white.

Produced by Robert Fellows. Directed

Billy Gilbert in *Maid's Night Out.*

by Ray Enright. Screenplay by Edwin Harvey Blum (based on a story by Jerry Cady and John Tucker Battle). Photographed by Frank Redman. Edited by Marvin Coll.

Starring Pat O'Brien (Speed), Adolphe Menjou (Kismet), Ellen Drew (Connie), Rudy Vallee (Gordon), Fortunio Bonanova (Zorado), Joseph Crehan (Doc Whitney), Jonathan Hale (Osborne), Minna Gombell (Aunt Sophie), Jason Robards, Sr. (Fletcher), Jack Norton (Willie), Myrna Dell (Sister), Carl "Alfalfa" Switzer (Ignatius), Gertrude Short (Frowsy Dame), Robert Clarke (Cabby), Robert Homans (Barney).

A husband thought to be dead comes back to haunt his wife's new beau.

Review: "The film cost $738,000, but the humor is only worth about $3" — *The Motion Picture Guide.*

527 *Man Hunt* (1933) Mystery. Running time: 64 minutes. Black and white.

Produced by J.G. Bachmann. Directed by Irving Cummings. Screenplay by Sam Mintz and Leonard Praskins. Photographed by Joseph Valentine.

Leon Errol in *Mama Loves Papa*.

Starring Junior Durkin (Junior), Charlotte Henry (Josie), Dorothy Reid (Mrs. Scott), Arthur Vinton (Wilkie), Edward Le Saint (Woodward), Richard Carle (Sheriff), Carl Gross, Jr. (Abraham).

Two kids try solving a diamond theft.

Note: Actor Durkin made one more film after this, then was killed in an auto crash that also took the life of Jackie Coogan's father.

528 *Man in the Vault* (1956)
Drama. Running time: 73 minutes. Black and white. Produced by John Wayne's Batjack productions for RKO release.

Produced by Robert E. Morrison. Directed by Andrew McLaglen. Screenplay by Burt Kennedy (based on the novel by Frank Gruber). Photographed by William Clothier. Edited by Everett Sutherland.

Starring William Campbell (Tommy), Karen Sharpe (Betty), Anita Ekberg (Flo), Berry Kroeger (Willis), Paul Fix (Herbie), James Seay (Paul), Mike Mazurki (Louie), Pedro Gonzales-Gonzales (Pedro).

A mobster forces a locksmith to open a safe deposit box.

529 *Man of Two Worlds* (1934)
Drama. Running time: 92 minutes. Black and white.

Produced by Pandro S. Berman. Directed by J. Walter Ruben. Screenplay by Howard J. Green (based on the novel by Ainsworth Morgan). Photographed by Henry Gerard. Edited by Jack Hively.

Starring Frances Lederer (Aigo), Elissa Landi (Joan Pemberton), Henry Stephenson (Sir Basil Pemberton), J. Farrell MacDonald (Michael), Walter Byron (Eric), Forrester Harvey (Tim), Ivan Simpson (Dr. Lott), Lumsden Hare (Capt. Swan), Steffi Duna (Guinana).

An Eskimo is brought to England and exposed to British culture.

Note: Lederer's first American film.

530 *Man on the Eiffel Tower* (1949) Drama. Running time: 97 minutes. Color. Available on videocassette.

Produced by Irving Allen. Directed by Burgess Meredith. Screenplay by Harry Brown (based on the story by Georges Simenon). Photographed by Stanley Cortez. Edited by Louis H. Sacken.

Starring Charles Laughton (Inspector Maigret), Franchot Tone (Radek), Burgess Meredith (Huertin), Robert Hutton (Bill Kirby), Jean Wallace (Edna Wallace), Patricia Roc (Helen Kirby), Belita (Gisella), George Thorpe (Comelieu), William Phipps (Janivier), Wilfrid Hyde-White (Grollet).

A killer defies an inspector to discover his identity.

531 *A Man to Remember* (1938)
Drama. Running time: 79 minutes. Black and white.

Produced by Robert Sisk. Directed by Garson Kanin. Screenplay by Dalton Trumbo. Photographed by J. Roy Hunt. Edited by Jack Hively.

Starring Anne Shirley (Jean), Edward Ellis (Dr. John Abbott), Lee Bowman, (Dick Abbott), William Henry (Howard Sykes), Granville Bates (George Sykes), Harlan Briggs (Homer Ramsey), Frank M. Thomas (Jode Harkness), Charles Halton (Perkins), John Wray (Johnson), Gilbert Emery (Dr. Robinson), Dickie Jones (Dick as a Child), Carole Leete (Jean as a Child), Joseph de Stephani (Jorgensen).

The saga of a kindly country doctor.

Note: Kanin's directorial debut, Trumbo's second screenplay. Became a box office smash through word-of-mouth. *Variety* liked it, but was skeptical about its lack of name stars.

Commentary: "It was a small, inexpensive film, but unlike the usual run of B pictures, did not insult the intelligence"—Garson Kanin.

532 *Man Who Found Himself* (1937) Drama. Running time: 67 minutes. Black and white.

Produced by Cliff Reid. Directed by Lew Landers. Screenplay by J. Robert Bren, Edmund L. Hartmann, Gladys Atwater, and Thomas Lennon (based on the story *Wings of Mercy* by Alice Curtis).

Starring John Beal, Joan Fontaine, Phillip Huston, Jane Walsh, George Irving, Jimmy Conlin, Frank M. Thomas, Diana Gibson, Dwight Frye, Edward Van Sloan, Billy Gilbert.

A cocky young surgeon alienates his peers.

533 *Marine Raiders* (1944) War. Running time: 91 minutes. Black and white. Available on videocassette.

Produced by Robert Fellows. Directed by Harold Schuster. Screenplay by Warren Duff. Photographed by Nicholas Musuraca. Edited by Phillip Martin, Jr. Music by Roy Webb and Constantin Bakaleinkoff.

Starring Pat O'Brien (Lockhard), Robert Ryan (Craig), Ruth Hussey (Ellen Foster), Frank McHugh (Leary), Barton

MacLane (Maguire), Richard Martin (Jimmy), Edmund Glover (Miller), Russell Wade (Tony Hewitt), Robert Anderson (Harrigan), Michael St. Angel (Sherwood), Martha MacVicar (Sally), Blake Edwards (Bit).

Two Marine buddies battle over lives and loves in Australia.

534 *The Marines Fly High* (1940) War. Running time: 68 minutes. Black and white. Available on videocassette.

Produced by Robert Sisk. Directed by George Nicholls, Jr., and Ben Stoloff. Screenplay by Jerry Cady and Lt. Cmdr. A.J. Bolton. Photographed by Frank Redman. Edited by Frederic Knudtson. Music by Roy Webb.

Starring Richard Dix (Lt. Darerick), Chester Morris (Lt. Malone), Lucille Ball (Joan Grant), Steffi Duna (Teresa), John Eldredge (John Henson), Paul Harvey (Col. Hill), Horace MacMahon (Monk), Robert Stanton (Hobbs), Ann Shoemaker (Mrs. Hill).

Two marines fight for the affection of a Central American cocoa plantation owner.

Note: Stoloff took over the direction when Nicholls was killed in an auto accident during production.

535 *Married and in Love* (1940) Drama. Running time: 58 minutes. Black and white.

Produced by Robert Sisk. Directed by John Farrow. Screenplay by S.K. Lauren. Photographed by J. Roy Hunt. Edited by Harry Marker.

Starring Alan Marshal (Leslie Yates), Barbara Read (Helen Yates), Patric Knowles (Paul Wilding), Frank Faylen (Man in Bar), Carol Hughes (Woman in Bar).

Two former lovers, now happily married to others, rekindle their old romance.

Note: Faylen and Hughes, playing a couple in a bar, were real-life husband and wife, and both suffered bouts with alcoholism in later years.

A rich girl's love
he couldn't afford...

A gangster's sinister
threat...

$200,000 waiting
in a safety
deposit box...

WHY DID
THE KEY HOLD
THE ANSWER
TO
ALL THREE?

"MAN IN THE VAULT"

Starring

WILLIAM CAMPBELL
KAREN SHARPE
ANITA EKBERG

with

BERRY KROEGER · PAUL FIX
MIKE MAZURKI · ROBERT KEYS

Screen Play by BURT KENNEDY
Produced by ROBERT E. MORRISON
Directed by ANDREW V. McLAGLEN

Distributed by
R K O
RADIO
PICTURES

Anita as a two-timing gal
— too much for one man

Publicity poster for *Man in the Vault*.

536 *Marry Me Again* (1953) Comedy. Running time: 73 minutes. Black and white.

Produced by Alex Gottlieb. Directed and written by Frank Tashlin (based on a story by Gottlieb). Photographed by Robert de Grasse. Edited by Edward Mann.

Starring Robert Cummings (Bill), Marie Wilson (Doris), Ray Walker (Mac), Mary Costa (Joan), Lloyd Corrigan (Taylor), Moroni Olsen (Courtney), Frank Cady (Dr. Day).

A fighter pilot returns home and finds his fiancee has inherited a million dollars.

Note: Costa was writer-director Tashlin's wife.

537 *The Marshal of Mesa City* (1939) Western. Running time: 62 minutes. Black and white.

Produced by Bert Gilroy. Directed by David Howard. Screenplay by Jack Lait, Jr. Photographed by Harry Wild. Edited by Frederic Knudtson.

Starring George O'Brien (Mason), Virginia Vale (Virginia), Leon Ames (Sheriff), Henry Brandon (Allison), Lloyd Ingraham (Mayor), Slim Whitaker (Butch), Mary Gordon (Ma), Harry Cording (Henderson), Joe McGuinn (Joe), Frank Ellis (Harry), Wilfred Lucas (Bit).

A former marshal is called in to clean up political corruption.

Note: A remake of *The Arizonian* (q.v.). Actress Vale won this role in a "Gateway to Hollywood" contest. Interestingly enough, she was already in some Paramount films under the name of Dorothy Howe.

538 *Mary of Scotland* (1936) Historical drama. Running time: 123 minutes. Black and white. Available on videocassette.

Produced by Pandro S. Berman. Directed by John Ford. Screenplay by Dudley Nichols (based on the play by Maxwell Anderson). Photographed by Joseph II. August. Edited by Jane Loring. Music by Max Steiner.

Starring Katharine Hepburn (Mary Stuart), Fredric March (Earl of Bothwell), Florence Eldridge (Elisabeth Tudor), Douglas Walton (Darnley), John Carradine (David Rizzio), Robert Barrat (Morton), Gavin Muir (Leicester), Ian Keith (James Moray), Moroni Olsen (John Knox), William Stack (Ruthven), Alan Mowbray (Throckmorton), Molly Lamont (Mary), Mary Gordon (Nurse), Monte Blue (Messenger), Lionel Belmore (Fisherman), Bobs Watson (Fisherman's Son), Robert Homans (Jailer).

A woman refuses to give up her claim to the English throne, despite opposition.

Review: "Events are walked through as though they were rooms in a museum, and closing time at three"—Otis Ferguson.

539 *Masked Raiders* (1949) Western. Running time: 60 minutes. Black and white.

Produced by Herman Schlom. Directed by Lesley Selander. Screenplay by Norman Houston. Photographed by George E. Diskant. Edited by Les Millbrook.

Starring Tim Holt (Tim), Richard Martin (Chito), Marjorie Lord (Gale), Gary Gray (Artie), Frank Wilcox (Copthrell), Charles Arndt (Doc), Tom Tyler (Trig), Harry Woods (Marshal Barlow), Clayton Moore (Matt).

Two marshals try stopping a Robin Hood–style gang of outlaws.

540 *The Master Race* (1944) Drama. Running time: 96 minutes. Black and white. Available on videocassette.

Produced by Robert Golden. Directed by Herbert J. Biberman. Screenplay by Biberman, Anne Froelick, and Rowland Leigh. Photographed by Russell Metty. Music by Roy Webb. Edited by Ernie Leadlay.

Starring George Coulouris (Von Beck),

Stanley Ridges (Phil Carson), Osa Massen (Helena), Carl Esmond (Andrei), Nancy Gates (Nina), Morris Carnovsky (Old Man Bartoc), Lloyd Bridges (Frank), Eric Feldary (Altmeier), Helen Beverly (Mrs. Varin), Gavin Muir (William Forsythe), Paul Guilfoyle (Katry), Richard Nugent (Sgt. O'Farrell), Gigi Perreau (Baby).

A German officer continues to spread Nazi hatred even after his empire is destroyed.

Note: Made by the same team that did *Hitler's Children* (q.v.).

541 *Mayor of 44th Street* (1942) Musical. Running time: 85 minutes. Black and white.

Produced by Cliff Reid. Directed by Alfred Green. Screenplay by Lewis Foster and Frank Ryan (based on a story by Robert Andrews, suggested by a *Collier's* magazine article by Luther Davis and John Cleveland). Photographed by Robert de Grasse. Edited by Irene Morra.

Starring George Murphy (Joe), Anne Shirley (Jessie Lee), William Gargan (Tommy), Richard Barthelmess (Ed), Jan Merril (Vicki), Freddy Martin (Himself), Rex Downing (Bit).

An ex-hoofer opens a dance band agency and hires a group of street kids to help out.

542 *Meanest Gal in Town* (1934) Comedy. Running time: 62 minutes. Black and white.

Directed by Russell Mack. Screenplay by Richard Schayer, Mack, and H.W. Hannemann (based on a story by Arthur Horman). Photographed by J. Roy Hunt. Edited by James Morely.

Starring ZaSu Pitts, El Brendel, Pert Kelton, James Gleason, Skeets Gallagher, Barney Furey, Bud Geary.

When a carnival is stranded in a small town, a loose woman with the troupe gets in the middle of a romance between a store owner and a barber.

543 *Meet Dr. Christian* (1939) Drama. Running time: 68 minutes. Black and white. Available on videocassette.

Produced by William Stephens. Directed by Bernard Vorhaus. Screenplay by Ian Hunter, Ring Lardner, Jr., Harvey Gates (based on a story by Gates). Photographed by Robert Pittack. Edited by Edward Mann.

Starring Jean Hersholt (Dr. Christian), Dorothy Lovett (Judy Price), Robert Baldwin (Roy Davis), Enid Bennett (Anne Hewitt), Paul Harvey (John Hewitt), Marcia Mae Jones (Marilee), Maude Eburne (Mrs. Hastings), Frank Coghlan, Jr. (Bud), Patsy Lee Parsons (Patsy Hewitt), Sarah Edwards (Mrs. Minnows), John Kelly (Cass), Eddie Acuff (Benson), Jackie Moran (Don Hewitt).

A country doctor is more concerned with the health of the patient than his own financial rewards.

Note: Based on a popular CBS radio series. First in the film series. The name of the character was borrowed from Hersholt's own favorite author, Hans Christian Andersen.

Review: "Profitable programme material for the family trade"—*Variety.*

544 *Meet the Missus* (1937) Comedy. Running time: 65 minutes. Black and white.

Produced by Albert Lewis. Directed by Joseph Santley. Screenplay by Jack Townley, Bert Granet, and Joel Sayre (based on the novel by Jack Goodman and Albert Rice). Photographed by Jack MacKenzie. Edited by Frederic Knudtson. Music by Roy Webb.

Starring Victor Moore (Otis Foster), Helen Broderick (Emma Foster), Anne Shirley (Louise Foster), Alan Bruce (Steve Walton), Edward H. Robins (Gordon Cutting), William Brisbane (Prentiss), Frank M. Thomas (Barney Lott), Ray Mayer (Mr. White), Ada Leonard (Princess Zarina), George Irving (Magistrate), Alec Craig (College President),

Willie Best (Mose), Virginia Sale (Mrs. Moseby), Jack Norton (Mrs. Norton), Valerie Bergere (Mrs. North-West), Fred Santley (Mr. Corn Belt), Don Wilson (Radio Announcer).

A meek man's domineering wife enters a series of contests, and is eventually defeated by her husband in the Happy Housewives competition.

Note: The 1940 Republic Studios feature is not a remake.

Review: "Destined for the lower half of duals" — *Variety.*

545 *Melody Cruise* (1933) Musical. Running time: 76 minutes. Black and white.

Produced by Merian C. Cooper. Directed by Mark Sandrich. Screenplay by Sandrich, Ben Holmes, Allen Rivkin, and P.J. Wolfson (based on a story by Sandrich and Holmes). Photographed by Bert Glennon. Edited by Jack Kitchin. Music by Val Burton and Will Jason.

Songs: "I Met Her at a Party," "He's Not the Marrying Kind," "Isn't This a Night for Love," "This Is the Hour."

Starring Charles Ruggles (Pete Wells), Phil Harris (Alan Chandler), Greta Nissen (Ann Von Rader), Helen Mack (Laurie Marlowe), Chick Chandler (Hickey), June Brewster (Zoe), Shirley Chambers (Vera), Florence Roberts (Miss Potts), Marjorie Gateson (Mrs. Wells), Betty Grable (Stewardess).

A playboy falls in love on a California-bound steamship.

Note: Sandrich's first feature-length directorial effort.

546 *Melody for Three* (1941) Drama. Running time: 67 minutes. Black and white. Available on videocassette.

Produced by William Stephens. Directed by Erle C. Kenton. Screenplay by Lee Loeb and Walter Ferris. Photographed by John Alton. Edited by Edward Mann.

Starring Jean Hersholt (Dr. Chris

tian), Fay Wray (Mary Stanley), Walter Woolf King (Antoine Pirelle), Schuyler Standish (Billy Stanley), Patsy Lee Parsons (Nancy Higby), Maude Eburne (Mrs. Hastings), Astrid Allwyn (Gladys McClelland), Irene Ryan (Mrs. Higby), Donnie Allen (Red Bates).

The good doctor tries to reunite a divorced couple.

547 *Melody Time* (1948) Animated musical. Running time: 75 minutes. Technicolor. Produced by Disney for release by RKO.

Produced by Walt Disney. Directed by Clyde Geronimi, Wilfred Jackson, Hamilton Luske, Jack Kinney. Screenplay by Winston Hibler, Erdman Penner, Harry Reeves, Homer Brightman, Ken Anderson, Ted Sears, Joe Rinaldi, Art Scott, Bill Cottrell, Bob Moore, Jesse Marsh, John Walbridge, Hardie Gramatsky. Photographed by Winton Hoch. Edited by Donald Halliday and Thomas Scott. Music by Bobby Worth, Ray Gilbert, Ernesto Nazareth, Eliot Daniel, Johnny Lange.

Songs: "Melody Time," "Little Toot," "The Lord Is Good to Me," "The Apple Song," "The Pioneer Song," "Once Upon a Wintertime," "Blame It on the Samba," "Blue Shadows on the Trail," "Pecos Bill."

Starring Roy Rogers, Bobby Driscoll, Ethel Smith, Bob Nolan, Sons of the Pioneers, and the voices of Buddy Clark, The Andrews Sisters, Fred Waring and His Pennsylvanians, Frances Langford, Dennis Day, Freddy Martin and His Orchestra, Jack Fina, The Dinning Sisters.

A variety show of cartoon segments, linked by narration and a magical paint brush.

Note: The last musical compilation film from the Disney studios.

548 *Men Against the Sky* (1940) Drama. Running time: 75 minutes. Black and white.

Produced by Howard Benedict. Directed by Leslie Goodwins. Screenplay by Nathaniel West (based on a story by John Twist). Photographed by Frank Redman. Edited by Desmond Marquette.

Starring Richard Dix (Phil), Kent Taylor (Martin), Edmund Lowe (Dan), Wendy Barrie (Kay), Granville Bates (Burdett), Grant Withers (Grant), Donald Briggs (Dick), Charles Quigley (Flynn), Selmer Jackson (Capt. Sanders), Terry Belmont (Capt. Wallen).

A once-famous flyer is now a heavy drinker who does stunt flying.

Note: Screenwriter West and his wife Eileen were killed in an auto crash shortly after this film was made. West also wrote *Day of the Locust.* He was only 36 years old. His wife was the inspiration for the story *My Sister Eileen.*

549 *Men Are Such Fools* (1933) Drama. Running time: 65 minutes. Black and white.

Produced by Joseph I. Schnitzer. Directed by William Nigh. Screenplay by Viola Brothers Shore and Edith Doherty (based on the story by Thomas Lloyd Lennon). Photographed by Charles Schoenbaum. A Jefferson production.

Starring Leo Carrillo (Tony), Vivienne Osborne (Lilli), Una Merkel (Molly), Joseph Cawthorn (Werner), Tom Moore (Tom Hyland), Earle Foxe (Joe), Paul Hurst (Styles).

An Italian immigrant, upon arriving in America, finds that his German wife is sleeping around with a cabaret owner.

Note: Jefferson was a production company briefly controlled by producer Schnitzer.

550 *Men of America* (1933) Western. Running time: 57 minutes. Black and white.

Directed by Ralph Ince. Screenplay by Samuel Ornitz and Jack Jungmeyer (based on a story by Humphrey Pearson and Henry McCarty). Photographed by J. Roy Hunt. Edited by Edward Schroeder. British title: *The Great Decision.*

Starring William Boyd (Jim Parker), Chic Sale (Smokey Joe), Dorothy Wilson (Annabelle), Ralph Ince (Cicero), Henry Armetta (Tony), Ling (Chinese Joe).

A newcomer to a small western town is implicated in several criminal undertakings.

Note: RKO had ideas of building a western action series around Boyd, but this would not happen until he appeared as Hopalong Cassidy at Paramount two years later.

551 *Men of Chance* (1932) Drama. Running time: 65 minutes. Black and white.

Directed by George Archainbaud. Screenplay by Louis Stevens and Wallace Smith. Photographed by Nicholas Musuraca. Edited by Archie Marshek.

Starring Mary Astor (Marthe), Ricardo Cortez (Johnny Silk), John Halliday (Dorval), Ralph Ince (Farley), Kitty Kelly (Gertie), James Donlan, George Davis (Bits).

Gamblers try to get info out of a man who has a knack for picking winning horses.

552 *Merely Mr. Hawkins* (1938) Comedy. Running time: 71 minutes. Black and white.

Produced by George Smith. Directed by Maclean Rogers. Screenplay by John Hunter. Photographed by Geoffrey Faithfull. Edited by Andy Buchanan.

Starring Eliot Makeham (Alfred Hawkins), Sybil Grove (Charlotte Hawkins), Dinah Sheridan (Betty Hawkins), George Pembroke (John Fuller), Jonathan Field (Richard), Jack Vyvyan (Harry).

A henpecked husband proves his worth to his spouse when he saves his daughter from marrying a crook.

Note: Produced in Great Britain.

553 *Mexican Spitfire* (1939) Comedy. Running time: 67 minutes. Black and white. Available on videocassette.

Produced by Cliff Reid. Directed by Leslie Goodwins. Screenplay by Joseph A. Fields and Charles E. Roberts. Photographed by Jack MacKenzie. Edited by Desmond Marquette.

Starring Lupe Velez (Carmelita Lindsay), Leon Errol (Uncle Matt, Lord Epping), Donald Woods (Dennis Lindsay), Linda Hayes (Elizabeth), Cecil Kellaway (Chumley), Elisabeth Risdon (Aunt Della), Charles Coleman (Butler).

A Mexican entertainer elopes with a young businessman. The man's former wife tries to break up the marriage.

Note: Although it was not a box office success, this was the first in a series.

554 *Mexican Spitfire at Sea* (1942)

Comedy. Running time: 73 minutes. Black and white.

Produced by Cliff Reid. Directed by Leslie Goodwins. Screenplay by Jerry Cady and Charles E. Roberts. Photographed by Jack MacKenzie. Edited by Theron Warth.

Starring Lupe Velez (Carmelita), Leon Errol (Uncle Matt, Lord Epping), Buddy Rogers (Dennis Lindsey), ZaSu Pitts (Miss Pepper), Elisabeth Risdon (Aunt Della), Florence Bates (Mrs. Baldwin), Marion Martin (Flo), Lydia Bilbrook (Lady Epping), Eddie Dunn (Mr. Skinner).

The Spitfire goes off to Hawaii to get an advertising contract.

555 *Mexican Spitfire Out West* (1940) Comedy. Running time: 76 minutes. Black and white.

Produced by Cliff Reid. Directed by Leslie Goodwins. Screenplay by Charles E. Roberts and Jack Townley. Photographed by Jack MacKenzie. Edited by Desmond Marquette.

Starring Lupe Velez (Carmelita), Leon Errol (Uncle Matt, Lord Epping), Donald Woods (Dennis), Elisabeth Risdon (Aunt Della), Cecil Kellaway (Chumley), Linda Hayes (Elizabeth), Lydia Billbrook (Lady Epping), Charles Coleman (Ponsby), Charles Quigley (Roberts), Eddie Dunn (Skinner), Grant Withers (Withers), Tom Kennedy (Taxi Driver), Gus Schilling (Desk Clerk), Charlie Hall (Elevator Boy).

The Spitfire fakes a divorce so that her husband will pay more attention to her.

556 *Mexican Spitfire Sees a Ghost* (1942) Comedy. Running time: 70 minutes. Black and white.

Produced by Cliff Reid. Directed by Leslie Goodwins. Screenplay by Charles E. Roberts and Monte Brice. Photographed by Russell Metty. Edited by Theron Warth.

Starring Lupe Velez (Carmelita), Leon Errol (Uncle Matt, Lord Epping), Buddy Rogers (Dennis), Elisabeth Risdon (Aunt Della), Donald MacBride (Percy Fitzpatten), Minna Gombell (Edith), Don Barclay (Fingers), John McGuire (Luders), Lillian Randolph (Hyacinth), Mantan Moreland (Lightnin'), Harry Tyler (Bascombe), Richard Martin (Chauffeur).

A supposedly haunted house is actually inhabited by enemy agents.

557 *Mexican Spitfire's Baby* (1941) Comedy. Running time: 69 minutes. Black and white.

Produced by Cliff Reid. Directed by Leslie Goodwins. Screenplay by Charles E. Roberts and Jerry Cady. Photographed by Jack MacKenzie. Edited by Harry Marker.

Starring Lupe Velez (Carmelita), Leon Errol (Uncle Matt, Lord Epping), Buddy Rogers (Dennis), Elisabeth Risdon (Aunt Della), Lydia Billbrook (Lady Epping), ZaSu Pitts (Mrs. Pepper), Fritz Feld (Pierre), Marion Martin (Suzanne), Lloyd Corrigan (Chumley), Tom Kennedy (Sheriff).

While staying in Arizona, the Spitfire befriends a lion cub.

558 *Mexican Spitfire's Blessed Event* (1943) Comedy. Running time: 63 minutes. Black and white.

Produced by Bert Gilroy. Directed by Leslie Goodwins. Screenplay by Charles E. Roberts and Dane Lussier. Photographed by Jack MacKenzie. Edited by Harry Marker.

Starring Lupe Velez (Carmelita), Leon Errol (Uncle Matt, Lord Epping), Walter Reed (Dennis), Elisabeth Risdon (Aunt Della), Lydia Billbrook (Lady Epping), Hugh Beaumont (Mr. Sharpe), Aileen Carlyle (Mrs. Pettibone), Alan Carney (Bartender), Wally Brown (Desk Clerk), Joan Barclay, Rita Corday (Bits).

The Spitfire borrows a baby so that a wealthy man will do business with her husband.

Note: Last film in the series. Velez committed suicide the following year.

559 *Mexican Spitfire's Elephant* (1942) Comedy. Running time: 63 minutes. Black and white.

Produced by Bert Gilroy. Directed by Leslie Goodwins. Screenplay by Charles E. Roberts. Photographed by Jack Mac-Kenzie. Edited by Harry Marker.

Starring Lupe Velez (Carmelita), Leon Errol (Uncle Matt, Lord Epping), Walter Reed (Dennis), Elisabeth Risdon (Aunt Della), Lydia Billbrook (Lady Epping), Marion Martin (Diana), Lyle Talbot (Reddy), Luis Alberni (Luigi), George Cleveland (Chief Inspector), Marten Lamont (Arnold), Keye Luke (Lao Lee), Tom Kennedy (Joe), Neely Edwards (Ship Bartender), Bess Flowers (Bit).

The Spitfire and company end up in possession of a glass elephant filled with stolen gems.

560 *Midnight Mystery* (1930) Mystery. Running time: 69 minutes. Black and white.

Produced by William LeBaron. Directed by George B. Seitz. Screenplay by Beulah Marie Dix (based on the play *Hawk Island* by Howard Irving Young). Photographed by Joseph Walker. Edited by Jack Kitchin.

Starring Betty Compson (Sally), Hugh Trevor (Gregory), Lowell Sherman (Tom), Rita La Roy (Madeline), Ivan Lebedeff (Mischa Kawelin), Raymond Hatton (Paul), Marcelle Corday (Harriet).

A mystery writer tries to solve a murder on board a ship.

561 *Midshipman Jack* (1933) Drama. Running time: 73 minutes. Black and white.

Directed by Christy Cabanne. Screenplay by Frank Wead and F. McGrew Willis. Photographed by Alfred Gilks. Edited by Basil Wrangell.

Starring Bruce Cabot (Jack Austin), Betty Furness (Ruth), Frank Albertson (Russell), Arthur Lake (Allan), Purnell Pratt (Capt. Rogers), Florence Lake (Sally), Margaret Seddon (Mrs. Burns), John Darrow (Clark).

A naval academy cadet has trouble adjusting to following orders.

Note: Both Albertson and Lake were up for the role of Dagwood Bumstead at Columbia some years later. This was remade as *Annapolis Salute* (q.v.), in which Lake again appears.

562 *Mighty Joe Young* (1949) Fantasy. Running time: 94 minutes. Black and white and colorized. Available on videocassette.

Produced by John Ford and Merian C. Cooper. Directed by Ernest B. Schoedsack. Screenplay by Ruth Rose. Photographed by J. Roy Hunt. Edited by Ted Cheesman.

Starring Terry Moore (Jill Young), Ben Johnson (Gregg), Robert Armstrong (Max), Frank McHugh (Windy), Douglas Fowley (Jones), Denis Green (Crawford), Paul Guilfoyle (Smith), Nestor Paiva (Brown), Regis Toomey (John Young), Lora Lee Michel (Jill as a Girl), Joseph Young (The Gorilla); Wee Willie Davis, Man Mountain Dean, Sammy Menacker (Strongmen); Selmer Jackson, Ellen Corby, Addison Richards, Iris Adrian (Bits).

A girl who lives in the African jungle raises a large gorilla from a baby, and is talked into exploiting him on Broadway.

563 *Millie* (1931) Drama. Running time: 85 minutes. Black and white.

Produced by Charles R. Rogers. Directed by John Francis Dillon. Screenplay by Charles Kenyon and Ralph

Murphy (based on the novel by Donald Henderson Clark). Photographed by Ernest Haller. Edited by Jack Kitchin.

Starring Helen Twelvetrees (Millie), Robert Ames (Tommy), Lilyan Tashman (Helen), Joan Blondell (Angie), John Halliday (Jimmy), James Hall (Jack), Anita Louise (Connie), Edmund Breese (Attorney), Frank McHugh (Holmes), Harry O. Stubbs (Mark), Geneva Mitchell (Clara), Marie Astaire (Bobbie).

A loose woman kills a man when she discovers his intentions toward her 16-year-old daughter.

564 *Millionaire Playboy* (1940)

Comedy. Running time: 64 minutes. Black and white.

Produced by Robert Sisk. Directed by Leslie Goodwins. Screenplay by Bert Granet and Charles E. Roberts (based on a story by Granet). Photographed by Jack MacKenzie. Edited by Desmond Marquette. British title: *Glamour Boy.*

Starring Joe Penner (Joe Zany), Linda Hayes (Lois), Russ Brown (Bob), Fritz Feld (Gorta), Tom Kennedy (Murph), Granville Bates (Stafford), Mantan Moreland (Bellhop).

A man who gets hiccups whenever he kisses a woman has his rich father offer five thousand dollars to anyone who can cure him.

565 *Millionaires in Prison* (1940)

Comedy. Running time: 63 minutes. Black and white.

Produced by Howard Benedict. Directed by Ray McCarey. Screenplay by Lynn Root and Frank Fenton (based on a story by Martin Mooney). Photographed by Harry Wild. Edited by Theron Warth.

Starring Lee Tracy (Nick Burton), Linda Hayes (Helen), Raymond Walburn (Vander), Morgan Conway (Brent), Truman Bradley (Dr. Collins), Virginia Vale (May Thomas), Cliff Edwards (Happy), Thurston Hall (Kellog), Shemp Howard (Professor), Thomas Jackson (Warden).

Four prison inmates agree to be guinea pigs for a doctor's experiment in exchange for parole.

566 *Miracle of the Bells* (1948)

Drama. Running time: 120 minutes. Black and white. Available on videocassette.

Produced by Jesse Lasky and Walter MacEwen. Directed by Irving Pichel. Screenplay by Ben Hecht, Quentin Reynolds and DeWitt Bodeen (based on the novel by Russell Janney). Photographed by Robert De Grasse. Edited by Elmo Williams.

Starring Fred MacMurray (Bill Dunnigan), Vallie (Olga), Frank Sinatra (Father Paul), Lee J. Cobb (Marcus Harris), Harold Vermilyea (Nick Orloff), Charles Meredith (Father Spinsky), Jim Nolan (Ted Jones), Veronica Pataky (Anna Klovina), Phillip Ahn (Ming Gow), Frank Ferguson (Dolan), Frank Wilcox (Jennings), Ray Teal (Koslick), Dorothy Sebastian (Katie), Billy Wayne (Tom).

The death of an actress results in a small town miracle.

Review: "I hereby declare myself the founding father of the Society for the Prevention of Cruelty to God" — James Agee.

567 *Mr. and Mrs. Smith* (1941)

Comedy. Running time: 95 minutes. Black and white. Available on videocassette.

Produced by Harry Edington. Directed by Alfred Hitchcock. Screenplay by Norman Krasna. Photographed by Harry Stradling. Edited by William Hamilton.

Starring Carole Lombard (Ann Smith, Ann Krausheimer), Robert Montgomery (David Smith), Gene Raymond (Jeff), Jack Carson (Chuck), Phillip Merivale (Custer), William Tracy (Sammy), Charles Halton (Deever), Esther Dale (Mrs. Krausheirmer), Emma Dunn (Martha).

A married couple find their marriage wasn't legal.

Cary Grant and Myrna Loy in *Mr. Blandings Builds His Dream House.*

Note: Lombard directed the Hitchcock cameo, playfully insisting he do it over and over again, adding powder to his reddening face with each take.

568 *Mr. Blandings Builds His Dream House* (1948) Comedy. Running time: 94 minutes. Black and white. Available on videocassette.
Produced by Norman Panama and Mel Frank. Directed by H.C. Potter. Screenplay by Panama and Frank (based on the novel by Eric Hodgins). Photographed by James Wong Howe. Edited by Harry Marker.
Starring Cary Grant (Jim Blandings), Myrna Loy (Muriel Blandings), Melvyn Douglas (Bill), Reginald Denny (Sims), Sharyn Moffett (Joan), Connie Marshall (Betsy), Louise Beavers (Gussie), Harry Shannon (W.D. Tesander), Ian Wolfe (Smith), Tito Vuolo (Mr. Zucca), Nestor Paiva (Joe Appollonio), Jason Robards, Sr. (John Retch), Lurene Tuttle (Mary), Lex Barker (Carpenter Foreman), Emory Parnell (Delford), Stanley Andrews (Murphy).
A New York advertising man decides to build his dream house in the Connecticut countryside.
Review: "A bulls-eye for middle-class middlebrows"—James Agee.

569 *Mr. Doodle Kicks Off* (1939) Comedy. Running time: 75 minutes. Black and white.

Produced by Robert Sisk. Directed by Leslie Goodwins. Screenplay by Bert Granet (based on the story by Mark Kelly). Photographed by Russell Metty. Edited by Ted Cheesman.

Starring Joe Penner (Doodle Bugs), June Travis (Janice), Richard Lane (Offside), Ben Alexander (Larry), Billy Gilbert (Minorous), Jack Carson (Rochet), Alan Bruce (Mickey), George Irving (Martin), William B. Davidson (Mr. Bugs), Pierre Watkin (Wondel), Frank M. Thomas (Coach Hammond), Wesley Barry, Robert Parrish (Sophomores).

A wealthy man insists his meek son graduate from his alma mater a star athlete.

Note: Re-vamped by Martin and Lewis as *That's My Boy* (Paramount, 1950).

570 *Mr. Lucky* (1943) Comedy-drama. Running time: 100 minutes. Black and white. Available on videocassette.

Produced by David Hempstead. Directed by H.C. Potter. Screenplay by Milton Holmes and Adrian Scott (from a story by Holmes). Photographed by George Barnes. Edited by Theron Warth.

Starring Cary Grant (Joe Adams), Laraine Day (Dorothy Bryant), Charles Bickford (Hard Swede), Gladys Cooper (Capt. Steadman), Alan Carney (Crunk), Henry Stephenson (Mr. Bryant), Paul Stewart (Zepp), Ray Johnson (Mrs. Ostrander), Erford Gage (Golfer), Walter Kingsford (Hargraves), J.M. Kerrigan (MacDougal), Ed Fielding (Foster), Vladimir Sokoloff (Greek Priest), Florence Bates (Mrs. Van Every).

A gambler takes the identity of a dead man, including his 4-F card, and proceeds to bilk a war charity out of its earnings.

Note: Became a TV series in 1959.

571 *M'liss* (1936) Drama. Running time: 66 minutes. Black and white.

Produced by Robert Sisk. Directed by George Nicholls, Jr. Screenplay by Dorothy Yost (based on the novel by Bret Harte). Photographed by Robert De Grasse. Edited by William Morgan.

Starring Anne Shirley (M'liss Smith), John Beal (Stephen), Guy Kibbee (Washoe Smith), Douglass Dumbrille (Lou Ellis), Moroni Olsen (Jake), Frank M. Thomas (Alf), Arthur Hoyt (Mayor), Barbara Pepper (Clytie), Billy Benedict (Bit).

A naive girl looks after her drunken father in a rough mining town.

572 *The Monkey's Paw* (1933) Horror. Running time: 58 minutes. Black and white.

Produced by Merian C. Cooper. Directed by Wesley Ruggles and Ernest B. Schoedsack. Screenplay by Graham John (based on the story by W.W. Jacobs and the stage play by Louis N. Parker). Photographed by Leo Tover, Jack MacKenzie, Edward Cronjager, and J. Taylor. Edited by Charles Kimball.

Starring Ivan Simpson, Louise Carter, C. Aubrey Smith, Branwell Fletcher, Betty Lawford, Winter Hall, Herbert Bunston, Nena Quartero, Nick Shaid, LeRoy Mason, Col. Gordon McGee, Gordon Jones, Aggie Steele, Joey Ray, Harry Strang, Harold Hughes.

An army sergeant brings a magical paw from India to England.

Note: Remade in England in 1948.

573 *Montana Belle* (1952) Western. Running time: 81 minutes. Trucolor.

Produced by Howard Welsch. Directed by Allan Dwan. Screenplay by Horace McCoy and Norman S. Hall. Photographed by Jack Marta. Edited by Arthur Roberts.

Starring Jane Russell (Belle Starr), George Brent (Tom Bradfield), Scott Brady (Bob Dalton), Forrest Tucker (Mac), Andy Devine (Pete), Jack Lambert

June Travis and Joe Penner in *Mr. Doodle Kicks Off.*

(Ringo), John Litel (Matt Towner), Ray Teal (Emmett Dalton), Rory Mallinson (Grant Dalton), Roy Barcroft (Jim Clark), Holly Bane (Ben Dalton), Gene Roth (Marshal Ripple), Glenn Strange, Pierce Lyden (Deputies), Kenneth Mac-Donald (Sheriff Irving).

When the Daltons rescue Belle Starr they make her pay back by involving herself in a dangerous raid.

Note: Completed in 1948, released in 1952. Originally this Fidelity Pictures production was to be released by Republic Pictures, but Howard Hughes, who had Russell under personal contract, decided he wanted to release it through RKO.

Commentary: "This epic was over so fast, I barely remember making it" — Jane Russell.

574 *Morning Glory* (1933) Drama.
Running time: 74 minutes. Black and white.

Produced by Pandro S. Berman. Di-rected by Lowell Sherman. Screenplay by Howard J. Green (based on a play by Zoe Akins). Photographed by Bert Glennon. Edited by George Nicholls, Jr.

Starring Katharine Hepburn (Eva Lovelace), Douglas Fairbanks, Jr. (Joseph Sheridan), Adolphe Menjou (Louis Easton), Mary Duncan (Rita Vernon), C. Aubrey Smith (Robert Harley Hedges), Don Alvarado (Pepe Velez), Fred Santley (Will Seymour), Richard Carle (Henry Lawrence), Tyler Brooke (Charles Van Dusen), Geneva Mitchell (Gwendolyn Hall), Helen Ware (Nellie Navarre), Theresa Harris (Maid), Jed Prouty (Seymour), Robert Grieg (Roberts).

An actress attempts to find success in New York City.

Note: Hepburn won her first Oscar for this film. Remade as *Stage Struck.*

575 *The Most Dangerous Game* (1932) Horror. Running time: 63 minutes. Black and white. Available on videocassette.

Leslie Banks, Fay Wray and Joel McCrea in *The Most Dangerous Game.*

Produced by Merian C. Cooper and Ernest B. Schoedsack. Directed by Schoedsack and Irving Pichel. Screenplay by James A. Creelman (from a story by Richard Connell). Photographed by Henry Gerard. Music by Max Steiner.

Starring Joel McCrea (Bob Rainsford), Fay Wray (Eve Trowbridge), Leslie Banks (Count Zaroff), Robert Armstrong (Martin Trowbridge), Steve Clemente, Noble Johnson (Servants), Hale Hamilton (Bit).

A sadistic hunter lures people onto his island so that he can hunt them like animals.

Note: Shot during the filming breaks on *King Kong,* which was made at the same time by the same people. Remade as *A Game of Death* and *Run for the Sun.*

576 *Mother Carey's Chickens*

(1938) Drama. Running time: 82 minutes. Black and white.

Produced by Pandro S. Berman. Directed by Rowland V. Lee. Screenplay by S.K. Lauren and Gertrude Purcell (based on the novel by Kate Douglas Wiggin). Photographed by J. Roy Hunt. Edited by George Hively.

Starring Anne Shirley (Nancy), Ruby Keeler (Kitty), James Ellison (Ralph), Fay Bainter (Mother), Walter Brennan (Popham), Frank Albertson (Tom), Alma Kruger (Aunt Bertha), Virginia Weidler (Lally Joy), Donnie Dunagan (Peter), Jackie Moran (Gilbert), Margaret Hamilton (Mrs. Fuller), Ralph Morgan (Captain Carey), Phyllis Kennedy (Annabelle), Harvey Clark (Fuller), Lucile Ward (Mrs. Popham), George Irving (Hamilton).

A widow, with two daughters and two sons, tries to keep ownership of her home.

Note: Katharine Hepburn was originally supposed to play the role that went to Ruby Keeler. Hepburn's refusal of

Bert Wheeler, Barbara Pepper and Bob Woolsey in *Mummy's Boys*.

this part resulted in RKO tearing up her contract. Remade as *Summer Magic*.

577 Mourning Becomes Electra
(1947) Drama. Running time: 173 minutes. Black and white.

Produced, directed, and written by Dudley Nichols (based on the play by Eugene O'Neill). Photographed by George Barnes. Edited by Roland Gross and Chandler House. Available on videocassette.

Starring Rosalind Russell (Lavinia), Michael Redgrave (Orin), Raymond Massey (Ezra), Katina Paxinou (Christine), Leo Genn (Adam), Kirk Douglas (Peter), Nancy Coleman (Hazel), Henry Hull (Seth), Thurston Hall (Blake), Jimmy Conlin (Abner), Emma Dunn (Mrs. Borden).

O'Neill's trilogy of "The Homecoming," "The Hunted," and "The Haunted" about the trials and tribulations of a post–Civil War family.

Review: "...proves that Greek trag-

edy doesn't always play well west of Athens"—*Motion Picture Guide*.

578 Mummy's Boys (1936)
Comedy. Running time: 68 minutes. Black and white.

Produced by Lee Marcus. Directed by Fred Guiol. Screenplay by Jack Townley, Phillip G. Epstein, and Charles E. Roberts. Photographed by Jack MacKenzie and Vernon Walker. Edited by John Lockert.

Starring Bert Wheeler (Stanley), Robert Woolsey (Whittaker), Barbara Pepper (Mary), Moroni Olsen (Doc Sterling), Frank M. Thomas (Browning), Willie Best (Catfish), Francis McDonald (El Bey), Frank Lackteen (Oriental), Charles Coleman (Butler), Mitchell Lewis (Sheik), Frederick Burton (Mr. Edwards).

Two ditch diggers become involved on an archaeological expedition in which the others are killed.

Review: "...net result of the dialogue is about four snickers"—*Variety*.

579 *Murder My Sweet* (1945)
Mystery. Running time: 95 minutes.
Black and white. Available on videocassette.

Produced by Adrian Scott. Directed by Edward Dmytryk. Screenplay by John Paxton (based on the novel *Farewell My Lovely* by Raymond Chandler). Photographed by Harry J. Wild. Edited by Joseph Noriega.

Starring Dick Powell (Phillip Marlowe), Claire Trevor (Velma, Mrs. Grayle), Anne Shirley (Ann), Otto Kruger, (Amthor), Mike Mazurki (Moose Malloy), Miles Mander (Mr. Grayle), Douglas Walton (Marriott), Don Douglas (Lt. Randall), Ralf Harolde (Dr. Sonderberg), Esther Howard (Mrs. Florian), John Indrisano (Chauffeur), Jack Carr Robinson (Boss), Larry Wheat (Butler).

A private eye searches for the girl friend of an ex-con, taking only $25 per day for his trouble.

Note: Powell begged for this role, as he was no longer believable as a singing juvenile. In order for the 6 foot 4 inch Mazurki to tower over the 6 foot 2 inch Powell, Mazurki had to stand on a box and Powell had to remove his shoes. The director also employed slanted ceilings so that when Mazurki moved from the high side to the low side, he would appear much larger on camera. The film was originally titled *Farewell My Lovely,* and retained that title in England, but American audiences figured a film with that title starring Powell was another light musical and did not bother attending. The title was changed to more accurately reflect its contents, and audiences flocked to see Powell in a new role. It was the beginning of a new career for the actor, who starred in many more detective films, and later starred on TV's *Dick Powell Theater.* This story had been used before in *The Falcon Takes Over* and was remade in 1975 as *Farewell My Lovely.*

Commentary: "The idea of the man who sang 'Tiptoe Through the Tulips' playing a tough private eye was beyond our imaginations"—Edward Dmytryk.

580 *Murder on a Bridle Path* (1936) Mystery. Running time: 63 minutes. Black and white.

Produced by William Sistrom. Directed by William Hamilton and Edward Killy. Screenplay by Dorothy Yost, Thomas Lennon, Edmund North, and James Gow (based on the novel by Stuart Palmer). Photographed by Nicholas Musuraca. Edited by Jack Hively.

Starring James Gleason (Inspector Piper), Helen Broderick (Hildegarde Withers), Louise Latimer (Barbara Foley), Owen Davis, Jr. (Eddie Fry), John Arledge (Joey), John Carroll (Latigo Wells), Leslie Fenton (Don Gregg), Christian Rub (Thomas), Sheila Terry (Violet), Willie Best (High Pockets).

A wealthy widow is found slain.

Note: Broderick was the mother of Broderick Crawford.

581 *Murder on a Honeymoon* (1935) Mystery. Running time: 74 minutes. Black and white.

Produced by Kenneth MacGowan. Directed by Lloyd Corrigan. Screenplay by Seton I. Miller and Robert Benchley (based on the novel by Stuart Palmer). Photographed by Nicholas Musuraca. Edited by William Morgan.

Starring Edna May Oliver (Hildegarde Withers), James Gleason (Piper), Lola Lane (Phyllis), Chick Chandler (Pilot French), George Meeker (Kelsey), Dorothy Libaire (Kay Deving), Harry Ellerbee (Marvin Deving), Spencer Charters (Chief Britt), DeWitt Jennings (Capt. Beegle), Leo G. Carroll (Joseph B. Tate), Arthur Hoyt (Dr. O'Rourke), Matt McHugh (Pilot Madden), Willie Best (Porter).

A nosy schoolteacher becomes involved in solving a murder while visiting Catalina.

582 *Murder on the Blackboard* (1934) Mystery. Running time: 71 minutes. Black and white.

Produced by Kenneth MacGowan. Directed by George Archainbaud. Screenplay by Willis Goldbeck (based on the story by Stuart Palmer). Photographed by Nicholas Musuraca. Edited by Archie Marshek.

Starring Edna May Oliver (Hildegarde Withers), James Gleason (Inspector Piper), Bruce Cabot (Addison Stevens), Gertrude Michael (Janey), Regis Toomey (Smiley), Edgar Kennedy (Donahue), Tully Marshall (MacFarland), Jackie Searl (Leland Jones).

A snooty school teacher discovers the murdered body of her school's music teacher.

Review: "Moderate entertainment for its class" — *Variety.*

583 *Music for Madame* (1937) Musical. Running time: 77 minutes. Black and white.

Produced by Jesse Lasky. Directed by John Blystone. Screenplay by Gertrude Purcell and Robert Hatari. Photographed by Joseph H. August. Edited by Desmond Marquette.

Starring Nino Martini (Nino), Joan Fontaine (Jean), Alan Mowbray (Leon), Billy Gilbert (Krause), Alan Hale (Flugelman), Grant Mitchell (Robinson), Erik Rhodes (Spaghetti Nacio), Lee Patrick (Nora Burns), Frank Conroy (Morton Harding), Bradley Page (Rollins), Ada Leonard (Bride).

An opera star tries to make it big in Hollywood.

Note: This film lost over $375,000. It was Lasky's first production for RKO and third attempt at making Martini a film star.

Review: "Seems that Nino just can't make the grade as a film star" — *Variety.*

584 *My Favorite Spy* (1942) Musical comedy. Running time: 86 minutes. Black and white.

Produced by Harold Lloyd. Directed by Tay Garnett. Screenplay by Sig Herzig. Photographed by Robert De Grasse. Edited by Desmond Marquette.

Starring Kay Kyser (Himself), Ellen Drew (Terry Kyser), Jane Wyman (Connie), Robert Armstrong (Harry), Helen Westley (Aunt Jessie), William Demarest (Cop), Una O'Connor (Maid), Lionel Royce (Winters), Moroni Olsen (Major Allen), George Cleveland (Gus), Vaughan Glaser (Col. Moffett), Hobart Cavanaugh (Jules), Chester Clute (Higgenbothan), Teddy Hart (Soldier), Ish Kabibble (Himself), Jack Norton (Drunk), Barbara Pepper (B Girl), Kay Kyser's Band featuring Harry Babbitt, Sully Mason, Dorothy Dunn, and Trudy Irwin (Themselves).

The bandleader postpones his honeymoon to act as a spy.

Note: Harold Lloyd's last production for RKO. The similarly titled Paramount feature with Bob Hope is not a remake.

585 *My Favorite Wife* (1940) Comedy. Running time: 88 minutes. Black and white and colorized. Available on videocassette.

Produced by Leo McCarey. Directed by Garson Kanin. Screenplay by Sam and Bella Spewack. Photographed by Rudolph Maté. Edited by Robert Wise.

Starring Irene Dunne (Ellen), Cary Grant (Nick), Randolph Scott (Stephen), Gail Patrick (Bianca), Ann Shoemaker (Ma), Scotty Beckett (Tim), Mary Lou Harrington (Chinch), Donald MacBride (Hotel Clerk), Hugh O'Connell (Johnson), Granville Bates (Judge), Pedro de Cordoba (Dr. Kohlmar), Brandon Tynan (Dr. Manning), Leon Belasco (Henri), Harold Gerald (Clerk), Murray Alper (Bartender).

A woman explorer returns after being shipwrecked for several years, only to find that she is presumed dead and her husband has remarried.

Note: Remade as *Move Over Darling.*

Review: "One of those comedies with a glow on it" — *Otis Ferguson.*

586 *My Forbidden Past* (1951) Drama. Running time: 81 minutes. Black and white. Available on videocassette.

Produced by Robert Sparks and Polan Banks. Directed by Robert Stevenson. Screenplay by Marion Parsonnet and Leopold Atlas. Photographed by Harry Wild. Edited by George Shrader.

Starring Robert Mitchum (Dr. Lucas), Ava Gardner (Barbara), Melvyn Douglas (Paul), Lucile Watson (Aunt Eula), Janis Carter (Corrine), Gordon Oliver (Clay), Basil Ruysdale (Dean Cazzley), Clarence Muse (Pompey), Walter Kingsford (Coroner), Jack Briggs (Phillipe).

A woman seeks revenge when family interferes with her marriage plans.

Note: Lost more than $700,000 at the box office.

587 *My Life with Caroline* (1941)

Comedy. Running time: 78 minutes. Black and white.

Produced and directed by Lewis Milestone. Screenplay by John Van Druten and Arnold Belgard (based on the play by Louis Verneuil and Georges Barr). Photographed by Victor Milner. Edited by Edward Donahue.

Starring Ronald Coleman (Anthony Mason), Anna Lee (Caroline Mason), Charles Winninger (Bliss), Reginald Gardiner (Paul), Gilbert Roland (Paco Del Valle), Katherine Leslie (Helen), Hugh O'Connell (Muirhead), Matt Moore (Butler), Murray Alper (Chauffeur), Richard Carle (Dr. Curtis).

A man believes his wife is cheating on him.

588 *My Pal Wolf* (1944)

Drama. Running time: 75 minutes. Black and white.

Produced by Adrian Scott. Directed by Alfred Werker. Screenplay by Lillie Hayward, Leonard Praskins, and John Paxton. Photographed by Jack MacKenzie. Edited by Harry Marker.

Starring Sharyn Moffett (Gretchen), Jill Esmond (Miss Munn), Una O'Connor (Mrs. Blevins), George Cleveland (Wilson), Charles Arnt (Papa), Claire Carleton (Ruby), Leona Maricle (Mrs. Antsey), Bruce Edwards (Mr. Antsey), Ed Fielding (Secretary of War), Larry Olsen (Fred), Jerry Michelson (Alf), Bobby Larson (Karl), Grey Shadow (Wolf).

A strict nanny comes between a little girl and her beloved dog.

589 *Mysterious Desperado* (1949)

Western. Running time: 61 minutes. Black and white.

Produced by Herman Schlom. Directed by Lesley Selander. Screenplay by Norman Houston. Photographed by Nicholas Musuraca. Edited by Les Millbrook.

Starring Tim Holt, Richard Martin, Edward Norris, Movita Castaneda, Robert Livingston, Frank Wilcox, William Tannen, Robert B. Williams, Kenneth MacDonald, Frank Lackteen, Leander DeCordova.

Chito's uncle is murdered and the man's son is falsely accused of the crime.

590 *Mystery in Mexico* (1948)

Mystery. Running time: 66 minutes. Black and white.

Produced by Sid Rogell. Directed by Robert Wise. Screenplay by Lawrence Kimble. Photographed by Jack Draper. Edited by Samuel E. Beetley.

Starring William Lundigan (Steve), Jacqueline White (Victoria), Ricardo Cortez (Norcross), Tony Barrett (Carlos), Jacqueline Dalya (Dolores), Walter Reed (Glenn), Jose Torvay (Swigart), Jaimie Himinez (Pancho).

When an insurance man disappears in Mexico, another is sent to find him.

591 *The Narrow Margin* (1952)

Crime drama. Running time: 71 minutes. Black and white. Available on videocassette.

Produced by Stanley Rubin. Directed by Richard Fleischer. Screenplay by Earl Fenton (based on a story by Martin Goldsmith and Jack Leonard). Photographed by George E. Diskant. Edited by Robert Swink.

Starring Charles McGraw (Walter),

Ava Gardner, Melvyn Douglas and Robert Mitchum in *My Forbidden Past.*

Marie Windsor (Mrs. Neil), Jacqueline White (Ann Sinclair), Gordon Gebert (Tommy), Queenie Leonard (Mrs. Troll), David Clarke (Kemp), Peter Virgo (Densel), Don Beddoe (Gus Forbes), Paul Maxey (Jennings), Harry Harvey (Train Conductor), Mike Lally (Cab Driver).

Police try guarding a prosecution witness on a train from Chicago to Los Angeles.

Note: Made for a meager $230,000, hence it was extremely profitable for the studio.

592 The Navy Comes Through

(1942) War drama. Running time: 81 minutes. Black and white. Available on videocassette.

Produced by Islin Auster. Directed by A. Edward Sutherland. Screenplay by Roy Chanslor, Earl Baldwin, John Twist, and Aeneas MacKenzie. Photographed by Nicholas Musuraca. Edited by Samuel E. Beetley.

Starring Pat O'Brien (Mallory), George Murphy (Sands), Jane Wyatt (Myra), Jackie Cooper (Babe), Carl Esmond (Kroner), Max Baer (Berringer), Desi Arnaz (Tarriba), Ray Collins (Captain McCall), Lee Bonnell (Kovac), Frank Jenks (Sampter), John Maguire (Bayliss), Frank Fenton (Hodum), Joey Ray (Dennis), Marten Lamont (Doctor).

An old freighter single handedly destroys a Nazi war fleet.

593 Nevada

(1944) Western. Running time: 62 minutes. Black and white.

Produced by Herman Schlom and Sid Rogell. Directed by Edward Killy. Screenplay by Norman Houston (based on the story by Zane Grey). Photographed by Harry Wild. Edited by Roland Gross.

Starring Robert Mitchum (Nevada),

Anne Jeffreys (Julie), Nancy Gates (Hattie), Craig Reynolds (Cash), Guinn "Big Boy" Williams (Dusty), Richard Martin (Chito), Harry Woods (Joe Powell), Edmund Glover (Ed), Alan Ward (William Brewer), Harry McKim (Marve), Wheaton Chambers (Dr. Darien).

A cowboy, searching for gold, is accused of murder.

Note: Remake of a 1927 silent. The 1938 Paramount film has nothing to do with this one.

594 *Never a Dull Moment* (1950)

Comedy. Running time: 89 minutes. Black and white.

Produced by Harriet Parsons. Directed by George Marshall. Screenplay by Lou Breslow and Doris Anderson (based on the novel by Kay Swift). Photographed by Joseph Walker. Edited by Robert Swink.

Starring Irene Dunne (Kay), Fred MacMurray (Chris), William Demarest (Mears), Andy Devine (Orvie), Gigi Perreau (Tina), Natalie Wood (Nan), Phillip Ober (Jed), Jack Kirkwood (Papa), Ann Doran (Jean), Margaret Gibson (Pokey), Lela Bliss (Mama), Irving Bacon (Tunk), Anne O'Neal (Julia).

A city girl tries to adapt to her new husband's country living.

Note: Has nothing to do with the 1943 Ritz Brothers or 1968 Disney films with the same title.

Never to Love see *A Bill of Divorcement*

595 *Never Wave at a WAC* (1952)

Comedy. Running time: 87 minutes. Black and white.

Produced by Frederick Brisson. Directed by Norman Z. McLeod. Screenplay by Ken Englund (based on a story by Fredrick Kohner and Fred Brady). Photographed by William Daniels. Edited by Stanley Johnson. British title: *The Private Wore Skirts*.

Starring Rosalind Russell (Jo McBain), Paul Douglas (Nadrew), Marie Wilson (Clara), William Ching (Fairchild), Arleen Whelan (Sgt. Wayne), Leif Erickson

(Noisy Jackson), Charles Dingle (Reynolds), Lurene Tuttle (Murchinson), Hillary Brooke (Phyllis), Frieda Inescort (Lily Mae Gorham), Regis Toomey (General Prager), Louise Beavers (Artamesa), General Omar Bradley (Himself).

A rich girl enters the WACs as a lark, but finds she gets no special treatment.

596 *New Faces of 1937* (1937)

Musical. Running time: 105 minutes. Black and white.

Produced by Edward Small. Directed by Leigh Jason. Screenplay by Nat Perrin, Phillip Epstein, Irving Brecher, Harold Kuell, Harry Clark, Howard Green, and David Friedman (based on the story "Shoestring" by George Bradshaw). Photographed by J. Roy Hunt. Edited by George Crone. Music by Sammy Fain, Hal Raynor, Charles Henderson, Ben Pollack, Harry James, Joe Penner, and Roy Webb.

Songs: "Our Penthouse on Third Avenue," "Love Is Never Out of Season," "It Goes to Your Feet," "If I Didn't Have You," "Take the World Off Your Shoulders," "It's the Doctor's Orders," "When the Berry Blossoms Bloom," "The Widow in Lace," "Peckin'."

Starring Joe Penner (Seymore), Milton Berle (Wellington), Parkyakarkus (Parky), Harriet Hilliard (Patricia), William Brady (Jimmy), Jerome Cowan (Hunt), Thelma Leeds (Elaine), Tommy Mack (Judge), Bert Gordon (Count Mischa Moody), Richard Lane (Broker), Patricia Wilder (Hunt's Secretary), Harry Bernard (Bridge Guard), Dewey Robinson (Joe).

A crooked producer sets out to make a flop and pocket the money from the backers.

Note: Remade as *The Producers* by Mel Brooks in 1968.

597 *Next Time I Marry* (1938)

Comedy. Running time: 64 minutes. Black and white.

Produced by Cliff Reid. Directed by Garson Kanin. Screenplay by John

Twist and Helen Meinardi (based on a story by Thames Williamson). Photographed by Russell Metty. Edited by Jack Hively.

Starring Lucille Ball (Nancy Fleming), James Ellison (Tony Anthony), Lee Bowman (Count Georgi), Granville Bates (H.E. Crocker), Mantan Moreland (Tilby), Eliott Sullivan (Red), Murray Alper (Joe), Robert E. Homans (Count Baliff), Dick Elliot (Justice of the Peace), Florence Lake (Justice's Wife), Cy Kendall (Lawyer), Jack Albertson (Reporter).

In order to inherit a fortune, a girl, in love with a foreigner, must marry an American.

598 *A Night of Adventure* (1944) Drama. Running time: 65 minutes. Black and white.

Produced by Herman Schlom. Directed by Gordon Douglas. Screenplay by Crane Wilbur. Photographed by Frank Redman. Edited by Les Millbrook.

Starring Tom Conway (Mark Latham), Audrey Long (Erica), Ed Brophy (Steve), Louis Borell (Tony Clark), Addison Richards (Branson), Jean Brooks (Julie), Nancy Gates (Connie), Russell Hopton (Benny), Clare Carlton (Ruby), Emory Parnell (Judge), Edmund Glover (Andrews).

A lawyer finds that his wife has taken up with an accused killer.

Note: Remake of *Hat, Coat, and Glove.*

599 *Night Parade* (1929) Drama. Running time: 72 minutes. Black and white.

Produced by William LeBaron. Directed by Malcolm St. Clair. Screenplay by James Green and George O'Hara (based on the play "Ringside" by George Abbott, Edward Paramoure, Gene Buck, Hyatt Daab). Photographed by William Marshall. Edited by Jack Kitchin. British title: *Sporting Life.*

Starring Hugh Trevor (Bobby), Lloyd Ingraham (Tom), Dorothy Gulliver (Doris), Aileen Pringle (Paula), Robert Ellis (John), Lee Shumway (Sid).

A middleweight champion is seduced by a woman and implicated with gangsters wanting him to throw the fight.

600 *Night Song* (1947) Drama. Running time: 101 minutes. Black and white.

Produced by Harriet Parsons. Directed by John Cromwell. Screenplay by DeWitt Bodeen, Frank Fenton, and Dick Irving Hyland. Photographed by Lucien Ballard. Edited by Harry Marker.

Starring Dana Andrews (Dan), Merle Oberon (Cathy), Ethel Barrymore (Miss Willey), Hoagy Carmichael (Chick), Arthur Rubenstein (Himself), Eugene Ormandy (Himself), Jacqueline White (Connie), Donald Curtis (George), Walter Reed (Jimmy), Jane Jones (Marnie), Whit Bissell (Ward).

A wealthy woman pretends to be poor and blind when she falls for a blind pianist.

601 *Night Waitress* (1936) Crime drama. Running time: 59 minutes. Black and white.

Produced by Joseph Henry Steele. Directed by Lew Landers. Screenplay by Marcus Goodrich (based on a story by Golda Draper). Photographed by Russell Metty. Edited by Desmond Marquette.

Starring Margot Grahame (Helen Roberts), Gordon Jones (Martin Rhodes), Vinton Haworth (Skinner), Marc Lawrence (Dorn), Billy Gilbert (Torre), Donald Barry (Margo Rigo), Otto Yamaoka (Fong), Paul Stanton (District Attorney), Arthur Loft (Borgum), Walter Miller (Inspector), Anthony Quinn (Hood), Frank Faylen, Dick Miller (Cops), Barbara Pepper (Bit).

A girl, newly released from prison, gets involved in a murder at the restaurant where she works.

602 *Nightspot* (1938) Comedy. Running time: 60 minutes. Black and white.

Produced by Robert Sisk. Directed by Christy Cabanne. Screenplay by Lionel Houser (based on a story by Anne Jordan).

Bert Wheeler, Betty Grable and Bob Woolsey in *The Nitwits*.

Photographed by Nicholas Musuraca. Edited by Harry Marker.

Starring Allan Lane (Pete), Parkyakarkus (Gashouse), Gordon Jones (Riley), Joan Woodbury (Marge), Lee Patrick (Flo), Bradley Page (Marty), Jack Carson (Shallen), Frank M. Thomas (Waiter).

A cop tries to prove a nightclub owner is actually a fenceman for jewel thieves.

Note: Woodbury's film debut; Lane's first leading role.

603 *Nine Till Six* (1932) Romance. Running time: 75 minutes. Black and white.

Produced and directed by Basil Dean. Screenplay by Beverly Nicholls, Alma Reville, John Paddy Carstairs (based on the play by Aimee and Phillip Stuart). Photographed by Robert Martin and Robert de Grasse.

Starring Louise Hampton, Elizabeth Allan, Florence Desmond, Isla Bevan, Richard Bird, Frances Doble, Jeanne de Casalis, Kay Hammond, Sunday Wil-shin, Alison Leggatt, Moore Marriott, George de Warfax, Hilda Simms.

Romantic episodes in a London dress shop.

Note: Screenwriter Reville was the wife of Alfred Hitchcock.

604 *The Nitwits* (1935) Comedy. Running time: 81 minutes. Black and white. Available on videocassette.

Produced by Lee Marcus. Directed by George Stevens. Screenplay by Fred Guiol, Al Boasberg. Photographed by Edward Cronjager. Edited by John Lockert.

Starring Bert Wheeler (Johnnie), Robert Woolsey (Newton), Fred Keating (Darrell), Betty Grable (Mary), Evelyn Brent (Mrs. Lake), Hale Hamilton (Lake), Arthur Aylesworth (Lurch), Erik Rhodes (Clark), Charles Wilson (Captain Jennings), Willie Best (Sleepy), Lew Kelley (Hazel), Dorothy Granger (Phyllis).

Two cigar store salesmen are implicated in a song publisher's murder.

605 *No Marriage Ties* (1933) Drama. Running time: 65 minutes. Black and white.

Produced by William Goetz. Directed by J. Walter Ruben. Screenplay by Arthur Caesar, Sam Mintz, and H.W. Hanemann. Photographed by Henry Cronjager. Edited by George Hively.

Starring Richard Dix (Bruce Foster), Elizabeth Allan (Peggy Wilson), Alan Dinehart (Perkins), David Landau (Zimmer), Hilda Vaughn (Olmstead), Hobart Cavanaugh (Smith), Doris Kenyon (Adrienne), Charles Wilson (Bit).

A drunken newspaperman, fired from his job, hooks up with an ad exec and becomes a business tyrant.

606 *No, No Nanette* (1940) Musical. Running time: 96 minutes. Black and white.

Produced and directed by Herbert Wilcox. Screenplay by Ken Englund (based on the musical by Frank Mandel, Otto Harbach, Emil Nyttray, and Vincent Youmans). Photographed by Russell Metty. Edited by Elmo Williams.

Starring Anna Neagle (Nanette), Richard Carlson (Tom), Victor Mature (William), Roland Young (Mr. Smith), Helen Broderick (Mrs. Smith), ZaSu Pitts (Pauline), Eve Arden (Winnie), Tamara (Sonya), Billy Gilbert (Styles), Stuart Robertson (Stillwater), Dorothea Kent (Betty), Benny Rubin (Max).

A Bible salesman helps three different women in trouble, and then the three all arrive at his vacation cottage.

Note: Second film version of the Broadway musical.

607 *No Other Woman* (1933) Drama. Running time: 58 minutes. Black and white.

Produced by David O. Selznick. Directed by J. Walter Ruben. Screenplay by Wanda Tuchock. Photographed by Edward Cronjager. Edited by William Hamilton.

Starring Irene Dunne (Ann Stanley), Charles Bickford (Big Jim), J. Carrol

Naish (Bonelli), Eric Linden (Joe), Gwili Andre (Margot Van Dearing), Buster Miles (Bobbie), Leila Bennett (Susie), Christian Rub (Eli).

A woman helps her man achieve wealth, with tragic results.

608 *No Time for Flowers* (1952) Comedy. Running time: 83 minutes. Black and white.

Produced by Mort Briskin. Directed by Don Siegel. Screenplay by Laslo Vadnay and Hans Wilhelm. Photographed by Toni Braun. Edited by Henrietta Brunsch.

Starring Viveca Lindfors (Anna), Paul Christian (Karl), Ludwig Stossel (Papa), Adrienne Gessner (Mama), Peter Preses (Emil), Manfred Inger (Kudelka), Peter Czeyke (Stefan), Fredrick Berger (Anton).

A Czech woman tries to control herself when surrounded by the temptations of the U.S.

609 *Nocturne* (1946) Crime drama. Running time: 88 minutes. Black and white.

Produced by Joan Harrison. Directed by Edwin L. Marin. Screenplay by Jonathan Latimer. Photographed by Harry J. Wild. Edited by Elmo Williams.

Starring George Raft (Lt. Joe Warne), Lynn Bari (Frances Ransom), Virginia Huston (Carol Page), Joseph Pevney (Fingers), Myrna Dell (Susan), Edward Ashley (Paul Vincent), Walter Sande (Halberson), Mabel Page (Mrs. Warne), Bernard Hoffman (Torp), Queenie Smith (Queenie), Mack Gray (Gratz), Pat Flaherty (Cop), Loring Ryker (Chemist), William Challee (Photographer).

A police lieutenant investigates the murder of a composer.

Note: Actor Joe Pevney later became a director.

Review: "Amusing, self-mocking..."
—Leslie Halliwell.

610 *None But the Lonely Heart* (1944) Drama. Running time: 113

Unknown actor and Cary Grant in *None But the Lonely Heart*.

minutes. Black and white. Available on videocassette.

Produced by David Hempstead. Directed and written by Clifford Odets (based on the novel by Richard Llewelyn). Photographed by George Barnes. Edited by Roland Gross.

Starring Cary Grant (Ernie), Ethel Barrymore (Ma), Barry Fitzgerald (Twite), June Duprez (Ada), Jane Wyatt (Aggie), George Coulouris (Jim Mordiney), Dan Duryea (Lew Tate), Konstantin Shayne (Ike), Eva Lernard Boyne (Chalmers), Morton Lowry (Taz), Roman Bohnen (Pettyjohn).

A shiftless Cockney is told that his mother, with whom he cannot get along, has cancer.

Ms. Barrymore's talents were acquired when RKO paid the expenses of closing the long-running play *The Corn Is Green* in which the actress was starring. This film was not a box office success, but is today considered a classic of its kind.

611 *The North Star* (1943) War drama. Running time: 105 minutes. Black and white. Available on videocassette.

Produced by William Cameron Menzies. Directed by Lewis Milestone. Screenplay by Lillian Hellman (from her play). Photographed by James Wong Howe. Edited by Daniel Mandell.

Starring Anne Baxter (Marina), Farley Granger (Damian), Jane Withers (Claudia), Dana Andrews (Kolya), Walter Brennan (Karp), Dean Jagger (Rodion), Ann Harding (Sophia), Carl Benton Reid (Boris), Ann Carter (Olga), Walter Huston (Dr. Kurin), Erich von Stroheim (Dr. Otto von Harden), Esther Dale (Anna), Ruth Nelson (Nadya), Paul Guilfoyle (Iakin), Martin Kosleck (Max Richter), Tonio Selwart (German Captain), Peter Pohlenz (German Lieutenant), Gene O'Donnell (Russian Gunner), Robert Lowery (Russian Pilot), Frank Wilcox (Petrov).

A Russian village defends itself against the Nazis.

Note: Goldwyn made this film at the request of FDR to do a movie honoring America's Russian allies. At the height of the McCarthy witchhunts, everyone involved with this film had to testify and give their reasons for making it. The film was edited by over twenty minutes in 1957 and retitled *Armored Attack.* Among the deletions included much character development and all uses of the word "comrade."

612 *Notorious* (1946) Suspense. Running time: 101 minutes. Black and white. Available on videocassette.

Produced and directed by Alfred Hitchcock. Screenplay by Ben Hecht. Photographed by Ted Tetzlaff. Edited by Theron Warth.

Starring Cary Grant (Devlin), Ingrid Bergman (Alicia), Claude Rains (Alexander), Louis Calhern (Paul), Mme. Konstantin (Sebastian), Reinhold Schunzel (Dr. Anderson), Moroni Olsen (Walter Beardsley), Ivan Triessault (Eric Mathis), Alex Minotis (Joseph), Wally Brown (Hopkins), Gavin Gordon (Ernest Weylin), Sir. Charles Mendl (Commodore), Ricardo Costa (Dr. Babosa), Eberhard Krumschmidt (Hupka), Fay Baker (Ethel), Antonio Moreno (Senor Ortiza), Frederick Ledebur (Knerr), Luis Serrano (Dr. Silva), William Gordon (Adams), Charles D. Brown (Judge).

An American agent is assigned to watch the daughter of a Nazi spy, but soon falls in love with her.

613 *Nurse Edith Cavell* (1939) Drama. Running time: 95 minutes. Black and white. Available on videocassette.

Produced and directed by Herbert Wilcox. Screenplay by Michael Hogan. Photographed by F.A. Young and Joseph H. August. Edited by Elmo Williams.

Starring Anna Neagle (Nurse Edith Cavell), Edna May Oliver (Countess), George Sanders (Heinrichs), May Robson (Rappard), ZaSu Pitts (Moulin), H.B. Warner (Gibson), Sophie Stewart (Sister Watkins), Mary Howard (Nurse O'Brien), Robert Coote (Cungey), Martin Kosleck (Perre).

The story of a nurse who was later executed as a spy.

Note: Controversial at the time of its initial release due to its brutal depiction of war.

614 *The Obliging Young Lady* (1941) Comedy. Running time: 80 minutes. Black and white.

Produced by Howard Benedict. Directed by Richard Wallace. Screenplay by Frank Ryan and Bert Granet. Photographed by Nicholas Musuraca. Edited by Henry Berman.

Starring Joan Carroll (Bridget Potter), Edmond O'Brien (Red Reddy), Ruth Warrick (Linda), Robert Smith (Charles), Eve Arden (Space), Charles Lane (Smith), Franklin Pangborn (Gibney), George Cleveland (Tom), Marjorie Gateson (Mira), John Miljan (George Potter), Luis Alberni (Riccardi).

A child is taken away by a secretary in order to reunite the parents.

615 *Of Human Bondage* (1934) Drama. Running time: 83 minutes. Black and white. Available on videocassette.

Produced by Pandro S. Berman. Directed by John Cromwell. Screenplay by Lester Cohen (based on the novel by W. Somerset Maugham). Photographed by Henry W. Gerard. Edited by William Morgan.

Starring Leslie Howard (Phillip Carey), Bette Davis (Mildred Rogers), Frances Dee (Sally Athelny), Reginald Owen (Thorpe Athelny), Reginald Denny (Harry Griffiths), Kay Johnson (Norah), Alan Hale (Emil Miller), Reginald Sheffield (Dunsford), Desmond Roberts (Jacobs).

A wealthy Englishman falls for a low-class waitress.

Review: "Stars and the novel rep will have to carry a lethargic romance"— *Variety.*

616 *Officer O'Brien* (1930) Crime drama. Running time: 72 minutes. Black and white. A Pathé production.

Directed by Tay Garnett. Screenplay by Tom Buckingham. Photographed by Arthur Miller. Edited by Jack Ogilvie.

Starring William Boyd, Ernest Torrence, Dorothy Sebastian, Russell Gleason, Clyde Cook, Ralf Harolde, Arthur Housman, Paul Hurst, Tom Maloney, Toyo Fujita.

A cop tries to reform his gangster father.

Old Greatheart see *Way Back Home*

617 *Old Man Rhythm* (1935) Musical. Running time: 74 minutes. Black and white.

Produced by Zion Meyers. Directed by Edward Ludwig. Screenplay by Sig Herzig, Ernest Pagano, and H.W. Hanemann. Photographed by Nicholas Musuraca. Edited by George Crone.

Starring Buddy Rogers (Johnny Roberts), George Barbier (John Roberts, Sr.), Barbara Kent (Edith), Grace Bradley (Marion), Betty Grable (Sylvia), Eric Blore (Phillips), Erik Rhodes (Frank), John Arledge (Pinky), Johnny Mercer (Colonel), Donald Meek (Parker), Dave Chasen (Andy).

A father enrolls in the college his son is attending.

618 *On Again—Off Again* (1937) Comedy. Running time: 60 minutes. Black and white.

Produced by Lee Marcus. Directed by Edward F. Cline. Screenplay by Nat Perrin and Benny Rubin. Photographed by Jack MacKenzie. Edited by John Lockert.

Starring Bert Wheeler (Hobbs), Robert Woolsey (Claude Horion), Marjorie Lord (Florence), Patricia Wilder (Gertie), Esther Muir (Nettie), Paul Harvey (Applegate), Russell Hicks (George Dilwig), George Meeker (Tony), Maxine Jennings (Miss Meeker), Kitty McHugh (Mrs. Parker).

Two pill factory partners decide to hold a wrestling match, with the winner to run the company.

619 *On Dangerous Ground* (1951) Crime drama. Running time: 82 minutes. Black and white.

Produced by John Houseman. Directed by Nicholas Ray. Screenplay by A.I. Bezzerides, Ray. Photographed by George Diskant. Edited by Roland Gross.

Starring Ida Lupino (Mary Malden), Robert Ryan (Jim Wilson), Ward Bond (Walter Brent), Charles Kemper (Bill Daly), Anthony Ross (Pete Antos), Ed Begley (Capt. Brawley), Ian Wolfe (Carrey), Sumner Williams (Danny Malden), Gus Schilling (Lucky).

A tough cop falls for a crook's blind sister.

620 *On the Loose* (1951) Drama. Running time: 74 minutes. Black and white.

Produced by Collier Young. Directed by Charles Lederer. Screenplay by Dale Eunson and Katherine Albert (based on a story by Young and Marvin Wald). Photographed by Archie Stout. Edited by Desmond Marquette.

Starring Joan Evans (Jill), Melvyn Douglas (Frank), Lynn Bari (Alice), Robert Arthur (Larry), Hugh O'Brien (Dr. Phillips), Constance Hilton (Susan), Michel Kuhn (Bob), Susan Morrow (Catherine).

A teenage girl becomes a delinquent when ignored by her parents.

621 *Once Upon a Honeymoon* (1942) Comedy. Running time: 117 minutes. Black and white. Available on videocassette.

Produced and directed by Leo McCarey. Screenplay by Sheridan Gibney. Photographed by George Barnes. Edited by Theron Warth.

Starring Ginger Rogers (Katie O'Hara), Cary Grant (Pat O'Toole), Walter Slezak (Baron Von Luber),

Albert Dekker (LeBlanc), Albert Basserman (Borelski), Ferike Boros (Elsa), Harry Shannon (Cumberland), John Banner (Kleinoch), Natsha Lytess (Anna), Peter Seal (Orderly).

A radio correspondent falls for a burlesque queen who has hooked up with a Nazi officer.

622 One Man's Journey (1933)

Drama. Running time: 72 minutes. Black and white.

Produced by Pandro S. Berman. Directed by John Robertson. Screenplay by Lester Cohen and Sam Ornitz. Photographed by Jack MacKenzie. Edited by Arthur Roberts.

Starring Lionel Barrymore (Dr. Eli Watt), May Robson (Sarah), Dorothy Jordan (Letty), Joel McCrea (Jimmy), Frances Dee (Joan), David Landau (McGinnis), James Bush (Bill Radford), Buster Phelps (Jimmy at Age 6), Oscar Apfel (John Radford), June Filmer (May Radford).

A small town doctor is devoted to the people he serves.

Note: Remade in 1938 as *A Man to Remember.*

623 One Minute to Zero (1952)

War drama. Running time: 105 minutes. Black and white.

Produced by Edmund Grainger. Directed by Tay Garnett. Screenplay by Milton Krims and William Wister Haines. Photographed by William Snyder. Edited by Robert Belcher.

Starring Robert Mitchum (Janowski), Ann Blyth (Linda), William Talman (Parker), Charles McGraw (Baker), Margaret Sheridan (Mary), Richard Egan (Ralston), Eduard Franz (Engstrand), Roy Roberts (General Thomas), Dorothy Granger (Nurse).

A soldier during the Korean War finds romance.

1000 Years from Now see Captive Women

Other Peoples Business see Way Back Home

624 Our Betters (1933) Comedy. Running time: 80 minutes. Black and white.

Produced by David O. Selznick. Directed by George Cukor. Screenplay by Jane Murfin and Harry Wagstaff Gribble (based on the play by W. Somerset Maugham). Photographed by Charles Rosher. Edited by Jack Kitchin.

Starring Constance Bennett (Lady Pearl Grayston), Gilbert Roland (Pepi d'Costa), Charles Starrett (Fleming Harvey), Anita Louise (Bessie), Alan Mowbray (Lord George Grayston), Minor Watson (Fenwick), Violet Kemble-Cooper (Duchess), Tyrell Davis (Ernest).

An American woman finds her British husband has been unfaithful.

Review: "They will really have to go for Constance Bennett to go for this picture" — *Variety.*

625 Our Very Own (1950) Drama.

Running time: 92 minutes. Black and white.

Produced by Samuel Goldwyn. Directed by David Miller. Screenplay by Hugh Herbert. Photographed by Lee Garmes. Edited by Sherman Todd.

Starring Ann Blyth (Gail), Jane Wyatt (Lois), Donald Cook (Fred), Farley Granger (Chuck), Joan Evans (Joan), Ann Dvorak (Mrs. Lynch), Natalie Wood (Penny), Gus Schilling (Frank).

An adoptee becomes curious about her birth mother.

626 Out of the Past (1947) Crime

drama. Running time: 97 minutes. Black and white. Available on videocassette.

Produced by Warren Duff. Directed by Jacques Tourneur. Screenplay by Geoffrey Homes. Photographed by Nicholas Musuraca. Edited by Samuel E. Beetley.

Starring Robert Mitchum (Jeff Bailey), Jane Greer (Kathie Moffett), Kirk Douglas (Whit Sterling), Rhonda Fleming (Meta), Richard Webb (Jim), Steve Brodie (Fisher), Virginia Huston (Ann), Paul Valentine (Joe), Dickie Moore (The Kid), Ken Niles (Eels), Lee Elson (Policeman), Frank Wilcox (Douglas).

A detective is hired to find a crook's girlfriend, and falls in love with her.

627 *Outcasts of Poker Flat* (1937) Western. Running time: 70 minutes. Black and white.

Produced by Robert Sisk. Directed by Christy Cabanne. Screenplay by John Twist and Harry Segall (based on the Bret Harte stories "The Outcasts of Poker Flat" and "The Luck of Roaring Camp"). Photographed by Robert De Grasse. Edited by Ted Cheesman.

Starring Preston Foster (John Oakhurst), Jean Muir (Helen Colby), Van Heflin (Reverend), Virginia Weidler (Luck), Margaret Irving (Duchess), Frank M. Thomas (Redford), Si Jenks (Kentuck), Dick Elliot (Stumpy), Al St. John (Uncle Billy), Monte Blue (Jim), Richard Lane (High Grade), Billy Gilbert (Charley), Barbara Pepper (Saloon Girl).

An alcoholic gambler adopts a little girl in an effort to go straight.

Note: Filmed before by John Ford in 1919 and then again for Fox in 1952.

628 *The Outlaw* (1943) Western. Running time: 126 minutes. Black and white. Available on videocassette.

Produced by Howard Hughes. Directed by Hughes, Howard Hawks. Screenplay by Jules Furthman. Photographed by Gregg Toland. Edited by Wallace Grissell.

Starring Jack Buetel (Billy the Kid), Jane Russell (Rio), Thomas Mitchell (Pat Garrett), Walter Huston (Doc Holliday), Mimi Aguglia (Guadalupe), Joe Sawyer (Charlie), Gene Rizzi (Stranger), Frank Darien (Shorty), Pat West (Bartender), Carl Stockdale (Minister), Nena Quartero (Chita), Lee "Lasses" White (Driver), Emory Parnell (Dolan), Martin Garralaga (Waiter).

Billy the Kid, Pat Garrett, and Doc Holliday fight over a half-breed girl with large breasts.

Note: Hughes chose Russell after seeing her photograph. She was 19, and this was her first film. Hughes would shoot as many as 100 takes on each scene. The film was briefly released in 1943, was picketed by civics groups due to Jane Russell's low cut blouses, and the obvious emphasis on her bust, and was withdrawn. For the next three years, Hughes had a publicity man plaster billboards with a photo from the film with Russell recoiled in a haystack. Then he re-released the film in 1946, garnering a good box office due to curiosity aroused by his publicity. The film is long known as being dreadful, and is now easily available in the public domain.

Commentary: "I honestly feel sorry if *The Outlaw* publicity campaign was responsible for the young girls who decided that the only way to make it in show business was to shove out their bosom or take their clothes off altogether"—Jane Russell.

629 *Outrage* (1950) Drama. Running time: 75 minutes. Black and white.

Produced by Collier Young. Directed by Ida Lupino. Screenplay by Lupino and Marvin Wald. Photographed by Archie Stout. Edited by Harvey Mager.

Starring Mala Powers (Ann Walton), Tod Andres (Ferguson), Robert Clarke (Jim Owens), Raymond Bond (Mr. Walton), Lilian Hamilton (Mrs. Walton), Rita Lupino (Stella), Hal March (Sgt. Hendrix), Kenneth Patterson (Harrison), Jerry Paris (Martini), Tristam Coffin (Judge), Angela Clark (Mrs. Harrison).

The effect of rape on a working girl who is engaged to a handsome young man.

630 *Overland Telegraph* (1951) Western. Running time: 60 minutes. Black and white.

Produced by Herman Schlom. Directed by Lesley Selander. Screenplay by Adele Buffington. Photographed by J. Roy Hunt. Edited by Samuel E. Beetley.

Starring Tim Holt (Tim), Gail Davis (Terry), Hugh Beaumont (Brad), Mari

Blanchard (Stella), George Nader (Paul Manning), Robert Wilke (Bellew), Cliff Clark (Muldoon), Russell Hicks (Colonel), Robert Bray (Steve), Fred Graham (Joe), Richard Martin (Chito).

A cowboy and his sidekick try to find who is sabotaging the new transcontinental telegraph.

631 *The Pace That Thrills* (1952)
Drama. Running time: 63 minutes. Black and white.

Produced by Lewis J. Rachmil. Directed by Leon Barsha. Screenplay by DeVallon Scott and Robert Lee Johnson. Photographed by Frank Redman. Edited by Samuel E. Beetley.

Starring Bill Williams (Dusty), Carla Balenda (Eve Drake), Robert Armstrong (Barton), Frank McHugh (Rocket), Steve Flagg (Chris), Cleo Moore (Ruby), John Mallory (Blackie), Diane Garrett (Opal), John Hamilton (Sour Puss), Claudia Drake (Pearl).

Two motorcycle enthusiasts fight over a woman.

632 *Pacific Liner* (1939)
Drama. Running time: 76 minutes. Black and white.

Produced by Robert Sisk. Directed by Lew Landers. Screenplay by John Twist. Photographed by Nicholas Musuraca. Edited by Harry Marker.

Starring Victor McLaglen (Crusher McKay), Chester Morris (Dr. Craig), Wendy Barrie (Ann Grayson), Alan Hale (Gallagher), Barry Fitzgerald (Britches), Allan Lane (Bilson), Halliwell Hobbes (Captain Mathews), Cy Kendall (Deadeye), Paul Guilfoyle (Wishart), Emory Parnell (Olaf).

A cholera epidemic on board an ocean liner.

633 *The Painted Desert* (1931)
Western. Running time: 59 minutes. Black and white.

Directed by Howard Higgins. Screenplay by Higgins and Tom Buckingham. Photographed by E.B. Derr.

Starring Bill Boyd, Helen Twelvetrees, William Farnum, J. Farrell MacDonald, Clark Gable, Charles Sellon, Hugh Adams, Wade Boteler, Will Walling, Edmund Breese, Guy Edward Hearn, William LeMaire, Richard Cramer.

Two prospectors find an abandoned child.

Note: Remade in 1938. Clark Gable's talkie debut.

634 *The Painted Desert* (1938)
Western. Running time: 59 minutes. Black and white. Available on videocassette.

Produced by Bert Gilroy. Directed by David Howard. Screenplay by John Rathmell and Oliver Drake. Photographed by Harry Wild. Edited by Frederic Knudtson.

Starring George O'Brien (Bob McVey), Laraine Johnson (Carol Banning), Ray Whitley (Steve), Stanley Fields (Placer Bill), Fred Kohler, Sr. (Fawcett), Max Wagner (Kincaid), Harry Cording (Burke), Lee Shumway (Bart), Lloyd Ingraham (Banning).

A cowboy and a bandit fight over a mine.

Note: Actress Johnson is Laraine Day.

635 *Panama Flo* (1932)
Drama. Running time: 72 minutes. Black and white.

Produced by Harry Joe Brown. Directed by Ralph Murphy. Screenplay by Garrett Fort. Photographed by Arthur Miller. Edited by Charles Craft.

Starring Helen Twelvetrees (Flo), Robert Armstrong (Babe), Charles Bickford (McTeague), Marjorie Peterson (Pearl), Maude Eburne (Sadie).

A showgirl becomes a housekeeper to avoid going to jail after being implicated with a gangster.

Note: Remade as *Panama Lady* (q.v.).

636 *Panama Lady* (1939)
Comedy. Running time: 64 minutes. Black and white. Available on videocassette.

Produced by Cliff Reid. Directed by

Jack Hively. Screenplay by Michael Kanin (based on a story by Garrett Fort). Photographed by J. Roy Hunt. Edited by Theron Warth.

Starring Lucille Ball (Lucy), Allan Lane (McTeague), Steffi Duna (Cheema), Evelyn Brent (Lenore), Donald Briggs (Roy Harmon), Bernadene Hayes (Pearl), Abner Biberman (Elisha).

A cabaret singer in Panama goes to work for a drunken oil man after she is caught trying to rob him.

Note: Remake of *Panama Flo.*

637 *Pan-Americana* (1945) Musical. Running time: 85 minutes. Black and white.

Produced and directed by John H. Auer. Screenplay by Lawrence Kimble (based on a story by Fredrick Kohner, Auer). Photographed by Frank Redman. Edited by Harry Marker.

Starring Phillip Terry (Dan), Audrey Long (Joanne), Robert Benchley (Charlie), Eve Arden (Hoppy), Ernest Truex (Rudy), Marc Cramer (Jerry), Isabelita (Lupita), Bill Gavin (Sancho), Frank Marasco (Miguel), Armando Gonzales (Carlos), Joan Beckstead (Miss Peru), Valerie Hall (Miss El Salvador), Luz Vasquez (Miss Mexico), Joy Curtis (Miss Bolivia), Goya Del Valle (Miss Panama), Carme Lopez (Miss Paraguay), Aldonna Gauvin (Miss Uruguay).

Several magazine writers go south of the border to find the prettiest girl.

638 *Parachute Battalion* (1941) War. Running time: 75 minutes. Black and white. Available on videocassette.

Produced by Howard Benedict. Directed by Leslie Goodwins. Screenplay by John Twist and Major Hugh Fite. Photographed by J. Roy Hunt. Edited by Theron Warth.

Starring Robert Preston (Donald), Nancy Kelly (Kit), Edmond O'Brien (Bill Burke), Harry Carey (Bill Richards), Buddy Ebsen (Jeff), Paul Kelly (Tex), Richard Cromwell (Spence), Robert Barrat (Col. Burke), Erville Alderson (Pa), Selmer Jackson (Morse).

A group of Army trainees prepare for a parachute corps.

639 *Park Avenue Logger* (1937) Drama. Running time: 65 minutes. Black and white.

Produced by George Hirliman. Directed by David Howard. Screenplay by Dan Jarrett and Ewing Scott (based on a story by Bruce Hutchison). Photographed by Frank B. Good. Edited by Robert Crandall.

Starring George O'Brien (Grant Curran), Beatrice Roberts (Peggy O'Shea), Willard Robertson (Ben Morton), Ward Bond (Paul Sanger), Bert Hanlon (Nick), Lloyd Ingraham (Mike Curran), George Rosener (Matt O'Shea).

A man sends his son to a lumber camp to become more masculine.

640 *Partners* (1932) Western. Running time: 62 minutes. Black and white.

Produced by Fred Allen. Screenplay by Donald W. Lee. Photographed by Harry Jackson. Edited by Walter Thompson.

Starring Tom Keene, Nancy Drexel, Bobby Nelson, Otis Harlan, Victor Potel, Lee Shumway, Billy Franey, Carlton King, Ben Corbett, Fred Burns.

An innocent man is accused of an old codger's murder.

641 *Partners in Time* (1946) Comedy. Running time: 74 minutes. Black and white.

Produced by Ben Hersh. Directed by William Nigh. Screenplay by Charles E. Roberts. Photographed by Jack MacKenzie. Edited by S. Roy Luby.

Starring Chester Lauck (Lum), Norris Goff (Abner), Pamela Blake (Elizabeth), John James (Tim), Teala Loring (Janet), Danny Duncan (Grandpappy Spears), Grady Sutton (Cedric).

How Lum and Abner meet upon arriving in Pine Ridge, Arkansas.

Note: The sixth and final Lum and Abner film for RKO.

642 *Passion* (1954) Western. Running time: 84 minutes. Color.

Produced by Benedict Bogeaus. Directed by Allan Dwan. Screenplay by Joseph Leytes, Beatrice Dresher, and Howard Estabrook. Photographed by John Alton. Edited by Carl Lodato.

Starring Cornel Wilde (Juan Obregon), Yvonne DeCarlo (Rosa Melo, Tonya Melo), Raymond Burr (Rodriguez), Lon Chaney, Jr. (Castro), Rodolfo Acosta (Salvador Sandro), John Qualen (Gaspar Melo), Anthony Caruso (Sgt. Munoz), Frank de Kova (Martinez), Peter Coe (Colfre).

Jealousy among ranchers in California's Spanish territory.

643 *Passport to Destiny* (1944) Drama. Running time: 65 minutes. Black and white.

Produced by Herman Schlom. Directed by Ray McCarey. Screenplay by Val Burton and Muriel Roy Bolton. Photographed by Jack MacKenzie. Edited by Robert Swink.

Starring Elsa Lanchester (Ella), Gordon Oliver (Franz), Lenore Aubert (Greta), Lionel Royce (Dietrich), Fritz Feld (Hausmeister), Joseph Vitale (Lt. Bosch), Gavin Muir (Lord Haw Haw), Lloyd Corrigan (Walters).

The widow of a British officer travels to Berlin to kill Hitler herself.

Review: Implausible story made bearable by Lanchester's commanding performance.

644 *The Past of Mary Holmes* (1933) Drama. Running time: 70 minutes. Black and white.

Produced by Bartlett Cormack. Directed by Harlan Thompson and Slavko Vorkapitch. Screenplay by Marion Dix and Edward Doherty. Photographed by Charles Rosher. Edited by Charles Kimball.

Starring Helen MacKellar (Mary), Eric Linden (Geoffrey), Jean Arthur (Joan), Skeets Gallagher (Pratt), Ivan Simpson (Jacob Riggs), Clay Clement (Etheridge), Franklin Parker (Brooks), Eddie Nugent (Flannagan), Roscoe Ates (Klondike), J. Carrol Naish (Kent), John Sheehan (Kinkaid), Rochelle Hudson, Jane Darwell (Bits).

A forgotten opera singer blames her son for her lack of recognition.

Note: Remake of the 1925 silent *The Goose Woman.*

645 *The Pay Off* (1930) Crime drama. Running time: 65 minutes. Black and white.

Produced by William LeBaron and Henry Hobart. Directed by Lowell Sherman. Screenplay by Jane Murfin (based on a play by Samuel Shipman and John Hymer). Photographed by J. Roy Hunt. Edited by Rose Smith.

Starring Lowell Sherman (Gene Fenmore), Marian Nixon (Annabelle), Hugh Trevor (Rocky), William Janney (Tommy), Helene Millard (Dot), Robert McWade (Frank), Alan Roscoe (District Attorney), Lita Chevret (Margy).

A master thief who only steals from other criminals and doesn't resort to violence against his victim, falls in love with a young girl, but finds she is engaged to another.

Note: Sherman was very active in the silent and early talking picture era, but only lived until 1934.

646 *Payment on Demand* (1951) Drama. Running time: 90 minutes. Black and white.

Produced by Jack H. Skirball and Bruce Manning. Directed by Curtis Bernhardt. Screenplay by Manning and Bernhardt. Photographed by Leo Tover. Edited by Harry Marker.

Starring Bette Davis (Joyce), Barry Sullivan (David Ramsey), Jane Cowl (Mrs. Hedges), Kent Taylor (Robert Townsend), Betty Lynn (Martha), John Sutton (Tunliffe), Frances Dee (Eileen), Peggy Castle (Diana), Otto Kruger (Prescott), Walter Sande (Swanson), Natalie Schaefer (Mrs. Blanton).

Tommy Kelly and Edgar Kennedy in *Peck's Bad Boy with the Circus*.

A woman is taken aback by her husband's request for a divorce.

Note: Made before Davis' bravura performance in *All About Eve*, but released after.

647 *Peach O'Reno* (1931) Comedy. Running time: 63 minutes. Black and white. Available on videocassette.

Produced by William LeBaron. Directed by William Seiter. Screenplay by Tim Whelan, Ralph Spence and Eddie Welch. Photographed by Jack MacKenzie. Edited by Jack Kitchin.

Starring Bert Wheeler (Wattles), Robert Woolsey (Swift), Dorothy Lee (Prudence), Joseph Cawthorn (Joe Bruno), Cora Witherspoon (Aggie), Sam Hardy (Judge Jackson), Zelma O'Neal (Pansy).

Two divorce lawyers run a gambling joint at night.

648 *Pearl of the South Pacific* (1955) Adventure. Running time: 86 minutes. Color. Available on videocassette.

Produced by Benedict Bogeaus. Directed by Allan Dwan. Screenplay by Talbot Jennings, Richard Landau, Jesse Lasky, Jr. Photographed by John Alton. Edited by James Leicester.

Starring Virginia Mayo (Rita), Dennis Morgan (Dan Merrill), David Farrar (Bully Hayes), Murvyn Vye (Halemano), Lance Fuller (George), Carol Thurston (Mother).

Thieves attempt to steal black pearls from a Pacific island.

649 *Peck's Bad Boy with the Circus* (1938) Comedy. Running time: 78 minutes. Black and white. Available on videocassette.

Produced by Sol Lesser. Directed by Edward F. Cline. Screenplay by Al Martin, David Boehm, Robert Neville. Photographed by Jack MacKenzie. Edited by Arthur Hilton.

Starring Tommy Kelly (Bill Peck), Ann Gillis (Fleurette), Edgar Kennedy (Bailey), Benita Hume (Myrna), "Spanky" George McFarland (Pee Wee), Billy Gilbert (Boggs), Grant Mitchell (Mr. Peck), William Demarest (Daro), Louise Beavers (Cassie).

Young Peck meets up with a circus rider on his way to camp.

650 *The People's Enemy* (1935) Crime drama. Running time: 65 minutes. Black and white.

Produced by Burt Kelly. Directed by Crane Wilbur. Screenplay by Gordon Kahn and Edward Dean Sullivan (based on a story by Sullivan). Photographed by Joseph Ruttenberg. Edited by William Thompson. A David O. Selznick production.

Starring Preston Foster (Vince), Lila Lee (Catherine), Melvyn Douglas (Traps), Shirley Grey (Ann), Roscoe Ates (Slip), William Collier, Jr. (Tony), Sybil Elaine (Mary), Herbert Rawlinson (Duke), Charles Coburn (Judge).

A once-heroic gangster is sent to prison for income tax evasion, and finds upon his release that he is a nobody.

651 *Peter Pan* (1953) Animated. Running time: 76 minutes. Color.

Produced by Walt Disney. Directed by Hamilton Luske, Clyde Geronimi, Wilfred Jackson. Screenplay by Ted Sears, Bill Peet, Joe Rinaldi, Erdman Penner, Winston Hibler, Milt Banta, Ralph Wright (based on the play by Sir James M. Barrie). Directing animators: Milt Kahl, Franklin Thomas, Wolfgang Reitherman, Ward Kimball, Eric Larson, Oliver Johnston Jr., Marc Davis, John Lunsbery, Les Clark, Norman Ferguson. Music by Sammy Cahn, Sammy Fain, Oliver Wallace, Erdman Penner, Ted Sears, Winston Hibler, Frank Churchill, Jack Lawrence. Available on videocassette.

Songs: "The Elegant Captain Hook," "The Second Star to the Right," "What Makes the Red Man Red," "You Can Fly," "Your Mother and Mine," "A Pirate's Life," "March of the Lost Boys," "Never Smile at a Crocodile."

Voices: Bobby Driscoll, Kathryn Beaumont, Hans Conried, Bill Thompson, Heather Angel, Paul Collins, Tommy Luske, Candy Candido, Tom Conway.

Animated version of the classic story of a boy who never grew up and the evil one-armed Captain Hook.

Note: The cost, which reached $4 million, was so high because Disney filmed a live-action version first to assist his animators. Disney had been negotiating for the rights to film this one since 1939. A silent version with Betty Bronson and a TV version with Mary Martin (who also had the role on stage) are also available.

652 *Petticoat Larceny* (1943) Comedy. Running time: 61 minutes. Black and white.

Produced by Bert Gilroy. Directed by Ben Holmes. Screenplay by Jack Townley and Stuart Palmer. Photographed by Frank Redman. Edited by John C. Grubb.

Starring Ruth Warrick (Pat Mitchell), Joan Carroll (Joan Mitchell), Walter Reed (Bill Morgan), Tom Kennedy (Pinky), Jimmy Conlin (Jitters), Vince Barnett (Stogie), Paul Guilfoyle (Foster), Grant Withers (Hogan), Wally Brown (Colfax).

A young radio actress tries to learn street-talk from a group of gangsters.

653 *The Phantom of Crestwood* (1932) Mystery. Running time: 77 minutes. Black and white.

Produced by David O. Selznick. Directed by J. Walter Ruben. Screenplay by Bartlett Cormack. Photographed by Carroll Clark. Edited by Henry Gerard.

Starring Karen Morley (Jenny Wren), Ricardo Cortez (Gary Curtis), H.B. Warner (Priam Andes), Pauline Frederick (Faith Andes), Robert McWade (Walcott), Aileen Pringle (Mrs. Walcott), Skeets Gallagher (Mack), Mary Duncan (Dorothy), Gavin Gordon (Will Jones), Anita Louise (Esther Wren).

Tim Holt in *Pirates of the Prairie.*

A woman assembles five former flames and tells them each to give her a large sum of money or she will expose her relationship with them. When she is found murdered, they are the likely suspects.

Note: RKO ran this as a six-week radio serial with the same cast concurrently with its filming. As the radio shows were ready to conclude, producers asked listeners to send in what they felt would be the best ending, offering a prize for the one used. Thus, when the film was released, all of the radio listeners attended to see how the story would end.

654 Pinocchio (1940) Animated feature. Running time: 88 minutes. Technicolor. Available on videocassette. A Walt Disney production released by RKO.

Produced by Walt Disney. Directed by Ben Sharpsteen, Hamilton Luske, Bill Roberts, Norman Ferguson, Jack Kinney, Wilfred Jackson, T. Hee (based on the story by Collodi). Music by Paul J. Smith.

Voices: Dickie Jones (Pinocchio), Christian Rub (Geppetto), Cliff Edwards (Jiminy Cricket), Evelyn Venable (The Blue Fairy), Walter Catlett (J. Worthington Foulfellow), Frankie Darro (Lampwick), Charles Judels (Stromboli), Don Brodie (Barker).

The story of a puppeteer whose wish is to have a boy of his own.

Note: Disney's second feature length cartoon, remains an enduring classic. Director T. Hee is Disney.

Review: "A work that gives you almost every possible kind of pleasure to be had from a motion picture" — Richard Mallen, *Punch.*

Pioneer Builders see *The Conquerors*

655 Pirates of the Prairie (1942) Western. Running time: 57 minutes. Black and white.

Produced by Bert Gilroy. Directed by Howard Bretherton. Screenplay by Doris Schroeder and J. Benton Cheney. Photographed by Nicholas Musuraca. Edited by John Lockert.

Starring Tim Holt, Cliff Edwards, Nel O'Day, John Elliott, Roy Barcroft, Karl Hackett, Dick Cramer, Edward Cassidy, Eddie Dew, Merrill McCormack, Reed Howes, Charles King, Bud Geary, Lee Shumway, Russell Wade, Ben Corbett, Frank McCarroll, Artie Ortego, George Morrell.

A cowboy poses as a vigilante to stop the terrorizing of farmers.

656 *Pistol Harvest* (1951) Western. Running time: 60 minutes. Black and white.

Produced by Herman Schlom. Directed by Lesley Selander. Screenplay by Norman Houston. Photographed by J. Roy Hunt. Edited by Douglas Biggs.

Starring Tim Holt (Tim), Joan Dixon (Felice), Robert Clarke (Jack), Mauritz Hugo (Norton), Robert Wilke (Baylor), William Griffith (Prouty), Guy Edward Hearn (Terry), Harper Carter (Johnny), Joan Freeman (Little Felice), F. Herrick (Capt. Rand), Richard Martin (Chito), Lee Phelps (Bit).

A shipping magnate kills a rancher to whom he owes money, and blames it on two strangers.

Note: Made for a budget of only $93,000 and more entertaining than many pretentious epics.

657 *Play Girl* (1940) Drama. Running time: 75 minutes. Black and white.

Produced by Cliff Reid. Directed by Frank Woodruff. Screenplay by Jerry Cady. Photographed by Nicholas Musuraca. Edited by Harry Marker.

Starring Kay Francis (Grace Herbert), James Ellison (Tom Dice), Mildred Coles (Ellen Daley), Nigel Bruce (Bill Vincent), Margaret Hamilton (Josie), Charles Quigley (Lock), Kane Richmond (Don), Stanley Andrews (Joseph Shawhan), Selmer Jackson (Fred Dice), Ralph Byrd (Doctor).

An aging golddigger tries to teach a younger girl her ways.

658 *Playmates* (1941) Comedy. Running time: 94 minutes. Black and white. Available on videocassette.

Produced by Cliff Reid. Directed by David Butler. Screenplay by James V. Kern and Arthur Phillips. Photographed by Frank Redman. Edited by Irene Morra.

Starring Kay Kyser (Himself), John Barrymore (Himself), Lupe Velez (Carmen del Torre), Ginny Simms (Giny), May Robson (Grandma), Patsy Kelly (Lulu), Peter Lind Hayes (Peter), George Cleveland (Pennypacker), Alice Fleming (Mrs. Pennypacker), Kay Kyser's Band featuring Harry Babbitt, Sully Mason and Ish Kabibble (Themselves).

John Barrymore is hired to coach Kay Kyser in playing the role of Hamlet.

Note: Barrymore's last film, and he seems to be having a good time.

Review: "Fairly funny in a high school kind of way"—Leslie Halliwell.

659 *The Plough and the Stars* (1936) Drama. Running time: 72 minutes. Black and white.

Produced by Cliff Reid and Robert Sisk. Directed by John Ford. Screenplay by Dudley Nichols (based on the play by Sean O'Casey). Photographed by Joseph H. August. Edited by George Hively.

Starring Barbara Stanwyck (Nora), Preston Foster (Jack), Barry Fitzgerald (Luther), Denis O'Dea (Cobey), Eileen Crow (Bessie), F.J. McCormick (Brennon), Arthur Shields (Padraic), Una O'Connor (Maggie), Moroni Olsen (Connolly), Bonita Granville (Mollser Cogan), Erin O'Brien-Moore (Rosie), Wesley Barry (Sniper).

A marriage is threatened in 1916 Dublin by the husband's appointment to the citizen army.

Review: "Skillfully made but not impressive as a money entry"—*Variety*.

660 *Pop Always Pays* (1940) Comedy. Running time: 66 minutes. Black and white. Available on videocassette.

Produced by Lee Marcus and Bert

Gilroy. Directed by Leslie Goodwins. Screenplay by Charles E. Roberts. Photographed by Jack MacKenzie. Edited by Desmond Marquette.

Starring Leon Errol (Henry Brewster), Dennis O'Keefe (Jeff), Adele Pearce (Edna), Walter Catlett (Tommy Lane), Marjorie Gateson (Mrs. Brewster), Tom Kennedy (Murphy).

A man will allow his daughter to marry if her intended can raise $1000.

661 *Postmark for Danger* (1956) Crime drama. Running time: 84 minutes. Black and white. Available on videocassette.

Produced by Frank Godwin. Directed by Guy Green. Screenplay by Green, Ken Hughes (based on the TV drama *Portrait of Allison* by Francis Dubridge). Photographed by Wilkie Cooper. Edited by Peter Taylor.

Starring Terry Moore (Allison), Robert Beatty (Tim), William Sylvester (Dave), Josephine Griffin (Jill), Geoffrey Keen (Inspector), Allan Cuthbertson (Henry).

Detectives break up a diamond smuggling ring.

662 *Powder Town* (1942) Drama. Running time: 79 minutes. Black and white.

Produced by Cliff Reid. Directed by Rowland V. Lee. Screenplay by David Boehm. Photographed by Frank Redman. Edited by Samuel E. Beetley.

Starring Victor McLaglen (Jeems), Edmond O'Brien (Pennant), June Havoc (Dolly), Dorothy Lovett (Sally), Eddie Foy, Jr. (Meeker), Damian O'Flynn (Oliver), Marten Lamont (Chick Parker).

An inventor creates an explosive formula for use in the army.

663 *Powdersmoke Range* (1935) Western. Running time: 71 minutes. Black and white. Available on videocassette.

Produced by Cliff Reid. Directed by Wallace Fox. Screenplay by Adele Buffington. Photographed by Harold Weinstrom. Edited by James Morley.

Starring Harry Carey (Tucson Smith), Hoot Gibson (Stony Brooke), Guinn "Big Boy" Williams (Lullaby Joslin), Tom Tyler (Sundown Saunders), William Farnum (Banker Orchan), Bob Steele (Guadalupe Kid), Wally Wales (Bud Taggert), Ethan Laidlaw (Fin), Adrian Morris (Brose), William Desmond (Happy), Frank Rice (Sourdough), Sam Hardy (Big Steve), Boots Mallory (Carolyn), Ray Mayer (Chap Bell), Art Mix (Rube), Buffalo Bill, Jr. (Tex), Buddy Roosevelt (Burnett), Irving Bacon (Storekeeper).

Three cowboys buy a ranch and attempts are made by some gunmen to overtake it.

The first official Three Mesquiteers film, and the last one for RKO. Hereafter, the films were made for Republic and would later feature John Wayne in the lineup.

664 *Prairie Law* (1940) Western. Running time: 59 minutes. Black and white.

Produced by Bert Gilroy. Directed by David Howard. Screenplay by Doris Schroeder and Arthur V. Jones. Photographed by J. Roy Hunt. Edited by Frederic Knudtson.

Starring George O'Brien (Brill), Virginia Vale (Priscilla), Dick Hogan (Larry), Slim Whitaker (Silent), J. Farrell MacDonald (Sheriff Austin), Cy Kendall (Pete), Paul Everton (Judge Curry), Henry Hall (Mr. Bramble), Monte Montague (Bit).

A war between cattlemen and settlers develops over irrigation wells.

665 *Prestige* (1932) Adventure. Running time: 73 minutes. Black and white.

Produced by Charles R. Rogers. Directed by Tay Garnett. Screenplay by Francis Edwards Faragoh, Rollo Lloyd, Garnett. Photographed by Lucien Andriot. Edited by Joe Kane.

Starring Ann Harding (Therese Du Flos), Adolphe Menjou (Capt. Remy

Baudoin), Melvyn Douglas (Lt. Andre Aerlaine), Ian MacLaren (Col. Du Flos), Guy Bates Post (Major), Carmelita Geraghty (Felice), Rollo Lloyd (Emil), Clarence Muse (Servant).

A woman follows her alcoholic husband to the Maylan prison colony where he works.

666 Primrose Path (1940) Drama. Running time: 92 minutes. Black and white.

Produced and directed by Gregory La Cava. Screenplay by Allan Scott and La Cava (based on the play by Robert L. Buckner and Walter Scott). Photographed by Joseph H. August. Edited by William Hamilton.

Starring Ginger Rogers (Ellie May Adams), Joel McCrea (Ed Wallace), Marjorie Rambeau (Mamie Adams), Henry Travers (Gramp), Miles Mander (Homer Adams), Queenie Vassar (Grandma), Joan Carroll (Honeybell Adams), Vivienne Osborne (Thelma), Carmen Morales (Carmelita), Gene Morgan (Hawkins).

The youngest in a long line of whores falls legitimately in love with a common working-class lout.

Note: Marjorie Rambeau was nominated for an Oscar.

667 The Princess and the Pirate (1944) Comedy. Running time: 94 minutes. Color. Available on videocassette.

Produced by Samuel Goldwyn. Directed by David Butler. Screenplay by Don Hartman, Melville Shavelson, Everett Freeman, Allen Boretz, and Curtis Kenyon. Photographed by Victor Milner and William Snyder. Edited by Daniel Mandell.

Starring Bob Hope (Sylvester), Virginia Mayo (Princess Margaret), Walter Brennan (Featherhead), Walter Slezak (La Roche), Victor McLaglen (The Hook), Marc Lawrence (Pedro), Hugo Haas (Bucket of Blood Proprietor), Maude Eburne (Landlady), Adia Kusne-

toff (Don Jose), Tom Kennedy (Alonzo), Stanley Andrews (Captain), Tom Tyler (Lieutenant), Rondo Hatton (Gorilla Man).

An actor tries to save the king's daughter from pirates.

Note: One of Hope's best films.

668 Professional Sweetheart (1933) Comedy. Running time: 68 minutes. Black and white.

Produced by H.N. Swanson. Directed by William Seiter. Screenplay by Maurine Watkins. Photographed by Edward Cronjager. Edited by James Morley.

Starring Ginger Rogers (Glory Eden), Norman Foster (Jim), ZaSu Pitts (Esmeralda), Frank McHugh (Speed), Allen Jenkins (O'Connor), Gregory Ratoff (Ipswitch), Edgar Kennedy (Kelsey), Lucien Littlefield (Announcer), Franklin Pangborn (Childress), Sterling Holloway (Scribe).

A radio "purity girl" attempts to have some romantic fun in real life, but sponsors worry she'll tarnish her pristine image.

Note: British title: *Imaginary Sweetheart.*

669 Public Defender (1931) Crime Drama. Running time: 70 minutes. Black and white.

Produced by Louis Sarecky. Directed by J. Walter Ruben. Screenplay by Bernard Schubert. Photographed by Edward Cronjager. Edited by Archie Marshek.

Starring Richard Dix (Pike Winslow), Shirley Grey (Barbara Gerry), Edmund Breese (Wells), Paul Hurst (Doctor), Purnell Pratt (Burns), Alan Roscoe (O'Neill), Boris Karloff (Professor).

When a vice president of a bank is sent to jail after the bank fails, a public defender tries to prove his innocence.

670 Public Pigeon No. 1 (1957) Comedy. Running time: 79 minutes. Color. A Val-Ritchie production for RKO, released through Universal.

Publicity poster for *Public Pigeon No. 1.*

Produced by Harry Tugend. Directed by Norman Z. McLeod. Screenplay by Tugend (based on a teleplay by Devery Freeman, from a story by Don Quinn and Larry Berns). Photographed by Paul C. Vogel. Edited by Otto Ludwig.

Starring Red Skelton (Rusty), Vivian Blaine (Rita), Janet Blair (Edith), Jay C. Flippen (Lt. Qualen), Allyn Joslyn (Harvey Baker), Benny Baker (Frankie), Milton Fromme (Avery), John Abbott (Dipso Dave), Howard McNear (Warden), James Burke (Harrigan), Herb Vigran (Club Manager).

A cafeteria worker gets mixed up with swindlers.

671 *Quality Street* (1937) Drama. Running time: 84 minutes. Black and white.

Produced by Pandro S. Berman. Directed by George Stevens. Screenplay by Mortimer Offner and Allan Scott (based on the play by Sir James M. Barrie). Photographed by Robert De Grasse. Edited by Henry Berman.

Starring Katharine Hepburn (Phoebe Thossel), Franchot Tone (Dr. Valentine Brown), Fay Bainter (Susan Thossel), Eric Blore (Recruiting Sergeant), Cora Witherspoon (Patty the Maid), Estelle Winwood (Mary Willoughby), Florence Lake (Henrietta Turnbull), Helena Grant (Fanny Willoughby), Bonita Granville (Isabella).

A man returns from the Napoleonic wars to find his sweetheart's beauty has faded over time, and, thus, he does not recognize her.

Note: Remake of a 1927 Marion Davies silent.

Review: "Such flutterings and jitterings and twitchings, such hand wringings and mouth quiverings, such runnings-about and eyebrow-raisings have not been on the screen in many a moon" — Frank Nugent, *The New York Times.*

672 *Quick Money* (1938) Drama. Running time: 59 minutes. Black and white.

Directed by Edward Killy. Screenplay by Arthur T. Horman, Franklin Coen, and Bert Granet. Photographed by Nicholas Musuraca. Edited by George Crone.

Starring Fred Stone (Jonas Tompkins), Gordon Jones (Bill), Dorothy Moore (Alice), Berton Churchill (Blueford Smythe), Paul Guilfoyle (Ambrose), Harlan Briggs (Barnstall), Dorothy Vaughan (Mrs. Tompkins), Sherwood Bailey (Freddie), Frank M. Thomas (Clark), Jack Carson (Football Coach), Kathryn Sheldon (Mrs. Otis), Dick Elliot (Walker), Fuzzy Knight (Potter), Hattie McDaniel (Bit).

A small town mayor goes against two crooks who want to change the town into a gambling resort.

673 *Race Street* (1948) Crime drama. Running time: 79 minutes. Black and white. Available on videocassette.

Produced by Nat Holt. Directed by Edwin L. Marin. Screenplay by Martin Rackin. Photographed by J. Roy Hunt. Edited by Samuel E. Beetley.

Starring George Raft (Dan Gannin), William Bendix (Runson), Marilyn Maxwell (Robbie), Frank Faylen (Phil Dickson), Harry Morgan (Hal Towers), Gale Robbins (Elaine Gannin), Cully Richards (Mike Hadley), Mack Gray (Stringy), Russell Hicks (Eassy Mason), Tom Keene (Al), Richard Benedict (Sam), George Chandler (Herman), Cy Kendall (Fatty Parker), Dean White (Big Jack).

A criminal attempts to go straight when he finds his pal has been murdered by gangsters. Vowing revenge, he ignores the advice of another friend, a cop, and goes after the killers himself.

674 *Rachel and the Stranger* (1948) Drama. Running time: 93 minutes. Black and white. Available on videocassette.

Produced by Richard H. Berger. Directed by Norman Foster. Screenplay by Waldo Salt. Photographed by Maury Gertsman. Edited by Les Millbrook.

Starring Loretta Young (Rachel), William Holden (Big Davey Harvey), Robert Mitchum (Jim), Gary Gray (Little Davey), Tom Tully (Parson Jackson), Sara Haden (Mrs. Jackson), Frank Ferguson (Mr. Green).

A farmer pays attention to his wife for the first time in a long while when he finds she's attracted to a handsome stranger.

Note: Released during Mitchum's marijuana conviction, which didn't hurt its box office. Studio head Dore Schary left RKO for MGM just after this one was made.

675 *Racing Lady* (1937) Drama. Running time: 59 minutes. Black and white.

Produced by William Sistrom. Directed by Wallace Fox. Screenplay by Dorothy Yost, Thomas Lennon and Cortland Fitzsimmons (based on stories by Damon Runyon). Photographed by Harry Wild. Edited by James Morely.

Starring Ann Dvorak (Ruth Martin), Smith Ballew (Steven Wendel), Harry Carey (Tom Martin), Berton Churchill (Judge), Frank M. Thomas (Bradford), Ray Mayer (Warbler), Willie Best (Brass), Hattie McDaniel (Abby), Harlan Tucker (Gilbert), Lew Payton (Joe).

A millionaire hires a horse woman to train a new addition to his stable.

676 *The Racket* (1951) Crime drama. Running time: 88 minutes. Black and white. Available on videocassette.

Produced by Edmund Grainger. Directed by John Cromwell and Nicholas Ray. Screenplay by William Wister Haines and W.R. Burnett. Photographed by George E. Diskant. Edited by Sherman Todd.

Starring Robert Mitchum (Capt. McQuigg), Lizabeth Scott (Irene), Robert Ryan (Scanlon), William Talman (Johnson), Ray Collins (Welch), Joyce MacKenzie (Mary McQuigg), Robert Hutton (Ames), Virginia Huston (Lucy Johnson), William Conrad (Turk), Walter Sande (Delaney), Les Tremayne (Chief Craig), Don Porter (Connolly), Walter Baldwin (Sullivan), Brett King (Scanlon), Richard Karlan (Enright).

A tough cop must battle the underworld as well as corrupt officials.

Note: Remake of a 1928 silent.

677 *Racketeers of the Range* (1939) Western. Running time: 62 minutes. Black and white. Available on videocassette.

Produced by Bert Gilroy. Directed by Ross Lederman. Screenplay by Oliver Drake. Photographed by Harry Wild. Edited by Frederic Knudtson.

Starring George O'Brien (Barney O'Dell), Chill Wills (Whopper), Mar-

jorie Reynolds (Helen), Gay Seabrook (Penny), Robert Fiske (Whitlock), John Dilson (Benson), Monte Montague (Larkin), Bud Osborne (Hank), Ben Corbett (Dutch), Ray Whitley (Ray), Cactus Mack (Flash), Frankie Marvin (Skeeter).

An evil packing-combine owner has been rustling the ranchers' cattle.

678 *Radio City Revels* (1937) Musical comedy. Running time: 84 minutes. Black and white.

Produced by Edward Kaufman. Directed by Ben Stoloff. Screenplay by Matt Brooks, Eddie Davis, Anthony Veiller, and Mortimer Offner (based on a story by Brooks). Photographed by J. Roy Hunt. Edited by Arthur Roberts.

Songs: "Goodnight Angel," "Speak Young Heart," "Take a Tip from the Tulip," "I'm Taking a Shine to You," "There's a New Moon Over the Old Mill," "Love Honor and Oh Baby, Why Must I Love You," "Morning Glories in the Moonlight," "You're the Apple of My Eye," "Swinging in the Corn."

Starring Robert Burns (Lester), Jack Oakie (Harry), Kenny Baker (Himself), Victor Moore (Plummer), Milton Berle (Teddy), Helen Broderick (Getie), Ann Miller (Billie), Richard Lane (Crane), Don Wilson (Announcer).

Two songwriters make a hit when they discover a man who sings catchy tunes in his sleep.

Note: Reworked by Frank Tashlin as *Artists and Models* for Dean Martin and Jerry Lewis.

679 *Radio Stars on Parade* (1945) Comedy. Running time: 69 minutes. Black and white.

Produced by Ben Stoloff. Directed by Leslie Goodwins. Screenplay by Robert E. Kent and Monte Brice. Photographed by Harry Walker. Edited by Edward W. Williams.

Starring Wally Brown (Jerry), Alan Carney (Mike), Frances Langford (Sally), Don Wilson (Himself), Tony Romano (Romano), Rufe Davis (Pinky), Robert

Clarke (Danny), Sheldon Leonard (Mad-doc), Ralph Edwards (Himself), Skinnay Ennis Band (Themselves).

The managers of a talent agency take their client to all the top radio shows in hopes of an audition.

680 *Rafter Romance* (1934) Comedy. Running time: 72 minutes. Black and white.

Produced by Alexander McKaig. Directed by William Seiter. Screenplay by Sam Mintz, H.W. Hanemann, Glenn Tryon. Photographed by David Abel. Edited by James Morley.

Starring Ginger Rogers (Mary), Norman Foster (Jack), George Sidney (Max), Robert Benchley (Hubbell), Laura Hope Crews (Elise), Guinn "Big Boy" Williams (Fritzie), Sidney Miller (Julius).

A working class couple, sharing a Greenwich Village apartment, never see each other as they work different shifts. Each believes the other is probably elderly and cranky, until they finally meet.

Note: Originally slated for Joel McCrea and Dorothy Wilson.

681 *Rainbow on the River* (1936) Drama. Running time: 87 minutes. Black and white.

Produced by Sol Lesser. Directed by Kurt Neumann. Screenplay by Earle Snell, Harry Chandlee, William Hurlburt, and Clarence Marks. Photographed by Charles Schoenbaum. Edited by Robert Crandall.

Starring Bobby Breen (Phillip), May Robson (Mrs. Ainsworth), Charles Butterworth (Barrett), Louise Beavers (Toinette), Alan Mowbray (Ralph Layton), Benita Hume (Julia Layton), Henry O'Neill (Father Josef), Marilyn Knowlden (Lucille), Eddie "Rochester" Anderson (Doctor).

A southern boy is forced to leave his beloved mammy and live with relatives in New York.

682 *The Rainmakers* (1935) Comedy. Running time: 75 minutes. Black and white.

Produced by Lee Marcus. Directed by Fred Guiol. Screenplay by Grant Garrett and Leslie Goodwins. Photographed by Ted McCord. Edited by John Lockert.

Starring Bert Wheeler (Billy), Robert Woolsey (Roscoe), Dorothy Lee (Margie Spencer), Berton Churchill (Simon Parker), George Meeker (Orville Parker), Frederic Roland (Henry Spencer), Edgar Dearing (Kelly).

Two men invent a rainmaking machine to end the drought plaguing farmers in California.

683 *The Ramparts We Watched* (1940) Documentary-drama. Running time: 90 minutes. Black and white.

Produced and directed by Louis de Rochemont. Screenplay by Robert L. Richards and Cedric R. Worth. Photographed by Charles E. Gilson and John Geisel. Edited by Lothar Wolff.

Starring John Adair, John Summers, Julia Kent, Ellen Prescott, Andrew Brummer, Myrtle Paseler, Alfred U. Wysse, Marguerite Brown, Frank McCabe, Myra Archibald, Elliot Reid.

A documentary style approach, using nonactors and actual footage, to illustrate the impact of World War One on Americans.

684 *Rancho Notorious* (1952) Western. Running time: 89 minutes. Color.

Produced by Howard Welsch. Directed by Fritz Lang. Screenplay by Daniel Taradash (based on the story "Gunsight Whitman" by Sylvia Richards). Photographed by Hal Mohr. Edited by Otto Ludwig. Available on videocassette.

Starring Marlene Dietrich (Altar), Arthur Kennedy (Vern), Mel Ferrer (Frenchy), Lloyd Gough (Kinch), Gloria Henry (Beth), William Frawley (Baldy), Lisa Ferraday (Maxine), John Raven (Delaer), Jack Elam (Geary), George Reeves (Wilson), Frank Ferguson (Preacher), Francis McDonald (Harbin), Dan Seymour (Paul), John Kellogg (Factor).

An innocent cowhand becomes obsessed with avenging his fiancee's murder.

Note: There was a lot of tension on the set of this film. Dietrich wanted to look glamorous as this was the first "aging" part she ever played. She begged the cameraman to do so, and even asked for his dismissal (she was refused). Director Lang was incensed that Producer Welsch ordered a recut of the film without his approval, removing much of the original ambiance. The tensions between Dietrich and Lang were so great that by the end of the filming the two were not speaking. None of these troubles are evident in the finished product.

685 *Rashomon* (1951) Japanese drama. Running time: 90 minutes. Black and white.

Produced by Jingo Minaura. Directed by Akira Kurosawa. Screenplay by Shinobu Hashimoto and Kurosawa (based on the short story "Yabu no Naka" and the novel by Ryunosuke Akutagawa). Photographed by Kazuo Miyagawa. Available on videocassette.

Starring Torisho Mifune, Machiko Kyo, Masayuki Mori, Takashi Shimura, Minoru Chiaki, Kichijiro Ueda, Fumiko Homma, Daisuke Kato.

Four people involved in a rape-murder trial offer varying accounts of what happened.

Note: A Japanese production released in the States by RKO. Kurosawa's first international success and a classic in every regard. Remade as *The Outrage.*

686 *Rebound* (1931) Drama. Running time: 67 minutes. Black and white.

Produced by Charles Rogers. Directed by Edward H. Griffith. Screenplay by Horace Jackson and Donald Ogden Stewart. Photographed by Norbert Brodine. Edited by Dan Mandell.

Starring Ina Claire (Sara Joffrey), Robert Ames (Bill Truesdale), Myrna Loy (Evie Lawrence), Hedda Hopper (Liz Crawford), Robert Williams (Johnnie Coles), Hale Hamilton (Lyman Patterson), Walter Walker (Mr. Henry Joffrey), Louise Closser Hale (Mrs. Joffrey), Leigh Allen (Les Crawford).

A woman attempts to forgive her cheating husband when he himself is jilted by his girlfriend.

Note: A strong rivalry existed on the set between Claire (age 40) and Loy (age 26), the older woman insisting the younger one could never be believable in a role that involved stealing a man from her. In any case, the film lost over $200,000.

687 *Red Morning* (1935) Drama. Running time: 66 minutes. Black and white.

Produced by Cliff Reid. Directed by Wallace Fox. Screenplay by John Twist and Fox. Photographed by Harold Wenstrom. Edited by Ted Cheesman.

Starring Steffi Duna, Regis Toomey, Lionel Belmore, Raymond Hatton, Mitchell Lewis, Charles Middleton, George J. Lewis, Francis McDonald, Willie Fung, Cap West, Brandon Hurst, Olaf Hytten.

A girl is involved in the mutiny on board her father's ship, then is accosted by angry islanders when she drifts ashore.

688 *Red River Robin Hood* (1943) Western. Running time: 57 minutes. Black and white.

Produced by Bert Gilroy. Directed by Lesley Selander. Screenplay by Bennett R. Cohen. Photographed by J. Roy Hunt. Edited by Archie Marshek.

Starring Tim Holt, Cliff Edwards, Barbara Moffett, Eddie Dew, Otto Hoffman, Russell Wade, Tom London, Earle Hodgins, Bud McTaggart, Reed Howes, Keene Duncan, David Sharpe, Bob McKenzie, Jack Rockwell, Jack Montgomery.

Two cowboys disguise themselves and thwart a crooked gang's plans.

Bert Wheeler, Dorothy Lee and Robert Woolsey in *The Rainmakers.*

689 *The Reluctant Dragon* (1941)
Animation–live action. Running time:
72 minutes. Technicolor. Available on
videocassette.

Produced by Alfred Werker. Directed
by Hamilton Luske, Jim Handley, Ford
Beebe, Erwin Verity, Jasper Blystone.
Screenplay by Ted Sears, Al Perkins,
Larry Clemmons, Bill Cottrell. Photographed by Bert Glennon and Winton
C. Hoch. Edited by Paul Weatherwax
and Earl Rettig.

Starring Robert Benchley (Himself),
Nana Bryant (Mrs. Benchley), Buddy
Pepper (Guide), Frances Gifford (Doris),
Barnett Parker (Dragon's Voice), Claude
Allister (Sir Giles' Voice), Billy Lee (Little Boy's Voice), Clarence Nash (Donald
Duck's Voice), Pinto Colvig (Goofy's
Voice), Alan Ladd (Bit).

A trip through the Disney studios with
humorist Robert Benchley.

Note: Disney's first live action feature.

An interesting look at the studio from
that period; portions of this film have
been released as short subjects. Just prior
to this film's release, the studio's
employees went on strike!

690 *Remedy for Riches* (1941)
Drama. Running time: 60 minutes.
Black and white.

Produced by William Stephens. Directed by Erle C. Kenton. Screenplay by
Lee Loeb. Photographed by John Alton.
Edited by Paul Weatherwax.

Starring Jean Hersholt (Dr. Christian), Dorothy Lovett (Judy), Edgar Kennedy (George Browning), Jed Prouty
(Emerson), Walter Catlett (Clem),
Robert Baldwin (Roy Davis), Warren
Hull (Tom Stewart), Maude Eburne
(Mrs. Hastings).

The good doctor helps thwart a phony
oil scheme and saves a small town.

691 Renegade Rancher (1938) Western. Running time: 60 minutes. Black and white. Available on videocassette.

Produced by Bert Gilroy. Directed by David Howard. Screenplay by Oliver Drake. Photographed by Harry Wild. Edited by Frederic Knudtson.

Starring George O'Brien (Capt. Jack Steele), Rita Hayworth (Judith Alvarez), Tim Holt (Larry Corwin), Ray Whitley (Happy), Lucio Villegas (Juan Capillo), William Royle (Ben Sanderson), Cecilia Callejo (Tonia Capillo), Neal Hart (Sheriff), Monte Montague (Monte), Tom Steele (Bit).

A Texas Ranger must bring in the murderer of a tax collector, but discovers it is a woman.

Review: "This was probably the best of the two dozen oaters O'Brien made for director Howard" — *The Motion Picture Guide.*

692 Renegades of the West (1932) Western. Running time: 55 minutes. Black and white.

Directed by Casey Robinson. Screenplay by Albert Shelby LeVino (based on the story by Frank Richardson Pierce). Photographed by Al Sieger. Edited by Jack Kitchin.

Starring Tom Keene, Betty Furness, Roscoe Ates, Rockliffe Fellowes, Jack Pennick, Max Wagner, James Mason, Joseph Girard, Joseph Ramos, Billy Franey, Roland Southern, Carl Miller, Josephene Ramous, Jules Cowles.

A cowboy goes undercover to catch the cattle thieves who killed his father.

Note: A remake of the 1923 silent *The Miracle Baby* which starred Harry Carey.

693 Reno (1939) Drama. Running time: 73 minutes. Black and white. Available on videocassette.

Produced by Robert Sisk. Directed by John Farrow. Screenplay by John Twist. Photographed by J. Roy Hunt. Edited by Harry Marker.

Starring Richard Dix (Bill Shear), Gail Patrick (Jessie), Anita Louise (Mrs. Ryder), Paul Cavanaugh (John), Laura Hope Crews (Mrs. Gardner), Louis Jean Heydt (Judge), Hobart Cavanaugh (Abe).

A lawyer builds up his divorce practices in Reno, as the city itself builds.

694 Repent at Leisure (1941) Drama. Running time: 66 minutes. Black and white.

Produced by Cliff Reid. Directed by Frank Woodruff. Screenplay by Jerry Cady. Photographed by Nicholas Musuraca. Edited by Harry Wild.

Starring Kent Taylor (Richard Hughes), Wendy Barrie (Emily Baldwin), George Barbier (R.C. Baldwin), Thurston Hall (Buckingham), Charles Lane (Morgan), Nella Walker (Mrs. Baldwin), Rafael Storm (Prince Paul), Ruth Dietrich (Miss Flynn), Cecil Cunningham (Mrs. Morgan), Fred "Snowflake" Toomes (Rufe).

A woman tries to marry for money.

695 The Return of Peter Grimm (1935) Fantasy. Running time: 83 minutes. Black and white.

Produced by Kenneth MacGowan. Directed by George Nicholls, Jr. Screenplay by Francis Edwards Faragoh. Photographed by Lucien Andriot. Edited by Arthur Schmidt.

Starring Lionel Barrymore (Peter Grimm), Helen Mack (Catherine), Edward Ellis (Dr. Macpherson), Donald Meek (Mayor Bartholomew), George Breakston (William Van Dam), Allen Vincent (Fredrik), James Bush (James), Lucien Littlefield (Lawton), Greta Mayer (Martha).

A dead man returns to fix the wrongs he committed during life.

Return of the Bad Men see *Return of the Badmen*

696 Return of the Badmen (1948) Western. Running time: 90 minutes. Black and white.

Produced by Jack J. Gross and Nat Holt. Directed by Ray Enright. Screenplay by Jack Natteford, Luci Ward, and Charles O'Neal (based on a story by Natteford and Ward). Photographed by J. Roy Hunt. Edited by Samuel Beetley.

Starring Randolph Scott, Robert Ryan, Anne Jeffreys, George "Gabby" Hayes, Jacqueline White, Steve Brodie, Richard Powers, Robert Bray, Lex Barker, Walter Reed, Dean White, Robert Armstrong, Tom Tyler, Lew Harvey, Gary Gray, Walter Baldwin, Minna Gombell Robert Clarke, Jason Robards, Sr., Ernie Adams, Billy Vincent, Forrest Taylor, Lane Chandler, Bud Osborne, Kenneth MacDonald, Ida Moore, Richard Thorne, Cyril Ring, John Hamilton, Earle Hodgins.

A marshall is forced out of retirement by a veritable Who's Who of outlaws, including the Youngers, the Daltons, and Billy the Kid.

Note: Sequel to *Badman's Territory.*

697 *The Richest Girl in the World* (1934) Comedy. Running time: 76 minutes. Black and white.

Produced by Pandro S. Berman. Directed by William Seiter. Screenplay by Norman Krasna. Photographed by Nicholas Musuraca. Edited by George Crone.

Starring Miriam Hopkins (Dorothy Hunter), Joel McCrea (Tony Travis), Fay Wray (Sylvia Vernon), Henry Stephenson (Jonathan Connors), Reginald Denny (Phillip Vernon), Beryl Mercer (Marie the Maid), George Meeker (Donald), Wade Boteler (Orsatti), Herbert Bunston (Cavendish).

A rich woman switches places with her secretary.

698 *Rider from Tucson* (1950) Western. Running time: 60 minutes. Black and white. Available on videocassette.

Produced by Herman Schlom. Directed by Lesley Selander. Screenplay by Ed Earl Repp. Photographed by Nicholas Musuraca. Edited by Robert Swink.

Starring Tim Holt (Dave), Elaine Riley (Jane), Richard Martin (Chito), Douglas Fowley (Rankin), Veda Ann Borg (Gypsy), Robert Shayne (Avery), William Phipps (Tug), Harry Tyler (Hardrock Jones), Luther Crocket (Sheriff), Dorothy Vaughan (Mrs. O'Reilly), Stuart Randall (Slim).

Two rodeo riders rescue the kidnapped bride of their pal.

699 *Riders of the Range* (1949) Western. Running time: 60 minutes. Black and white.

Produced by Herman Schlom. Directed by Lesley Selander. Screenplay by Norman Houston. Photographed by J. Roy Hunt. Edited by Robert Swink.

Starring Tim Holt (Kansas), Richard Martin (Chito), Jacqueline White (Dusty), Reed Hadley (Burrows), Robert Barrat (Sheriff), Robert Clarke (Harry), Tom Tyler (Ringo), William Tannen (Trump).

Two ranch hands come to the aid of the boss' son, who takes up rustling to pay off a gambling debt.

Note: By the late 1940s, at the end of perhaps the western's most popular decade, television was just beginning to eclipse the movie western; hence this film lost about $50,000 at the box office.

700 *Riding on Air* (1937) Comedy. Running time: 70 minutes. Black and white. Available on videocassette.

Produced by David L. Loew. Directed by Edward Sedgwick. Screenplay by Richard Flournoy and Richard Macaulay. Photographed by Al Gilks. Edited by Jack Ogilvie.

Starring Joe E. Brown (Elmer), Guy Kibbee (Doc), Florence Rice (Betty), Vinton Haworth (Harvey), Anthony Nace (Bill), Harlan Briggs (Harrison), Andrew Tombes (Byrd), Clem Bevans (Sheriff).

A newspaper editor gets mixed up with smugglers when he invents a new radio beam.

701 *Riding the Wind* (1942) Western. Running time: 60 minutes. Black and white.

Produced by Bert Gilroy. Directed by Edward Killy. Screenplay by Earle Snell and Morton Grant. Photographed by Harry Wild. Edited by Frederic Knudtson.

Starring Tim Holt (Clay Stewart), Ray Whitley (Smokey), Mary Douglas (Joan), Lee "Lasses" White (Whopper), Eddie Dew (Henry Dodge), Earle Hodgins (Burt McLeod), Kate Harrington (Martha).

A crook builds a dam that cuts ranchers' land off from the river, and charges them extra for water.

702 *Riffraff* (1947) Drama. Running time: 80 minutes. Black and white.

Produced by Nat Holt. Directed by Ted Tetzlaff. Screenplay by Martin Rackin. Photographed by George E. Diskant. Edited by Phillip Martin.

Starring Pat O'Brien (Dan), Walter Slezak (Molinar), Anne Jeffreys (Maxine), Percy Kilbride (Pop), Jerome Cowan (Walter Gredson), George Givot (Rues), Jason Robards, Sr. (Dominguez).

A dying man releases a map of oil deposits, and several go after its riches.

703 *The Right to Romance* (1933) Drama. Running time: 67 minutes. Black and white.

Produced by Merian C. Cooper. Directed by Alfred Santell. Screenplay by Sidney Buchman and Henry McCarty (based on a story by Myles Connolly). Photographed by Lucien Andriot. Edited by Ralph Dieterle.

Starring Ann Harding (Dr. Margaret Simmons), Robert Young (Bob Preble), Nils Asther (Heppling), Sari Maritza (Lee Joyce), Irving Pichel (Beck), Helen Freeman (Mrs. Preble), Stephen Chase (Bunny), Delmar Watson (Bill).

A stuffy plastic surgeon finds romance, but the couple soon grows apart. When the ex-boyfriend is severely disfigured in a plane crash, she rushes to his aid.

704 *Rio Grande Patrol* (1950) Western. Running time: 60 minutes. Black and white.

Produced by Herman Schlom. Directed by Lesley Selander. Screenplay by Norman Houston. Photographed by J. Roy Hunt. Edited by Desmond Marquette.

Starring Tim Holt (Nebraska), Richard Martin (Chito), Jane Nigh (Sherry), Douglas Fowley (Bragg), Cleo Moore (Peppie), Rick Vallin (Trevino), John Holland (Fowler), Tom Tyler (Vance).

Two cowboys try to thwart smugglers at the Mexican border.

705 *Rio Rita* (1929) Musical comedy. Running time: 135 minutes. Black and white and color.

Produced by William LeBaron. Directed by Luther Reed. Screenplay by Reed and Russell Mack (based on the musical by Guy Bolton and Fred Thompson). Photographed by Robert Kurrie and Lloyd Knetchel. Edited by William Hamilton.

Starring Bert Wheeler (Chick), Bob Woolsey (Lovett), Bebe Daniels (Rita), John Boles (Stewart), Dorothy Lee (Dolly), Don Alvarado (Roberto Ferguson), Georges Renavent (Ravenoff), Eva Rosita (Carmen), Sam Nelson (McGinn), Fred Scott (Ranger).

A Texas Ranger falls in love while in pursuit of a bandit.

Note: Based on the 1927 Ziegfeld show, this was Wheeler and Woolsey's film debut and one of the first musical spectaculars ever done. The duo had starred in the stage version. Shot in only 24 days, this one made a fortune for RKO. Remade at MGM in 1942 with the story updated and Abbott and Costello in the comedy roles.

706 *Riverboat Rhythm* (1946) Comedy. Running time: 65 minutes. Black and white.

Produced by Nat Holt. Directed by Leslie Goodwins. Screenplay by Charles E. Roberts (based on a story by Robert

Faber). Photographed by Robert De Grasse. Edited by Marvin Coil.

Starring Leon Errol (Matt Lindsey), Glenn Vernon (John Beeler), Walter Carlett (Witherspoon), Marc Cramer (Lionel Beeler), Jonathan Hale (Edward Beeler), Joan Newton (Midge), Dorothy Vaughan (Belle), Mantan Moreland, Ben Carter, Frankie Carle and His Orchestra.

A riverboat captain gets mixed up in a feud when he docks near the grounds of a southern resort hotel.

707 *Road Agent* (1952) Western. Running time: 60 minutes. Black and white. Available on videocassette.

Produced by Herman Schlom. Directed by Lesley Selander. Screenplay by Norman Houston. Photographed by J. Roy Hunt. Edited by Paul Weatherwax.

Starring Tim Holt (Tim), Noreen Nash (Cora Drew), Mauritz Hugo (Milo Brand), Dorothy Patrick (Sally Clayton), Bob Wilke (Slab), Tom Tyler (Larkin), Guy Edward Hearn (Sheriff).

Cowboys discover bandits trying to bankrupt ranchers by forcing them to pay tolls on certain trails.

708 *Roadblock* (1951) Crime drama. Running time: 73 minutes. Black and white.

Produced by Lewis Rachmil. Directed by Harold Daniels. Screenplay by Steve Fisher and George Bricker. Photographed by Nicholas Musuraca. Edited by Robert Golden.

Starring Charles McGraw (Joe Peters), Joan Dixon (Diane), Lowell Gilmore (Kendall), Louis Jean Heydt (Harry Miller), Milburn Stone (Egan), Joseph Crehan (Thompson), Joe Forte (Brissard).

A woman with a taste for spending big money marries an insurance agent and tricks him into unlawful schemes.

709 *The Roadhouse Murder* (1932) Drama. Running time: 77 minutes. Black and white.

Produced by Willis Goldbeck. Di-

rected by J. Walter Ruben. Screenplay by Ruben and Gene Fowler. Photographed by J. Roy Hunt. Edited by Jack Kitchin.

Starring Eric Linden (Chick Brian), Dorothy Jordan (Mary Agnew), Bruce Cabot (Fred Dykes), Phyllis Clare (Louise Rand), Roscoe Ates (Joyce), Purnell Pratt (Inspector), Roscoe Karns (Dale).

A rookie reporter poses as a murderer so that he can write about it from the inside.

710 *Roar of the Dragon* (1932) Action. Running time: 68 minutes. Black and white.

Produced by William LeBaron. Directed by Wesley Ruggles. Screenplay by Howard Estabrook. Photographed by Edward Cronjager. Edited by William Hamilton.

Starring Richard Dix (Carson), Gwili Andre (Natscha), Edward Everett Horton (Busby), Arline Judge (Helen), ZaSu Pitts (Tourist), C. Henry Gordon (Voronsky).

A group of Americans are stranded in war-torn Manchuria.

711 *Robbers of the Range* (1941) Western. Running time: 61 minutes. Black and white.

Produced by Bert Gilroy. Directed by Edward Killy. Screenplay by Morton Grant and Arthur V. Jones. Photographed by Harry Wild. Edited by Frederic Knudtson.

Starring Tim Holt (Drummond), Virginia Vale (Alice), Ray Whitley (Smokey), Emmett Lynn (Whopper), LeRoy Mason (Rankin), Howard Hickman (Tremaine), Ernie Adams (Greeley), Frank LaRue (Higgins), Ray Bennett (Daggett), Tom London (Monk).

A landowner is framed when he refuses to sell to a railroad company.

712 *Roberta* (1935) Musical. Running time: 105 minutes. Black and white. Available on videocassette.

Ginger Rogers and Fred Astaire in *Roberta*.

Produced by Pandro S. Berman. Directed by William Seiter. Screenplay by Jane Murfin, Sam Mintz, Allan Scott, and Glenn Tryon (from the play by Jerome Kern and Otto Harbach and the novel *Gowns by Roberta* by Alice Duer Miller). Photographed by Edward Cronjager. Edited by William Hamilton. Music by Jerome Kern.

Starring Irene Dunne (Stephanie), Fred Astaire (Huck), Ginger Rogers (Lizzie), Randolph Scott (John Kent), Helen Westley (Roberta, Aunt Minnie), Victor Varconi (Ladislaw), Claire Dodd (Sophie), Luis Alberni (Voyda), Ferdinand Munier (Lord Delves), Lucille Ball (Mannequin).

A football player travels to Paris with a jazz band.

Note: Famous Broadway musical starred George Murphy and Bob Hope. Remade as *Lovely to Look At.*

713 *Rockabye* (1932) Drama. Running time: 71 minutes. Black and white.

Produced by David O. Selznick. Directed by George Cukor. Screenplay by Jane Murfin and Kubec Glasmon. Photographed by Charles Rosher. Edited by George Hively.

Starring Constance Bennett (Judy Carroll), Joel McCrea (Jake), Paul Lukas (Antony de Sola), Walter Pidgeon (Howard), Jobyna Howland (Snooks), Virginia Hammond (Mrs. Van Riker Pell).

A Broadway performer loses her career to scandal.

714 *Romance in Manhattan*
(1935) Drama. Running time: 79 minutes. Black and white.

Produced by Pandro S. Berman. Directed by Stephen Roberts. Screenplay by Jane Murfin and Edward Kaufman. Photographed by Nicholas Musuraca. Edited by Jack Hively.

Starring Frances Lederer (Karel Novak), Ginger Rogers (Sylvia), Arthur Hohl (Attorney), Jimmy Butler (Frank), J. Farrell MacDonald (Officer Murphy), Helen Ware (Miss Anthrop).

A Czech immigrant adjusts to life in the U.S.

715 *Rookie Cop* (1939) Drama. Running time: 60 minutes. Black and white.

Produced by Bert Gilroy. Directed by David Howard. Screenplay by Morton Grant and Jo Pagano (based on the story by Guy K. Austin and Earl Johnson). Photographed by Harry Wild. Edited by Frederic Knudtson.

Starring Tim Holt, Virginia Weidler, Janet Shaw, Frank M. Thomas, Robert Emmett Keane, Monte Montague, Don Brodie, Ralf Harolde, Muriel Evans, Ace the Wonder Dog.

A young policeman tries to convince his superiors to use canine patrols.

716 *Rookies in Burma* (1943) Comedy. Running time: 62 minutes. Black and white.

Produced by Bert Gilroy. Directed by Leslie Goodwins. Screenplay by Edward James. Photographed by Harry Wild. Edited by Harry Marker.

Starring Wally Brown (Jerry), Alan Carney (Mike), Erford Gage (Sergeant), Claire Carleton (Janie), Joan Barclay (Connie).

Two soldiers wander through Burma after escaping a Japanese concentration camp.

Note: Sequel to *Adventures of a Rookie* (q.v.).

717 *Room Service* (1938) Comedy. Running time: 78 minutes. Black and white. Available on videocassette.

Produced by Pandro S. Berman. Directed by William Seiter. Screenplay by Morrie Ryskind (based on the play by John Murray and Allen Boretz). Photographed by J. Roy Hunt. Edited by George Crone.

Starring Groucho Marx (Gordon Miller), Chico Marx (Binelli), Harpo Marx (Faker), Lucille Ball (Christine), Ann Miller (Hilda), Frank Albertson (Leo Davis), Donald MacBride (Gregory Wagner), Cliff Dunstan (Gribble), Phillip Loeb (Hogarth), Phillip Wood (Jenkins), Alexander Asro (Sasha), Charles Halton (Dr. Glass).

Three men try putting on a stage show while skipping on their hotel rent.

Note: Remade as *Step Lively* (q.v.). Originally a stage show, with MacBride, Wood, Astro, Dunstan, and Loeb repeating their roles. Despite longtime Marx writer Ryskind's attempts to adapt the play to the brothers' unique style, and although the budget was very low, the film lost nearly $400,000, even though it was released just after two Marxian blockbusters—*A Night at the Opera* and *A Day at the Races.* Even today, this is considered an offbeat entry for the comic siblings.

718 *Roseanna McCoy* (1949) Drama. Running time: 100 minutes. Black and white.

Produced by Samuel Goldwyn. Directed by Irving Reis. Screenplay by John Collier (based on the novel by Alberta Hannum). Photographed by Lee Garmes. Edited by Daniel Mandell.

The Marx Brothers with Frank Albertson in *Room Service.*

Starring Farley Granger (Johnse Hatfield), Joan Evans (Roseanna McCoy), Charles Bickford (Devil Anse Hatfield), Raymond Massey (Old Randall McCoy), Richard Basehart (Mounts Hatfield), Gigi Perreau (Allifair McCoy), Aline MacMahon (Suarie McCoy), Marshall Thompson (Tolbert McCoy), Lloyd Gough (Phamer McCoy), Peter Miles (Young Randall McCoy), Arthur Franz (Thad Wilkins).

Amidst the notorious Hatfield-McCoy feud, a romance blossoms.

Note: Film debut of fourteen-year-old Evans, a Goldwyn discovery.

719 *Roughshod* (1949) Western. Running time: 88 minutes. Black and white.

Produced by Richard H. Berger. Directed by Mark Robson. Screenplay by Geoffrey Homes and Hugo Butler. Photographed by Joseph F. Biroc. Edited by Marston Fay.

Starring Robert Sterling (Clay), Gloria Grahame (Mary), Claude Jarman, Jr. (Steve), John Ireland (Lednov), Jeff Donnell (Elaine), Myrna Dell (Helen), Martha Hyer (Marcia), George Cooper (Jim Clayton), Jeff Corey (Jed), Sara Haden (Ma Wyatt), James Bell (Pa Wyatt), Shawn McGlory (Fowler), Robert Williams (McCall), Steve Savage (Peters), Edward Cassidy (Sheriff), Brian Weiher (Grant).

Two brothers traveling with a herd of horses and group of stranded dance hall girls meet with troubles on the trail.

720 *The Royal Bed* (1930). Comedy. Running time: 76 minutes. Black and white.

Directed by Lowell Sherman. Screenplay by J. Walter Ruben (based on the play *The Queen's Husband* by Robert E. Sherwood). Photographed by Leo Tover. Edited by Arthur Roberts.

Starring Lowell Sherman (the King), Nance O'Neil (the Queen), Mary Astor (Princess Anne), Anthony Bushell (Granton), Robert Warwick (Premiere Northrup), Alan Roscoe (Birtern), Hugh Trevor (Clown Prince), J. Carrol Naish (Laker).

While the queen is away in America, the king of a small island in the North Sea is forced to make decisions on his own.

721 Run of the Arrow (1957) Western. Running time: 86 minutes. Color/Scope. Available on videocassette.

Produced, directed, and written by Samuel Fuller. Photographed by Joseph Biroc. Edited by Gene Fowler, Jr.

Starring Rod Steiger (O'Meara), Sarita Montiel (Yellow Moccasin), Brian Keith (Capt. Clark), Ralph Meeker (Lt. Driscoll), Jay C. Flippen (Walking Coyote), Charles Bronson (Blue Buffalo), Olive Carey (Mrs. O'Meara), H.M. Wyant (Crazy Wolf), Col. Tim McCoy (General Allan), Stuart Randall (Col. Taylor).

Saga of the man who shot the last bullet of the Civil War.

Note: Completed during the tail end of RKO's production-distribution days and picked up by Universal-International for release.

722 Runaway Bride (1930) Comedy. Running time: 69 minutes. Black and white.

Produced by William Sistrom. Directed by Donald Crisp. Screenplay by Jane Murfin. Photographed by Leo Tover. Edited by Archie Marshek.

Starring Mary Astor (Mary), Lloyd Hughes (Blaine), David Newell (Heavy), Natalie Moorehead (Clara), Maurice Black (Dugan), Paul Hurst (Daly), Edgar Norton (Williams).

A crook stashes jewels in a woman's purse, unbeknownst to her; and when he is killed, his gang goes after the loot.

723 Rustlers (1949) Western. Running time: 61 minutes. Black and white.

Produced by Herman Schlom. Directed by Lesley Selander. Screenplay by Jack Natteford and Luci Ward. Photographed by J. Roy Hunt. Edited by Frank Doyle.

Starring Tim Holt (Dick), Richard

Martin (Chito), Martha Hyer (Ruth), Steve Brodie (Wheeler), Lois Andrews (Trixie), Harry Shannon (Sheriff), Addison Richards (Abbott), Stanley Blystone (Cook).

After winning marked bills in a roulette game, two cowboys get involved in a rustling scheme.

724 Saddle Buster (1932) Western. Running time: 59 minutes. Black and white.

Directed by Fred Allen. Screenplay by Oliver Drake. Photographed by Ted McCord. Edited by William Clemens.

Starring Tom Keene, Helen Foster, Charles Quigley, Ben Corbett, Fred Burns, Marie Quillan, Richard Carlyle, Robert Frazer, Harry Bowen, Al Taylor, Charles "Slim" Whitaker.

A rodeo cowboy gives up riding after he's almost killed by a wild bronco.

Note: Made for $38,000 and turned a profit of $25,000.

725 Saddle Legion (1951) Western. Running time: 61 minutes. Black and white.

Produced by Herman Schlom. Directed by Lesley Selander. Screenplay by Ed Earl Repp. Photographed by J. Roy Hunt. Edited by Desmond Marquette.

Starring Tim Holt (Dave Saunders), Dorothy Malone (Ann Rollins), Robert Livingston (Regan), Mauritz Hugo (Kelso), James Bush (Gabe), Movita Casteneda (Mercedes), Cliff Clark (Warren), Stanley Andrews (Chief Layton), George J. Lewis (Rurales Captain), Richard Martin (Chito).

A cattle inspector uses a disease as a scam to rustle herds.

726 Sagebrush Law (1943) Western. Running time: 56 minutes. Black and white.

Produced by Bert Gilroy. Directed by Sam Nelson. Screenplay by Bennett Cohen. Edited by John Lockert.

Starring Tim Holt, Cliff Edwards, Joan Barclay, John Eliot, Ed Cassidy,

Publicity poster for *Run of the Arrow*.

Karl Hackett, Roy Barcroft, Ernie Adams, John Merton, Bud McTaggart.

Bank president is wrongly accused of embezzlement.

727 *The Saint in London* (1939) Mystery. Running time: 72 minutes. Black and white. Available on videocassette.

Produced by William Sistrom. Directed by John Paddy Carstairs. Screenplay by Lynn Root and Frank Fenton (based on the novel by Leslie Charteris). Photographed by Claude Friese Green. Edited by Harry Marker.

Starring George Sanders (Simon Templar), Sally Gray (Penelope), David Burns (Dugan), Gordon McLeod (Inspector Teal), Henry Oscar (Bruno Lang), Ralph Truman (Kussella), Carl Jaffe (Stengler), Ben Williams (Wilkins).

The Saint travels to London to thwart counterfeiters.

728 *The Saint in New York* (1938) Mystery. Running time: 71 minutes. Black and white. Available on videocassette.

Produced by William Sistrom. Directed by Ben Holmes. Screenplay by Charles Kaufman and Mortimer Offner (based on the novel by Leslie Charteris). Photographed by Joseph August and Frank Redman. Edited by Harry Marker.

Starring Louis Hayward (Simon Templar), Kay Sutton (Faye), Sig Rumann (Hutch), Jonathan Hale (Inspector Fernack), Jack Carson (Red), Paul Guilfoyle (Hymie), Ben Welden (Papinoff).

The Saint must stop a notorious gangster known as the Big Fellow.

729 *The Saint in Palm Springs* (1941) Mystery. Running time: 65 minutes. Black and white.

Produced by Howard Benedict. Directed by Jack Hively. Screenplay by Jerry Cady (based on a story by Leslie Charteris). Photographed by Harry Wild. Edited by George Hively.

Starring George Sanders (Simon Templar), Wendy Barrie (Elna), Paul Guilfoyle (Pearly), Jonathan Hale (Inspector Fernack), Linda Hayes (Margaret), Ferris Taylor (Evans), Richard Crane (Whitey).

The Saint goes after the smugglers of three rare stamps.

Note: Sanders' last appearance as the Saint. In the 1960's, a TV series featuring Roger Moore was telecast.

730 *The Saint Meets the Tiger* (1943) Mystery. Running time: 70 minutes. Black and white.

Produced by William Sistrom. Directed by Paul Stein. Screenplay by Leslie Arliss, James Seymour and Wolfgang Wilhelm (based on the novel by Leslie Charteris). Photographed by Bob Krasker. Edited by Ralph Kempton.

Starring Hugh Sinclair (Simon Templar), Jean Gillie (Pat), Gordon McLeod (Teal), Clifford Evans (Sidmarsh), Wylie Watson (Horace), Dennis Arundell (Bentley), Charles Victor (Bittle).

The Saint tries to solve a string of murders when a man is found dead on his doorstep.

Note: RKO's attempt to revive the series after a two year hiatus. The studio was wary after producing the film and handed it to Republic Pictures for release. Made in England.

731 *The Saint Strikes Back* (1939) Mystery. Running time: 67 minutes. Black and white. Available on videocassette.

Produced by Robert Sisk. Directed by John Farrow. Screenplay by John Twist (based on a novel by Leslie Charteris). Photographed by Frank Redman. Edited by Jack Hively.

Starring George Sanders (Simon Templar), Wendy Barrie (Val), Jonathan Hale (Inspector Fernack), Jerome Cowan (Cullis), Neil Hamilton (Allan Breck), Barry Fitzgerald (Zipper), Robert Elliot (Webster).

The Saint tries to prove a woman's murdered father was innocent of another series of murders.

732 *The Saint Takes Over* (1940)
Mystery. Running time: 68 minutes.
Black and white. Available on videocassette.

Produced by Howard Benedict. Directed by Jack Hively. Screenplay by Lynn Root and Frank Fenton (based on characters created by Leslie Charteris). Photographed by Frank Redman. Edited by Desmond Marquette.

Starring George Sanders (Simon Templar), Wendy Barrie (Ruth), Jonathan Hale (Inspector Fernack), Paul Guilfoyle (Pearly), Morgan Conway (Sam Reese), Robert Emmett Keane (Leo Sloan), Cy Kendall (Max).

The Saint comes to the aid of the inspector when he is framed by race track touts.

Note: The only Saint entry not derived from one of the original novels (i.e. an original screenplay).

733 *The Saint's Double Trouble* (1940) Mystery. Running time: 68 minutes. Black and white.

Produced by Cliff Reid. Directed by Jack Hively. Screenplay by Ben Holmes (based on a story by Leslie Charteris). Photographed by J. Roy Hunt. Edited by Theron Warth.

Starring George Sanders (Simon Templar, Duke Piato), Helen Whitney (Anne Bitts), Jonathan Hale (Inspector Fernack), Bela Lugosi (Partner), Donald MacBride (Inspector Bohlen), John Hamilton (Limpy).

The Saint discovers a jewel thief he's after is his exact double.

734 *The Saint's Girl Friday* (1954)
Mystery. Running time: 70 minutes.
Black and white.

Produced by Julian Lesser and Anthony Hinds. Directed by Seymour Friedman. Screenplay by Allan MacKinnon (based on characters created by Leslie Charteris). Photographed by Walter Harvey. Edited by James Needs.

Starring Louis Hayward (Simon Templar), Sidney Tafler (Max), Naomi Chance (Carol), Charles Victor (Teal), Harold Lang (Jarvis), Thomas Gallagher (Hoppy Uniatz), Diana Dors (Margie).

The Saint finds that an old girlfriend has been murdered in London.

Note: Last of the Saint films, and done by Hammer studios for RKO release twelve years after the previous one. Hayward, who appeared in the first film, now appears in the last. British title: *The Saint's Return.*

735 *The Saint's Vacation* (1941)
Mystery. Running time: 60 minutes.
Black and white. Available on videocassette.

Produced by William Sistrom. Directed by Leslie Fenton. Screenplay by Jeffrey Dell and Leslie Charteris. Photographed by Bernard Knowles. Edited by Al Barnes.

Starring Hugh Sinclair (Simon Templar), Sally Gray (Mary Langdon), Arthur Macrae (Monty), Cecil Parker (Rudolph), Leueen MacGrath (Valerie), Gordon McLeod (Teal), John Warwick (Gregory).

The Saint hunts for a music box containing a secret code while vacationing in Switzerland.

736 *San Quentin* (1946) Crime drama. Running time: 66 minutes. Black and white.

Produced by Martin Mooney. Directed by Gordon Douglas. Screenplay by Lawrence Kimble, Arthur Ross and Howard Green. Photographed by Frank Redman. Edited by Marvin Coil.

Starring Lawrence Tierney (Jim), Barton MacLane (Nick), Marian Carr (Betty), Harry Shannon (Warden), Carol Forman (Ruthie), Tom Keene (Schaeffer), Joe Devlin (Broadway), Raymond Burr (Torrance), Lee Bonnell (Carzoni).

A group of prisoners form a welfare league on the inside, but it is nearly ruined when one of the founders escapes.

Note: The 1937 Warner Bros. film has nothing to do with this one.

WHAT DOES IT TAKE TO STOP *THE SAINT*?

Bullets? Blackmail? Or the most desirable, dangerous blonde in London's underworld!

LOUIS HAYWARD in

THE SAINT'S GIRL FRIDAY

Based on Characters Created by LESLIE CHARTERIS with

NAOMI CHANCE
SIDNEY TAFLER
CHARLES VICTOR

Story and Screenplay by ALLAN MacKINNON · Directed by SEYMOUR FRIEDMAN · Produced by ANTHONY HINDS · Presented by JULIAN LESSER

Publicity poster for *The Saint's Girl Friday*.

737 *Saturday's Heroes* (1937) Drama. Running time: 58 minutes. Black and white.

Produced by Robert Sisk. Directed by Edward Killy. Screenplay by Paul Yawitz, David Silverstein, and Charles Kaufman (based on the story by George Templeton). Photographed by Nicholas Musuraca. Edited by Frederic Knudtson.

Starring Van Heflin (Val), Marian Marsh (Frances), Richard Lane (Red), Alan Bruce (Burgeson), Minor Watson (Doc), Frank Jenks (Dubrowsky), Willie Best (Sam), Walter Miller (Coach Banks), Al St. John (Andy), Frank Coghlan, Jr. (Student).

A college football star balks at his special treatment.

Scandals see *George White's Scandals*

738 *Scarlet River* (1933) Western. Running time: 62 minutes. Black and white.

Produced by David O. Selznick. Directed by Otto Brower. Screenplay by Harold Shumate. Photographed by Nicholas Musuraca. Edited by Frederic Knudtson.

Starring Tom Keene, Dorothy Wilson, Lon Chaney, Jr. Edgar Kennedy, Betty Furness, Hooper Atchley, Roscoe Ates, Yakima Canutt, James Mason, Jack Raymond, Billy Butts, Myrna Loy, Rochelle Hudson, Joel McCrea, Julie Haydon, Bruce Cabot.

A movie cowboy finds himself caught up in real life trouble.

739 *Scattergood Baines* (1941) Comedy. Running time: 69 minutes. Black and white.

Produced by Jerrold Brandt. Directed by Christy Cabanne. Screenplay by Michael L. Simmons and Edward T. Lowe (based on the stories by Clarence Budington Kelland). Photographed by Jack MacKenzie. Edited by Henry Berman.

Starring Guy Kibbee (Scattergood Baines), Carol Hughes (Helen), John Archer (Johnny), Dink Trout (Pliny), Emma Dunn (Mirandy), Lee "Lasses" White (Ed Potts), Fern Emmett (Clara Potts), Willie Best (Hipp).

Life with the owner of a small-town hardware store.

740 *Scattergood Meets Broadway* (1941) Comedy. Running time: 68 minutes. Black and white.

Produced by Jerrold Brandt. Directed by Christy Cabanne. Screenplay by Michael L. Simmons and Ethel B. Stone (based on the stories by Clarence Budington Kelland). Photographed by Jack MacKenzie. Edited by John Sturges.

Starring Guy Kibbee (Scattergood Baines), Emma Dunn (Mirandy), Joyce Compton (Diana), Bradley Page (Bard), Frank Jenks (Bent), William Henry (Davy), Mildred Coles (Peggy), Paul White (Hipp).

Scattergood travels to the Big Apple to aid a local boy who gets involved with folks of the fast life.

741 *Scattergood Pulls the Strings* (1941) Comedy. Running time: 69 minutes. Black and white.

Produced by Jerrold T. Brandt. Directed by Christy Cabanne. Screenplay by Cabanne and Bernard Schubert (based on stories by Clarence Budington Kelland). Photographed by Jack MacKenzie. Edited by Desmond Marquette.

Starring Guy Kibbee (Scattergood), Bobs Watson (Jimmy), Susan Peters (Ruth), James Corner (Urban Downs), Emma Dunn (Mirandy), Dink Trout (Pliny), Monte Blue (Ben), Fern Emmett (Clara).

Scattergood helps a runaway boy.

742 *Scattergood Rides High* (1942) Comedy. Running time: 63 minutes. Black and white.

Produced by Jerrold T. Brandt. Directed by Christy Cabanne. Screenplay by Michael L. Simmons (based on the stories by Clarence Budington Kelland). Photographed by Jack MacKenzie. Edited by Henry Berman.

Starring Guy Kibbee (Scattergood), Jed Prouty (Van Pelt), Dorothy Moore (Helen), Charles Lind (Dan), Kenneth Howell (Phillip), Regina Wallace (Mrs. Van Pelt), Frances Carson (Mrs. Dane).

Scattergood helps a neighbor keep from losing his father's horse stable.

743 *Scattergood Survives a Murder* (1942) Comedy. Running time: 66 minutes. Black and white.

Produced by Jerrold T. Brandt. Directed by Christy Cabanne. Screenplay by Michael Simmons (based on the stories by Clarence Budington Kelland). Photographed by Jack MacKenzie. Edited by Richard Cahoon.

Starring Guy Kibbee (Scattergood), John Archer (Dunker), Margaret Hayes

(Gail), Wallace Ford (Wally), Spencer Charters (Sheriff), Eily Malyon (Mrs. Grimes), John Miljan (Rolfe), George Chandler (Sam), Dick Elliot (Mathew Quentin), Florence Lake (Phoebe), Willie Best (Hipp).

Two old women die and leave their fortune to a cat.

Note: Last of the Scattergood Baines films.

Scattergood Swings It see Cinderella Swings It

744 *Sea Devils* (1937) Drama. Running time: 85 minutes. Black and white.

Produced by Edward Small. Directed by Ben Stoloff. Screenplay by Frank Wead, John Twist, and P.J. Wolfson. Photographed by J. Roy Hunt. Edited by Arthur Roberts.

Starring Victor McLaglen (Medals Malone), Preston Foster (Mike), Ida Lupino (Doris), Donald Woods (Steve), Helen Flint (Sadie), Gordon Jones (Puggy), Billy Gilbert (Cop), Barbara Pepper (Flo).

Conflict between a father and daughter over whom she should marry.

745 *Sea Devils* (1953) Adventure. Running time: 91 minutes. Color.

Produced by David E. Rose. Directed by Raoul Walsh. Screenplay by Borden Chase (from a book by Victor Hugo). Photographed by Wilkie Cooper. Edited by John Seabourne.

Starring Yvonne DeCarlo (Drouette), Rock Hudson (Gillatt), Maxwell Reed (Rantaine), Denis O'Dea (Lethierry), Michael Goodliffe (Ragan), Bryan Forbes (Willie).

A British agent poses as French royalty.

746 *Sealed Cargo* (1951) Drama. Running time: 90 minutes. Black and white.

Produced by William Duff. Directed by Alfred Werker. Screenplay by Dale Van Every, Oliver H.P. Garrett, Roy Huggins. Photographed by George E. Diskant. Edited by Ralph Dawson.

Starring Dana Andrews (Pat), Carla Balenda (Margaret), Claude Raines (Skalder), Phillip Dorn (Conrad), Onslow Stevens (McLean), Skip Homeier (Steve), Eric Feldary (Holger), J.M. Kerrigan (Skipper Ben), Arthur Shields (Dolan), Morgan Farley (Caleb), Whit Bissell (Schuster), Donald Dillaway (Owen).

A fisherman stumbles upon a vessel containing Nazi weapons and supplies.

747 *Second Chance* (1953) Drama. Running time: 82 minutes. Color. Available on videocassette.

Produced by Sam Wisenthal. Directed by Rudolph Maté. Screenplay by Oscar Millard and Sydney Boehm. Photographed by William Snyder. Edited by Robert Ford.

Starring Robert Mitchum (Russ Lambert), Linda Darnell (Clare Shepard), Jack Palance (Cappy Gordon), Sandro Giglio (Cable Car Conductor), Rodolfo Hoyos (Vasco), Reginald Sheffield (Woburn), Margaret Brewster (Mrs. Woburn), Roy Roberts (Malloy), Dan Seymour (Felipe).

A boxer in Mexico falls for a girl on the run from a mob hit man.

Note: Made in 3-D and Stereophonic sound. Mitchum's last film for RKO (although the earlier made *She Couldn't Say No* was released after this one).

748 *Second Wife* (1930) Drama. Running time: 67 minutes. Black and white.

Directed by Russell Mack. Screenplay by Hugh Herbert and Bert Glennon (based on the play "All the King's Men" by Fulton Oursler). Photographed by William Marshall.

Starring Conrad Nagel (Walter Fairchild), Lila Lee (Florence Wendell), Hugh Huntley (Gilbert), Mary Carr (Mrs. Rhodes), Freddie Burke (Jr.).

A man cannot stop grieving for his first wife, even after his second wife becomes pregnant.

749 *Second Wife* (1936) Drama. Running time: 59 minutes. Black and white.

Produced by Lee Marcus. Directed by Edward Killy. Screenplay by Thomas Lennon (based on the play "All the Kings Men" by Fulton Oursler). Photographed by Nicholas Musuraca. Edited by George Crone.

Starring Gertrude Michael (Virginia Howard), Walter Abel (Kenneth Carpenter), Erik Rhodes (Dave Bennett), Emma Dunn (Mrs. Brown), Lee Van Atta (Jr.).

Remake of the 1930 feature.

750 *The Secret Fury* (1950) Comedy. Running time: 86 minutes. Black and white.

Produced by Jack H. Skirball and Bruce Manning. Directed by Mel Ferrer. Screenplay by Lionel Houser. Photographed by Leo Tover. Edited by Harry Marker.

Starring Claudette Colbert (Ellen), Robert Ryan (David), Jane Cowl (Aunt Clara), Paul Kelly (Eric Lowell), Phillip Ober (Kent), Elisabeth Risdon (Dr. Twining), Doris Dudley (Pearl), Dave Barbour (Lucian), Vivian Vance (Leah), Percy Helton (Justice of the Peace).

A couple stall their plans to get married when it is announced the woman is already wed.

751 *The Secret Life of Walter Mitty* (1947) Comedy. Running time: 105 minutes. Color. Available on videocassette.

Produced by Samuel Goldwyn. Directed by Norman Z. McLeod. Screenplay by Ken Englund and Everett Freeman (based on the story by James Thurber). Photographed by Lee Garmes. Edited by Monica Underwood.

Starring Danny Kaye (Walter Mitty), Virginia Mayo (Rosalind), Boris Karloff (Dr. Hugo Hollingshead), Fay Bainter (Mrs. Mitty), Ann Rutherford (Gertrude), Thurston Hall (Pierce), Konstantin Shayne (Peter van Hoorn), Florence Bates (Mrs. Griswold), Gordon Jones (Tubby), Reginald Denny (Colonel).

A hopeless daydreamer imagines himself heroic in a variety of settings.

Note: Based on Thurber's short story, which the author offered Goldwyn $10,000 *not* to film. Thurber hated Danny Kaye's work, and stated "It began to be bad with the first git-gat-gittle." The author disclaimed the film to his dying day, although Goldwyn tried hard to please him. Thurber even went so far as to write a long sarcastic condemnation of the movie in *Life* magazine (8/18/47 issue), which also ran a letter from Goldwyn stating he did his best. Nevertheless, the film, made for three million, was a box office smash.

752 *Secret Service* (1931) War drama. Running time: 69 minutes. Black and white.

Produced by Louis Sarecky. Directed by J. Walter Ruben. Screenplay by Gerrit Lloyd and Bernard Schubert. Photographed by Edward Cronjager. Edited by Jack Kitchin.

Starring Richard Dix (Lewis Dumont), Shirley Grey (Edith), William Post, Jr. (Lt. Dumont), Gavin Gordon (Archford), Fred Warren (Gen. Grant), Nance O'Neil (Mrs. Varney), Virginia Sale (Mrs. Kittridge).

A Union officer and his brother must get information behind confederate lines.

The Secret Sharer see *Face to Face*

753 *Secrets of the French Police* (1932) Mystery. Running time: 59 minutes. Black and white.

Directed by A. Edward Sutherland. Screenplay by Samuel Ornitz and Robert Tasker. Photographed by Al Gilks. Edited by Jack Kitchin.

Starring Gwili Andre (Eugenie), Frank Morgan (Francois), Gregory Ratoff (Moloff), Murray Kinnell (Bertillon), John Warburton (Leon Renault).

An evil hypnotist puts a woman under his spell to commit crimes.

754 *The Set-Up* (1949) Drama. Running time: 72 minutes. Black and white. Available on videocassette.

Produced by Richard Goldstone. Directed by Robert Wise. Screenplay by Art Cohn. Photographed by Milton Krasner. Edited by Roland Gross.

Starring Robert Ryan (Stroker Thompson), Audrey Totter (Julie), George Tobias (Tiny), Alan Baxter (Little Boy), Wallace Ford (Gus), Percy Helton (Red), Hal Fieberling (Tiger Nelson), Darryl Hickman (Shaley), Kenny O'Morrison (Moore), James Edwards (Luther Hawkins), David Clarke (Gunboat).

A washed-up boxer is too proud to throw his final fight, and is therefore a victim of gangsters.

Note: Like *High Noon*, each minute in the film is a minute in real-life, with no editing transitions for time. Ryan actually did box for four years in college.

Review: "One of the most realistic and gripping boxing films ever made . . . a unique and fascinating film" — *The Motion Picture Guide.*

755 *Seven Days Ashore* (1944) Comedy. Running time: 74 minutes. Black and white. Available on videocassette.

Produced and directed by John H. Auer. Screenplay by Edward Verdier, Irving Phillips, and Lawrence Kimble. Photographed by Russell Metty. Edited by Harry Marker.

Starring Wally Brown (Monty), Alan Carney (Orval), Marcy McGuire (Dot), Gordon Oliver (Dan Arland), Virginia Mayo (Carol), Amelita Ward (Lucy), Elaine Shepard (Annabelle), Dooley Wilson (Jason).

A playboy cons two navy buddies into helping him with girl troubles.

Note: Obviously influenced by Abbott and Costello's *In the Navy* (Universal, 1941).

756 *Seven Days Leave* (1942) Comedy. Running time: 87 minutes. Black and white.

Produced and directed by Tim Whelan. Screenplay by William Bowers, Ralph Spence, Curtis Kenyon, Kenneth Earl. Photographed by Robert De Grasse. Edited by Robert Wise.

Starring Victor Mature (Johnny Grey), Lucille Ball (Terry), Harold Peary (Gildersleeve), Mapy Cortes (Mapy), Ginny Simms (Ginny), Marcy McGuire (Mickey), Peter Lind Hayes (Jackson), Walter Reed (Ralph Bell), Wallace Ford (Sgt. Mead), Arnold Stang (Bitsy), Buddy Clark (Clarky), Charles Victor (Charles), King Kennedy (Gifford), Addison Richards (Capt. Collins).

A serviceman will gain a big inheritance if he marries a socialite.

757 *Seven Keys to Baldpate* (1930) Comedy. Running time: 72 minutes. Black and white.

Produced by Louis Sarecky. Directed by Reginald Barker. Screenplay by Jane Murfin (based on the play by George M. Cohan, and the story by Earl Derr Biggers). Photographed by Edward Cronjager. Edited by Archie Marshek.

Starring Richard Dix (William Magee), Miriam Segar (Mary Norton), Margaret Livingston (Myra), Joseph Allen (Peters), Lucien Littlefield (Thomas Hayden).

A writer attempts to complete his overdue novel before his marriage.

Note: First of three versions by RKO, it had been filmed before in 1917 and 1925.

758 *Seven Keys to Baldpate* (1935) Comedy. Running time: 80 minutes. Black and white.

Produced by William Sistrom. Directed by William Hamilton and Edward Killy (based on the play by George M. Cohan, and the story by Earl Derr Biggers). Photographed by Robert De Grasse. Edited by Desmond Marquette.

Starring Gene Raymond (Magee),

Marcy McGuire in *Seven Days Ashore.*

Margaret Callahan (Mary), Eric Blore (Bolton), Erin O'Brien Moore (Myra), Moroni Olsen (Cagan), Grant Mitchell (Hayden).

Remake of the above.

759 *Seven Keys to Baldpate*

(1947) Comedy. Running time: 68 minutes. Black and white.

Produced by Herman Schlom. Directed by Lew Landers. Screenplay by Lee Loeb (based on the play by George M. Cohan, and the story by Earl Derr Biggers). Photographed by Jack MacKenzie. Edited by J.R. Whittridge.

Starring Phillip Terry (Magee), Jacqueline White (Mary), Eduardo Ciannelli (Cargan), Margaret Lindsay (Connie), Arthur Shields (Bolton), Jimmy Conlin (Hermit).

Remake of the above.

760 *Seven Miles from Alcatraz*

(1942) Drama. Running time: 62 minutes. Black and white. Available on videocassette.

Produced by Herman Schlom. Directed by Edward Dmytryk. Screenplay by Joseph Krumgold (based on a story by John Klorer). Photographed by Robert De Grasse. Edited by George Crone.

Starring James Craig (Larkin), Bonita Granville (Anne Porter), Frank Jenks (Jimbo), Cliff Edwards (Stormy), George Cleveland (Porter).

Two prison escapees thwart Nazi spies.

761 *Seventh Victim* (1943) Horror. Running time: 71 minutes. Black and white.

Produced by Val Lewton. Directed by Mark Robson. Screenplay by DeWitt Bodeen, Charles O'Neal. Photographed by Nicholas Musuraca. Edited by John Lockert.

Starring Tom Conway (Dr. Louis Judd), Kim Hunter (Mary Gibson), Jean Brooks (Jacqueline Gibson), Hugh Beaumont (Gregory Ward), Erford Gage (Jason), Isabel Jewell (Frances Fallon), Chef Milani (Romani), Evelyn Brent

Fred Astaire and Ginger Rogers in *Shall We Dance.*

(Natalie), Milton Kibbee (Joseph), Joan Barclay (Gladys).

While searching for her missing sister, a woman discovers links to Satanism.

762 *Shall We Dance* (1937) Musical. Running time: 116 minutes. Black and white. Available on videocassette.

Produced by Pandro S. Berman. Directed by Mark Sandrich. Screenplay by Allan Scott, Ernest Pagano, P.J. Wolfson. Photographed by David Abel. Edited by William Hamilton. Music by George and Ira Gershwin.

Songs: "Slap That Bass," "Beginner's Luck," "Let's Call the Whole Thing Off," "Walking the Dog," "They All Laughed," "They Can't Take That Away from Me," "Shall We Dance."

Starring Fred Astaire (Pete Peters), Ginger Rogers (Linda Keene), Edward Everett Horton (Jeffrey Baird), Eric Blore (Cecil Flintridge) Jerome Cowan (Arthur), Ketti Gallian (Lady Tarrington), William Brisbane (Montgomery), Ann

Shoemaker (Mrs. Fitzgerald), Ben Alexander (Bandleader).

Dancing partners pretend to be married.

763 *She* (1935) Fantasy. Running time: 95 minutes. Black and white.

Produced by Merian C. Cooper. Directed by Irving Pichel and Lansing C. Holden. Screenplay by Ruth Rose and Dudley Nichols. Photographed by J. Roy Hunt. Edited by Archie Marshek.

Starring Helen Gallaghan (She), Randolph Scott (Leo), Helen Mack (Tanya), Nigel Bruce (Holly), Gustav Von Seyffertitz (Prime Minister), Samuel S. Hinds (Vincey), Jim Thorpe (Captain of Guards).

A group finds a lost city where a queen cannot die unless she falls in love.

Note: Gallaghan once ran for Senate against Richard Nixon. This was her last film appearance. *The Motion Picture Guide* reports this film as missing, but it

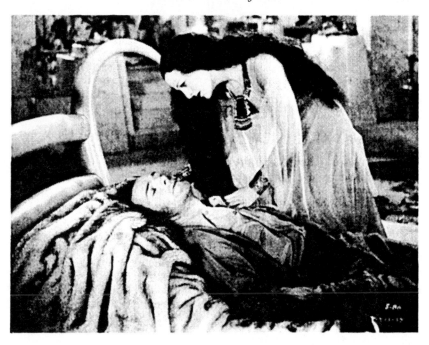

Randolph Scott and Helen Gallaghan in *She*.

is available to TV albeit often in a truncated 89 minute print.

764 *She Couldn't Say No* (1954)
Comedy. Running time: 88 minutes. Black and white.

Produced by Robert Sparks. Directed by Lloyd Bacon. Screenplay by D.D. Beauchamp, William Bowers, and Richard Flournoy (based on the story "Enough for Happiness" by Beauchamp). Photographed by Harry Wild. Edited by George Amy. Available on videocassette.

Starring Robert Mitchum (Doc), Jean Simmons (Corby), Arthur Hunnicutt (Otley), Edgar Buchanan (Ad), Wallace Ford (Joe), Raymond Walburn (Judge), Jimmy Hunt (Digger), Ralph Dumke (Sheriff), Hope Landin (Mrs. McMurty), Gus Schilling (Gruman), Florence Lake (Mrs. Gruman), Eleanor Todd (Sally), Pinky Tomlin (Elmer), Burt Mustin (Amos).

A rich woman decides to assist those who helped her on the way up.

Note: This was shot in 1953 but withheld from release while Howard Hughes thought up a title. The one he finally decided upon was also the title of a 1930 Warner release, the same studio's 1941 remake, and a 1939 British film. The British title of this one was *Beautiful But Dangerous*. Jean Simmons' last RKO film.

765 *She Wore a Yellow Ribbon* (1949) Western. Running time: 103 minutes. Color. Available on videocassette.

Produced by John Ford and Merian C. Cooper. Directed by Ford. Screenplay by Frank S. Nugent and Laurence Stallings. Photographed by Winton C. Hoch and Charles P. Boyle. Edited by Jack Murray.

Starring John Wayne (Brittles), Joanne Dru (Olivia), John Agar (Cohill), Ben Johnson (Tyree), Harry Carey, Jr.

(Pennel), Victor McLaglen (Quincannon), Mildred Natwick (Abby), George O'Brien (Allshard), Arthur Shields (Dr. O'Laughlin), Francis Ford (Barman), Harry Woods (Rynders), Tom Tyler (Quayne).

Saga of a cavalry officer's last days before retirement.

Oscar: Best Photography.

766 She's Got Everything (1938)

Comedy. Running time: 72 minutes. Black and white.

Produced by Albert Lewis. Directed by Joseph Santley. Screenplay by Joseph Hoffman and Monroe Shaff. Photographed by Jack MacKenzie. Edited by Frederic Knudtson.

Starring Gene Raymond (Fuller Partridge), Ann Sothern (Carol Rogers), Victor Moore (Waldo Eddington), Helen Broderick (Aunt Jane), Parkyakarkus (Mick), Billy Gilbert (Chaffee), William Brisbane (Roger).

A girl gets a secretarial job after she finds herself in debt upon the death of her father.

767 She's My Weakness (1930)

Comedy. Running time: 75 minutes. Black and white.

Produced by Henry Hobart. Directed by Melville Brown. Screenplay by J. Walter Ruben. Photographed by Leo Tover. Edited by Jack Kitchin.

Starring Sue Carol (Marie), Arthur Lake (Tommy), William Collier, Sr. (David), Lucien Littlefield (Walter), Alan Bruce (Bernard), Walter Gilbert (Wilson).

A girl's uncle believes she is too young to marry her sweetheart.

768 Shooting Straight (1930)

Drama. Running time: 72 minutes. Black and white.

Produced by Louis Sarecky. Directed by George Archainbaud. Screenplay by J. Walter Ruben and Wallace Smith. Photographed by Edward Cronjager. Edited by Otto Ludwig.

Starring Richard Dix (Lucky Sheldon), Mary Lawlor (Doris Powell), James Neill (Reverend Powell), Matthew Betz (Martin), George Cooper (Chick), William Janney (Tommy Powell), Robert Emmett O'Connor (Hagen), Clarence Wurtz (Stevens), Eddie Sturgis (Spike), Dick Curtis (Butch).

A big time gambler hiding out in a small town falls for a minister's daughter and saves her brother from two-bit gamblers.

769 Side Street (1929) Drama.

Running time: 70 minutes. Black and white.

Produced by William LeBaron. Directed by Malcolm St. Clair. Screenplay by John Russell, St. Clair, George O'Hara, Eugene Walter. Photographed by William Marshall and Nicholas Musuraca.

Starring Tom Moore (Jimmy), Matt Moore (John), Owen Moore (Dennis), Kathryn Perry (Kathleen), Frank Sheridan (Mr. O'Farrell), Emma Dunn (Mrs. O'Farrell), Arthur Housman (Silk), Mildred Harris (Bunny), Charles Bryer (Maxie), Edwin August (Mac), Irving Bacon (Slim).

A cop must go after a killer only to find that it is his own brother.

770 The Silken Affair (1957) Comedy. Running time: 96 minutes. Black and white.

Produced by Douglas Fairbanks, Jr. and Fred Feldkamp. Directed by Roy Kellino. Screenplay by Robert Lewis Taylor. Photographed by Gilbert Taylor. Edited by Robert Best.

Starring David Niven (Roger), Genevieve Page (Genevieve), Ronald Squire (Marberry), Beatrice Straight (Theora), Wilfrid Hyde White (Sir Horace Hogg), Howard Marion-Crawford (Baggott), Dorothy Allison (Mrs. Tweakham), Miles Malleson (Blucer), Richard Wattis (Worthington).

A silk company owner juggles the books to make things look more prosperous, while doing the same to make his rival's business look bleak.

771 *Silly Billies* (1936) Comedy. Running time: 63 minutes. Black and white.

Produced by Lee Marcus. Directed by Fred Guiol. Screenplay by Al Boasberg and Jack Townley. Photographed by Nicholas Musuraca. Edited by John Lockert.

Starring Bert Wheeler (Roy), Robert Woolsey (Doc), Dorothy Lee (Mary), Harry Woods (Hak), Ethan Laidlaw (Trigger), Chief Thunderbird (Chief Cyclone), Delmar Watson (Morton), Richard Alexander (John Little).

A dentist and his assistant head west to cash in on the dental needs of gold prospectors.

772 *Silver Cord* (1933) Drama. Running time: 75 minutes. Black and white.

Produced by Pandro S. Berman. Directed by John Cromwell. Screenplay by Jane Murfin (based on the play by Sidney Howard). Photographed by Charles Rosher. Edited by George Nicholls Jr.

Starring Irene Dunne (Christina Phelps), Joel McCrea (David), Frances Dee (Hester), Eric Linden (Robert), Laura Hope Crews (Mrs. Phelps), Helen Cromwell (Delilah).

A mother clings to her youngest child.

Note: It has been said that Linden was so broken up when Dee married McCrea, he took a trip to Europe to forget her. All three are in this movie, so it must have been pretty wild on the set.

773 *Silver Horde* (1930) Drama. Running time: 76 minutes. Black and white.

Produced by William LeBaron. Directed by George Archainbaud. Screenplay by Wallace Smith. Photographed by Leo Tover. Edited by Otto Ludwig.

Starring Evelyn Brent (Cherry), Louis Wolheim (George), Joel McCrea (Boyd Emerson), Raymond Hatton (Fraser), Blanche Sweet (Queenie), Purnell Pratt (Wayne Wayland), Jean Arthur (Mildred).

A fisherman fights for control of his life.

774 *Silver Lode* (1954) Western. Running time: 80 minutes. Color.

Produced by Benedict Bogeaus. Directed by Allan Dwan. Screenplay by Karen De Wolf. Photographed by John Alton. Edited by James Leicester.

Starring John Payne (Dan), Dan Duryea (Ned), Lizabeth Scott (Rose), Dolores Moran (Dolly), Emile Meyer (Sheriff), Harry Carey, Jr. (Johnson), Morris Ankrum (Zachary), John Hudson (Mitch).

A cowboy is accused of murder on his wedding day, and must then clear himself.

775 *The Silver Streak* (1935) Drama. Running time: 85 minutes. Black and white. Available on videocassette.

Produced by Glendon Allvine. Directed by Tommy Atkins. Screenplay by H.W. Hannemann, Jack O'Donnell, and Roger Whatley. Photographed by Roy Hunt. Edited by Vernon Walker.

Starring Sally Blaine (Ruth), Charles Starrett (Tom), Hardie Albright (Allan), William Farnum (B.J.), Irving Pichel (Bronte), Arthur Lake (Crawford), Theodore Von Eltz (Ed Tyler), Guinn "Big Boy" Williams (Higgins), Edgar Kennedy (O'Brien), Murray Kinnell (Dr. Flynn).

Lives are intertwined on a train from Chicago to Nevada.

Note: This one made a $107,000 profit, which was quite good for 1935.

776 *Sin Ship* (1931) Drama. Running time: 65 minutes. Black and white.

Produced by Myles Connolly. Directed by Louis Wolheim. Screenplay by Hugh Herbert. Photographed by Nicholas Musuraca. Edited by Otto Ludwig.

Starring Louis Wolheim (McVeigh), Mary Astor (Kitty), Ian Keith (Marsden), Hugh Herbert (Charlie), Russell Powell (Tourist), Alan Roscoe (Dave).

Two crooks pose as a minister and his wife while on board a two-masted schooner.

777 Sin Takes a Holiday (1930) Drama. Running time: 81 minutes. Black and white.

Produced by E.B. Derr. Directed by Paul Stein. Screenplay by Horace Jackson. Photographed by Jack Mescall. Edited by Daniel Mandell.

Starring Constance Bennett (Sylvia), Kenneth MacKenna (Gaylord), Basil Rathbone (Durant), Rita La Roy (Grace), Louis John Bartels (Richards), ZaSu Pitts (Anna).

A stenographer marries her boss to save him from marrying his divorcee girl friend.

778 Sinbad the Sailor (1947) Adventure. Running time: 117 minutes. Color. Available on videocassette.

Produced by Stephen Ames. Directed by Richard Wallace. Screenplay by John Twist. Photographed by George Barnes. Edited by Sherman Todd. Music by Roy Webb.

Starring Douglas Fairbanks, Jr. (Sinbad), Maureen O'Hara (Shireen), Walter Slezak (Melik), Anthony Quinn (Emir), George Tobias (Abbu), Jane Greer (Priouze), Mike Mazurki (Yusuf), Sheldon Leonard (Auctioneer), Alan Napier (Aga), John Miljan (Moga), Barry Mitchell (Mualin), Glenn Strange (Slave Master), George Chandler (Commoner), Louis Jean Heydt (Mercenary), Cy Kendall (Crier at Execution).

Sinbad sails the seas to find a hidden treasure.

779 Sing and Like It (1934) Comedy. Running time: 71 minutes. Black and white.

Produced by Howard J. Green. Directed by William Seiter. Screenplay by Marion Dix and Laird Doyle. Photographed by Nicholas Musuraca. Edited by George Crone.

Starring ZaSu Pitts (Annie), Pert Kelton (Ruby), Edward Everett Horton (Adam Fink), Nat Pendleton (Fenny),

Ned Sparks (Toots), John Qualen (Oswald), Stanley Fields (Butch), Steve Morelli (Barney).

A hardened gangster is reduced to tears every time an off-key singer warbles a sentimental song about mothers.

780 Sing Your Way Home (1945) Musical. Running time: 72 minutes. Black and white.

Produced by Bert Granet. Directed by Anthony Mann. Screenplay by William Bowers. Photographed by Frank Redman. Edited by Harry Marker.

Starring Jack Haley (Steve), Marcy McGuire (Bridget), Glenn Vernon (Jimmy), Anne Jeffreys (Kay), Donna Lee (Terry), Patti Brill (Dottie), Nancy Marlowe (Patsy), Emory Parnell (Captain), Ed Gargan (Jailer).

A war correspondent puts on a show featuring young European entertainers.

781 Sing Your Worries Away (1942) Comedy. Running time: 71 minutes. Black and white.

Produced by Cliff Reid. Directed by A. Edward Sutherland. Screenplay by Monte Brice. Photographed by Frank Redman. Edited by Henry Berman.

Starring Bert Lahr (Chow Brewster), June Havoc (Rocksey Rochelle), Buddy Ebsen (Tommy Jones), Patsy Kelly (Bebe), Dorothy Lovett (Carol), Sam Levene (Smiley Clark), Margaret Dumont (Flo).

A songwriter inherits $300,000.

The Sinner see **Desert Desperadoes**

782 Sister Kenny (1946) Biography. Running time: 116 minutes. Black and white. Available on videocassette.

Produced and directed by Dudley Nichols. Screenplay by Nichols, Alexander Knox, Mary McCarthy and Milton Gunzberg (uncredited) (based on the book *And They Shall Walk* by Elizabeth Kenny with Martha Otenso). Photographed by George Barnes. Edited by Roland Gross.

Starring Rosalind Russell (Elizabeth Kenny), Alexander Knox (Dr. McDonnell), Dean Jagger (Kevin Connors), Phillip Merivale (Dr. Black), Beulah Bondi (Mary Kenny), Charles Dingle (Michael Kenny), John Litel (Medical Director), Doreen McCann (Dirrie), Fay Helm (Mrs. McIntyre), Charles Kemper (Mr. McIntyre), Dorothy Peterson (Agnes), Gloria Holden (Mrs. McDonnell).

Biography of woman who brought her own system of treating polio victims into the limelight.

Note: Russell was nominated for an Oscar, but the film lost $700,000.

783 *Six Gun Gold* (1941) Western. Running time: 57 minutes. Black and white.

Produced by Bert Gilroy. Directed by David Howard. Screenplay by Norton S. Parker. Photographed by Harry Wild. Edited by Frederic Knudtson.

Starring Tim Holt (Don), Ray Whitley (Smokey), Jan Clayton (Penny), Lee "Lasses" White (Whopper), LeRoy Mason (Marshal), Eddy Walker (Ben Blanchard), Davison Clark (Robinson).

A cowboy attempts to rescue his kidnapped brother.

784 *Sixty Glorious Years* (1938) Drama. Running time: 90 minutes. Color.

Produced and directed by Herbert Wilcox. Screenplay by Charles de Brandcourt, Miles Malleson, and Robert Vansittart. Photographed by F.A. Young.

Starring Anna Neagle, Anton Walbrook, C. Aubrey Smith, Walter Rilla, Charles Carson, Felix Aylmer, Lewis Casson, Henry Hallatt, Wyndham Goldie, Derrick De Marney, Joyce Bland.

A sequel to *Victoria the Great* about the Queen's engagement to Prince Albert and ensuing complications.

Note: The American public was so interested in the initial story about Queen Victoria that RKO and Herbert Wilcox formed a contract that ensured distribution of British films in the U.S. and an exchange of American and British talent for various productions. Wilcox featured his wife, Neagle, in the American RKO feature *Nurse Edith Calwell* (q.v.) as his next project.

785 *Sky Giant* (1938) Adventure. Running time: 81 minutes. Black and white.

Produced by Robert Sisk. Directed by Lew Landers. Screenplay by Lionel Houser. Photographed by Nicholas Musuraca. Edited by Harry Marker.

Starring Richard Dix (Stag), Chester Morris (Ken), Joan Fontaine (Meg), Harry Carey (Col. Stockton), Paul Guilfoyle (Fergie), Robert Strange (Weldon), Vicki Lester (Edna).

Three people crash land an airplane in the arctic.

786 *The Sky's the Limit* (1943) Musical. Running time: 89 minutes. Black and white. Available on videocassette.

Produced by David Hempstead and Sherman Todd. Directed by Edward Griffith. Screenplay by Frank Fenton and Lynn Root. Photographed by Russell Metty. Edited by Roland Gross. Music by Johnny Mercer and Harold Arlen.

Songs: "One for My Baby," "My Shining Hour," "I've Got a Lot in Common with You."

Starring Fred Astaire (Fred), Joan Leslie (Joan), Robert Benchley (Phil), Robert Ryan (Reg), Elizabeth Patterson (Mrs. Fisher), Marjorie Gateson (Canteen Hostess), Richard Davies (Merlin), Clarence Kolb (Sloan), Eric Blore (Jackson), Freddie Slack and His Orchestra (Themselves).

A flying tiger on leave falls for a magazine writer.

787 *Slaughter Trail* (1951) Western. Running time: 78 minutes. Color.

Produced and directed by Irving

Allen. Screenplay by Sid Kuller. Photographed by Jack Greenhaigh. Edited by Fred Allen.

Starring Brian Donlevy (Dempster), Gig Young (Vaughn), Virginia Grey (Lorabelle), Andy Devine (McIntosh), Robert Hutton (Morgan), Terry Wilkesson (Singalong), Lew Bedell (Hardsaddle), Myron Healey (Heath), Eddie Parks (Rufus Black), Lois Hall (Susan).

The Indians are on the warpath when two braves are killed by cavalry men.

788 *Slightly Scarlet* (1956) Drama. Running time: 90 minutes. Color. Available on videocassette.

Produced by Benedict Bogeaus. Directed by Allan Dwan. Screenplay by Robert Blees, story by James M. Cain. Photographed by John Alton. Edited by James Leicester.

Starring John Payne (Ben Grace), Arlene Dahl (Dorothy Lyons), Rhonda Fleming (June Lyons), Kent Taylor (Frank Jansen), Ted de Corsia (Sol Caspar), Lance Fuller (Gauss), Frank Gerstle (Dave).

The mayor's secretary falls for a gangleader.

789 *Smart Woman* (1931) Comedy. Running time: 68 minutes. Black and white.

Produced by Bertram Millhauser. Directed by Gregory La Cava. Screenplay by Salisbury Field. Photographed by Nicholas Musuraca. Edited by Ann McKnight.

Starring Mary Astor (Nancy), Robert Ames (Donald), Edward Everett Horton (Ross), Noel Francis (Peggy), John Halliday (Sir Guy Harrington), Gladys Gale (Mrs. Preston), Ruth Weston (Sally Ross).

A woman returns from a trip to find her husband has found another.

790 *Smartest Girl in Town* (1936) Comedy. Running time: 58 minutes. Black and white.

Produced by Edward Kaufman. Directed by Joseph Santley. Screenplay by Viola Brothers Shore. Photographed by J. Roy Hunt. Edited by Jack Hively. Music and lyrics to "Will You" by Gene Raymond.

Starring Gene Raymond (Dick Smith), Ann Sothern (Francis), Helen Broderick (Gwen), Eric Blore (Philbean), Erik Rhodes (Torine).

A millionaire falls for a model.

791 *Smashing the Rackets* (1938) Crime drama. Running time: 65 minutes. Black and white.

Produced by B.P. Fineman. Directed by Lew Landers. Screenplay by Lionel Houser. Photographed by Nicholas Musuraca. Edited by Harry Marker.

Starring Chester Morris (Jim Conway), Frances Mercer (Susan Lane), Bruce Cabot (Steve Lawrence), Rita Johnson (Letty Lane), Donald Douglas (Spaulding), Ben Welden (Whitey), Ed Pawley (Chin).

A rugged D.A. cleans up New York City.

Note: Based loosely on the exploits of Thomas Dewey.

792 *Snow White and the Seven Dwarfs* (1937) Animated feature. Running time: 82 minutes. Technicolor.

Produced by Walt Disney. Directed by David Hand, Perce Pearce, Larry Morey, William Cottrell, Wilfred Jackson, Ben Sharpsteen. Screenplay by Ted Sears, Otto Englander, Earl Hurd, Dorothy Ann Blank, Richard Creedon, Dick Richard, Merrill De Maris, Webb Smith.

Voices: Adriana Caselotti (Snow White), Harry Stockwell (Prince Charming), Lucille LaVerne (Queen), Moroni Olsen (Magic Mirror), Billy Gilbert (Sneezy), Pinto Colvig (Sleepy, Grumpy), Otis Harlan (Happy), Scotty Mattraw (Bashful), Roy Atwell (Doc), Stuart Buchanan (Huntsman).

Classic animated version of the fairy tale.

Note: The first feature-length cartoon,

employing larger animation cells and a multiplane camera process for the first time. Made for $1.5 million, it was released on December 21, 1937, and grossed over $8 million in its first run. Some of the sequences are frightening — in England, no one under 16 was admitted. Disney later stated that one of his first moviegoing experiences was to view a silent version of this fairy tale. The results here are a true milestone in animation, and in filmmaking. At the Oscars the following year, Disney was presented, by Shirley Temple, the special award of one regular size statuette and seven little ones.

Comment: "Who'd pay to see a drawing of a fairy princess when they can watch Joan Crawford's boobs for the same price?" — Louis B. Mayer.

Review: "The romantic leads are wishy-washy, but the comic and villainous characters turned the film into a worldwide box office bombshell" — Leslie Halliwell.

793 *So Dear to My Heart* (1948)

Musical. Running time: 82 minutes. Color.

Produced by Walt Disney and Perce Pearce. Directed by Harold Schuster and Hamilton Luske. Screenplay by John Tucker Battle, Maurice Rapf, and Ted Sears (based on the book *Midnight and Jerimiah* by Sterling North). Photographed by Winton Hoch. Edited by Thomas Scott and Lloyd Richardson.

Starring Burl Ives (Hiram), Beulah Bondi (Granny), Harry Carey, Jr. (Judge), Luana Patten (Tildy), Bobby Driscoll (Jerimiah).

The story of a boy and his love for a horse.

794 *So This Is Washington* (1943)

Comedy. Running time: 64 minutes. Black and white. Available on videocassette.

Produced by Ben Hersh. Directed by Ray McCarey. Screenplay by Leonard Praskins and Roswell Rogers. Photographed by Harry Wild. Edited by Duncan Mansfield.

Starring Chester Lauck (Lum), Norris Goff (Abner), Alan Mowbray (Mr. Marshall), Roger Clark (Robert Blevins), Mildred Coles (Jane), Sarah Padden (Aunt Charity), Minerva Urecal (Mrs. Pomeroy), Matt McHugh (Stranger), Barbara Pepper (Taxi Driver).

Lum and Abner invent a synthetic rubber which they plan to use to help the war effort.

795 *So Well Remembered* (1947)

Drama. Running time: 114 minutes. Black and white.

Produced by Adrian Scott. Directed by Edward Dmytryk. Screenplay by John Paxton (based on the novel by James Hilton). Photographed by Fredrick A. Young. Edited by Harry Gerstad.

Starring John Mills (Boswell), Martha Scott (Olivia), Patricia Roc (Julie), Trevor Howard (Whitesade), Richard Carlson (Charles), Reginald Tate (Mangin), Beatrice Verley (Annie), Juliet Mills (Baby Julie).

Episodic story of several people in a small Lancashire town on the eve of the victory in Europe of WW2.

Note: Scott, Dmytryk and composer Hans Eisler were suspicioned as possible communist sympathizers at the time, thus many right wingers found this film to be communist-inspired. It was based on a novel by the author of *Lost Horizon*.

796 *Soldier and the Lady* (1937)

Drama. Running time: 83 minutes. Black and white.

Produced by Pandro S. Berman. Directed by George Nicholls. Screenplay by Mortimer Offner, Anthony Veiller, Anne Morrison Chapin (based on the novel by Jules Verne). Photographed by Frederic Knudtson.

Starring Anton Walbrook (Strogoff), Elizabeth Allan (Nadia), Margot Grahame (Zangarra), Akim Tamiroff (Ogareff), Fay Bainter (Mother), Eric Blore (Blount), Ed Brophy (Packer).

A courier is entrusted to deliver a new military strategy to Siberian forces.

797 *Son of Kong* (1933) Adventure. Running time: 70 minutes. Black and white.

Produced by Archie Marshek. Directed by Ernest B. Schoedsack. Screenplay by Ruth Tose. Photographed by Edward Linden, Vernon Walker, J. Taylor. Music by Max Steiner. Edited by Ted Cheesman. Available on videocassette.

Starring Robert Armstrong (Carl), Helen Mack (Hilda), Frank Reicher (Englehorn), John Marston (Helstrom), Victor Wong (Cook), Ed Brady (Red), Lee Hohlmar (Mickey), Clarence Wilson (Peterson), Katherine Ward (Mrs. Hudson), Gertrude Short (Reporter), Noble Johnson (Chief), Steve Clemente (Witch King), Leo Hendrian (Dutch).

The promotions man responsible for King Kong is being sued for the damages done by the beast, so he sets off again to Skull Island and finds Kong's 25-foot-tall offspring.

Note: With the exception of the brontosaurus, all characters in *Son of Kong* were newly built for this film. Willis O'Brien reluctantly returned to do the work, balking at the humor element being the focal point of this sequel. The large hand from the first film was also reconstructed and fitted with white fur.

798 *Son of Sinbad* (1955) Adventure. Running time: 88 minutes. Color.

Produced by Robert Sparks. Directed by Ted Tetzlaff. Screenplay by Aubrey Wisberg and Jack Pollexfen. Photographed by William Snyder. Edited by Roland Gross and Frederic Knudtson. Available on videocassette.

Starring Dale Robertson (Sinbad), Sally Forrest (Ameer), Lilli St. Cyr (Nerissa), Vincent Price (Omar Khayam), Mari Blanchard (Kristina), Leon Askin (Khalif), Jay Novello (Jiddah), Raymond Grenleaf (Simon), Woody Strode (Guard).

Sinbad and his partner sail off to encounter adventure.

Review: "Sinbad just cavorts with the beauties in a story that has no plot, no anything really except for skin"—*The Motion Picture Guide.*

799 *Son of the Border* (1933) Western. Running time: 55 minutes. Black and white.

Produced by David Lewis. Directed by Lloyd Nosler. Screenplay by Wellyn Totman and Harold Shumate (based on a story by Totman). Photographed by Nicholas Musuraca. Edited by Frederic Knudtson.

Starring Tom Keene, Edgar Kennedy, Julie Haydon, Dave Durand, Creighton Chaney, Charles King, Al Bridge, Claudia Coleman.

A cowboy faces a gang of outlaws terrorizing stagecoach passengers.

800 *A Song Is Born* (1948) Musical comedy. Running time: 113 minutes. Color.

Produced by Samuel Goldwyn. Directed by Howard Hawks. Screenplay by Harry Tugend (based on a story by Thomas Monroe and Billy Wilder). Photographed by Gregg Toland. Edited by Daniel Mandell.

Starring Danny Kaye (Prof. Frisbee), Virginia Mayo (Honey Swanson), Benny Goodman (Magenbruch), Hugh Herbert (Twingle), Steve Cochran (Tony), J. Edward Bromberg (Elfini), Felix Bressart (Gerikhoff), Ludwig Stossel (Traumer), O.Z. Whitehead (Oddly), Esther Dale (Mrs. Bragg), Sidney Blackmer (Adams), Ben Welden (Monte), Lane Chandler (Policeman), Joe Devlin (Gangster), Tommy Dorsey and His Orchestra, Louis Armstrong and His Orchestra, Charlie Barnet and His Orchestra, Mel Powell and Orchestra, The Page Cavannaugh Trio, The Golden Gate Quartet, Buck and Bubbles (Themselves).

A group of professors get together to trace the history of music.

Note: Musical remake of *Ball of Fire*

Danny Kaye and Virginia Mayo in *A Song Is Born*.

with the same director, editor, cinematographer, and most of the same crew. Kaye's last film for RKO and for Goldwyn (who'd discovered him).

801 *Song of the South* (1946) Fantasy. Running time: 94 minutes. Color.

Produced by Walt Disney. Directed by Harve Foster and Wilfred Jackson. Screenplay by Dalton Raymond, Morton Grant, and Maurice Rapf (based on "Tales of Uncle Remus" by Joel Chandler Harris). Photographed by Gregg Toland. Edited by William Morgan.

Starring Ruth Warrick (Sally), James Baskett (Uncle Remus), Bobby Driscoll (Johnny), Luana Patten (Ginny), Lucile Watson (Grandmother), Hattie McDaniel (Aunt Tempy), Glenn Leedy (Toby), George Nokes and Gene Holland (The Favers Boys).

A young boy living on his grandmother's plantation is taught to use his imagination by a kindly plantation worker.

Note: James Baskett died shortly after the film's release. He was posthumously awarded an honorary Oscar for his performance.

802 *Sorority House* (1939) Drama. Running time: 64 minutes. Black and white.

Produced by Robert Sisk. Directed by John Farrow. Screenplay by Dalton Trumbo (based on the three-act comedy "Chi House" by Mary Coyle Chase). Photographed by Nicholas Musuraca. Edited by Harry Marker.

Starring Anne Shirley (Alice Fisher), James Ellison (Bill Loomis), Barbara Read (Dotty Spencer), Helen Wood (Mme. President), J.M. Kerrigan (Lew Fisher), Doris Jordan (Neva Simpson), June Storey (Norman Hancock), Elisabeth Risdon (Mme. Scott), Margaret Armstrong (Mrs. Dawson).

A working class girl lies about her status in order to be accepted into a top sorority.

Note: Look quickly for Veronica Lake in a bit role, billed as Constance Keane.

803 *The Spanish Main* (1945) Adventure. Running time: 100 minutes. Technicolor. Available on videocassette.
Produced by Stephen Ames. Directed by Frank Borzage. Screenplay by George Worthington Yates, Herman J. Mankiewicz. Photographed by George Barnes. Edited by Ralph Dawson.

Starring Paul Henried (Laurent Van Horn), Maureen O'Hara (Francisca), Walter Slezak (Don Alvarado), Binnie Barnes (Anne Bonney), John Emery (DuBillar), Barton MacLane (Capt. Black), J.M. Kerrigan (Pillery), Fritz Leiber (Bishop), Nancy Gates (Lupita), Jack LaRue (Escobar), Mike Mazurki (Swaine), Victor Kilian (Captain).

A pirate kidnaps a girl and tries to win her over.

804 *Special Investigator* (1936) Crime drama. Running time: 61 minutes. Black and white.
Produced by Cliff Reid. Directed by Louis King. Screenplay by Louis Stevens, Thomas Lennon, and Ferdinand Reyher (based on the novel by Erle Stanley Gardner). Photographed by Edward Cronjager. Edited by George Crone.

Starring Richard Dix (Bill Fenwick), Margaret Callahan (Virginia), Erik Rhodes (Denny), Owen Davis, Jr. (George), Ray Mayer (Dutchman), Joe Sawyer (Plummer), J. Carrol Naish (Selton), Sheila Terry (Judy), Jed Prouty (Dr. Reynolds).

An unethical attorney, who has made a fortune keeping crooks out of prison, finds that his brother, an FBI agent, is killed by the criminals he's been defending.

805 *The Spellbinder* (1939) Crime drama. Running time: 69 minutes. Black and white.
Produced by Cliff Reid. Directed by Jack Hively. Screenplay by Thomas Lennon and Joseph A. Fields. Photographed by Russell Metty. Edited by Theron Warth.

Starring Lee Tracy (Jed Marlowe), Barbara Read (Janet), Patric Knowles (Tom Dixon), Allan Lane (Steve Kendall), Linda Hayes (Miss Simpson), Morgan Conway (Carrington), Robert Emmett Keane (Judge Butler).

An attorney who frees guilty men finds his daughter is to marry one of his clients.

806 *The Spiral Staircase* (1946) Mystery. Running time: 83 minutes. Black and white.
Produced by Dore Schary. Directed by Robert Siodmak. Screenplay by Mel Dinelli (based on the novel *Some Must Watch* by Ethel Lina White). Photographed by Nicholas Musuraca. Edited by Harry Marker. A Vanguard production.

Starring Dorothy McGuire (Helen), George Brent (Warren), Ethel Barrymore (Mrs. Warren), Kent Smith (Dr. Parry), Rhonda Fleming (Blanche), Gordon Oliver (Steve Warren), Elsa Lanchester (Mrs. Oates), James Bell (Constable), Ellen Corby (Neighbor).

A young mute girl is servant to a bedridden widowed invalid in a spooky old mansion at the turn-of-the-century.

Note: The first in a planned series of co-productions between David O. Selznick's Vanguard films and RKO, bringing in a profit of more than one million dollars, split evenly between the two production companies. Remade in England in 1975.

807 *Spitfire* (1934) Drama. Running time: 88 minutes. Black and white.
Produced by Pandro S. Berman and John Cromwell. Directed by Jane Murfin and Lula Vollmer. Photographed by Edward Cronjager. Edited by William H. Morgan.

Starring Katharine Hepburn (Trigger), Robert Young (John Stafford), Ralph Bellamy (George Fleetwood),

Martha Sleeper (Eleanor Stafford), Louis Mason (Bill Grayson), Sara Haden (Etta Dawson), Virginia Howell (Granny), Sidney Toler (Mr. Sawyer), High Ghere (West Fry).

A backwoods girl believes she can heal through faith.

Note: Comedian Bob Burns went under the billing of High Ghere. Lead originally slated for Dorothy Jordan; Hepburn campaigned for the part "to extend her range" and won it. The film was a flop at the box office, one of many low grossing films for Hepburn. From here she went to New York and appeared in a play, which also flopped. Fortunately for us, she kept trying. Leslie Howard's *Spitfire,* made in England for Misbourne–British Aviation and was the actor's last film, is not a remake. Its original title is *The First of the Few.*

808 *Split Second* (1953) Drama. Running time: 85 minutes. Black and white.

Produced by Edmund Grainger. Directed by Dick Powell. Screenplay by William Bowers and Irving Wallace. Photographed by Nicholas Musuraca. Edited by Robert Ford. Available on videocassette.

Starring Stephen McNally (Sam Hurley), Alexis Smith (Kay Garven), Jan Sterling (Dottie), Keith Andes (Larry Fleming), Arthur Hunnicutt (Asa), Paul Kelly (Bart Moore), Robert Paige (Arthur Ashton), Richard Egan (Dr. Garven).

A gangleader holds a group of people hostage in a small Nevada town, soon discovering that the town is a government nuclear test site.

Note: Powell's directorial debut.

Splitface see *Dick Tracy*

809 *Sport Parade* (1932) Drama. Running time: 67 minutes. Black and white.

Produced by Dudley Murphy. Screenplay by Corey Ford, Tom Wenning, and Francis Cockrell, with additional dialogue by Robert Benchley. Photographed by J. Roy Hunt. Edited by Otto Ludwig.

Starring Joel McCrea (Sandy), William Gargan (Johnny), Marian Marsh (Irene), Walter Catlett (Morrison), Skeets Gallagher (Dizzy), Robert Benchley (Announcer), Clarence Wilson (Bit).

A college all-pro athlete becomes a professional wrestler.

Note: Lots of stock footage of sporting events, and made at a time when wrestling was, ostensibly, legitimate. That humorists Corey Ford and Robert Benchley are among the writers is curious, for this is a dramatic film. Benchley does some funny stuff as a radio announcer.

810 *Squadron Leader X* (1943) War drama. Running time: 99 minutes. Black and white.

Produced by Victor Hanbury. Directed by Lance Comfort. Screenplay by Wolfgang Wilhelm and Miles Malleson (based on the story *Four Days in a Hero's Life* by Emeric Pressburger). Photographed by Mutz Greenbaum. Edited by Michael C. Chorlton.

Starring Eric Portman, Ann Dvorak, Walter Fitzgerald, Martin Miller, Beatrice Varley, Henry Oscar, Barry Jones, Charles Victor, Mary Merrall, Carl Jaffe, Marjorie Rhodes, Frederick Richter, David Peel.

Two German soldiers attempt to infiltrate the RAF.

811 *Stage Door* (1937) Drama. Running time: 83 minutes. Black and white. Available on videocassette.

Produced by Pandro S. Berman. Directed by Gregory La Cava. Screenplay by Morrie Ryskind, Anthony Veiller (based on the play by Edna Ferber and George S. Kaufman). Photographed by Robert De Grasse. Edited by William Hamilton.

Starring Katharine Hepburn (Terry), Ginger Rogers (Joan), Adolphe Menjou (Anthony Powell), Gail Patrick (Linda), Constance Collier (Catherine), Andrea Leeds (Kaye Hamilton), Samuel S.

Hinds (Henry), Lucille Ball (Judy), Pierre Watkin (Richard Carmichael), Franklin Pangborn (Harcourt), Elizabeth Dunne (Mrs. Orcutt), Grady Sutton (Butcher), Jack Carson (Milbank), Eve Arden (Eve), Ann Miller (Annie), Jack Rice (Playwright).

The lives of girls in a theatrical boarding house.

Review: "Zest, pace, and photographic elegance" — Frank S. Nugent, *The New York Times.*

812 *Stage Struck* (1958) Drama. Running time: 95 minutes. Color.

Produced by Stuart Miller. Directed by Sidney Lumet. Screenplay by Ruth and Augustus Goetz (based on the play *Morning Glory* by Zoe Akins). Photographed by Frank Planer and Maurice (Morris) Hartzband. Edited by Stuart Gilmore.

Starring Henry Fonda (Lewis Easton), Susan Strasberg (Eva Lovelace), Joan Greenwood (Rita), Herbert Marshall (Hedges), Christopher Plummer (Joe), Daniel Ocko (Constantine), Pat Harrington (Benny), John Fiedler (Adrian), Frank Campanella (Jack), Jack Weston (Frank), Roger C. Carmel (Stagehand).

A small town girl is determined to make it on stage.

Note: Remake of *Morning Glory* (1932) (q.v.), which won Katharine Hepburn an Oscar. Strasberg is the daughter of the late Lee Strasberg of the actor's studio. Her mother was reportedly on the set almost always, inhibiting Susan's performance.

813 *Stage to Chino* (1940) Western. Running time: 59 minutes. Black and white.

Produced by Bert Gilroy. Directed by Edward Killy. Screenplay by Morton Grant, Arthur V. Jones (based on a story by Norton S. Parker). Photographed by J. Roy Hunt. Edited by Frederic Knudtson.

Starring George O'Brien, Virginia Vale, Hobart Cavanaugh, Roy Barcroft, William Haade, Carl Stockdale, Glenn Strange, Harry Cording, Martin Garralaga, Ethan Laidlaw, Tom London, Elmo Lincoln, Billy Franey, Bruce Mitchell, Pals of the Golden West.

Postal inspector works undercover to foil a plot to put his niece out of business.

814 *Stagecoach Kid* (1949) Western. Running time: 60 minutes. Black and white.

Produced by Herman Schlom. Directed by Lew Landers. Screenplay by Norman Houston. Photographed by Nicholas Musuraca. Edited by Les Millbrook.

Starring Tim Holt (Dave), Richard Martin (Chito), Jeff Donnell (Jessie), Joe Sawyer (Thatcher), Thurston Hall (Arnold), Carol Hughes (Birdie), Robert Bray (Clint), Robert B. Williams (Parnell), Kenneth MacDonald (Sheriff).

Stagecoach owners try to save a fellow's ranch when he finds many of his employees are crooks.

815 *Star of Midnight* (1935) Mystery. Running time: 90 minutes. Black and white. Available on videocassette.

Produced by Pandro S. Berman. Directed by Stephen Roberts. Screenplay by Howard J. Green, Anthony Veiller, and Ed Kaufman. Photographed by J. Roy Hunt. Edited by Arthur Roberts.

Starring William Powell (Clay), Ginger Rogers (Donna), Paul Kelly (Kinland), Gene Lockhart (Swayne), Ralph Morgan (Roger), Leslie Fenton (Winthrop), J. Farrell MacDonald (Inspector), Russell Hopton (Tommy), Vivian Oakland (Gerry).

A man must clear himself as a suspect when a stage star is murdered.

816 *Station West* (1948) Western. Running time: 92 minutes. Black and white.

Produced by Robert Sparks. Directed by Sidney Lanfield. Screenplay by Frank Fenton and Winston Miller. Photographed by Harry J. Wild. Edited by Frederic Knudtson.

William Powell in *Star of Midnight.*

Starring Dick Powell (Haven), Jane Greer (Charlie), Agnes Moorehead (Mrs. Carlson), Burl Ives (Hotel Clerk), Tom Powers (Capt. Iles), Gordon Oliver (Prince), Steve Brodie (Stallman), Guinn "Big Boy" Williams (Mick), Raymond Burr (Mark Bristow), Regis Toomey (Goddard), Olin Howland (Cook).

In an attempt to locate the gang who murdered two soldiers, a man falls in love with the woman behind the crime.

817 *Step by Step* (1946) Drama. Running time: 62 minutes. Black and white.

Produced by Sid Rogell. Directed by Phil Rosen. Screenplay by Stuart Palmer (based on the story by George Callahan). Photographed by Frank Redman. Edited by Robert Swink.

Starring Lawrence Tierney (Johnny Christopher), Anne Jeffreys (Evelyn Smith), Lowell Gilmore (Van Dorn), George Cleveland (Simpson), Jason Robards, Sr. (Bruckner), Myrna Dell (Gretchen), Harry Harvey (Remmy).

An ex–Marine and a government secretary are wanted for the murder of a federal agent, and are also pursued by Nazis who want the dead man's secret documents.

818 *Step Lively* (1944) Musical. Running time: 88 minutes. Black and white. Produced by Robert Fellows. Directed by Tim Whelan. Screenplay by Warren Duff and Peter Milne (based on the play *Room Service* by John Murray and Allen Boretz). Photographed by Robert De Grasse. Edited by Gene Milford. Music by Sammy Cahn and Jule Styne.

Songs: "Some Other Time," "As Long as There's Music," "Where Does Love Begin," "Come Out Come Out Wherever You Are," "Why Must There Be an Opening Song," "And Then You Kissed Me," and "Ask the Madame."

Starring Frank Sinatra (Glen), George Murphy (Miller), Adolphe Menjou (Wagner), Gloria DeHaven (Christine), Walter Slezak (Gribble), Eugene Pallette (Jenkins), Wally Brown (Binion), Alan Carney (Harry), Grant Mitchell (Dr. Glass), Anne Jeffreys (Miss Abbott), Frances King (Mother), Harry Noble (Father), George Chandler (Bit).

A playwright from upstate New York falls victim to a fast-talking producer who owes everybody money.

Note: Remake of the 1938 Marx Brothers feature *Room Service* (q.v.).

819 *Stingaree* (1934) Musical. Running time: 76 minutes. Black and white. Produced by Pandro S. Berman. Directed by William Wellman. Screenplay by Becky Gardiner, Lynn Riggs, and Leonard Spigelgass. Photographed by James Van Trees. Edited by James Morley.

Starring Irene Dunne (Hilda), Richard Dix (Stingaree), Mary Boland (Mrs. Clarkson), Conway Tearle (Kent), Andy Devine (Howie), Henry Stephenson (Mr. Clarkson), Una O'Connor (Annie).

A thief falls for an Australian opera singer.

Note: The story was originally filmed as a 12-part serial for Kalem known as *The Adventures of Stingaree.*

820 *Storm Over Wyoming* (1950) Western. Running time: 60 minutes. Black and white. Available on videocassette.

Produced by Herman Schlom. Directed by Lesley Selander. Screenplay by Ed Earl Repp. Photographed by J. Roy Hunt. Edited by Robert Swink.

Starring Tim Holt (Dave), Noreen Nash (Chris), Richard Powers (Tug), Betty Underwood (Ruby), Kenneth MacDonald (Dawson), Holly Bane (Scott), Don Haggerty (Marshal), Richard Martin (Chito Rafferty).

Two law-abiding drifters get involved in a feud between cattlemen and sheep herders. Actor Powers is Tom Keene.

821 *The Story of Robin Hood* (1952) Adventure. Running time: 84 minutes. Color.

Produced by Perce Pearce. Directed by Ken Annakin. Screenplay by Lawrence E. Watkin. Photographed by Guy Green. Edited by Gordon Pilkington.

Starring Richard Todd (Robin Hood), Joan Rice (Maid Marian), Peter Finch (Sheriff of Nottingham), James Hayter (Friar Tuck), James Robertson Justice (Little John), Martita Hunt (Queen Eleanor), Hubert Gregg (Prince John), Bill Owen (Stutley), Reginald Tate (Fitzooth).

Story of the adventurer who robbed from the rich and gave to the poor.

822 *The Story of Vernon and Irene Castle* (1939) Musical biography. Running time: 90 minutes. Black and white. Available on videocassette.

Produced by George Haight. Directed by H.C. Potter. Screenplay by Richard Sherman, Oscar Hammerstein, Dorothy Yost (based on books by Irene Castle). Photographed by Robert De Grasse. Edited by William Hamilton.

Starring Fred Astaire (Vernon Castle), Ginger Rogers (Irene Castle), Edna May Oliver (Maggie Sutton), Walter Brennan (Walter), Lew Fields (Himself), Etienne Girardot (Papa Aubel), Janet Beecher (Mrs. Foote), Rolfe Sedan (Emile),

Leonid Kinsky (Artist), Robert Strange (Dr. Foote).

Biography of the famed dance team of the early 20th century.

Note: Astaire had seen the Castles dance when he was a lad of 14, and found the opportunity to work in this film with Irene Castle to be quite an honor.

823 *Strange Bargain* (1949) Crime drama. Running time: 68 minutes. Black and white.

Produced by Sid Rogell. Directed by Will Price. Screenplay by Lillie Hayward (based on a story by J.H. Wallis). Photographed by Harry Wild. Edited by Frederic Knudtson.

Starring Martha Scott (Georgia Wilson), Jeffrey Lynn (Sam Wilson), Harry Morgan (Webb), Katherine Emery (Edna Jarvis), Richard Gaines (Malcolm Jarvis), Henry O'Neill (Timothy Herne), Walter Sande (Sgt. Cord), Robert Bray (McTay).

A business owner plans suicide because of his failure, getting a troubled bookkeeper to help him dispose of the weapon.

824 *Strange Justice* (1932) Crime drama. Running time: 72 minutes. Black and white.

Produced by J.G. Bachmann. Directed by Victor Schertzinger. Screenplay by William Drake. Photographed by Merritt Gerstad.

Starring Marian Marsh, Reginald Denny, Richard Bennett, Norman Foster, Irving Pichel, Thomas Jackson, Nydia Westman, Larry Steers.

Two bankers fake a murder, sending an innocent man to prison.

825 *The Stranger* (1946) Drama. Running time: 95 minutes. Black and white. Available on videocassette.

Produced by S.P. Eagle. Directed by Orson Welles. Screenplay by Anthony Veiller, John Huston, Welles. Photographed by Russell Metty. Edited by Ernest Nims.

Starring Edward G. Robinson (Wil-

son), Loretta Young (Mary), Orson Welles (Rankin, Kindler), Phillip Merivale (Judge), Richard Long (Noah), Byron Keith (Lawrence), Billy House (Potter).

A Nazi criminal settles in America when he marries a girl unaware of his past.

Review: "Some striking effects with lighting and interesting angles much relied on" — Bosley Crowther, *The New York Times.*

826 *Stranger on the Third Floor* (1940) Mystery. Running time: 64 minutes. Black and white.

Produced by Lee Marcus. Directed by Boris Ingster. Screenplay by Frank Partos. Photographed by Nicholas Musuraca. Edited by Harry Marker.

Starring Peter Lorre (Stranger), John McGuire (Michael Ward), Margaret Tallichet (Jane), Charles Waldron (District Attorney), Elisha Cook, Jr. (Joe Briggs), Charles Halton (Meg), Ethel Griffies (Mrs. Kane), Cliff Clark (Martin), Oscar O'Shea (Judge), Alec Craig (Defense Attorney), Otto Hoffman (Police Surgeon), Charles Judels (Nick), Frank Yaconelli (Jack), Paul McVey (Lt. Jones).

A newspaper reporter's testimony helps convict an innocent man.

Note: Considered the first film noir. Directorial debut of Ingster, a screenwriter who owed a great deal to German Expressionism filmmaking in the style of Lang or Murnau.

827 *Strangers All* (1935) Drama. Running time: 70 minutes. Black and white.

Produced by Cliff Reid. Directed by Charles Vidor. Screenplay by Milton Krims. Photographed by John Boyle. Edited by Jack Hively.

Starring May Robson (Mom Carter), Preston Foster (Murray), Florine McKinney (Lily), William Bakewell (Dick Carter), James Bush (Lewis Carter), Samuel S. Hinds (Mr. Green), Clifford Jones (Pat Gruen), Suzanne Kaaren (Frances Farrell).

A mother tries to make her three sons and one daughter more than strangers to each other.

828 *Street Girl* (1929) Musical. Running time: 91 minutes. Black and white.

Produced by William LeBaron. Directed by Wesley Ruggles. Screenplay by Jane Murfin. Photographed by Leo Tover. Music by Oscar Levant and Sidney Claire.

Songs: "My Dream Melody," "Broken Up Tune," "Huggable and Sweet."

Starring Betty Compson (Freddie), John Harron (Mike), Ned Sparks (Happy), Jack Oakie (Joe), Guy Buccola (Pete), Joseph Cawthorn (Keppel).

A street girl becomes the business manager for a jazz combo.

Note: Remade as *That Girl from Paris* and *Four Jacks and a Jill.*

829 *Strictly Dynamite* (1934) Comedy. Running time: 71 minutes. Black and white.

Produced by Pandro S. Berman. Directed by Elliott Nugent. Screenplay by Maurine Watkins, Milton Raison, Jack Harvey, and Ralph Spence (based on the play by Robert T. Colwell and Robert A. Simon). Photographed by Edward Cronjager. Edited by George Crone.

Starring Jimmy Durante (Maxie), Lupe Velez (Vera), Norman Foster (Nick), William Gargan (Georgie), Marian Nixon (Sylvia), Eugene Pallette (Sam), Minna Gombell (Miss LeSeur), Sterling Holloway (Fleming), Stanley Fields and Tom Kennedy (Bodyguards), The Mills Brothers.

A radio comedian runs out of jokes and hires a comedy writer.

830 *Stromboli* (1950) Drama. Running time: 81 minutes. Black and white. Available on videocassette.

Produced and directed by Roberto Rossellini. Screenplay by Rossellini, Art Cohn, Renzo Cesana, Sergio Amedi, C.P. Callagari. Photographed by Otello Martelli. Edited by Roland Gross and Jolanda Bevenuti.

Starring Ingrid Bergman (Karin), Mario Vitale (Antonio), Renzo Cesana (Priest), Mario Sponza (Lighthouse Keeper).

A Czech woman marries an Italian soldier to escape the terrors of the displaced person's camp.

Note: Bergman and Rossellini had an affair while working on this film, producing a child out of wedlock. This was news across the world, as Bergman was married at the time. Women's groups boycotted the picture, and it took some time for Bergman's career to recover. Times have since changed.

831 *Success at Any Price* (1934) Drama. Running time: 75 minutes. Black and white.

Produced by J. Walter Ruben. Screenplay by John Howard Lawson and Howard J. Green. Photographed by Henry Gerard. Edited by George Hively.

Starring Douglas Fairbanks, Jr. (Joe), Genevieve Tobin (Agnes), Frank Morgan (Raymond Merritt), Colleen Moore (Sarah), Edward Everett Horton (Fisher), Allen Vincent (Jeffrey Hallibuton), Nydia Westman (Dinah), Henry Kolker (Hadfield), Spencer Charters (Crawford).

The rise and fall of an unscrupulous capitalist.

832 *Sudden Fear* (1952) Suspense. Running time: 110 minutes. Black and white.

Produced by Joseph Kaufman. Directed by David Miller. Screenplay by Lenore Coffee, Robert Smith. Photographed by Charles Lang, Jr. Edited by Leon Barsha. Music by Elmer Bernstein.

Starring Joan Crawford (Myra), Jack Palance (Lester), Gloria Grahame (Irene), Bruce Bennett (Steve Kearney), Virginia Huston (Ann Taylor), Mike Connors (Junior).

A woman discovers her husband is planning to kill her.

833 *Sued for Libel* (1940) Mystery. Running time: 66 minutes. Black and white.

Produced by Cliff Reid. Directed by Leslie Goodwins. Screenplay by Jerry Cady. Photographed by Jack MacKenzie. Edited by Desmond Marquette.

Starring Kent Taylor (Steve), Linda Hayes (Maggie), Lillian Bond (Muriel), Morgan Conway (Pomeroy), Richard Lane (Smiley), Roger Pryor (Corbin), Thurston Hall (Hastings).

A radio station is sued for libel when an announcer accuses a man of murder.

834 *Suicide Fleet* (1931) Drama. Running time: 84 minutes. Black and white.

Produced by Charles R. Rogers. Directed by Albert Rogell. Screenplay by Lew Lipton and F. McGrew Willis. Photographed by Sol Polito. Edited by Joe Kane.

Starring Bill Boyd (Baltimore Clark), Robert Armstrong (Dutch), James Gleason (Skeets), Ginger Rogers (Sally), Harry Bannister (Commander), Frank Reicher (Capt. Holtzman), Henry Victor (Capt. Von Stuben), Ben Alexander (Kid), Hans Joby (Schwartz).

Three Navy shipmates fight over the same girl.

835 *Sundown Trail* (1931) Western. Running time: 56 minutes. Black and white.

Produced by Fred Allen. Written and directed by Robert Hill. Photographed by Ted McCord.

Starring Tom Keene, Marion Shilling, Nick Stuart, Hooper Atchley, Louise Beavers, Stanley Blystone, Alma Chester, William Welsh, Murdock MacQuarrie.

A ranch foreman co-inherits the property on which he works, along with a lady from the East who despises the West.

Note: Keene's first of eleven RKO westerns.

836 *Sunny* (1941) Musical. Running time: 98 minutes. Black and white.

Produced and directed by Herbert Wilcox. Screenplay by Sig Herzig. Photographed by Russell Metty. Edited by Elmo Williams. Music by Jerome Kern.

Starring Anna Neagle (Sunny), Ray Bolger (Bunny), John Carroll (Larry), Edward Everett Horton (Henry Bates), Grace Hartman (Juliet), Paul Hartman (Egghead), Frieda Inescort (Elizabeth).

A circus girl falls in love with an automobile magnate.

Note: Remake of a 1930 First National feature.

837 *Sunset Pass* (1946) Western. Running time: 58 minutes. Black and white.

Produced by Herman Schlom. Directed by William Berke. Screenplay by Norman Houston (based on the novel by Zane Grey). Photographed by Frank Redman. Edited by Samuel E. Beetley.

Starring James Warren, Nan Leslie, John Laurenz, Jane Greer, Robert Barrat, Harry Woods, Robert Clarke, Steve Brodie, Harry Harvey, Slim Balch, Roy Bucko, Steve Stevens, George Plues, Clem Fuller, Bob Dyer, Artie Ortego, Buck Bucko, Slim Hightower, Boyd Stockman, Frank O'Connor, Florence Pepper, Robert Bray, Marcia Dodd.

A lawman tracks train robbers working the Arizona border.

Note: Third film version of the novel, the first being a silent with Jack Holt, the second a 1933 Paramount feature starring Randolph Scott.

838 *Super Sleuth* (1937) Comedy. Running time: 75 minutes. Black and white.

Produced by Edward Small. Directed by Ben Stoloff. Screenplay by Gertrude Purcell and Ernest Pagano. Photographed by Joseph H. August. Edited by William Hamilton.

Starring Jack Oakie (Bill), Ann Sothern (Mary), Eduardo Ciannelli (Horman), Alan Bruce (Larry), Edgar Kennedy (Garrison), Joan Woodbury (Doris

Dunne), Bradley Page (Ralph Waring), Paul Guilfoyle (Gibbons), Willie Best (Warts), Richard Lane (Barker).

A movie detective takes his persona so seriously he tries to solve real-life crimes.

Note: Remade as *Genius at Work* (q.v.).

839 *Susan Slept Here* (1954) Comedy. Running time: 98 minutes. Color.

Produced by Harriet Parsons. Directed by Frank Tashlin. Screenplay by Alex Gottlieb. Photographed by Nicholas Musuraca. Edited by Harry Marker. Music by Jack Lawrence and Richard Myers.

Starring Dick Powell (Mark), Debbie Reynolds (Susan), Anne Francis (Isabella), Alvy Moore (Virgil), Glenda Farrell (Maude), Horace MacMahon (Maizel), Herb Vigran (Hanlon), Les Tremayne (Lawyer).

A writer befriends a teenage girl to assist on his screenplay about juvenile delinquency.

Review: "...a surprisingly bad outing..." — *The Motion Picture Guide.*

840 *Suspicion* (1941) Suspense. Running time: 99 minutes. Black and white. Available on videocassette.

Produced and directed by Alfred Hitchcock. Screenplay by Samson Raphaelson, Joan Harrison, Alma Reville. Photographed by Harry Stradling. Edited by William Hamilton.

Starring Cary Grant (Johnnie), Joan Fontaine (Lina), Sir Cedric Hardwicke (McLaidlaw), Nigel Bruce (Beakey), Dame May Whitty (Mrs. McLaidlaw), Isabel Jeans (Mrs. Newsham), Heather Angel (Ethel), Auriol Lee (Isobel), Reginald Sheffield (Reggie), Leo G. Carroll (Melbeck), Clyde Cook (Photographer).

A woman believes her husband is plotting to murder her.

841 *Sweepings* (1933) Drama. Running time: 80 minutes. Black and white.

Produced by Pandro S. Berman. Directed by John Cromwell. Screenplay by Lester Cohen, Howard Estabrook, H.W. Hannemann (based on the novel by Cohen). Photographed by Edward Cronjager. Edited by George Nicholls. Music by Max Steiner.

Starring Lionel Barrymore (Daniel Pardway), Alan Dinehart (Thane Pardway), Eric Linden (Fred Pardway), William Gargan (Gene Pardway), Gloria Stuart (Phoebe Pardway), Gregory Ratoff (Abe Ullman), Lucien Littlefield (Grimson), Ninetta Sunderland (Abigail Pardway), Helen Mack (Maimie Donahue), Ivan Lebedeff (Prince Niko).

A department store owner finds his children are not worthy of inheriting his business.

Note: Remade as *Three Sons.*

842 *Sweepstakes* (1931) Comedy. Running time: 75 minutes. Black and white.

Produced by Charles Rogers. Directed by Albert Rogell. Screenplay by Lew Lipton, Ralph Murray (based on a story by Lipton). Photographed by Ed Snyder. Edited by Joe Kane.

Starring Eddie Quillan (Bud), James Gleason (Sleepy), Marian Nixon (Babe), Lew Cody (Wally), Paul Hurst (Bartender), Frederick Burton (Pop), King Baggott (Trainer), Billy Sullivan (Speed), Lillian Leighton (Ma), Mike Donlin (Dude), Thomas Jackson (Cop).

A jockey becomes a singer when he is barred from racing.

843 *Swing High* (1930) Drama. Running time: 95 minutes. Black and white.

Produced by E.B. Derr. Directed by Joseph Santley. Screenplay by Santley and James Seymour. Photographed by Dave Abel. Edited by Daniel Mandell.

Starring Helen Twelvetrees, Fred Scott, Dorothy Burgess, John Sheehan, Daphne Pollard, George Fawcett, Bryant Washburn, Billy Curtis, Ben Turpin, Chester Conklin.

A circus aerialist becomes involved in a sordid love triangle.

LOVE
IS GRAND BUT IN
SUPERSCOPE
ITS
SENSATIONAL!

TECHNICOLOR

SUSAN
SLEPT
HERE

RKO
RADIO

Dick POWELL
Debbie
REYNOLDS

Publicity poster for *Susan Slept Here.*

844 Swing Time (1936) Musical. Running time: 105 minutes. Black and white. Available on videocassette.

Produced by Pandro S. Berman. Directed by George Stevens. Screenplay by Howard Lindsay and Allan Scott. Photographed by David Abel. Edited by Henry Berman. Music by Jerome Kern.

Starring Fred Astaire (Lucky), Ginger Rogers (Penny), Victor Moore (Pop), Helen Broderick (Mabel), Eric Blore (Gordon), Betty Furness (Margaret Watson), George Metaxa (Ricardo Romero), Landers Stevens (Judge Watson), John Harrington (Dice Raymond), Pierre Watkin (Al Simpson), Abe Reynolds (Schmidt).

A dance team runs into problems when the girl falls for the guy, while he has a girl back home.

Oscar: Song, "The Way You Look Tonight."

845 Swiss Family Robinson (1940) Adventure. Running time: 92 minutes. Black and white.

Produced by Gene Towne and Graham Baker. Directed by Edward Ludwig. Screenplay by Walter Ferris and Towne Baker (based on the novel by Johann David Wyss).

Starring Thomas Mitchell (William Robinson), Edna Best (Elizabeth Robinson), Freddie Bartholomew (Jack Robinson), Terry Kilburn (Ernest Robinson), Tim Holt (Fritz Robinson), Bobby Quillan (Francis Robinson), Christian Rub (Thoren).

A London family are shipwrecked on their way to Australia.

Note: A big loser at the box office, although the Disney version twenty years later was quite a hit. Filmed before as a serial in 1925.

846 Sword and the Rose (1953) Adventure. Running time: 91 minutes. Color.

Produced by Perce Pearce. Directed by Ken Annakin. Screenplay by Lawrence Watkin. Photographed by Geoffrey Unsworth. Edited by Gerald Thomas.

Starring Richard Todd (Brandon), Glynis Johns (Princess), James Robertson Justice (King Henry VIII), Michael Gough (Duke of Buckingham), Jane Barrett (Lady Margaret), Peter Copely (Sir Edwin), Rosalie Crutchley (Queen Catherine).

The love life of Mary Tudor.

Ginger Rogers and Fred Astaire in *Swing Time*.

847 *Sword of Venus* (1953) Adventure. Running time: 73 minutes. Black and white.

Produced by Aubrey Wisberg and Jack Pollexfen. Directed by Harold Daniels. Screenplay by Wisberg and Pollexfen. Photographed by John Russell. Edited by W. Donn Hayes.

Starring Robert Clarke (Dantes), Catherine McLeod (Claire), Dan O'Herlihy (Danglars), William Schallert (Valmont), Stuart Randall (Hugo).

An unscrupulous man tries to obtain wealth from the son of the Count of Monte Cristo.

848 *Sylvia Scarlett* (1936) Drama. Running time: 97 minutes. Black and white. Available on videocassette.

Produced by Pandro S. Berman. Directed by George Cukor. Screenplay by Gladys Unger, John Collier, and Mortimer Offner. Photographed by Joseph August. Edited by Jane Loring.

Starring Katharine Hepburn (Sylvia), Cary Grant (Jimmy), Brian Aherne (Michael), Edmund Gwenn (Henry), Natalie Paley (Lily), Dennis Moore (Maudie Tilt), Lennox Pawle (Drunk).

A girl masquerades as a boy and escapes to France with her father.

Note: A big box office flop, it has a cult following today.

849 *Symphony of Six Million* (1932) Drama. Running time: 85 minutes. Black and white.

Produced by Pandro S. Berman. Directed by Gregory La Cava. Screenplay by Bernard Schubert, J. Walter Ruben, James Seymour (based on the novel by Fannie Hurst). Photographed by Leo Tover. Edited by Archie Marshek. Music by Max Steiner.

Starring Ricardo Cortez (Felix Kaluber), Irene Dunne (Jessica), Anna Appel (Hannah), Gregory Ratoff (Meyer), Lita Chevret (Birdie), Noel Madison (Magnus), Helen Freeman (Miss Spencer), Julie Haydon (Nurse), Oscar Apfel (Doctor).

A surgeon moves from the ghetto where he is happy, to Manhattan where he works on eccentric rich folks, but for much more money. When he must operate on his father, and the operation is not successful, he leaves the medical profession.

Note: Ratoff's first film, and Steiner's first complete score.

850 *Syncopation* (1929) Musical. Running time: 83 minutes. Black and white.

Produced by Robert Kane. Directed by Bert Glennon. Screenplay by Frances Agnew and Paul Haschke. Photographed by Dal Clawson, George Weber, and Frank Landi. Edited by Edward Pfizenmeier.

Starring Barbara Bennett (Flo), Bobby Watson (Benny), Morton Downey (Lew), Ian Hunter (Winston), Dorothy Lee (Peggy), Osgood Perkins (Hummel), Verree Teasdale (Rita), Fred Waring (Himself).

The rocky romance of two vaudeville partners.

Note: Bennett, sister of Joan and Constance, was married to Downey and the mother of Morton, Jr.

851 *Syncopation* (1942) Musical. Running time: 88 minutes. Black and white.

Produced and directed by William Dieterle. Screenplay by Phillip Yordan and Frank Cavett. Photographed by J. Roy Hunt. Edited by John Sturges.

Starring Adolphe Menjou (Latimer), Jackie Cooper (Johnnie), Bonita Granville (Kit), George Bancroft (Mr. Porter), Ted North (Paul Porter), Todd Duncan (Rex Tearborne), Connee Boswell (Singer), Gene Krupa, Benny Goodman, Harry James, Charlie Barnett (Themselves).

A girl and a boy who adore music soon fall in love.

Note: Not a remake of the 1929 film.

852 *Tall in the Saddle* (1944) Western. Running time: 87 minutes. Black and white and colorized. Available on videocassette.

Produced by Robert Fellows. Directed by Edwin L. Marin. Screenplay by Michael Hogan and Paul Fix. Photographed by Robert De Grasse. Edited by Phillip Martin.

Starring John Wayne (Rocklin), Ella Raines (Arly), Audrey Long (Clara), George Gabby Hayes (Dave), Elisabeth Risdon (Miss Martin), Ward Bond (Judge), Don Douglas (Harolday), Russell Wade (Clint), Frank Puglia (Juan), Paul Fix (Bob), Harry Woods (George), Emory Parnell (Sheriff), Cy Kendall (Bartender), Bob MacKenzie (Doc), Raymond Hatton (Zeke).

A ranch hand who is too macho for women has two ladies out to get him.

853 *Tanned Legs* (1929) Musical. Running time: 68 minutes. Black and white.

Produced by Louis Sarecky. Directed by Marshall Neilan. Screenplay by Tom Geraghty. Photographed by George Hull and Leo Tover. Edited by Archie Marshek.

Starring June Clyde (Peggy), Arthur Lake (Bill), Sally Blaine (Janet), Allen

John Wayne in *Tall in the Saddle*.

Kearns (Roger), Albert Grant (Mr. Reynolds), Edmund Burns (Clinton Darrow), Dorothy Reiver (Mrs. Lyons King), Ann Pennington (Tootsie), Lloyd "Ham" Hamilton (Detective).

A husband and wife try to stay young by romancing younger partners.

Note: Actress Blaine is Loretta Young's real-life sister.

854 *Target* (1952) Western. Running time: 60 minutes. Black and white.

Produced by Herman Schlom. Directed by Stuart Gilmore. Screenplay by Norman Houston. Photographed by J. Roy Hunt. Edited by George Schrader.

Starring Tim Holt (Tim), Linda Douglas (Marshal Terry), Walter Reed (Controy), Harry Harvey (Carson), John

Hamilton (Bailey), Lane Bradford (Garrett), Riley Hill (Foster), Mike Ragan (Higgins), Richard Martin (Chito).

A lady marshal taking over for her deceased father is assisted by two cowhands.

855 *Tarnished Angel* (1938) Drama. Running time: 67 minutes. Black and white.

Produced by B.P. Fineman. Directed by Leslie Goodwins. Screenplay by Jo Pagano. Photographed by Nicholas Musuraca. Edited by Desmond Marquette.

Starring Sally Eilers (Connie), Lee Bowman (Paul), Ann Miller (Violet), Alma Kruger (Mrs. Stockton), Paul Guilfoyle (Eddie), Jonathan Hale (Detective Cramer).

A phony evangelist actually does find religion.

856 *Tarzan and the Amazons* (1945) Adventure. Running time: 76 minutes. Black and white.

Produced by Sol Lesser. Directed by Kurt Neumann. Screenplay by Hans Jacoby and Marjorie Pfaelzer (based on characters created by Edgar Rice Burroughs). Photographed by Archie Stout. Edited by Robert Crandall.

Starring Johnny Weissmuller (Tarzan), Brenda Joyce (Jane), Johnny Sheffield (Boy), Henry Stephenson (Henderson), Maria Ouspenskaya (Amazon Queen), Barton MacLane (Ballister).

Tarzan protects wealthy Amazon women from greedy archaeologists.

Note: Joyce's first fling as Jane.

857 *Tarzan and the Huntress* (1947) Adventure. Running time: 72 minutes. Black and white.

Produced by Sol Lesser. Directed by Kurt Neumann. Screenplay by Jerry Gruskin and Rowland Leigh (based on characters created by Edgar Rice Burroughs). Photographed by Archie Stout. Edited by Merrill White.

Starring Johnny Weissmuller (Tarzan), Brenda Joyce (Jane), Johnny Sheffield (Boy), Patricia Morrison (Tanya), Barton MacLane (Weir), John Warburton (Marley), Wallace Scott (Smithers).

Tarzan fights a zoo expedition coming to trap animals from the jungle.

Note: Sheffield left the series after this one to become Bomba at Monogram studios.

858 *Tarzan and the Leopard Woman* (1946) Adventure. Running time: 72 minutes. Black and white.

Produced by Sol Lesser. Directed by Kurt Neumann. Screenplay by Carroll Young (based on characters created by Edgar Rice Burroughs). Photographed by Karl Struss. Edited by Robert Crandall.

Starring Johnny Weissmuller (Tarzan), Brenda Joyce (Jane), Johnny Sheffield (Boy), Acquanetta (Lea), Edgar Barrier (Lazar), Tommy Cook (Kimba), Dennis Hoey (Commissioner), Anthony Caruso (Mongo), George J. Lewis (Corporal).

Tarzan battles a secret cult who kill people with iron claws.

859 *Tarzan and the Mermaids* (1948) Adventure. Running time: 68 minutes. Black and white.

Produced by Sol Lesser. Directed by Robert Florey. Screenplay by Carroll Young (based on characters created by Edgar Rice Burroughs). Photographed by Jack Draper. Edited by Merrill White.

Starring Johnny Weissmuller (Tarzan), Brenda Joyce (Jane), Linda Christian (Mara), John Lanenz (Benji), Fernando Wagner (Varga), George Zucco (Palanth).

Tarzan helps a woman tribe overthrow their evil male leader.

Note: Weissmuller's final appearance as Tarzan (after 16 years). He put on some clothes and went to Monogram for the Jungle Jim series.

860 *Tarzan and the She-Devil*
(1953) Adventure. Running time: 74
minutes. Black and white.

Produced by Sol Lesser. Directed by
Kurt Neumann. Screenplay by Karl
Lamb and Carroll Young (based on characters created by Edgar Rice Burroughs).
Photographed by Russell Harlan. Edited
by Christian Nyby.

Starring Lex Barker (Tarzan), Vanessa
Brown (Jane), Robert Alda (Neil), Hurd
Hatfield (Prince), Arthur Shields (Randini), Robert Warwick (High Priest),
Anthony Caruso (Sengo).

A lion-worshipping tribe captures
Jane when they are overcome by a mysterious plague.

Note: Brown's first appearance as Jane.

861 *Tarzan Triumphs* (1943) Adventure. Running time: 78 minutes.
Black and white.

Produced by Sol Lesser. Directed by
William Thiele. Screenplay by Carroll
Young and Roy Chanslor (based on characters created by Edgar Rice Burroughs).
Photographed by Harry Wild. Edited by
Hal Kern.

Starring Johnny Weissmuller (Tarzan), Johnny Sheffield (Boy), Frances
Gifford (Zandra), Stanley Ridges (Col.
von Reichart), Sig Rumann (Sergeant),
Pedro de Cordoba (Patriarch), Phillip
Van Zandt (Bausch).

Nazi paratroopers descend upon the
jungles.

862 *Tarzan's Desert Mystery*
(1943) Adventure. Running time: 70
minutes. Black and white.

Produced by Sol Lesser. Directed by
William Thiele. Screenplay by Edward
T. Lowe (based on characters created by
Edgar Rice Burroughs). Photographed
by Harry Wild. Edited by Ray Lockert.

Starring Johnny Weissmuller (Tarzan), Johnny Sheffield (Boy), Nancy
Kelly (Connie), Otto Kruger (Hendrix),
Joe Sawyer (Karl), Robert Lowery
(Prince), Lloyd Corrigan (Sheik).

Tarzan is again mixed up with Nazis as
well as an American showgirl and a giant
spider.

863 *Tarzan's Hidden Jungle*
(1955) Adventure. Running time: 73
minutes. Black and white.

Produced by Sol Lesser. Directed by
Harold Schuster. Screenplay by William
Lively (based on characters by Edgar Rice
Burroughs). Photographed by William
Whitley. Edited by Leon Barsha.

Starring Gordon Scott (Tarzan), Vera
Miles (Jill), Peter Van Eyck (Celliers),
Don Beddoe (Johnson), Jester Hairston
(Witch Doctor), Rex Ingram (Sukulu),
Jack Elam (Burger).

Tarzan battles hunters after skins and
ivory.

Note: Scott's first appearance as Tarzan; RKO's last Tarzan production. The
series returned to MGM.

864 *Tarzan's Magic Fountain*
(1949) Adventure. Running time: 73
minutes. Black and white.

Produced by Sol Lesser. Directed by
Lee Sholem. Screenplay by Curt Siodmak and Harry Chandlee (based on characters created by Edgar Rice Burroughs).
Photographed by Karl Struss. Edited by
Merrill White.

Starring Lex Barker (Tarzan), Brenda
Joyce (Jane), Evelyn Ankers (Gloria
James), Albert Dekker (Trask), Charles
Drake (Dodd), Alan Napier (Jessup),
Henry Kulky (Vredak), Henry Brandon
(Seka).

An aviatrix crashes in the jungle,
discovers a fountain of youth, and remains young for twenty years. When she
is rescued by Tarzan and returned to
civilization, her age catches up with her.

Note: Barker's first appearance as Tarzan, Joyce's last as Jane, and the last Tarzan effort filmed while Burroughs was
alive. He was on the set during filming.

865 *Tarzan's Peril* (1951) Adventure. Running time: 79 minutes. Black
and white.

Produced by Sol Lesser. Directed by

Publicity poster for *Tarzan's Hidden Jungle*.

Byron Haskin and Phil Brandon. Screenplay by Samuel Newman, Francis Swann, and John Cousins (based on characters created by Edgar Rice Burroughs). Photographed by Karl Struss. Edited by John Murray.

Starring Lex Barker (Tarzan), Virginia Houston (Jane), George Macready (Radijeck), Douglas Fowley (Trask), Glenn Anders (Andrews), Fredrick O'Neal (Bulom), Alan Napier (Peter), Dorothy Dandridge (Queen Melemendi).

Gunrunners instigate dissension between African tribes.

866 *Tarzan's Savage Fury* (1952) Adventure. Running time: 80 minutes. Black and white.

Produced by Sol Lesser. Directed by Cy Endfield. Screenplay by Cyril Hume, Hans Jacoby, and Shirley White (based on characters created by Edgar Rice Burroughs). Photographed by Karl Struss. Edited by Frank Sullivan.

Starring Lex Barker (Tarzan), Dorothy Hart (Jane), Patric Knowles (Edwards), Charles Korvin (Rokov), Tommy Carlton (Joey).

Tarzan unwittingly aids diamond thieves.

867 *The Tattooed Stranger* (1950) Crime drama. Running time: 64 minutes. Black and white.

Produced by Jay Bonafield. Directed by Edward J. Montagne. Screenplay by Phil Reisman, Jr. Photographed by William Steiner. Edited by David Cooper.

Starring John Miles, Patricia White, Walter Kinsella, Frank Tweddell, Rod McLennan, Henry Lasko.

A detective tries to find the murderer of a young woman in Central Park, whose only distinguishing feature is a Marine corps tattoo on her wrist.

Note: First of an intended series of low-budget features Howard Hughes planned to have made on the East Coast. This one was made for only $124,000. Bonafield and Montagne had originally been documentary short subject filmmakers for RKO.

868 *Taxi 13* (1928) Comedy. Running time: 64 minutes. Black and white.

Directed by Marshall Neilan. Screenplay by George LeMaire and W. Scott Darling (based on a story by Darling). Photographed by Phillip Tannura. Edited by Pandro S. Berman.

Starring Chester Conklin (Angus MacTavish), Ethel Wales (Mrs. MacTavish), Martha Sleeper (Flora), Hugh Trevor (Dan), Lee Moran (Dennis), Jerry Miley (Mason), Charles Byer (Berger).

A cab driver gets caught up as a getaway driver for two bank robbers.

Note: An FBO production, largely silent with a few talking sequences, and a direct precursor to RKO Radio Pictures.

869 *Tender Comrade* (1943) Drama. Running time: 102 minutes. Black and white.

Produced by David Hempstead. Directed by Edward Dmytryk. Screenplay by Dalton Trumbo. Photographed by Russell Metty. Edited by Roland Gross.

Starring Ginger Rogers (Joe), Robert Ryan (Chris), Ruth Hussey (Barbara), Patricia Collinge (Helen), Mady Christians (Manya), Kim Hunter (Doris), Jane Darwell (Mrs. Henderson), Mary Forbes (Mother), Richard Martin (Mike).

A woman struggles on the homefront when her husband is killed in WWII.

Note: When Trumbo and Dmytryk were called before the House UnAmerican Activities Committee in the fifties, this film's liberal message was used against them. Rogers testified against them.

870 *Tennessee's Partner* (1955) Western. Running time: 87 minutes. Color.

Produced by Benedict Bogeaus. Directed by Allan Dwan. Screenplay by Milton Krims, D.D. Beauchamp, Graham Baker, and Teddie Sherman (based on the story by Bret Harte). Photographed by John Alton. Edited by James Leicester.

Starring John Payne (Tennessee),

Ronald Reagan (Cowpoke), Rhonda Fleming (Duchess), Coleen Gray (Goldie Slater), Anthony Caruso (Turner), Morris Ankrum (Judge), Chubby Johnson (Grubstake).

When a gambler's life is saved by a cowpoke the two become inseparable pals.

871 *Tension at Table Rock* (1956) Western. Running time: 93 minutes. Color.

Produced by Sam Wisenthal. Directed by Charles Marquis Warren. Screenplay by Winston Miller. Photographed by Joseph Biroc. Edited by Harry Marker.

Starring Richard Egan (Wes Tancred), Dorothy Malone (Lorna Miller), Cameron Mitchell (Sheriff Miller), Billy Chapin (Jody), Royal Dano (Jameson).

A cowboy is scorned when he kills a supposed hero who was actually a rat.

872 *Texas Lady* (1955) Western. Running time: 86 minutes. Color. Available on videocassette.

Produced by Nat Holt. Directed by Tim Whelan. Screenplay by Horace McCoy. Photographed by Ray Rennahan. Edited by Richard Farrell.

Starring Claudette Colbert (Prudence), Barry Sullivan (Chris), Greg Walcott (Jess), James Bell (Gower), Horace MacMahon (Stringy), Ray Collins (Ralston), Walter Sande (Sturdy), Don Haggerty (Sheriff), Douglas Fowley (Ballard), Florenz Ames (Wilson), Kathleen Mulqueen (Nanny).

A newspaperwoman incurs the wrath of crooked cattle barons.

873 *That Girl from Paris* (1937) Musical. Running time: 110 minutes. Black and white.

Produced by Pandro S. Berman. Directed by Leigh Jason. Screenplay by P.J. Wolfson, Dorothy Yost, Joseph A. Fields (based on a story by Jane Murfin which itself was suggested by a magazine article by W. Carey Wonderly). Photo-

graphed by J. Roy Hunt. Edited by William Morgan.

Starring Lily Pons (Nikki), Gene Raymond (Windy), Jack Oakie (Whammo), Herman Bing (Hammacher), Lucille Ball (Claire), Mischa Auer (Butch), Frank Jenks (Laughing Boy).

A French opera star hiding from immigration officials hooks up with a swing band.

Note: Remade as *Four Jacks and a Jill* (q.v.).

874 *That Night* (1957) Drama. Running time: 88 minutes. Black and white.

Produced by Himan Brown. Directed by John Newland. Screenplay by Robert Wallace and Jack Rowles (based on his story and TV drama "The Long Way Home"). Photographed by Maurice (Morris) Hartzband. Edited by David Cooper.

Starring John Beal (Chris), Augusta Dabney (Maggie), Malcolm Bordrick (Tommy), Dennis Kohler (Chrissy), Beverly Lunsford (Betsy), Shepperd Strudwick (Fischer).

An ad exec must change his lifestyle after suffering a heart attack.

875 *That's Right—You're Wrong* (1939) Musical. Running time: 91 minutes. Black and white.

Produced and directed by David Butler. Screenplay by William Conselman and James V. Kern. Photographed by Russell Metty. Edited by Irene Morra.

Starring Kay Kyser (Kay), Adolphe Menjou (Stacey), May Robson (Grandma), Lucille Ball (Sandra), Dennis O'Keefe (Chuck), Edward Everett Horton (Tom), Roscoe Karns (Mal), Moroni Olsen (Forbes), Ginny Simms (Ginny), Sully Mason (Sully), Harry Babbitt (Harry), Ish Kabibble (Ish), Sheilah Graham and Hedda Hopper (Themselves).

Kyser's band travels to Hollywood to be in their first movie.

876 *Their Big Moment* (1934) Comedy. Running time: 68 minutes. Black and white.

Directed by James Cruze. Screenplay by Arthur Caesar and Marion Dix (based on a story by Walter Hackett). Photographed by Harold Wenstrom. Edited by William Hamilton.

Starring ZaSu Pitts (Tillie), Slim Summerville (Bill), Julie Haydon (Fay), Ralph Morgan (Portman), William Gaxton (Lasalle), Bruce Cabot (Franklyn), Kay Johnson (Eve), Tamara Geva (Lottie).

A magician hires two assistants as psychics and they attempt to break a spell.

Note: Released in England as *Afterwards.*

877 **There Goes My Girl** (1937)
Comedy. Running time: 74 minutes. Black and white.

Produced by William Sistrom. Directed by Ben Holmes. Screenplay by Harry Segall. Photographed by Joseph H. August. Edited by Desmond Marquette.

Starring Gene Raymond (Jerry Martin), Ann Sothern (Connie), Gordon Jones (Dunn), Richard Lane (Tim), Frank Jenks (Tate), Bradley Page (Joe), Joan Woodbury (Margot), Marla Shelton (Grace), Alec Craig (Bum).

A newspaper editor tries to ruin the marriage of his star reporter.

Review: "Watch *His Girl Friday* fifteen times instead" — *The Motion Picture Guide.*

878 **There Goes the Groom**
(1937) Comedy. Running time: 64 mintes. Black and white.

Produced by Albert Lewis. Directed by Joseph Santley. Screenplay by S.K. Lauren, Dorothy Yost, and Harold Kusell (based on a story by David Garth). Photographed by Milton Krasner. Edited by Jack Hively.

Starring Ann Sothern (Betty), Burgess Meredith (Dick), Mary Boland (Mrs. Russell), Onslow Stevens (Becker), William Brisbane (Potter), Louise Henry (Janet), Roger Imhoff (Hank), George Irving (Yacht Captain).

A college grad sets off to find the frontier of Alaska and possible wealth in the gold fields. When he returns home, he finds his girl isn't interested.

879 **They Got Me Covered** (1943)
Comedy. Running time: 95 minutes. Black and white. Available on videocassette.

Produced by Samuel Goldwyn. Directed by David Butler. Screenplay by Harry Kurnitz. Photographed by Rudolph Mate. Edited by Daniel Mandell.

Starring Bob Hope (Robert Kittridge), Dorothy Lamour (Christina Hill), Lenore Aubert (Mrs. Margo Vanescu), Otto Preminger (Otto), Eduardo Ciannelli (Balandacco), Marion Martin (Gloria), Donald Meek (Little Old Man), Phillip Ahn (Nichimuro), Donald MacBride (Norman), Mary Treen (Helen), Walter Catlett (Hotel Manager), George Chandler (Smith), Stanley Clements (Office Boy), Diana Lynn (Bit).

A fired newspaper reporter tries to prove himself by uncovering a Nazi spy ring.

880 **They Knew What They Wanted** (1940) Drama. Running time: 96 minutes. Black and white. Available on videocassette.

Produced by Erich Pommer. Directed by Garson Kanin. Screenplay by Robert Ardrey. Photographed by Harry Stradling. Edited by John Sturges.

Starring Carole Lombard (Amy), Charles Laughton (Tony), William Gargan (Joe), Harry Carey (Doctor), Frank Fay (Father McKee), Joe Bernard (R.F.D.), Janet Fox (Mildred), Lee Tung-Foo (Ah Gee).

A man proposes through correspondence, sending the woman a photo of his handsome hired hand. She accepts, but resents it when she finds he is overweight and unattractive.

881 **They Live by Night** (1949)
Drama. Running time: 95 minutes. Black and white. Available on videocassette.

Produced by John Houseman. Directed by Nicholas Ray. Screenplay by Charles Schnee and Ray (based on the novel *Thieves Like Us* by Edward Anderson). Photographed by George Diskant. Edited by Sherman Todd.

Starring Cathy O'Donnell (Eechie), Farley Granger (Bowie), Howard DaSilva (Chickamaw), Jay C. Flippen (Dub), Helen Craig (Mattie), Will Wright (Mobley), Ian Wolfe (Hawkins), Tom Kennedy (Cop).

A young boy and girl get mixed up in a criminal life.

Note: First film by director Ray. Its original title was to have been *The Twisted Road.* The film was shot in 1947, but shelved during the shakeup in which when Dore Schary left and was replaced by Howard Hughes. It was initially released in England, then the States a year later. Ray had released two other films before this one finally came out.

882 *They Made Her a Spy* (1939)
Drama. Running time: 69 minutes. Black and white.

Produced by Robert Sisk. Directed by Jack Hively. Screenplay by Michael Kanin, Jo Pagano (based on a story by Lionel Houser and George Bricker). Photographed by Nicholas Musuraca. Edited by Harry Marker.

Starring Sally Eilers (Irene), Allan Lane (Huntley), Frank M. Thomas (Col. Shaw), Fritz Leiber (Krull), Larry Blake (Dawson), Charles Halton (Belden), Theodore von Eltz (Page), Pierre Watkin (Col. Wilson).

A woman joins Army Intelligence to avenge the death of her brother.

Note: Screenwriter Michael Kanin is the brother of writer-director Garson Kanin.

883 *They Meet Again* (1941)
Drama. Running time: 69 minutes. Black and white. Available on videocassette.

Produced by William Stephens. Di-

rected by Erle C. Kenton. Screenplay by Peter Milne and Maurice Leo. Edited by Alexander Troffey.

Starring Jean Hersholt (Christian), Dorothy Lovett (Judy), Robert Baldwin (Roy), Maude Eburne (Mrs. Hastings), Neil Hamilton (Webster), Anne Bennett (Janie).

The good doctor aids a man accused of embezzlement.

Note: Last film of this series.

884 *They Met in Argentina* (1941)
Musical. Running time: 77 minutes. Black and white.

Produced by Lou Brock. Directed by Leslie Goodwins. Screenplay by Jerry Cady. Photographed by J. Roy Hunt. Edited by Desmond Marquette. Music by Rodgers and Hart.

Starring Maureen O'Hara (Lolita), James Ellison (Tim Kelly), Alberto Vila (Alberto), Buddy Ebsen (Duke), Robert Barrat (Don), Joseph Buloff (Santiago), Diossa Costello (Panchita), Robert Middlemass (George), Chester Clute (Secretary).

An oil baron's rep tries to secure a prized Argentinean horse.

885 *They Wanted to Marry* (1937)
Comedy. Running time: 60 minutes. Black and white.

Produced by Zion Meyers. Directed by Lew Landers. Screenplay by Paul Yawitz and Ethel Borden (based on a story by Larry Bachmann and Darwin L. Teilher). Photographed by Russell Metty. Edited by Desmond Marquette.

Starring Betty Furness, Gordon Jones, E.E. Clive, Patsy Lee Parsons, Henry Kolker, Charles Wilson, Billy Benedict, Diana Ibson, Frank M. Thomas.

A photographer covering a society wedding falls for the bride's younger sister, but is thwarted by her stuffy father.

886 *They Won't Believe Me* (1947) Crime drama. Running time: 95 minutes. Black and white. Available on videocassette.

Produced by Joan Harrison. Directed by Irving Pichel. Screenplay by Jonathan Latimer. Photographed by Harry Wild. Edited by Elmo Williams.

Starring Robert Young (Larry), Susan Hayward (Verna), Jane Greer (Janice), Rita Johnson (Greta), Tom Powers (Trenton), George Tyne (Lt. Carr), Don Beddoe (Thomasan), Frank Ferguson (Cahill), Harry Harvey (Fletcher), Paul Maxey (Bowman), Dot Farley (Emma), Jack Rice (Tour Conductor).

A playboy is accused of his wife's murder.

887 The Thing (1951) Sci-fi. Running time: 87 minutes. Black and white and colorized. Available on videocassette.

Produced by Howard Hawks. Directed by Christian Nyby. Screenplay by Charles Lederer. Photographed by Russell Harlan. Edited by Roland Gross.

Starring Kenneth Tobey (Hendry), James Arness (Thing), Margaret Sheridan (Nikki), Robert Cornthwaite (Carrington), Doug Spencer (Scotty), James Young (Lt. Dykes), Dewey Martin (Bob), Robert Nichols (Kerickson), William Self (Barnes), Eduard Franz (Stern), John Dierkes (Chapman), Billy Curtis (The Thing While Shrinking).

Scientists in the arctic stumble across a frozen monster.

Note: Remade in 1982.

Review: "One of the greatest science-fiction films ever made" — *The Motion Picture Guide*.

888 Thirteen Women (1932) Drama. Running time: 74 minutes. Black and white.

Produced by David O. Selznick. Directed by George Archainbaud. Screenplay by Bartlett Cormack and Samuel Ornitz. Photographed by Leo Tover. Edited by Buddy Kimball.

Starring Ricardo Cortez (Clive), Irene Dunne (Laura), Myrna Loy (Ursula), Jill Esmond (Jo Turner), Florence Eldridge (Grace Coombs), Kay Johnson (Helen), Julie Haydon (Mary), Harriet Hagman (May), Peg Entwhistle (Hazel).

A half–Japanese, half–Indian girl must leave a sorority because its other members are racist.

Note: Entwhistle made history when, after this film, and saddened by a career that never seemed to take off, she climbed to the top of the "H" on the HOLLYWOOD sign and jumped to her death.

889 This Land Is Mine (1943) Drama. Running time: 103 minutes. Black and white. Available on videocassette.

Produced by Jean Renoir and Dudley Nichols. Directed by Renoir. Screenplay by Nichols. Photographed by Frank Redman. Edited by Frederic Knudtson.

Starring Charles Laughton (Arthur), Maureen O'Hara (Louise), George Sanders (George), Walter Slezak (von Keller), Kent Smith (Paul), Una O'Connor (Emma), Phillip Merivale (Sorel), Thurston Hall (Mayor), George Coulouris (Prosecuting Attorney), Nancy Gates (Julie).

A European village battles for its freedom against Nazi rule.

890 This Man Is Mine (1934) Drama. Running time: 76 minutes. Black and white.

Produced by Pandro S. Berman. Directed by John Cromwell. Screenplay by Jane Murfin. Photographed by David Abel. Edited by William Morgan.

Starring Irene Dunne (Toni), Ralph Bellamy (Jim), Constance Cummings (Fran), Kay Johnson (Bee), Charles Starrett (Jud), Sidney Blackmer (Holmes).

A woman comes between a happily married couple.

This Man Is Mine see *The Lusty Man*

891 This Marriage Business (1938) Comedy. Running time: 70 minutes. Black and white.

Produced by Cliff Reid. Directed by Christy Cabanne. Screenplay by Gladys

Rita Johnson and Robert Young in *They Won't Believe Me.*

Atwater. Photographed by Joseph H. August. Edited by Harry Marker.

Starring Victor Moore (Jud), Allan Lane (Bill), Vicki Lester (Nancy), Cecil Kellaway (Hardy), Jack Carson (Candid), Richard Lane (Joe), Kay Sutton (Bella), Paul Guilfoyle (Frankie), Jack Arnold (Lloyd), Frank M. Thomas (Frisbee), Leona Roberts (Mrs. Platt).

A marriage license clerk brags that none of his couples has ever divorced, causing a slew of marriage-minded couples to descend upon his office.

892 *Those Endearing Young Charms* (1945) Comedy. Running time: 81 minutes. Black and white. Available on videocassette.

Produced by Bert Granet. Directed by Lewis Allen. Screenplay by Jerome Chodorov (based on the play by Edward Chodorov). Photographed by Ted Tetzlaff. Edited by Roland Gross. Music by Roy Webb.

Starring Robert Young (Hank), La-raine Day (Helen), Ann Harding (Mrs. Brandt), Marc Cramer (Capt. Stowe), Anne Jeffreys (Suzanne), Glenn Vernon (Sailor), Norma Varden (Floor Lady), Lawrence Tierney (Pilot).

A soldier introduces his buddy to his girlfriend, only to have the two fall for each other.

893 *The Threat* (1949) Crime drama. Running time: 66 minutes. Black and white. Available on videocassette.

Produced by Hugh King. Directed by Felix Foist and Dick Hyland. Photographed by Harry J. Wild. Edited by Samuel E. Beetley.

Starring Michael O'Shea (Williams), Virginia Grey (Carol), Charles McGraw (Klugger), Julie Bishop (Ann), Frank Conroy (Mac), Robert Shayne (Murphy), Anthony Caruso (Nick), Don McGuire (Joe).

A killer escapes prison and tries to get even with those responsible for his sentence.

James Arness and Billy Curtis in *The Thing*.

894 *The Three Caballeros* (1944)
Animation/Live action. Running time:
70 minutes. Black and white. Available
on videocassette.

Produced by Norman Ferguson. Di-
rected by Ferguson, Clyde Geronimi,
Jack Kinney, Bill Roberts, Harold
Young.

Starring Aurora Miranda, Carmen
Molina, Dora Luz, Nestor Amarale,
Alimrante, Trio Calvarez; voices of Clar-
ence Nash, Jose Oliveria, Joaquim
Garay.

Donald Duck takes a tour of South
America.

895 *The Three Musketeers* (1935)
Adventure. Running time: 90 minutes.
Black and white.

Produced by Cliff Reid. Directed by
Rowland V. Lee. Screenplay by Dudley
Nichols (based on the story by Alexandre
Dumas). Photographed by Peverell Marley. Edited by George Hively.

Starring Walter Abel (D'Artagnan),
Paul Lukas (Athos), Margot Grahame
(Milade de Winter), Heather Angel
(Constance), Ian Keith (de Rochefort),
Moroni Olsen (Porthos), Onslow Stevens
(Aramis), Rosamond Pinchot (Queen
Anne).

First talkie version of classic story,
filmed before in 1921, and again as a
comedy in 1939 and 1948 (as part of a
short series).

896 *Three Sons* (1939) Drama.
Running time: 72 minutes. Black and
white.

Produced by Robert Sisk. Directed by
Jack Hively. Screenplay by John Twist.
Photographed by Russell Metty. Edited
by Theron Warth.

Starring Edward Ellis (Pardway), William Gargan (Thane), Kent Taylor
(Gene), J. Edward Bromberg (Abe),
Katherine Alexander (Abagail), Virginia
Vale (Phoebe), Robert Stanton (Bert),
Dick Hogan (Freddie), Grady Sutton
(Grimson), Barbara Pepper (Viola).

A store owner, who built himself up
from nothing, finds his children are not
interested in taking over the business
when he's gone.

Note: Filmed before as *Sweepings.*
Gargan was in both films.

897 *Three Who Loved* (1931)
Drama. Running time: 72 minutes.
Black and white.

Produced by Bertram Millhauser. Directed by George Archainbaud. Screenplay by Beulah Marie Dix. Photographed by Nicholas Musuraca. Edited
by Jack Kitchin.

Starring Betty Compson, Conrad
Nagel, Robert Ames, Robert Emmett

O'Connor, Bodil Rosing, Dickie Moore,
Fred Santley.

After sending for his sweetheart from
Sweden, a bank teller is accused of embezzlement.

898 *Thunder Mountain* (1947)
Western. Running time: 60 minutes.
Black and white.

Produced by Herman Schlom. Directed by Lew Landers. Screenplay by
Norman Houston (based on a novel by
Zane Grey). Photographed by Jack MacKenzie. Edited by Phillip Martin.

Starring Tim Holt (Marvin), Martha
Hyer (Ellen), Richard Martin (Chito),
Steve Brodie (Chick), Virginia Owen
(Ginger), Harry Woods (Trimble), Jason
Robards, Sr. (James Gardner), Tom
Keene (Johnny Blue).

A cowboy comes home from college to
find a family feud is reignited.

Note: Filmed before in 1923.

899 *Thundering Hoofs* (1941)
Western. Running time: 60 minutes.
Black and white.

Produced by Bert Gilroy. Directed by
Lesley Selander. Screenplay by Paul
Franklin. Photographed by J. Roy Hunt.
Edited by Frederic Knudtson.

Starring Tim Holt (Bill), Ray Whitley
(Smoky), Lee "Lasses" White (Whopper), Luana Walters (Nancy), Archie
Twitchell (Farley), Gordon DeMain
(Underwood), Charles Phipps (Kellogg),
Monte Montague (Slick).

A cowboy tries to save his father from
being victimized by crooks.

900 *Till the End of Time* (1946)
Drama. Running time: 105 minutes.
Black and white. Available on videocassette.

Produced by Dore Schary. Directed by
Edward Dmytryk. Screenplay by Allen
Rivkin. Photographed by Harry J. Wild.
Edited by Harry Gerstad.

Starring Dorothy McGuire (Pat), Guy
Madison (Cliff), Robert Mitchum (Tabeshaw), Bill Williams (Kincheloe), Tom

Tully (Harper), William Gargan (Watrous), Jean Porter (Helen), Johnny Sands (Tommy), Loren Tindall (Pinky), Ruth Nelson (Amy), Harry Von Zell (Scuffy).

World War II veterans return home and attempt to re-adjust to civilian life.

Note: Released months before *The Best Years of Our Lives* but totally eclipsed by that film.

901 *Timber Stampede* (1939) Western. Running time: 59 minutes. Black and white.

Produced by Bert Gilroy. Directed by David Howard. Screenplay by Morton Grant (based on stories by Bernard McConville and Paul Franklin). Edited by Frederic Knudtson.

Starring George O'Brien (Scott), Chill Wills (Whopper), Marjorie Reynolds (Anne), Morgan Wallace (Dunlap), Robert Fiske (Matt), Guy Usher (Jones), Earl Dwire (Henry), Frank Hagney (Champ), Robert Burns (Sheriff), Monte Montague (Jake), Bud Osborne (Brady), Billy Benedict, Elmo Lincoln, Hank Worden (Bits).

A rancher tries to stop land grabbers from ruining timberland.

Note: The only RKO O'Brien western that failed to turn a profit.

902 *The Tip Off* (1931) Comedy. Running time: 70 minutes. Black and white. Available on videocassette.

Produced by Charles Rogers. Directed by Albert Rogell. Screenplay by Earl Baldwin. Photographed by Edward Snyder. Edited by Charles Craft.

Starring Eddie Quillan (Tommy), Robert Armstrong (Kayo), Ginger Rogers (Baby Face), Joan Peers (Edna), Ralf Harolde (Nick Vatelli), Charles Sellon (Pop), Mike Donlin (Swanky Jones), Ernie Adams (Slug McGee), Dorothy Granger (Bit).

A mild-mannered man falls for a mobster's girl, and is aided by a dimwitted prizefighter.

Note: British title: *Looking for Trouble.*

903 *To Beat the Band* (1935) Comedy. Running time: 68 minutes. Black and white.

Produced by Zion Meyers. Directed by Ben Stoloff. Screenplay by Brian James. Photographed by Nicholas Musuraca. Edited by George Crone.

Starring Hugh Herbert (Hugo), Helen Broderick (Freeda), Roger Pryor (Larry), Fred Keating (Carson), Eric Blore (Hawkins), Phyllis Brooks (Roweena), Johnny Mercer (Band Member), The Fred Keating Orchestra (Themselves).

A man tries to marry a widow in order to get his aunt's inheritance.

904 *Toast of New York* (1937) Biographical drama. Running time: 109 minutes. Black and white. Available on videocassette.

Produced by Edward Small. Directed by Rowland V. Lee. Screenplay by Dudley Nichols, John Twist, Joel Sayre. Photographed by Peverell Marley. Edited by George Hively.

Starring Edward Arnold (Jim Fiske), Cary Grant (Nick Boyd), Frances Farmer (Josie), Jack Oakie (Luke), Donald Meek (Drew), Thelma Leeds (Fleurique), Clarence Kolb (Vanderbilt).

Biography of Jim Fisk.

905 *Tokyo File 212* (1951) Drama. Running time: 84 minutes. Black and white.

Produced by George Breakston and Dorrell McGowan. Directed and written by Dorell and Stuart McGowan. Photographed by Herman Schopp. Edited by Martin G. Cohn.

Starring Florence Marley (Steffi), Robert Peyton (Jim Carter), Katsu Kaika Haida (Taro), Reiko Otani (Taro's Girl).

A U.S. agent tries to curb communist activities in Japan.

906 *Tom Brown's Schooldays* (1940) Drama. Running time: 86 minutes. Black and white.

Produced by Gene Towne and Graham Baker. Directed by Robert Steven-

Ginger Rogers and Robert Armstrong in *The Tip Off*.

son. Screenplay by Walter Ferris, Frank Cavett, Towne, Baker, Stevenson (based on the novel by Thomas Hughes). Photographed by Nicholas Musuraca. Edited by William Hamilton.

Starring Sir Cedric Hardwicke, Freddie Bartholomew, Jimmy Lydon, Josephine Hutchinson, Billy Halop, Polly Moran, Hughie Green, Ernest Cossart, Alec Craig, Gale Storm, Charles Smith.

A young lad leaves his wealthy home and is forced to live in a boarding school with tough delinquents.

Note: Filmed before in 1914 and again in 1951.

907 *Tom, Dick, and Harry* (1941)

Comedy. Running time: 86 minutes. Black and white. Available on videocassette.

Produced by Robert Sisk. Directed by Garson Kanin. Screenplay by Paul Jarrico. Photographed by Merritt Gerstad. Edited by John Sturges.

Starring Ginger Rogers (Janie), George Murphy (Tom), Alan Marshal (Dick), Burgess Meredith (Harry), Joe Cunningham (Pop), Jane Seymour (Mom), Lenore Lonergan (Babs), Vicki Lester (Paula), Phil Silvers (Ice Cream Boy).

A girl wants a millionaire but ends up choosing from among three working class boys.

Note: Sisk's last film for RKO, after which he moved to Paramount. Ginger Rogers' last film for RKO. Remade as *The Girl Most Likely.*

Oscar: Script.

908 *Tomorrow at Seven* (1933)

Mystery. Running time: 62 minutes. Black and white.

Produced by Joseph I. Schnitzer and Samuel Zierler. Directed by Ray Enright. Screenplay by Ralph Spence. Photographed by Charles Schoenbaum. Edited by Rose Loewinger. Available on videocassette.

Starring Chester Morris (Neil), Vivienne Osborne (Martha), Frank McHugh (Clancy), Allen Jenkins (Dugan), Henry

Stephenson (Drake), Grant Mitchell (Winters), Charles Middleton (Simons), Oscar Apfel (Marsden).

A mystery writer attempts to track down the notorious killer known as the Ace of Spades.

909 *Tomorrow Is Forever* (1946) Drama. Running time: 105 minutes. Black and white.

Produced by David Lewis. Directed by Irving Pichel. Screenplay by Lenore Coffee (based on the novel by Gwen Bristow). Photographed by Joseph Valentine. Edited by Ernest Nims. Music by Max Steiner.

Starring Claudette Colbert (Elizabeth MacDonald Hamilton), Orson Welles (John MacDonald/Erich Kessler), George Brent (Larry Hamilton), Lucile Watson (Aunt Jessie), Richard Long (Drew), Natalie Wood (Margaret), Sonny Howe (Brian), John Wengraf (Dr. Ludwig), Tom Wirick (Pudge), Lane Watson (Secretary).

When a man is scarred and crippled in the war, he gets word to his wife that he's been killed, so he does not have to face her. She remarries, but runs into him again years later.

Note: Film debut of six-year-old Natalie Wood.

910 *Too Many Cooks* (1931) Comedy. Running time: 77 minutes. Black and white.

Produced by Douglas MacLean. Directed by William Seiter. Screenplay by Jane Murfin and Frank Craven (based on the play by Craven). Photographed by Nicholas Musuraca. Edited by Jack Kitchin.

Starring Bert Wheeler (Al Bennett), Dorothy Lee (Alice Cook), Sharon Lynn (Ella Mayer), Roscoe Ates (Wilson), Robert McWade (Uncle George), Hallam Cooley (Andrews), Florence Roberts (Mrs. Cook), Clifford Dempsey (Mr. Cook), George Chandler (Cousin Ned), Ruth Weston (Bit).

A young couple try to build their dream house despite the intrusion of relatives.

Note: Wheeler's only film without partner Bob Woolsey until after Woolsey's death in 1938.

Comment: "While we were making this one, Bert and I kept saying it's getting worse every day, but we're getting paid"—Dorothy Lee.

911 *Too Many Girls* (1940) Comedy. Running time: 85 minutes. Black and white.

Produced and directed by George Abbott. Screenplay by John Twist. Photographed by Frank Redman. Edited by William Hamilton. Music by Rodgers and Hart.

Starring Lucille Ball (Connie), Richard Carlson (Clint), Ann Miller (Pepe), Eddie Bracken (Jojo), Frances Langford (Eileen), Desi Arnaz (Mauelito), Hal LeRoy (Al Terwillinger), Libby Bennett (Tallulah Lu), Harry Shannon (Casey), Douglas Walton (Waverly), Chester Clute (Lister), Van Johnson (Bit).

An heiress tries college life.

Note: Lucy and Desi met on this film.

912 *Too Many Wives* (1937) Comedy. Running time: 61 minutes. Black and white.

Produced by William Sistrom. Directed by Ben Holmes. Screenplay by Dorothy Yost, Lois Eby, and John Grey (based on a story by Richard English). Photographed by Nicholas Musuraca. Edited by Desmond Marquette.

Starring John Morely (Barry Trent), Anne Shirley (Winifred Jackson), Gene Lockhart (Her Father), Dudley Clements (Horation), Barbara Pepper (Secretary), Frank Melton (Holden), Dot Farley (Mrs. Potts), Jack Carson (Hodges), George Irving (Otto).

A young couple look for a valuable missing stamp. The scheming husband has another spouse.

913 *Top Hat* (1935) Musical. Running time: 101 minutes. Black and white. Available on videocassette.

Ginger Rogers and Fred Astaire in *Top Hat*.

Produced by Pandro S. Berman. Directed by Mark Sandrich. Screenplay by Dwight Taylor and Allen Cott. Photographed by David Abel. Edited by William Hamilton. Music by Cole Porter.

Starring Fred Astaire (Jerry), Ginger Rogers (Dale), Edward Everett Horton (Horace), Helen Broderick (Madge), Erik Rhodes (Alberto Beddini), Eric Blore (Bates), Lucille Ball (Flower Clerk), Donald Meek (Curate), Gino Corrado (Hotel Manager), Dennis O'Keefe, Charlie Hall (Bits).

A romantic comedy of mistaken identities.

Oscar nominations: Best Picture and Best Song (Cole Porter's "Cheek to Cheek").

Review: "The theaters will hold their own World Series with this one" — *Variety.*

914 *Trail Guide* (1952) Western. Running time: 60 minutes. Black and white.

Produced by Herman Schlom. Directed by Lesley Selander. Screenplay by Arthur Orloff. Photographed by Nicholas Musuraca. Edited by Samuel Beetley.

Starring Tim Holt (Tim), Linda Douglas (Peg), Frank Wilcox (Regan), Robert Sherwood (Kenny), John Pickard (Dawson), Kenneth MacDonald (Wheeler).

Cowboys help farmer immigrants across the West.

915 *Trail Street* (1947) Western. Running time: 84 minutes. Black and white. Available on videocassette.

Produced by Nat Holt. Directed by Ray Enright. Screenplay by Norman Houston and Gene Lewis. Photographed by J. Roy Hunt. Edited by Lyle Boyer.

Starring Randolph Scott (Bat Masterson), Robert Ryan (Allen), Anne Jeffreys (Ruby Stone), George Gabby Hayes (Billy Jones), Madge Meredith (Susan), Steve Brodie (Logan Maury), Billy House (Carmondy), Virginia Sale (Hannah).

Bat Masterson rides into Kansas.

Note: Made $360,000 at the box office.

916 *Transgression* (1931) Drama. Running time: 72 minutes. Black and white.

Produced by William LeBaron. Directed by Herbert Brenon. Screenplay by Elizabeth Meehan and Benn Levy. Photographed by Leo Tover.

Starring Kay Francis (Elsie Maury), Paul Cavanaugh (Robert Maury), Ricardo Cortez (Don Arturo), Nance O'Neil (Honora Maury), John St. Polis (Serafin), Adrienne d'Ambricourt (Julie).

A bored wife leaves her husband for her Spanish lover.

917 *Traveling Husbands* (1931) Comedy. Running time: 73 minutes. Black and white.

Produced by William LeBaron. Directed by Paul Sloane. Screenplay by Humphrey Pearson. Photographed by Leo Tover.

Starring Evelyn Brent (Ruby), Frank Albertson (Barry), Constance Cummings (Ellen), Hugh Herbert (Hymie), Carl Miller (Ben), Frank McHugh (Pinkie), Spencer Charters (Joe), Dorothy Peterson (Martha), Purnell Pratt (J.C. Wilson).

Salesmen romance call girls.

918 *Treasure Island* (1950). Adventure. Running time: 96 minutes. Color.

Produced by Perce Pearce. Directed by Byron Haskin. Screenplay by Lawrence E. Watkin (based on the novel by Robert Louis Stevenson). Photographed by F.A. Young. Edited by Alan L. Jaggs. Available on videocassette.

Starring Bobby Driscoll (Jim Hawkins), Robert Newton (Long John Silver), Basil Sydney (Capt. Smollett), Walter Fitzgerald (Squire), Denis O'Dea (Livelsy), Ralph Truman (George Merry), Finlay Currie (Capt. Bones), Frances De Wolf (Black Dog).

Disney version of the classic novel.

Note: When re-released in 1970 after the MPAA ratings were in, it was given a PG rating. The Disney people balked and snipped some of the violence to ensure a G rating. Filmed before in 1918 (with a girl, Shirley Mason, playing Jim) and in a classic 1934 production by MGM.

919 *Treasure of Pancho Villa* (1955) Western. Running time: 96 minutes. Available on videocassette.

Produced by Edmund Grainger. Directed by George Sherman. Screenplay by Niven Busch. Photographed by William Snyder. Edited by Harry Marker.

Starring Rory Calhoun (Tom Bryan), Shelley Winters (Ruth), Gilbert Roland (Juan), Joseph Calleia (Pablo), Carlos Mosquiz (Commandant), Fanny Schiller (Laria Morales).

Mercenaries try to transport a gold shipment.

920 *Triple Justice* (1940) Western. Running time: 65 minutes. Black and white.

Produced by Bert Gilroy. Directed by David Howard. Screenplay by Arthur V. Jones and Morton Grant. Photographed by J. Roy Hunt. Edited by Frederic Knudtson.

Starring George O'Brien (Brad), Virginia Vale (Lorna), Harry Woods (Reeves), Peggy Shannon (Mary), Leroy Mason (Gregory), Paul Fix (Cleary), Glenn Strange (Wiley).

A cowboy is mistaken for a bank robber.

Note: O'Brien's last film for RKO.

921 *Trouble in Sundown* (1939) Western. Running time: 60 minutes. Black and white.

Produced by Bert Gilroy. Directed by David Howard. Screenplay by Oliver Drake, Dorrell McGowan, and Stuart McGowan (based on a story by Charles F. Royal—aka George F. Royal). Photographed by Harry Wild. Edited by Frederick Knudtson. Music by Ray Whitley.

Songs: "Prairie Winds," "Home on the Prairie."

Starring George O'Brien, Rosalind Keith, Ray Whitley, Chill Wills, Ward Bond, Cy Kendall, Howard Hickman, Monte Montague, John Dislon, Otto Yamaoka, Ken Card, Earl Dwire, Robert Burns, The Phelps Brothers.

A crooked real estate man robs a bank and frames the banker.

922 *The Truth About Murder* (1946) Drama. Running time: 63 minutes. Black and white.

Produced by Herman Schlom. Directed by Lew Landers. Screenplay by Lawrence Kimble, Hilda Gordon, and Eric Taylor. Photographed by Frank Redman. Edited by Edward W. Williams.

Starring Bonita Granville (Chris Allen), Morgan Conway (Les Ashton), Rita Corday (Peggy), Don Douglas (Paul Marvin), June Clayworth (Marsha Crane), Gerald Mohr (Johnny Lacka), Michael St. Angel (Hank), Tommy Noonan (Jonesy), Edward Norris (Bill Crane).

A woman photographer is found dead; her husband is arrested, but is defended by the D.A.'s wife.

Note: Released in Great Britain as *The Lie Detector.*

923 *The Tuttles of Tahiti* (1942) Comedy. Running time: 91 minutes. Black and white. Available on videocassette.

Produced by Sol Lesser. Directed by Charles Vidor. Screenplay by S. Lewis Meltzer, Robert Carson, and James Hilton (based on the novel *No More Gas* by Charles Nordhoff and James Norman Hall). Photographed by Nicholas Musuraca. Edited by Frederic Knudtson.

Starring Charles Laughton (Jonas Tuttle), Jon Hall (Charles Tuttle), Peggy Drake (Tamara Taio), Victor Francen (Dr. Blondin), Gene Reynolds (Ru), Florence Bates (Emily), Curt Bois (Jensen), Adeline Reynolds (Mama Rusu Tuttle), Mala (Nat), Leonard Sues (Fana), Jody Gilbert (Effie), Jim Spencer (Tupa), Teddy Infuhr (Ala), Alma Ross (Hio).

Saga of a carefree island family.

Note: Based on a novel by the authors of *Mutiny on the Bounty,* in which Laughton also starred (in 1939 for MGM). Film did not make its $847,000 production costs back.

924 *Twelve Crowded Hours* (1939) Crime drama. Running time: 64 minutes. Black and white.

Produced by Robert Sisk. Directed by Lew Landers. Screenplay by John Twist. Photographed by Nicholas Musuraca. Edited by Harry Marker.

Starring Richard Dix (Nick Green), Lucille Ball (Paula Sanders), Allan Lane (Dave Sanders), Donald MacBride (Inspector), Cy Kendall (Costain), Granville Bates (McEwan), John Arledge (Red).

11

Peggy Drake and Jon Hall in *The Tuttles of Tahiti.*

A reporter avenges the murder of his editor.

The Twisted Road see *They Live by Night*

925 *Two Alone* (1934) Drama. Running time: 75 minutes. Black and white.

Produced by David Lewis. Directed by Elliott Nugent. Screenplay by Josephine Lovett and Joseph Moncure March. Photographed by Lucien Andriot. Edited by Arthur Roberts.

Starring Jean Parker (Mazie), Tom Brown (Adam), ZaSu Pitts (Esther), Arthur Byron (Slog), Beulah Bondi (Mrs. Slag), Nydia Westman (Corie), Willard Robertson (Marshall), Charley Grapewin (Sandy), Emerson Treacy (Milt).

A man saves an orphan farm girl from her evil guardian.

926 *Two in Revolt* (1936) Children's. Running time: 65 minutes. Black and white.

Produced by Robert Sisk. Directed by

Glenn Tryon. Screenplay by Frank Howard Clark. Photographed by Jack MacKenzie. Edited by Frederic Knudtson.

Starring John Arledge (John Woods), Louise Latimer (Gloria), Moroni Olsen (Cyrus), Emmett Vogan (Mason), Harry Jans (Crane), Murray Alper (Andy), Max Wagner (Davis).

The exploits of a dog and a horse, born on the same day.

927 *Two in the Dark* (1936)
Mystery. Running time: 72 minutes. Black and white.

Produced by Zion Meyers. Directed by Ben Stoloff. Screenplay by Seton Miller. Photographed by Nicholas Musuraca. Edited by George Crone.

Starring Walter Abel (The Man), Margot Grahame (Marie), Wallace Ford (Hillyer), Gail Patrick (Irene), Alan Hale (Floria), Leslie Fenton (Eldridge), Eric Blore (Edmund Fish).

A man who suffered a loss of memory finds he's wanted for murder.

Note: Remade as *Two O'Clock Courage* (see below).

928 *Two O'Clock Courage* (1945)
Mystery. Running time: 66 minutes. Black and white.

Produced by Ben Stoloff. Directed by Anthony Mann. Screenplay by Robert E. Kent. Photographed by Jack MacKenzie. Edited by Phillip Martin, Jr.

Starring Tom Conway (The Man), Ann Rutherford (Patty), Richard Lane (Haley), Lester Matthews (Mark Evans), Roland Drew (Maitland), Emory Parnell (Brenner), Jane Greer (Helen), Jean Brooks (Barbara).

Note: Remake of *Two in the Dark* (see above).

929 *Two Thoroughbreds* (1939)
Drama. Running time: 62 minutes. Black and white.

Produced by Cliff Reid. Directed by Jack Hively. Screenplay by Joseph Fields and Jerry Cady. Photographed by Frank Redman. Edited by Theron Warth.

Starring Jimmy Lydon (David), Joan Brodel (Wendy), Arthur Hohl (Carey), J.M. Kerrigan (Jack), Marjorie Main (Hildegarde Carey), Selmer Jackson (Bill), Spencer Charters (Doc Purdy).

A farm boy raises a wild colt on his own.

Note: Actress Brodel later went by the name of Joan Leslie.

930 *Two Tickets to Broadway*
(1951) Musical comedy. Running time: 106 minutes. Color.

Produced by Howard Hughes. Directed by James V. Kern. Screenplay by Sid Silvers and Hal Kanter (based on a story by Sammy Cahn). Photographed by Edward Cronjager. Edited by Harry Marker. Choreography by Busby Berkeley.

Starring Tony Martin (Dan), Janet Leigh (Nancy), Gloria DeHaven (Hannah), Eddie Bracken (Lew), Ann Miller (Joyce), Barbara Lawrence (Foxy), Bob Crosby (Himself), Joe Smith (Harry), Charlie Dale (Leo), Taylor Holmes (Willard Glendon), Buddy Baer (Sailor).

A small town girl leaves home to make it big in New York.

931 *Two Weeks to Live* (1943)
Comedy. Running time: 76 minutes. Black and white. Available on videocassette.

Produced by Ben Hersh. Directed by Malcolm St. Clair. Screenplay by Michael Simmons and Roswell Rogers. Photographed by Jack MacKenzie. Edited by Duncan Mansfield.

Starring Chester Lauck (Lum), Norris Goff (Abner), Franklin Pangborn (Mr. Pinkey), Kay Linaker (Mrs. Carmen), Irving Bacon (Gimpel), Herbert Rawlinson (Stark, Sr.), Ivan Simpson (Prof. Frisby), Rosemary LaPlanche (Nurse), Danny Duncan (Postman), Evelyn Knapp (Secretary), Charles Middleton (Kelton), Jack Riche (Hotel Clerk), Tim Ryan (Higgens).

Lum and Abner travel to Chicago to claim a railroad they've inherited. When Abner is duped into thinking he's terminally ill, he agrees to take a rocket trip to Mars as an experiment.

932 *Tycoon* (1947) Drama. Running time: 128 minutes. Black and white.

Produced by Stephen Ames. Directed by Richard Wallace. Screenplay by Borden Chase and John Twist (based on a novel by C.E. Scoggins). Photographed by Harry Wild. Edited by Frank Doyle.

Starring John Wayne (Munroe), Laraine Day (Maura), Sir Cedric Hardwicke (Alexander), Anthony Quinn (Ricky), Grant Withers (Harris), Paul Fix (Joe), Fernando Alvarado (Chico), Michael Harvey (Curly), Harry Woods (Holden), Martin Garralaga (Chavez).

A man sets out to build a railroad for a wealthy American.

Note: Lost over one million dollars at the box office. Day's husband, baseball shortstop Leo Durocher, allegedly grew very jealous whenever his wife played love scenes with Wayne. He hung around the set inhibiting Wayne, until the actor insisted upon a closed set—the only time the otherwise easygoing actor made such a demand.

933 *Under the Tonto Rim* (1947) Western. Running time: 61 minutes. Black and white.

Produced by Herman Schlom. Directed by Lew Landers. Screenplay by Norman Houston (based on the novel by Zane Grey). Photographed by J. Roy Hunt. Edited by Lyle Boyer.

Starring Tim Holt (Brad), Nan Leslie (Lucy), Richard Martin (Chito), Tom Keene (Dennison), Carol Forman (Juanita), Tony Barrett (Patton), Harry Harvey (Sheriff), Jason Robards, Sr. (McClean).

A stagecoach operator plans to avenge the death of his driver.

934 *Under Water* (1955) Adventure. Running time: 99 minutes. Black and white. Available on videocassette.

Produced by Harry Tatelman. Directed by John Sturges. Screenplay by Walter Newman. Photographed by Harry Wild. Edited by Stuart Gilmore.

Starring Jane Russell (Theresa), Gilbert Roland (Dominic), Richard Egan (Johnny), Lori Nelson (Gloria), Robert Keith (Father Cannon), Joseph Calleia (Rico), Eugene Iglesias (Miguel), Ric Roman (Jesus).

A husband and wife diving team discover sunken treasures.

Note: The last Hughes-Russell film to be completed.

935 *Unexpected Uncle* (1941) Comedy. Running time: 67 minutes. Black and white.

Produced by Tay Garnett. Directed by Peter Godfrey. Screenplay by Delmer Davies and Noel Langley. Photographed by Robert De Grasse. Edited by William Hamilton.

Starring Anne Shirley (Kathleen Brown), James Craig (Johnny), Charles Coburn (Seton Manley), Ernest Truex (Wilkins), Renee Godfrey (Carol), Russell Gleason (Tommy), Astrid Allwyn (Sara), Jed Prouty (Sanderson), Thurston Hall (Jerry), Virginia Engles (Mrs. Carter), Hans Conried (Clayton), Arthur Aylesworth (Quenton).

A salesgirl asks an older man for advice when she gets involved with a wealthy manufacturer.

936 *The Unholy Wife* (1957) Drama. Running time: 94 minutes. Color. Available on videocassette. An RKO–Treasure Films production, released by Universal-International.

Produced and directed by John Farrow. Screenplay by Jonathan Latimer (based on a story by William Durkee). Photographed by Lucien Ballard. Edited by Eda Warren.

Starring Diana Dors (Phyllis), Rod Steiger (Paul), Tom Tryon (Sam), Beulah Bondi (Emma), Marie Windsor (Gwen), Arthur Franz (Rev. Hochen), Luis Van Rooten (Ezra), Argentina Brunetti (Theresa), James Burke (Sheriff).

A woman marries a wealthy wine seller, but then falls for a rodeo star. *Note:* Dors' first American film.

937 *Vacation in Reno* (1946) Comedy. Running time: 60 minutes. Black and white.

Produced and directed by Leslie Goodwins. Screenplay by Charles E. Roberts and Arthur Ross. Photographed by George E. Diskant. Edited by Les Millbrook.

Starring Jack Haley (Jack Carroll), Anne Jeffreys (Eleanor), Wally Brown (Eddie), Iris Adrian (Bunny), Morgan Conway (Joe), Alan Carney (Angel), Myrna Dell (Mrs. Dumont), Matt McHugh (Dumont).

A young married couple tries to survive its first big spat.

938 *Vagabond Lover* (1929) Musical. Running time: 65 minutes. Black and white.

Produced by James Ashmore Creelman and Louis Sarecky. Directed by Marshall Neilan. Screenplay by Creelman. Photographed by Leo Tover. Available on videocassette.

Starring Rudy Vallee, Marie Dressler, Sally Blane, Charles Sellon, Eddie Nugent, Nella Walker, Malcolm Waite, Alan Roscoe, the Connecticut Yankees.

A small town man learns the saxophone by correspondence and joins a band.

939 *Valley of the Sun* (1942) Western. Running time: 84 minutes. Black and white. Available on videocassette.

Produced by Grahame Baker. Directed by George Marshall. Screenplay by Horace McCoy. Photographed by Harry Wild. Edited by Desmond Marquette.

Starring Lucille Ball (Christine), James Craig (Jonathan), Sir Cedric Hardwicke (Warrick), Dean Jagger (Sawyer), Peter Whitney (Willie), Billy Gilbert (Justice), Tom Tyler (Geronimo), Antonio Moreno (Cochise), Hank Bell (Shotgun),

Richard Fiske (Lieutenant), Al St. John, Chester Conklin (Bits), Iron Eyes Cody, Jay Silverheels (Bits as Indians).

An evil Indian agent is thwarted by a renegade scout.

940 *The Vandergilt Diamond Mystery* (1936) Comedy. Running time: 60 minutes. Black and white.

Produced and directed by Randall Faye. Screenplay by Margaret Houghton.

Starring Betty Astell, Bruce Seton, Hilary Pritchard, Charles Patton, Ethel Royale, Ben Graham Soutten.

941 *Variety Time* (1951) Musical variety. Running time: 80 minutes. Black and white.

Collection of novelty acts and musical numbers staged like a vaudeville show. Includes a Leon Errol short and other attractions. See also *Footlight Varieties.*

942 *The Velvet Touch* (1948) Mystery. Running time: 97 minutes. Black and white.

Produced by Frederick Brisson. Directed by John Gage. Screenplay by Leo Rosten and Walter Reilly. Photographed by Joseph Walker. Edited by Chandler House.

Starring Rosalind Russell (Valerie), Leo Genn (Michael), Claire Trevor (Marian), Sydney Greenstreet (Danbury), Leon Ames (Gordon Dunning), Frank McHugh (Ernie Boyle), Walter Kingsford (Gunther), Dan Tobin (Jeff Trent), Lex Barker (Paul).

A stage star murders her producer.

943 *Vendetta* (1950) Drama. Running time: 84 minutes. Black and white.

Produced by Howard Hughes. Directed by Mel Ferrer. Screenplay by W.R. Burnett and Peter O'Crotty. Photographed by Frank Planer and Al Gilks. Edited by Stuart Gilmore.

Starring Faith Domergue (Columba), George Dolenz (Orso), Hillary Brooke (Lydia), Nigel Bruce (Sir Thomas),

Joseph Calleia (Mayor), Hugo Haas (Brando).

A girl avenges the murder of her father.

944 *The Very Idea* (1929) Comedy. Running time: 65 minutes. Black and white.

Produced by Myles Connolly. Directed by Richard Rosson and William LeBaron. Screenplay by LeBaron (based on his play). Photographed by Leo Tover. Edited by Ann McKnight.

Starring Frank Craven (Alan Camp), Theodore Von Eltz (Green), Doris Eaton (Edith), Allen Kearns (Gilbert), Hugh Trevor (Joe), Sally Blane (Nora).

A couple's inability to conceive causes them to ask their maid and chauffeur to do it for them.

945 *Vigil in the Night* (1940) Drama. Running time: 96 minutes. Black and white.

Produced and directed by George Stevens. Screenplay by Fred Guiol, P.J. Wolfson, Rowland Leigh. Photographed by Robert De Grasse. Edited by Henry Berman.

Starring Carole Lombard (Anna Lee), Brian Aherne (Dr. Prescott), Anne Shirley (Lucy), Julien Mitchell (Matthew), Robert Coote (Dr. Caley), Brenda Forbes (Nora), Peter Cushing (Joe).

Two sisters who are nurses are stunned when one's bad judgment leads to a child's death.

Note: Pandro Berman and George Stevens left RKO after this one.

946 *Village Tale* (1935) Drama. Running time: 80 minutes. Black and white.

Produced by David Hempstead. Directed by John Cromwell. Screenplay by Allan Scott. Photographed by Nicholas Musuraca. Edited by William Morgan.

Starring Randolph Scott (Slaughter Sommerville), Kay Johnson (Janet Stevenson), Arthur Hohl (Elmer Stevenson), Robert Barrat (Drury Stevenson),

Janet Beecher (Amy), Edward Willis (Ike).

Gossip among townsfolk results in a rivalry between two men.

Review: "Depressing story without marquee strength"—*Variety.*

947 *The Villain Still Pursued Her* (1940) Comedy. Running time: 65 minutes. Black and white. Available on videocassette.

Produced by Harold B. Franklin. Directed by Edward F. Cline. Screenplay by Elbert Franklin. Photographed by Lucien Ballard. Edited by Arthur Hilton.

Starring Hugh Herbert (Healy), Anita Louise (Mary), Alan Mowbray (Cribbs), Buster Keaton (William), Joyce Compton (Hazel), Richard Cromwell (Edward), Billy Gilbert (Announcer), Margaret Hamilton (Mrs. Wilson), William Farnum (Vagabond), Franklin Pangborn (Bartender), Diane Fisher (Julia).

Hiss the villain, cheer the hero in wacky melodramatic farce regarding demon alcohol.

Note: Franklin was one-time head of RKO theater chain.

948 *The Violators* (1957) Drama. Running time: 76 minutes. Black and white. An RKO-Galahad Production released by Universal-International.

Produced by Himan Brown. Directed by John Newland. Screenplay by Ernest Pendrell. Photographed by Maurice (Morris) Hartzband. Edited by David Cooper.

Starring Arthur O'Connell (Solomon), Nancy Malone (Debbie), Fred Beir (Jimmy), Clarice Blackburn (Eva), Henry Sharp (David), Mary Michael (Mrs. Riley), Joe Julian (Riley), Bill Darrid (Calini).

A probation officer's daughter's fiance commits a felony.

949 *Vivacious Lady* (1938) Comedy. Running time: 90 minutes. Black and white. Available on videocassette.

Produced and directed by George

Stevens. Screenplay by P.J. Wolfson and Ernest Pagano. Photographed by Robert De Grasse. Edited by Henry Berman.

Starring Ginger Rogers (Frances Brent), James Stewart (Peter Morgan), James Ellison (Keith Beston), Charles Coburn (Dr. Morgan), Beulah Bondi (Mrs. Morgan), Frances Mercer (Helen), Phyllis Kennedy (Jenny), Alec Craig (Joseph the Chauffeur), Franklin Pangborn (Apartment Manager), Grady Sutton (Culpepper), Hattie McDaniel (Maid), Jack Carson (Waiter), Willie Best (Porter), George Chandler (Bit).

A nightclub singer marries a shy botany professor, and must deal with his overbearing parents.

Oscar nomination: Photography.

950 *Wagon Train* (1940) Western. Running time: 62 minutes. Black and white.

Produced by Bert Gilroy. Directed by Edward Killy. Screenplay by Morton Grant. Photographed by Harry Wild. Edited by Frederic Knudtson.

Starring Tim Holt, Ray Whitley, Emmett Lynn, Martha O'Driscoll, Bud McTaggart, Cliff Clark, Ellen Lowe, Wade Crosby, Ethan Laidlaw, Monte Montague, Carl Stockdale, Bruce Dane, Glenn Strange.

A supply train fights off Indian attacks.

951 *Wagonmaster* (1950) Western. Running time: 86 minutes. Black and white and colorized. Available on videocassette.

Produced and directed by John Ford. Screenplay by Frank S. Nugent and Patrick Ford (based on a story by John Ford). Photographed by Bert Glennon. Edited by Jack Murray.

Starring Ward Bond (Elder), Ben Johnson (Travis), Harry Carey, Jr. (Sandy Owens), Joanne Dru (Denver), Charles Kemper (Shiloh), Jane Darwell (Sister Ledeyard), Alan Mowbray (Hall), Ruth Clifford (Fleuretty), Russell Simpson (Adam Perkins), Kathleen O'Malley

(Prudence), James Arness (Floyd), Hank Worden (Luke), Jim Thorpe (Navajo).

Adventures of a wagon train's journey towards Utah. The travelers are Mormons who were ousted due to their religious beliefs.

952 *Walk Softly Stranger* (1950) Drama. Running time: 81 minutes. Black and white.

Produced by Robert Sparks. Directed by Robert Stevenson. Screenplay by Frank Fenton. Photographed by Harry Wild. Edited by Frederic Knudtson.

Starring Joseph Cotten (Chris Hale), Alida Valli (Elaine), Spring Byington (Mrs. Brentman), Paul Stewart (Whitey), Jack Parr (Ray), Jeff Donnell (Gwen).

A gambler moves into a small town in an attempt to escape his past.

953 *Walking on Air* (1936) Comedy. Running time: 70 minutes. Black and white.

Produced by Edward Kaufman. Directed by Joe Santley. Screenplay by Bert Kalmar and Harry Ruby. Photographed by J. Roy Hunt. Edited by George Hively.

Starring Gene Raymond (Pete Quinlan), Ann Sothern (Kit Bennett), Jessie Ralph (Evelyn Bennett), Henry Stephenson (Mr. Bennett), Gordon Jones (Joe), George Meeker (Tom Quinlan), Maxine Jennings (Flo), Alan Curtis (Fred).

A girl gets a man to pose as her suitor to drive her parents crazy.

954 *Wanderer of the Wasteland* (1945) Western. Running time: 67 minutes. Black and white.

Produced by Herman Schlom. Directed by Edward Killy and Wallace Grissell. Screenplay by Norman Houston (based on the novel by Zane Grey). Photography by Harry J. Wild. Edited by J.R. Whittridge.

Starring James Warren (Adam), Richard Martin (Chito), Audrey Long (Jean),

Robert Clarke (Jay), Robert Barrat (Collinshaw), Robert Clarke (Jay), Harry Woods (Eliott), Minerva Urecal (Mama), Harry D. Brown (Papa), Tommy Cook (Chito as a Boy), Harry McKim (Adam as a Boy).

A cowboy searches for the killer of his father.

955 *Wanted: Jane Turner* (1936) Crime drama. Running time: 67 minutes. Black and white.

Produced by Cliff Reid. Directed by Ed Killy. Screenplay by John Twist. Photographed by Robert De Grasse. Edited by Ted Cheesman.

Starring Lee Tracy (Mallory), Gloria Stuart (Doris), Judith Blake (Jane), John McGuire (Jerry), Frank M. Thomas (Banks), Patricia Wilder (Babe), Barbara Pepper (Marge).

A postal investigator smashes the gang who robbed from a mail truck and murdered the driver.

956 *Way Back Home* (1932) Drama. Running time: 81 minutes. Black and white.

Produced by Pandro S. Berman. Directed by William Seiter. Screenplay by Jane Murfin. Photographed by J. Roy Hunt.

Starring Phillips Lord (Seth Parker), Effie Palmer (Ma Parker), Mrs. Phillips Lord (Liz), Bennett Kilpack (Cephius), Frank Albertson (David), Bette Davis (Mary Lucy), Oscar Apfel (Wobblin), Stanley Fields (Rube Turner), Frankie Darro (Robbie Turner).

A preacher shelters a young boy from his alcoholic father.

Note: Bette Davis, an unknown at the time, received $900 for three weeks' work on this film. Alternate titles: *Old Greatheart* and *Other People's Business.*

957 *Way Down South* (1939) Musical. Running time: 62 minutes. Black and white.

Produced by Sol Lesser. Directed by Bernard Vorhaus. Screenplay by Clarence Muse and Langston Hughes. Photographed by Charles Schoenbaum. Edited by Arthur Hilton.

Starring Bobby Breen, Alan Mowbray, Ralph Morgan, Clarence Muse, Steffi Duna, Sally Blane, Ed Maxwell, Charles Middleton, Matthew "Stymie" Beard.

An orphaned youngster tries taking over the family plantation in pre–Civil War Louisiana.

Note: Rare in that it was a general release film co-authored by black artists: veteran actor Muse and poet-writer Hughes.

958 *The Way Out* (1956) Crime drama. Running time: 86 minutes. Black and white.

Produced by Alec Snowden. Written and directed by Montgomery Tully. Photographed by Phillip Grindrod. Edited by Geoffrey Miller.

Starring Gene Nelson (Greg), Mona Freeman (Terry), John Bentley (Seagrave), Michael Goodliffe (Moffat), Sidney Tafler (Alf), Charles Victor (Smithers), Arthur Lovegrove (George).

A man escapes with his wife and brother when he kills a man in a bar during a drunken brawl.

959 *We Who Are About to Die* (1937) Drama. Running time: 82 minutes. Black and white. Available on videocassette.

Produced by Edward Small. Directed by Christy Cabanne. Screenplay by John Twist. Photographed by Robert Planck. Edited by Arthur Roberts.

Starring Preston Foster (Mathews), Ann Dvorak (Connie), John Beal (John), Ray Mayer (Bright Boy), Gordon Jones (Slim Tolliver), Russell Hopton (Mac), J. Carrol Naish (Nick), Paul Hurst (Tip), Frank Jenks (Clyde).

An inmate's friends try proving his innocence while he sits on death row.

960 *Weekend for Three* (1941) Comedy. Running time: 65 minutes. Black and white.

Produced by Tay Garnett. Directed by Irving Reis. Screenplay by Dorothy Parker and Alan Campbell (based on a story by Budd Schulberg). Photographed by Russell Metty. Edited by Desmond Marquette.

Starring Dennis O'Keefe (Jim), Jane Wyatt (Ellen), Phillip Reid (Randy), Edward Everett Horton (Stonebraker), ZaSu Pitts (Anna), Franklin Pangborn (Number Seven), Marion Martin (Mrs. Weatherby), Hans Conried (Desk Clerk).

A newlywed tries to make her husband jealous.

961 *We're on the Jury* (1937) Comedy. Running time: 71 minutes. Black and white.

Produced by Lee Marcus. Directed by Ben Holmes. Screenplay by Franklin Coen. Photographed by Nicholas Musuraca. Edited by Ted Cheesman.

Starring Victor Moore (J. Clarence Beaver), Helen Broderick (Mrs. Ashley), Phillip Huston (Steve), Louise Latimer (Mrs. Clyde), Vinton Haworth (M. Williams), Robert McWade (Judge Prime), Maxine Jennings (Clara Simpson), Billy Gilbert (E. Allen).

A jury holdout insists a man is innocent and expects the others to see it her way.

962 *We're Only Human* (1936) Crime drama. Running time: 67 minutes. Black and white.

Produced by Edward Kaufman. Directed by James Flood. Screenplay by Brian James. Photographed by J. Roy Hunt. Edited by Archie Marshek.

Starring Preston Foster (McCaffrey), Jane Wyatt (Sally), James Gleason (Danny Walsh), Arthur Hohl (John Martin), John Arledge (Johnny O'Brien), Jane Darwell (Mrs. Walsh), Mischa Auer (Lefty).

A tough cop overdoes it while capturing crooks.

963 *We're Rich Again* (1934) Comedy. Running time: 73 minutes. Black and white.

Directed by William Seiter. Screenplay by Ray Harris. Photographed by Nicholas Musuraca.

Starring Edna May Oliver (Maude), Billie Burke (Mrs. Page), Marian Nixon (Arabella), Reginald Denny (Booky), Joan Marsh (Carolyne Page), Buster Crabbe (Erp), Grant Mitchell (Wilbur Page).

A wedding is overlooked by a family trying to scrape together money for a stock market gamble.

964 *West of the Pecos* (1935) Western. Running time: 68 minutes. Black and white.

Produced by Cliff Reid. Directed by Phil Rosen. Screenplay by Milton Krims and John Twist (based on the novel by Zane Grey). Photographed by James Van Trees. Edited by Archie Marshek.

Starring Richard Dix (Pecos Smith), Martha Sleeper (Terrell), Samuel S. Hinds (Mabeth), Fred Kohler, Sr. (Sawtelle), Louise Beavers (Mauree), Willie Best (Jonah).

A woman poses as a man while traveling through post–Civil War Texas.

965 *West of the Pecos* (1945) Western. Running time: 66 minutes. Black and white.

Produced by Herman Schlom. Directed by Edward Killy. Screenplay by Norman Houston (based on the novel by Zane Grey). Photographed by Harry J. Wild. Edited by Roland Gross.

Starring Robert Mitchum (Pecos Smith), Barbara Hale (Rill), Richard Martin (Chito), Thurston Hall (Lambeth), Rita Corday (Suzanne), Russell Hopton (Jeff Stinger).

Remake of the above.

966 *Western Heritage* (1948) Western. Running time: 61 minutes. Black and white.

Produced by Herman Schlom. Directed by Wallace Grissell. Screenplay by Norman Houston. Photographed by Alfred Keller. Edited by Desmond Marquette.

Starring Tim Holt (Ross), Nan Leslie (Beth), Richard Martin (Chito), Lola Andrews (Cleo), Tom Barrett (Trig), Walter Reed (Joe Powell), Harry Woods (Arnold), Tom Keene (Spade), Jason Robards, Sr. (Judge).

Outlaws trick ranchers out of their land, and a cowboy tries to right things.

967 *Westward Passage* (1932) Romance. Running time: 72 minutes. Black and white.

Produced by Harry Joe Brown. Directed by Robert Milton. Screenplay by Bradley King. Photographed by Lucien Andriot. Edited by Charles Craft.

Starring Ann Harding (Olivia), Laurence Olivier (Nick), ZaSu Pitts (Mrs. Truesdale), Irving Pichel (Harry), Juliette Compton (Henriette), Irene Purcell (Diane), Emmett King (Ottendorf), Bonita Granville (Little Olivia), Edgar Kennedy (Elmer), Florence Lake (Elmer's wife), Henry Bing (Dutchman), Joyce Compton (Bit).

A struggling writer, despondent over his lack of success, tries to keep his marriage together.

968 *What a Blonde* (1945) Comedy. Running time: 71 minutes. Black and white.

Produced by Ben Stoloff. Directed by Leslie Goodwins. Screenplay by Charles E. Roberts. Photographed by J. Roy Hunt.

Starring Leon Errol (Fowler), Richard Lane (Pomeroy), Michael St. Angel (Andrew), Elaine Riley (Cynthia), Veda Ann Borg (Pat), Lydia Billbrook (Mrs. Fowler), Clarence Kolb (Dafoe), Ann Shoemaker (Mrs. Dafoe).

A man opens his home to showgirls while his wife fumes.

969 *What Price Hollywood?* (1932) Drama. Running time: 88 minutes. Black and white.

Produced by David O. Selznick. Directed by George Cukor. Screenplay by Jane Murfin, Ben Markson, Gene Fowler, and Rowland Brown (based on a story by Adela Rogers St. John). Photographed by Charles Rosher. Edited by Jack Kitchin.

Starring Constance Bennett (Mary Evans), Lowell Sherman (Maximillan Carey), Neil Hamilton (Lenny Borden), Gregory Ratoff (Julius Saxe), Brooks Benedict (Muto), Louise Beavers (Bonita), Eddie "Rochester" Anderson (James).

A former waitress rises in show business as her husband's star fades.

Note: Remade as *A Star Is Born* in 1937, 1954 and 1976.

970 *When's Your Birthday* (1937) Comedy. Running time: 77 minutes. Black and white. Available on videocassette.

Produced by Robert H. Harris. Directed by Harry Beaumont. Screenplay by Harry Clork, Harvey Gates, Malcolm Stuart Boylan, and Samuel Pike. Photographed by George Robinson. Edited by Jack Ogilvie.

Starring Joe E. Brown (Dustin), Marian Marsh (Gerry), Fred Keating (Larry), Edgar Kennedy (Bascomb), Maude Eburne (Mrs. Bascombe), Suzanne Kaaren (Diane), Margaret Hamilton (Mossy), Minor Watson (Regan), Frank Jenks (Lefty), Granville Bates (Judge), Bull Montana (Himself).

A boxer uses the stars to predict his ring success.

Note: Cartoon sequence in color.

971 *Where Danger Lives* (1950) Crime drama. Running time: 84 minutes. Black and white.

Produced by Irving Cummings, Jr. Directed by John Farrow. Screenplay by Charles Bennett. Photographed by Nicholas Musuraca. Edited by Eda Wharton.

Starring Robert Mitchum (Jeff), Faith Domergue (Margo), Claude Raines (Frederick Lannington), Maureen O'Sullivan (Julie), Charles Kemper (Police Chief), Ralph Dumke (Klauber), Billy House

(Bogardus), Harry Shannon (Dr. Maynard), Phillip Van Zandt (Milo), Jack Kelly (Mullenbach).

A doctor falls for a suicidal patient.

972 *Where Sinners Meet* (1934) Comedy. Running time: 73 minutes. Black and white.

Directed by J. Walter Ruben. Screenplay by H.W. Hannemann (based on the play *The Dover Road* by A.A. Milne). Photographed by Nicholas Musuraca. Edited by George Hively.

Starring Diana Wynyard (Anne), Clive Brook (Latimer), Billie Burke (Eustacia), Reginald Owen (Leonard), Alan Mowbray (Nicholas), Gilbert Emery (Dominic), Vernon Steele (Saunders), Phyllis Barry, Katherine Williams (Maids), Walter Armitage, Robert Adair (Footmen).

A millionaire, victim of several failed marriages, holds two eloping couples captive in his mansion to keep them from making the same mistake.

973 *While the City Sleeps* (1956). Crime drama. Running time: 100 minutes. Black and white.

Produced by Bert Friedlob. Directed by Fritz Lang. Screenplay by Casey Robinson. Photographed by Ernest Laszlo. Edited by Gene Fowler, Jr.

Starring Dana Andrews (Mobley), Rhonda Fleming (Dorothy), Sally Forrest (Nancy), Thomas Mitchell (John Day Griffith), Vincent Price (Walter), Howard Duff (Kaufman), Ida Lupino (Mildred), George Sanders (Loving), Maes Craig (Kitzer), John Barrymore, Jr. (Manners), Vladimir Sokoloff (Plasky), Robert Warwick (Kyner), Mae Marsh (Mrs. Manners).

A newspaper owner offers a top position to the reporter who can crack the case of the notorious "Lipstick Killer."

Note: Lang's favorite among his films, next to the 1936 feature *Fury*. Originally set for release by United Artists, this film was produced independently.

974 *The Whip Hand* (1951) Drama. Running time: 82 minutes. Black and white.

Produced by Lewis J. Rachmil. Directed by William Cameron Menzies. Screenplay by George Bricker, Frank L. Moss (based on a story by Roy Hamilton). Photographed by Nicholas Musuraca. Edited by Robert Golden.

Starring Carla Balenda (Janet), Elliot Reid (Matt), Edgar Barrier (Dr. Koller), Raymond Burr (Steve Loomis), Otto Waldis (Dr. Bucholz), Michael Steele (Chick), Lurene Tuttle (Molly).

A reporter on vacation uncovers a communist plot.

975 *White Soldiers* (1931) Drama. Running time: 80 minutes. Black and white.

Produced by Henry Hobart. Directed by Melville Brown. Screenplay by J. Walter Ruben and Jane Murfin. Photographed by Jack MacKenzie. Edited by Archie Marshek.

Starring Mary Astor (Norma), Jack Holt (Gordon), Ricardo Cortez (Lawrence), Sidney Toler (Southern), Kitty Kelly (Marie), Robert Keith (Bit).

A millionaire rescues a girl from poverty.

976 *The White Tower* (1950) Adventure. Running time: 98 minutes. Black and white. Available on videocassette.

Produced by Sid Rogell. Directed by Ted Tetzlaff. Screenplay by Paul Jarrico. Photographed by Ray Rennahan. Edited by Samuel E. Beetley.

Starring Glenn Ford (Martin), Alida Valli (Carla), Claude Rains (Paul Delmabe), Oscar Homolka (Andreas), Sir Cedric Hardwicke (Nicholas), Lloyd Bridges (Mr. Hein), June Clayworth (Astrid Delambre), Lotte Stein (Frau Andreas), Fred Essler (Knubel).

A group of people and their reasons for wanting to climb a mountain.

Robert Mitchum and Faith Domergue in *Where Danger Lives.*

977 *Wild Cargo* (1934) Jungle documentary. Black and white.

Produced by Frank Buck and the Van Beuren Corporation. Directed by Armand Denis. Dialogue and narration by Courtney Ryley Cooper. Photographed by Nicholas Cavaliere and Leroy G. Phelps.

Frank Buck's methods of trapping wild animals.

978 *The Wild Heart* (1952) Drama. Running time: 82 minutes. Black and white.

Produced by David O. Selznick. Directed and written by Michael Powell and Emeric Pressburger. Photographed by Christopher Challis. Edited by Reginald Mills.

Starring Jennifer Jones (Hazel), David Farrar (Jack), Cyril Cusack (Marston), Sybil Thorndike (Mrs. Marston), Edward Chapman (Mr. James), Esmond Knight (Abel Woodus), Hugh Griffith (Vessons).

A young woman who tries saving animals from hunters marries a clergyman but finds her life sexually unfulfilled.

979 *Wild Horse Mesa* (1947) Western. Running time: 61 minutes. Black and white.

Produced by Herman Schlom. Directed by Wallace Grissell. Screenplay by Norman Houston (based on the novel by Zane Grey). Edited by Desmond Marquette.

Starring Tim Holt (Dave Jordan), Nan Leslie (Sue Melbern), Richard Martin (Chito), Tom Keene (Hod Slack), Jason Robards, Sr. (Pop), Harry Woods (Olmstead).

A horse trainer objects to roundup methods using barbed wire.

980 *Windjammer* (1931) Crime drama. Running time: 60 minutes. Black and white.

Produced by George A. Hirliman and David Howard. Directed by Ewing Scott.

Screenplay by Dan Jarrett and James Green (based on a story by Major Raoul Haig). Photographed by Frank B. Good. Edited by Robert Crandall.

Starring George O'Brien (Lane), Constance Worth (Betty), William Hall (Morgan), Brandon Evans (Commodore), Gavin Gordon (Forsythe), Stanley Blystone (Peterson), Ben Hendricks, Jr. (Dolan), Lee Shumway (Captain).

A deputy state's attorney joins a yacht race in order to serve a supoena on a wealthy yachtsman.

981 The Window (1949) Crime drama. Running time: 73 minutes. Black and white. Available on videocassette.

Produced by Fredric Ullman. Directed by Ted Tetzlaff. Screenplay by Mel Dinelli. Photographed by William Steiner. Edited by Frederick Knudtson.

Starring Barbara Hale (Mrs. Woodry), Bobby Driscoll (Tommy), Arthur Kennedy (Mr. Woodry), Paul Stewart (Kellerton), Ruth Roman (Mr. Kellerton), Anthony Ross (Ross), Richard Benedict (Drunk), Jim Nolan (Stranger).

A boy witnesses a murder, but nobody believes him.

Oscar: Bobby Driscoll, Actor.

982 Wings and the Woman (1942) Biographical drama. Running time: 96 minutes. Black and white.

Produced and directed by Herbert Wilcox. Screenplay by Miles Malleson. Photographed by Mutz Greenbaum and Fredrick A. Young. Edited by Alan Jaggs.

Starring Anna Neagle (Amy Johnson), Robert Newton (Jim Mollison), Edward Chapman (Mr. Johnson), Nora Swinburne (ATA Commandant), Joan Kemp-Welch (Mrs. Johnson), Charles Carson (Lord Wakefield), Brefini O'Rorke (Mac), Muriel George (Housekeeper), Martita Hunt (Schoolmistress), Eliot Markham (Mayor).

The biography of fliers Jim Mollison and Amy Johnson and their exploits during WW2.

Wings Over Wyoming see *Hollywood Cowboy*

983 Winterset (1936) Drama. Running time: 78 minutes. Black and white. Available on videocassette.

Produced by Pandro S. Berman. Directed by Alfred Santell. Screenplay by Anthony Veiller (based on the play by Maxwell Anderson). Photographed by Peverell Marley. Edited by William Hamilton.

Starring Burgess Meredith (Mio), Margo (Miramme), Eduardo Ciannelli (Trock), Paul Guilfoyle (Garth), John Carradine (Romangna), Edward Ellis (Judge), Stanley Ridges (Shadow), Myron McCormick (Carr), Willard Robertson (Policeman), Mischa Auer (Radical), Barbara Pepper, Lucille Ball (Bits).

A man tries to prove his executed father's innocence, fifteen years after the fact.

984 Wise Girl (1937) Drama. Running time: 70 minutes. Black and white.

Produced by Edward Kaufman. Directed by Leigh Jason. Screenplay by Allan Scott. Photographed by Peverell Marley. Edited by Jack Hively.

Starring Miriam Hopkins (Susan), Ray Milland (John), Walter Abel (Karl), Henry Stephenson (Fletcher), Alec Craig (Dermont O'Neil), Guinn "Big Boy" Williams (Mike), Margaret Dumont (Bell-Rivington), James Finlayson (Jailer).

An heiress poses as an artist and seeks custody of her sister's children.

985 Without Orders (1936) Drama. Running time: 64 minutes. Black and white.

Produced by Cliff Reid. Directed by Lew Landers. Screenplay by J. Robert Bren and Edmund L. Hartmann. Photographed by J. Roy Hunt. Edited by Desmond Marquette.

Starring Sally Eilers (Kay Armstrong), Robert Armstrong (Wad Madison), Frances Sage (Penny Armstrong), Charley Grapewin (J.P. Kendrick), Vinton Haworth (Len Kendrick), Ward Bond (Tim Casey), Frank M. Thomas (Trueman).

Two pilots vie for the attention of an attractive stewardess.

986 *Without Reservations* (1946)
Comedy. Running time: 107 minutes. Black and white. Available on videocassette.

Produced by Jesse Lasky. Directed by Mervyn Leroy. Screenplay by Andrew Solt. Photographed by Milton Krasner. Edited by Jack Ruggiero.

Starring Claudette Colbert (Kit), John Wayne (Rusty), Don DeFore (Dink), Anne Triola (Connie), Phil Brown (Soldier), Frank Puglia (Oraga), Thurston Hall (Baldwin), Dona Drake (Dolores), Louella Parsons, Jack Benny, Cary Grant (Themselves).

An author traveling incognito meets two Marine fliers en route, who hate her book, but don't realize she's the writer.

987 *The Witness Chair* (1936)
Mystery. Running time: 64 minutes. Black and white.

Produced by Cliff Reid. Directed by George Nicholls, Jr. Screenplay by Rian Jones and Gertrude Purcell (based on the story by Rita Weiman). Photographed by Robert De Grasse. Edited by William Morgan.

Starring Ann Harding (Paula), Walter Abel (Jim), Douglass Dumbrille (Whittaker), Frances Sage (Connie), Moroni Olsen (Lt. Poole), Margaret Hamilton (Grace Franklin), Maxine Jennings (Tillie Jones), Billy Benedict (Benny Ryan), Paul Harvey (Martin), Frank Jenks (Levino).

A woman watches as her lover goes to trial for a murder she herself committed.

988 *Woman Between* (1931) Drama. Running time: 81 minutes. Black and white.

Produced by William LeBaron. Directed by Victor Schertzinger. Screenplay by Howard Estabrook (based on the play *Madame Julie* by Irving Kaye Davis). Photographed by J. Roy Hunt. Edited by William Hamilton.

Starring Lily Damita, O.P. Heggie, Lester Vail, Miriam Seeger, Anita Louise, Ruth Weston, Halliwell Hobbes, Lincoln Stedman, Blanche Frederici, William Morris.

A French woman married to a wealthy man falls for his son.

989 *A Woman Commands* (1932)
Drama. Running time: 83 minutes. Black and white.

Produced by Charles R. Rogers. Directed by Paul L. Stein. Screenplay by Horace Jackson. Photographed by Hal Mohr. Edited by Dan Mandell.

Starring Pola Negri (Maria Draga), Roland Young (King Alexander), Basil Rathbone (Capt. Pasitsch), H.B. Warner (Col. Stradmirovitsch), Anthony Bushell (Iwan), Reginald Owen (Prime Minister).

A dancer romances both a king and a soldier.

Note: Negri's first talking picture, and last American film until a cameo in the 1943 release *Hi Diddle Diddle*. This film lost over a quarter of a million dollars, with Negri taking most of the blame.

990 *The Woman I Love* (1937)
Drama. Running time: 85 minutes. Black and white.

Produced by Albert Lewis. Directed by Anatole Litvak. Screenplay by Mary Borde. Photographed by Charles Rosher. Edited by Henri Rust.

Starring Paul Muni (Claude), Miriam Hopkins (Helene), Louis Hayward (Herbillion), Colin Clive (Thelis), Minor Watson (Deschamps), Elisabeth Risdon (Madame Herbillion), Paul Guilfoyle (Berthier), Wally Albright (Georges), Mady Christians (Florence), Alec Craig (Doctor).

A WW1 pilot is considered a jinx when many of his partners die in action while flying with him.

991 *Woman in the Dark* (1934)
Drama. Running time: 68 minutes. Black and white.

Produced by Burt Kelly. Directed by Phil Rosen. Screenplay by Sada Cowan, Marcy Klauber, and Charles Williams (based on the story by Dashiel Hammett). Photographed by Joseph Ruttenberg.

Starring Fay Wray (Louise Lorimer), Ralph Bellamy (Bradley), Melvyn Douglas (Robson), Roscoe Ates (Tommy Logan), Reed Brown (Conroy), Ruth Gillette (Lil Logan), Nel O'Day (Helen Grant), Granville Bates (Sheriff).

A bad-tempered ex-con tries to lead a straight life after three years in prison.

992 *Woman in the Window* (1945) Drama. Running time: 99 minutes. Black and white. Available on videocassette.

Produced by Nunnally Johnson. Directed by Fritz Lang. Screenplay by Johnson. Photographed by Milton Krasner. Edited by Marjorie Gateson.

Starring Edward G. Robinson (Wanley), Joan Bennett (Alice), Raymond Massey (Frank Lalor), Edmond Breon (Barkstone), Dan Duryea (Heidt), Thomas Jackson (Inspector), Arthur Loft (Frank Howard), Frank Dawson (Collins).

A staid college professor has an affair while his wife is away.

993 *A Woman of Experience* (1931) Drama. Running time: 65 minutes. Black and white.

Produced by Charles R. Rogers. Directed by Harry Joe Brown. Screenplay by John Farrow and Ralph Murphy (based on the play *The Registered Woman* by Farrow). Photographed by Hal Mohr. Edited by Fred Allen.

Starring Helen Twelvetrees, William Bakewell, Lew Cody, ZaSu Pitts, H.B. Warner, C. Henry Gordon, Franklin Pangborn, Nance O'Neil, George Fawcett, Bertha Mann, Edward Earle, Max Waizman, William Tooker, Alfred Hickman.

Shady lady joins intelligence agents to trap a German spy.

994 *Woman on Pier 13* (1950) Drama. Running time: 73 minutes. Black and white.

Produced by Jack J. Gross. Directed by Robert Stevenson. Screenplay by Charles Grayson, Robert Hardy Andrews (based on a story by George W. George and George F. Slavin). Photographed by Nicholas Musuraca. Edited by Roland Gross.

Starring Laraine Day (Nan Collins), Robert Ryan (Brad Collins), John Agar (Don Lowry), Thomas Gomez (Vanning), Janis Carter (Christine), Richard Rober (Jim Travis), William Talman (Bailey), Paul Burns (Arnold), Paul Guilfoyle (Ralston), G. Pat Collins (Charles Dover).

A former Communist Party member is forced back into the operation.

Note: Alternate title: *I Married a Communist.*

995 *Woman on the Beach* (1947) Drama. Running time: 71 minutes. Black and white.

Produced by Jack Gross. Directed by Jean Renoir. Screenplay by Renoir, Frank Davis, Michael Hogan. Photographed by Leo Tover. Edited by Roland Gross.

Starring Joan Bennett (Peggy), Robert Ryan (Lt. Scott Burnett), Charles Bickford (Ted Butler), Nan Leslie (Eve Geddes), Walter Sande (Otto Wernecke), Irene Ryan (Mrs. Wernecke), Frank Darien (Lars), Jay Norris (Jimmy), Glenn Vernon (Kirk), Hugh Chapman (Fisherman).

A man comes between a woman and her sadistic husband.

Note: Renoir's last American film.

996 *A Woman Rebels* (1936) Drama. Running time: 86 minutes. Black and white. Available on videocassette.

Produced by Pandro S. Berman. Directed by Mark Sandrich. Screenplay by Anthony Veiller and Ernest Vajda. Photographed by Robert De Grasse. Edited by Jane Loring.

Starring Katharine Hepburn (Pamela),

Herbert Marshall (Thomas), Elizabeth Allan (Flora), Donald Crisp (Judge), Doris Dudley (Young Flora), David Manners (Alan), Lucile Watson (Betty), Van Heflin (Gerald).

A Victorian woman fights for female rights and has a baby out of wedlock.

997 *A Woman's Secret* (1949) Drama. Running time: 85 minutes. Black and white.

Produced by Herman J. Mankiewicz. Directed by Nicholas Ray. Screenplay by Mankiewicz (based on the novel by Vicki Baum). Photographed by George Diskant. Edited by Sherman Todd.

Starring Maureen O'Hara (Marian), Melvyn Douglas (Luke), Gloria Grahame (Susan), Bill Williams (Lee), Victor Jory (Brook), Mary Phillips (Fowler), Jay C. Flippen (Fowler), Robert Warwick (Roberts).

An ex-singer kills her protege.

Note: This one lost $760,000.

998 *Wonder Man* (1945) Comedy. Running time: 98 minutes. Color.

Produced by Samuel Goldwyn. Directed by Bruce Humberstone. Screenplay by Don Hartman, Melville Shavelson, Phillip Rapp, Jack Jevne, Eddie Moran (based on a story by Arthur Sheekman). Photographed by Victor Milner. Edited by Daniel Mandell.

Starring Danny Kaye (Buzzy, Edwin), Virginia Mayo (Ellen Shanley), Vera-Ellen (Midge), Donald Woods (Monte), S.Z. "Cuddles" Sakall (Schmidt), Allen Jenkins (Chimp), Ed Brophy (Torso), Steve Cochran (Ten Grand), Otto Kruger (D.A.), Richard Lane (Grossett), Natalie Schaefer (Mrs. Hume), Huntz Hall (Mike).

When a showman is murdered by gangsters, his bookish twin assumes his identity.

Review: "...possibly his best vehicle..."—Leslie Halliwell.

999 *The Yellow Canary* (1944) Mystery. Running time: 84 minutes. Black and white.

Produced and directed by Herbert Wilcox. Screenplay by Miles Malleson and DeWitt Bodeen. Photographed by Mutz Greenbaum. Edited by Vera Campbell.

Starring Anna Neagle (Sally), Richard Greene (Garrick), Nova Pilbeam (Betty), Lucie Manneim (Mme. Orlock), Albert Lieven (Jan Orlock), Cyril Fletcher (Himself), Margaret Rutherford (Mrs. Towcester).

A female British agent is accused as a Nazi spy.

1000 *Yellow Dust* (1936) Western. Running time: 68 minutes. Black and white.

Produced by Cliff Reid. Directed by Wallace Fox. Screenplay by Cyril Hume and John Twist. Photographed by Earl Woolcott. Edited by James Morley.

Starring Richard Dix (Bob), Leila Hyams (Nellie), Moroni Olsen (Missouri), Jessie Ralph (Mrs. Brian), Andy Clyde (Solitaire), Onslow Stevens (Hanaway), Victor Potel (Jugger), Ethan Laidlaw (Bogan), Ted Oliver (McLearney), Art Mix (Crook).

A gold miner must clear his name of robberies.

1001 *You Can't Beat Love* (1937) Comedy. Running time: 82 minutes. Black and white.

Produced by Robert Sisk. Directed by Christy Cabanne. Screenplay by David Silverstein and Maxwell Shane. Photographed by Russell Metty. Edited by Ted Cheesman.

Starring Preston Foster (Jimmy), Joan Fontaine (Trudy), Herbert Mundin (Jasper), William Brisbane (Clem), Alan Bruce (Scoop), Paul Hurst (Butch).

A playboy runs for mayor on a dare.

1002 *You Can't Buy Luck* (1937) Crime drama. Running time: 61 minutes. Black and white.

Directed by Lew Landers. Screenplay by Martin Mooney and Arthur T. Horman. Photographed by J. Roy Hunt. Edited by Jack Hively.

Starring Onslow Stevens (Baldwin), Helen Mack (Betty), Vinton Haworth (Paul), Maxine Jennings (Jean), Paul Guilfoyle (Frank), Frank M. Thomas (Bond), Richard Lane (McGrath), Murray Alper (Spike), Hedda Hopper (Mrs. White), Dudley Clements (Ben), George Irving (Mr. White), Barbara Pepper (Clerk), Eddie Gribbon (Chuck).

A racehorse owner believes good deeds will bring him luck on the track, but he is soon accused of murder.

1003 *You Can't Fool Your Wife* (1940) Comedy. Running time: 68 minutes. Black and white.

Produced by Cliff Reid. Directed by Ray McCarey. Screenplay by Jerry Cady. Photographed by J. Roy Hunt. Edited by Theron Warth.

Starring Lucille Ball (Clara Merecedes), James Ellison (Andrew), Robert Coote (Battincourt), Virginia Vale (Sally), Emma Dunn (Mom), Elaine Shepard (Peggy), William Haligan (Gillespie).

A mother-in-law annoys a newly married couple.

1004 *You'll Find Out* (1940) Comedy. Running time: 97 minutes. Black and white.

Produced and directed by David Butler. Screenplay by James V. Kern, Monte Brice, Andrew Bennison, R.T.M. Scott. Photographed by Frank Redman. Edited by Irene Morra. Music by Johnny Mercer and Jimmy McHugh.

Starring Kay Kyser (himself), Peter Lorre (Fenninger), Boris Karloff (Mainwaring), Bela Lugosi (Saliano), Helen Parrish (Janis), Dennis O'Keefe (Chuck), Alma Kruger (Aunt Margo), Ginny Simms, Harry Babbitt, Sully Mason, Ish Kabibble, Kay Kyser's Band (Themselves).

A radio big band is stuck in a creepy old house.

Comment: "This picture is one of the happiest I ever did" — David Butler.

Young Bride* see *Love Starved

1005 *Young Donovan's Kid* (1931) Drama. Running time: 72 minutes. Black and white.

Produced by Louis Sarecky. Directed by Fred Niblo. Screenplay by J. Walter Ruben (based on the novel *Big Brother* by Rex Beach). Photographed by Edward Cronjager.

Starring Richard Dix (Jim Donovan), Jackie Cooper (Midge Murray), Marion Shilling (Kitty Costello), Frank Sheridan (Father Dan), Boris Karloff (Cokey Joe), Dick Rush (Burke), Fred Kelsey (Colins), Wilfred Lucas (Duryea).

A gangster takes a dead buddy's kid brother under his wing, but the boy is removed by child care officials. The badman then attempts to go straight in an effort to win back the boy.

Comment: "Boris Karloff played a character called Cokey Joe and he was trying to make me sniff some white powder. Then Richard Dix burst in to save me; he beat Karloff up and carried me to safety. I kept asking everybody what the white powder was. They told me it was a drug. It wasn't until recently that I have seen any film in which cocaine was shown so clearly." — Jackie Cooper in his autobiography.

1006 *Young Stranger* (1957) Drama. Running time: 84 minutes. Black and white.

Produced by Stuart Miller. Directed by John Frankenheimer. Screenplay by Robert Dozier. Photographed by Robert Planck. Edited by Robert Swink.

Starring James MacArthur (Hal), Kim Hunter (Helen), James Daly (Tom), James Gregory (Shipley), Whit Bissell (Grubbs), Jeff Silver (Jerry), Jack Mullaney (Confused Boy), Eddy Ryder (Theater Patron).

A juvenile delinquent is arrested for battery.

1007 *Youth Runs Wild* (1944) Drama. Running time: 67 minutes. Black and white.

Produced by Val Lewton. Directed by Mark Robson. Screenplay by John Fante, Ardel Wray (based on a story by Fante and Herbert Kline). Photographed by John Mescall. Edited by John Lockert.

Starring Bonita Granville (Toddy), Kent Smith (Danny), Jean Brooks (Mary), Glenn Vernon (Frank), Teresa Brind (Sarah), Ben Baird (Mr. Taylor), Arthur Shields (Dunlap), Dickie Moore (Georgie), Rod Rodgers (Rocky), Juanita Alvarez (Lucy), Harold Barnitz (Stevie), Gloria Donovan (Nancy).

Teenagers get into trouble while their parents are away.

Note: Horror director Lewton's attempt at a social drama was botched by studio chiefs, who edited it down and shot new scenes, toning down the harsh realities Lewton had intended. Angered, Lewton fought to keep his name off the film, but without success.

1008 *Zombies on Broadway* (1945) Comedy. Running time: 68 minutes. Black and white. Available on videocassette.

Produced by Ben Stoloff. Directed by Gordon Douglas. Screenplay by Lawrence Kimble. Photographed by Jack MacKenzie. Edited by Phillip Martin, Jr.

Starring Wally Brown (Jerry), Alan Carney (Mike), Bela Lugosi (Renault), Anne Jeffreys (Jean), Sheldon Leonard (Ace), Frank Jenks (Gus), Russell Hopton (Hopkins), Joseph Vitale (Joseph).

Press agents must come up with a zombie to please a wicked nightclub owner.

British title: *Loonies on Broadway*.

Index

References are to entry numbers, not pages.